FRENCH TRENCH WARFARE
1917 – 1918
A REFERENCE MANUAL

FRENCH GENERAL STAFF

The Naval & Military Press Ltd

Published by

The Naval & Military Press Ltd
Unit 10 Ridgewood Industrial Park,
Uckfield, East Sussex,
TN22 5QE England

Tel: +44 (0) 1825 749494
Fax: +44 (0) 1825 765701

www.naval-military-press.com
www.nmarchive.com

In reprinting in facsimile from the original, any imperfections are inevitably reproduced and the quality may fall short of modern type and cartographic standards.

TABLE OF CONTENTS.

Pages.

Préamble 7

PART I.
PRINCIPLES OF COMMAND.

CHAPTER I. — The chief. 9
           Advice to a young officer 10
CHAPTER II. — General functions of the different grades in the company 14
CHAPTER III. — Seniority. — Rights to command 16

PART II.
ELEMENTARY TRAINING OF THE INFANTRY.

CHAPTER I. — Omitted.
CHAPTER II. — Omitted.
CHAPTER III. — **Rifle fire.** 17
CHAPTER IV. — **Training of the grenadier** 20
CHAPTER V. — **Organization, formation, movements, and deployment of the platoon** 27
        Organization and formation of the platoon 27
        Movements of the platoon in line and in column 30
        Deployment of the platoon as skirmishers. 33
        Assault 37
CHAPTER VI. — **Organization, formations and movements of the company** 38
        Organization and formations of the company 38
        Movements of the company 44
CHAPTER VII. — **The company on the march** 46

	Pages.
CHAPTER VIII. — **School of the sapper**...............	49
Normal types......................	53
Construction of a trench..............	65
Construction of a sap................	65
Construction of a wire entanglement....	71
Fascine and hurdle work.............	74

PART III.

MATERIEL.

CHAPTER I. — Omitted.	
CHAPTER II. — **The automatic rifle**...................	79
CHAPTER III. — **The machine guns**...................	83
Hotchkiss model 1914................	83
CHAPTER IV. — **The grenades**......................	84
CHAPTER V. — **The 37 mm. gun**....................	95
CHAPTER VI. — **Explosives and destruction**...........	97
CHAPTER VII. — Omitted.	
CHAPTER VIII. — **The wagons and horses of the company.**	
The wagons........................	106
The horses.........................	108
CHAPTER IX. — **Illuminating fireworks and signalling apparatus**..........................	109
Illuminating fireworks................	109
Signalling apparatus.................	111
CHAPTER X. — **The telephone**......................	118
CHAPTER XI. — **Means of observation and reconnaissance**...............................	121
Compass...........................	121
Maps and plans.....................	129
Conventional signs...................	131
CHAPTER XII. — Omitted.	
CHAPTER XIII. — **Defensive and offensive war materiel (Miscellaneous)**......................	134
CHAPTER XIV. — Omitted.	
CHAPTER XV. — **Effects of projectiles**.................	138
CHAPTER XVI. — **Information on the 75**...............	144

PART IV.

MISCELLANEOUS INFORMATION USEFUL TO PLATOON LEADERS.

		Pages.
CHAPTER I.	— The principles.	145
CHAPTER II.	— Notes on organization.	146
CHAPTER III.	— Tactical qualities of the infantry	149
CHAPTER IV.	— Rifle fire.	150
CHAPTER V.	— Tactical employment of machine guns, automatic rifles, grenades, trench weapons and 37 mm. gun.	155
	The machine guns.	155
	The automatic rifles.	158
	The grenades.	161
	The rifle grenades V. B. and D. R.	168
	Trench weapons. — Omitted.	
	37 millimeter gun.	171
CHAPTER VI.	— Principles of field fortification	173
	Principles of different traces	179
	Elements of a position. — Different organizations.	187
	Ground observation.	204
	Shelters.	217
CHAPTER VII.	— Ideas relative to the tactical qualities of the different arms and relative to the staff service.	225
	Artillery.	225
	Cavalry.	229
	Engineers.	230
	Staff service.	230
CHAPTER VIII.	— Omitted.	
CHAPTER IX.	— Methods of liaison and signal communication.	231
CHAPTER X.	— Sanitation and alimentation.	249
CHAPTER XI.	— Supply of ammunition and materiel.	256
CHAPTER XII.	— Railway transport.	262
CHAPTER XIII.	— Notes on the service of the rear.	265
CHAPTER XIV.	— Notes on the rules of warfare.	26

PART V.

GENERAL DISCIPLINE.

Pages.

CHAPTER I. -- Measures to be taken to communicate information to higher authority and to secure secrecy.......................... 268
CHAPTER II. — Omitted.
CHAPTER III. — Omitted.
CHAPTER IV. — Omitted.
CHAPTER V. — Omitted.
CHAPTER VI. — Omitted.

PART VI.

CANTONMENT REGULATION FOR INFANTRY.

CHAPTER I. — Preparation of the cantonment.......... 271
    Bivouac............................... 276
CHAPTER II. — Administration in the field............. 277
CHAPTER III. — Regulation as to the guard and security in the cantonment.................... 281

PART VII.

INFANTRY IN THE TRENCHES.

CHAPTER I. — Infantry in waiting..................... 286
    Tactical memorandum of chief of platoon. 291
    Internal service in the trenches.......... 299
CHAPTER II. — Infantry attacked in trenches........... 307
    Counter-attacks....................... 311

PART VIII.

AN ATTACK UPON A POSITION BY THE INFANTRY.

CHAPTER I. — The aspect of an infantry combat........ 315
    Preparation for the assault............... 315
    The assault........................... 318
    Front breaking attack; following up the success............................ 318
    Notions on the part played by the artillery in the offensive....................... 324

	Pages.
CHAPTER II. — Combat of the platoon and the group....	325
CHAPTER III. — The company engaged.................	330
The battalion engaged...............	339
CHAPTER IV. — Liaison during the progression..........	344

PART IX.

PURSUIT AND WAR OF MOVEMENT.

CHAPTER I. — Protection on the march................	351
CHAPTER II. — Service of security in camp. — Outposts.	356

PART X.

METHODS OF INSTRUCTION.

CHAPTER I. — Training in the billets in rear of the lines.	367
Organization of combat drill for platoons and companies......................	371
Instruction of specialists................	379
CHAPTER II. — Instruction camps and depots...........	380

PREAMBLE.

GENERAL PRESCRIPTIONS.

The present mode of recruiting the subaltern officers of infantry, and the conditions in which they must **acquire,** and then **maintain** their military instruction, have brought about the necessity of assembling in a single volume the fundamental notions which are indispensable to them, as well as the various details, advices, informations and numbers most frequently useful.

In the domain of the platoon leaders as well as of others, the war has brought such modifications and innovations that the regulation texts can be read only with precaution.

It is necessary to proceed to a temporary adjustment and to assemble in the same collection some of the previous texts which have never ceased to have their full value, and some of the new prescriptions, extracted from or inspired by the most recent documents.

Such is the object of this present **Manual.**

It is intended for the platoon leaders and for the non commissioned officers susceptible of being proemoted to that grade. It will form the foundation of th-training given in the units **at rest** and in the **Schools of instruction in the Armies.**

It is intended also for the officer-instructors at **depots** and in **camps of instruction in the interior.** It will guide them in such a manner that the men of the reenforcements may be ready, after a very short acclimation to conduct themselves and to fight like their comrades at the front. This community of instruction between the field regiments and their depots is indispensable for the arrival of the reenforcements on the fighting line at their full value.

It remains with company and battalion commanders to pursue the instruction of their subordinates both by practical exercises and by inciting them to acquire a more complete knowledge of the regulations, instructions and studies which have been utilized in compiling this present **Manual** such as:

Infantry Drill Regulations;

Instruction on the Combat of Small Units, 8 january, 1916;

Supplement or Annex to the latter, 27 september, 1916;

Instruction of 16 december, 1916, on the Object and Conditions of a Combined Offensive Action;

Field Service Regulations;

Small arms firing regulations;

Instruction on Field Works, 21 december, 1915;

Note on the Tactical Employment of Machine Guns, 24 november, 1915;

Aide-Memoire on Infantry Machine Guns, 15 april, 1916;

Instruction on the Employment of the Automatic rifle, 13 february, 1916;

Note on the Organization and Employment of Infantry Bombardiers;

Note on the Pneumatic Howitzers, 31 october, 1916;

Note on the different models of Grenades in Service, 2 april, 1916;

Instruction on Grenade Combat, 7 april, 1916;

Note on the Organization of Grenadiers, 5 april, 1915;

Instruction on the Liaison, 1917;

Note on Illuminating fireworks and their Projecting Apparatus, 3 september, 1916;

Note on Protection against Asphyxiating gas, 1 april, 1916;

Note of 25 october, 1916, on the Instruction to be given to Officers and Men;

Note of 28 august, 1915, on the Instruction of Infantry in the Depots.

PART I.

PRINCIPLES OF COMMAND.

CHAPTER I.

THE CHIEF. — ADVICE TO A YOUNG OFFICER.

The chief.

The action of the chief has a decisive influence on the value of the unit.

The chief must : be well informed, set an example, and command.

The instruction. — For one who must propagate confidence, the lack of knowledge is intolerable, because it creates timidity. The chief who «knows his business» rek quires from his men only the effort that counts, does not wear them out prematurely and does not carelessly ristheir lives in combat.

The example. — The unit is the reflection of its chief. It is his most severe judge, it remembers his least word and watches his attitude. It only asks to be able to admire him and to follow him blindly. Its good behavior under fire is the chief s best recompense.

To command. — The chief leads on his men because he knows how to be the keenest of them, but he is also the master of them because he knows how to see clearly and to keep his head. He must see everything and the men must give him their entire confidence. To command does not consist only in issuing orders : **to command is to give an order and to have it executed.** It is also to keep the mind always alive, to know everything that happens, to call for orders if he does not receive any, or to take **the initiative**, to give the necessary instructions in good time, and constantly orient his subordinates.

The authority of a chief makes itself felt first of all by **the discipline** of his troop ; i.e., in the execution of orders, appearance, exterior marks of respect, cleanliness care of weapons, exactitude in tne drill.

The disciplined unit fights well; in actual combat, the undisciplined unit escapes from its chiefs, throws away its arms, surrenders or gives way.

Advice to a young officer.

The influence. — A chief must make an impression on his men by a certain number of superiorities. A single type of chief does not exist which young officers can take as a model. But all must think and ask of themselves which are the natural or the acquired qualities which give to the best chiefs in their vicinity their **influence** over their men.

An officer newly promoted should not think himself **a chief** because he is obeyed under everyday circumstances. This indicates only that his rank is respected. He should feel satisfied only when he has patiently gained the **confidence** and the **heart** of his men, when he has acquired the certainty that they have given themselves up to him and that they will obey him even in face of death.

A young chief must always consider that in the critical hours **the authority due to himself alone** will always be more efficient than that which he gets from regulations.

The moral qualities. — A chief maintains the esteem of his men, first of all, by the qualities of his **character,** and this is only just, because **energy, initiative, will, perseverance, precision, judgment, selfcontrol, spirit of duty, self-denial** are aptitudes in the absence of which the finest gifts of the mind remain worthless.

Amongst qualities of mind, **a broad military and general knowledge** is not extemporised during the period of a campaign, but every officer can and must endeavor to know thoroughly all things which concern his functions. If he knows things with great **precision,** he will acquire confidence in himself, the common sense solutions will easily come to his mind, he will express himself with **calm** and **without hesitation** and he will be listened to by the soldier; on the contrary, unprecise or contradictory orders, given in an uncertain or nervous tone will raise doubts as to their efficacity. The soldier obeys blindly only when he has a blind confidence.

A chief is **loved** by his men when he shows a spirit of justice, when he is absolutely **straight,** when he looks closely after their welfare, and when he performs his duties in person. The soldier accepts quite well all strictness within reason, and at heart gives to excessive indulgence and to weakness the condemnation they deserve. Justice does not consist in treating every man in the same way, but in exacting from each one the full employment of his faculties or means, and in rewarding merit according to the effort it has cost.

The everyday **attitude** of the officer has also its importance: lack of restraint in dress and language, and certain vulgarities and familiarities, an officer should **never** indulge in. Anybody can be **correct, simple** and **dignified**, without keeping his subordinates far off and without depriving himself of the **good humor** and **gaity** which, like **tenacity in hope** and **absolute faith** in **victory**, are so eminently and happily contagious.

In dark hours, when discouragement appears, officers and non-commissioned officers act in unity in order to drive it from the company: they remind all that whatever happens, one must never despair, that there is no good reason why the enemy should not be quite as much reduced and depressed as anybody else, that in war, fortune has most sudden returns for those who do not give up and that «complete victory belongs to him who can suffer one quarter of an hour longer than the other ».

The spirit of precision. — The importance of the details. — As regards these moral qualities, which endure always, it is important that the young officer should thoroughly acquaint himself with all the new requirements of a war, which, for the first time, gives such a large share to scientific qualifications.

Nowadays, any attack, any resisting to the last, runs the risk of failing, if the troops engaged have not prepared their terrain, their implements, and their personnel, **with a minuteness superior to that of the enemy.**

In this preparation, the least neglect has to be paid for ; all details are important.

The N. C. O. and the platoon leader, must know then that, whatever their personal qualities of intrepidity may be, their task will not be accomplished if they do not put a daily ardor into the minute details of duty which **no other chief can do for them.** Order, method, desire for numerical precision; horror of the pretty-near, and of the incompleted, have become essential qualities, the lack of which is enough to expose a chief to the gravest disappointments.

Orders received and the initiative. — Command is exercised according to the following principle : the superior determines the objective to be attained, indicates his intentions and defines the tasks which are to be carried out by the subordinate echelons : he leaves to the latter the choice of means of execution. The officers and N. C. O's must make a good use of that **initiative** by choosing the best means of accomplishing the desired end.

Initiative consists then, in no way, as might be sometimes thought, of the right to alter an order received, even if one judges that the result would be better. This is disobedience.

On the contrary, a N. C. O. must show **initiative :**

1° In completing and developing an order, when, intentionally or otherwise the chief who has given it to him, has remained mute on certain details which he intends to leave to his judgment;

2° When from some reason or other, no order has arrived and there is an opportunity however to take a decision. In this case, an order must be given and a report made. One may be mistaken as to the emergency, but the chief will always consider that **the only errors which merit reproach are inaction and fear of responsibility.**

Finally, in some **very exceptional cases,** for instance, that of a situation entirely changed between the moment an order has been written and the time it arrives, initiative may cause one to act contrary to all or to part of the order given : he must then be absolutey certain that «to disobey the text of the order, is to obey the **intention** of the chief» and, then besides, one must make a report without delay.

In all other cases, discipline requires that orders should be **punctually** obeyed, even to the smallest details into which a chief has judged it well to enter. Initiative comes into play only for those details that he has not mentioned, and it must only be used according to what one knows according to his intentions and of his way of thinking.

The orders given. — The principal quality of an order, is **clearness.** « In war there exists a more dangerous enemy than lack of discipline : it is misinterpretation which, more frequently than the former, interferes with the strict execution of orders. »

A subordinate chief finds very often an advantage in explaining and commenting upon the orders he gives to his men : in this manner their intelligence comes into play, and they execute more cheerfully the orders the utility of which they understand.

But it is necessary also that the soldiers keep well in mind that he employs such proceedings only in the interest of the service.

Nevertheless, the troops must be well trained in executing strictly, without hesitation or murmur, a **firm order, issued without** any explanation. Such is the actual basis of discipline, and it cannot be repeated too often, if only for practice.

Non commissioned officers are often imperfectly obeyed when they give orders to a number of men for a work that is to be executed by some of them only. Each one relies on his neighbor. The one who gives orders must always divide the work and assign the responsibilities by name: it is rarely that anyone who receives a personal order will try to shirk it, whereas any ambiguity will be taken advantage of.

Before an order is given it must be seen that **it can be entirely executed and cannot be evaded;** say very exactly what is wanted and no more; refrain from the idea of asking too much to have enough: this is bargaining. « What is ordered must be obtained: the difficulty is to measure out what is reasonable and what is useful. »

When an order is given in these conditions of precision, equilibrium and common sense, a prompt and severe punishment must follow its non-execution.

It cannot be admitted that a N. C. O. or an officer can overlook a flagrant fault, committed under his eyes, on the pretext that the culprit is not under his direct command. This happens frequently; either through indolence or by fear of hurting the misplaced susceptibility of the man's chief. Any officer whatsoever is the superior of all soldiers of the Army holding a rank inferior to his own. He must have the feeling of his own authority and not make himself a tacit accomplice of the man who behaves irregularly in his presence. He must interfere then with tact and firmness, and see that orders and regulations are respected wherever he happens to be. All laxness in cantonment and in trenches arises from the non-observation of this principle.

In the Company, the non-commissioned officers must be the councillors of their squads or platoons and never refuse a man the advice he is seeking or the solution of a difficulty. An excellent way to have little to repress in the internal everyday life of a company is to make it a principle that a soldier is never at fault when he is covered by the previous approbation of a N. C. O., but that he is always to blame for not applying to him, if there was the least doubt of what he had to do; on the other hand, the N. C. O. will be considered unworthy of command if he shirks his responsibility by avoiding a firm answer.

Thus, the young officers and N. C. O's must never forget that they hold a portion of the principle of authority, and that it has been entrusted to them to never allow it to perish.

Relations between officers. — The officers of a company mess together. Meal-times are moments of relaxation during which it is convenient that they should remain together. Whatever affectionate familiarity reigns around the table, no one should ever forget the deference due to experience, age and rank.

Respect shown by the Lieutenant to the Captain, his promptitude and punctuality in carrying out his least orders will soon be observed by the soldiers and will teach them obedience and military spirit by the best of theories: **Example.**

CHAPTER II.

GENERAL FUNCTIONS OF THE DIFFERENT GRADES IN THE COMPANY.

The company. — The company is the unit which the soldier takes the most to his heart. It is the strongest unit in which all N. C. O's and soldiers can know one another individually. It is the smallest to which an elementary tactical operation can be entrusted.

It has its own designation and its own customs; it does not resemble its neighbor. To his men the captain is the chief par excellence, the confidant of their troubles, as the obligatory channel of their wants. Nothing that concerns them is done without his action.

He has a somewhat universal role which need not be further described here.

He is responsible for everything in the company and consequently has complete control of his subordinates.

The platoon-leader. — The platoon-leader is a chief purely military; he is the head of the strongest unit which it is possible to command by voice and to take in at a glance, even when deployed. The platoon is the cellular element of combat; in principle, it is engaged, fires and fights as a single unit; everything takes place as if its power were concentrated on one single head, the platoon-leader. For this reason the function of this chief is **capital.**

Having under his command about 5o men only, whom he hardly ever leaves, the platoon-leader is the only officer who can know exactly the temper and aptitudes of each one, and he is the best qualified to influence always their morale. He is, in the platoon, the one most concerned about the tactical situation, of which he **must always be thinking.** (Security, liaisons, observation, wearing down the enemy, etc).

He must then' for all his other duties, exact a complete support from his N. C. O.' s in order to be able to devote himself before everything else, to his **moral** and **tactical** function.

The sergeant of the half-platoon. — The sergeant is practically, the first N. C. O. who enjoys a strong authority, and on the other side, he commands a number of men small enough to remember and to note all details concerning them : dress, equipment, armament, food supplies, etc. Such is his lot. His multiple duties can be condensed in one sentence : to do what is necessary to have the personnel and materiel of his half-platoon always present and in good condition. In a half-platoon well in hand, the officers only have to make daily verifications and do not have to do the work of a sergeant.

In combat, the sergeant of a half-platoon has an essential function, that of **file-closer**. He must be told of that often, he must be told that fear is contagious, that the salvation of his country demands that all weakness, all beginning of stampede, must be nipped in the bud, that to hesitate to shoot down a coward, is perhaps to save twenty enemies or to cause the death of twenty friends.

In the progression, the sergeant does not place his rifle in a firing position, but sees that all others do.

To allow him to perform his duty with an implacable energy, he must be given, in the field, a far greater authority than in peace time.

The corporal. — The corporal lives in intimate contact with his men, he is their mess-chief and their justice of the peace.

The best corporal is the one whose group cooks its food in spite of all and manages to eat it hot. It is not right that the sergeant should shift on to him a part of the permanent responsibilities he must himself assume ; the actual function of a corporal consists in trusting him with the execution of well defined and successive tasks.

This rank is a stage which allows choosing future sergeants from amongst the corporals who have revealed the taste and aptitude of command.

Selection of trained specialists in the companies.
— The qualities to be sought in selecting specialists are :

Headquarters or Company clerks	A spirit of order and scrupulousness, discretion.
Agents of liaison	Absolute devotion, discretion, good handwriting, aptitude to make reports on what happens, and memory of the terrain.
Observers	Good eye-sight, coolness.
Signalmen	Good eye-sight, good memory.
Grenadiers	Sporting proclivities.
Automatic riflemen...	Vigor, audacity.
Stretcher-Bearers.....	Physical strength.

It is difficult to make a selection of specialists without diminishing the average value of the remainder of the platoon. This is a great drawback which platoon-leaders will lessen by training many substitutes and in taking care that none of the trained specialists remaining under their authority shall loose the ordinary qualities and aptitudes of trained soldiers.

CHAPTER III.

SENIORITY. — RIGHTS TO COMMAND.

It is important that sergeants, corporals and privates Ist class in the company should always exactly know their relative seniority, in order that, should the case occur, there would be no hesitation as to who should automatically take command and become responsible.

The relative list must be kept up to date and communicated to new comers.

The principle is that, as soon as two or more soldiers are assembled for service, one of them should always be in command, the highest in rank, or, when of equal rank, the senior.

The lieutenant will find it profitable to establish the seniority even among the soldiers of his platoon.

But in combat, when the leaders are disabled, a soldier, more brave than his comrades, must spring from the ranks — not **necessarily the senior.** — He leads on the others : he is the chief.

This notion must be inculcated in the head of soldiers : if rules of seniority hold good in every day life, they no longer exist between soldiers in combat.

Of equal rank, the regularly commissionned officer has command over the officer of temporary rank.

PART II.

ELEMENTARY TRAINING OF THE INFANTRYMAN.

EXERCISE GROUND. — RIFLE RANGE.

Part II is especially intended for the instruction battalions.

In the period of war, time is lacking to give elementary instruction with the same minuteness as in time of peace : all hasten toward the application.

The movements of the school of the soldier and of the school of the platoon are executed mostly by **imitation** and at the indication of the instructor, without explanations from the text. **Energy** and **tradition** often replace without detriment the exact knowledge of the regulations.

Certain elementary matters are placed in Part II only for reference for the instructors, so as to avoid too great divergencies which might result if they could not at times consult the precise text. They have in no sense been assembled with the intention of their being taught fully to the soldier in all their details. The result obtained is the only thing that counts.

. . . .

CHAPTER III.

RIFLE FIRE.

TACTICAL INSTRUCTION OF THE ISOLATED RIFLEMAN.

The tactical instruction of the rifleman is to teach him how to use his rifle to advantage when he is isolated, that is to say under circumstances where his fire is not conducted by the commands of his chief (when sentinel, scout, patrol, agent of liaison).

He applies then the two following rules, which he must know by heart and which he must often be made to repeat.

Rules and limits for the employment
of individual fire.

Fire discipline. — The isolated soldier should fire as little as possible.

On principle, he fires only :

1° **When he has received an order to do so ;**
2° **In self-defense ;**
3° **As a warning to the troops he is guarding.**

If it is in the first case (order to fire on any objective that appears) — which will however be the general case **in the trenches** — he must **estimate the distance** and be governed by the second rule which is as follows:

Limit for the employment of individual fire. — On principle, the isolated soldier should not fire at more than :

400 meters at a lone man or horseman;
600 meters at a group of at least 4 men.

The rules of **fire discipline** and of the **limits of employment of individual fire** find their application especially in war of movement, but also in all cases where the necessity of not revealing one's presence and of springing a surprise must take precedence over the pleasure of taking a shot at a most tempting target. The alarm clumsily given by one individual may rob an enterprise of most interesting results.

If the isolated rifleman must shoot, it is often advantageous for him to wait for his objective to approach before opening fire.

The point to aim at is the lower edge of the visible portion of the target. If the objective moves across the field of vision, aim at the edge toward the direction of march. With a wind from the flank, aim at the edge toward the wind. The chances are very small of hitting an individual at more than 250 meters moving across the field of view or standing in a strong cross wind.

Under no circumstances should fire be opened upon an avion or dirigible without the order of an officer.

Estimation of distance. — Choice of sight elevation. — The estimation of distance for a man temporarily isolated consists in judging where an objective is, relative to 400, to 600 meters.

On account of the flatness of the trajectory, there are as many chances of hitting the target at short ranges with the battle sight as with a more exact setting.

The following simple rule may therefore be given to the isolated rifleman:

From 0 to 600 meters, use the battle sight.

Beyond 600 meters, never fire.

Utilisation of the terrain. — **Cover** is the term applied to such obstacles as hedges, fields of grain or high vegetation, brushwood, etc., which mask the firer without protecting him against bullets.

Shelter is the term applied to walls, embankments, etc., which protect a man from bullets.

A tree of medium thickness is not very safe shelter; it should be as large as a man to stop bullets at short range.

Walls of stone or brick even when quite thin are shelter against fire at all distances.

To shoot, the soldier must endeavour above all to see, then to cover himself, then shelter and lastly to find a rest for his rifle. **Action** takes precedence over **protection.**

The rifleman places himself as close as possible to the shelter and fires from the right side of it.

He uses the cartridges from the right hand side while engaged in shooting. During lulls he uses his time to transfer cartridges from left side to right. Exceptionally in defense he may place cartridges on the ground but keeps them off the soil. He must never stick them into the earth.

CHAPTER IV.

TRAINING OF THE GRENADIER.

INDIVIDUAL INSTRUCTION. – INSTRUCTION OF THE GRENADIER. INSTRUCTION OF THE GROUP.

Individual instruction.

Individual instruction is given to all soldiers without exception.
It includes : throwing exercises and some theories on the fabrication, the dismounting and handling of grenades.

1° Throwing.

«*Throwing*» *is the basis of grenadier training.*
Precision in throwing is of the utmost importance for, besides the advantage it secures during the fight, it lessens the risks of accidents and the waste of grenades.
The moral effect of a grenade bursting in a trench must be added to its destructive effect.

Fig. 10 *bis*. — Tearing the safety-pin out of the igniter.

The grenade should never be thrown low, nor thrown with the bent arm. *Grenade fire should be plunging.*

Fig. 11. — Aiming at the objective with extended left arm, the grenade being held in the right hand.

Fig. 12. — Left arm kept in the direction of the objective. Right arm carried back.

Fig. 13. — Left arm without change, right hand back, arm extended. Look at the grenade and see that nothing will hinder its throwing.

Fig. 14. — Look again at the objective. Describe with right arm an arc in a vertical plane.

Fig. 15. — Let go the grenade,
right shoulder and body following right arm movement.
Left arm follows left shoulder which is refused.
The grenades will go in the direction aimed at with the left arm.

The normal process of throwing is shown in fig. 10 *bis*, 11, 12, 13, 14, 15. — This process, however, is modified according to the various positions in which soldiers may find themselves (kneeling, lying, or behind an obstacle).

Grenade throwing exercises. — At first the men are trained to throw dummy grenades in the open field and at registered distances. The trenches, represented by two lines drawn on the ground one meter apart are situated at the following distances: 20, 25, 30, 35 meters, etc (fig. 16).

The throwers in trench A take their places. Then they try to throw their grenades in B trench. Afterwards they try longer ranges by degrees so as to reach C D., etc.

The groups may be divided into halves, one at the firing line, the other at the target. The latter hrow back the grenades in their turn and so on. In this way

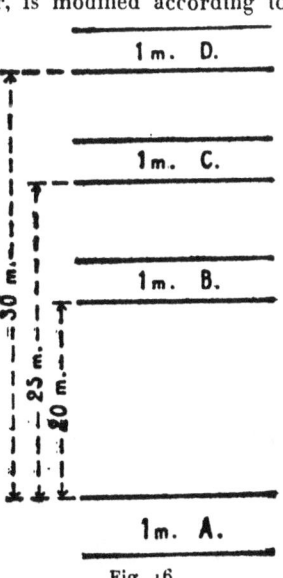

Fig. 16.

time is saved and the interest taken in the exercise is increased for all.

Skill and precision can be developed by the use of targets drawn on the ground.

Men must be trained to throw grenades in standing, kneeling and prone positions.

When the student grenadiers have acquired sufficient precision, they are trained to throw grenades from one real trench into another and to progress along a trench by throwing grenades over the traverses.

2° Dismounting grenades. — Handling.

The object of this part of the instruction is to make the soldiers understand the normal working of grenades, the defects to be found in their fabrication, the dangers that may arise in certain cases, for instance in the case of non-bursting, and the care to be taken in their handling.

It is strictly forbidden to take to pieces loaded grenades or even dummy grenades with loaded detonators.

Accordingly, exercises will take place with entirely inert grenades especially made for that purpose.

It is absolutely necessary to arrange a training trench. It may be sufficient to dig — 20 meters apart — two trench elements with two traverses separated by a firing interval.

Every time a body of troops is brought to the rear for rest or reserve it is the instructor's duty to rapidly prepare an exercise ground. Hollow roads, hillocks, natural obstacles, that he can adapt to his purpose in a few hours, will constitute shelters during exercises with real grenades.

Instruction of the grenadier.

Besides the ordinary instructions given to all soldiers in common the grenadier undergoes a particular instruction and a more complete training.

This instruction includes :

— The fabrication of explosive charges;

— The fabrication of dummy grenades;

— The utilization of German grenades and detonators;

— The handling of low power trench mortars.

The special training for grenadiers aims at making them expert throwers, confident in their skill, monitors capable of setting an example to their comrades and of organizing grenade fighting.

Grenadiers must be particulary trained to fire rifle-grenades. Constantly on the look out and quick to seize an opportunity, they will daily cause many casualties in the ennemy's ranks.

Instruction of the group of grenadiers.

Collective drill aims at:

Teaching any group of grenadiers (and particularly the first group of every platoon) how to prepare a grenade fight and how to pass into that kind of fighting rapidly, as soon as circumstances allow it;

Teaching how to carry out a raid by means of grenades. As a rule, the men in a group of grenadiers are divided, for the fight, into:

Throwers,

Ammunition carriers,

Assistant-grenadiers (formerly called riflemen).

Each grenadier must be able to play any one of those parts as soon as he is designated «thrower, ammunition carrier, assistant...»

The group of 1 corporal and 7 grenadiers will then constitute, under the command of its chief, a team including for instance: 2 throwers, 2 carriers, 2 assistants and one spare grenadier. Or it will fight in two teams of 3 grenadiers each, lead one by the corporal, the other by the most energetic grenadier.

More important detachments will often be constituted, under the command of a sergeant, or a grenadier officer, to take a more extensive point of resistance. Sometimes it will be necessary to assemble into a detachment all the grenadiers of a company or of a battalion.

The fight of such a detachment consists in the juxtaposition of smaller fights carried on by the detachment of 4 to 8 grenadiers, among which the grenadier officer has divided the entire objective, giving to each detachment a carefully chosen point.

Instruction of the small group is therefore the basis of grenade fighting.

ROLE OF THE CHIEF OF THE GROUP.

The group or detachment chief conducts the fight: he places his men according to their abilities, he arranges them so as to avoid crowding in the trenches or boyaux, he organises the relief of throwers and carriers; he supervizes the replenishment of the supply of grenades.

The chief of the detachment rapidly seizes all opportunities for gaining ground; if advance becomes impossible he keeps himself ready to fight for every foot of ground while multiplying the barricades.

The grenadier officer, being chief of a more numerous group, has **two essential tasks** :

1° Reconnoitring the objective and arranging the groups or detachments ;

2° Assuring the supply for these detachments.

This **latter task** requires, by far, the more energy, the more intelligence and initiative.

ROLE OF EACH SOLDIER
IN A GROUP FIGHTING WITH GRENADES.

Throwers. — The «throwers» must have their hands absolutely free so as to handle their grenades without difficulty; they carry their rifle slung during the fight. For their defense they have a pistol and a trench knife besides.

Throwers need not to take their rifles when the fight is not to be pushed too far, as in the carrying out of a raid.

Ammunition carriers. — The «carriers» assure the grenade supply. They replace disabled throwers. They are equipped in the same manner.

Assistant-grenadiers. — The «assistants» must be chosen from the most energetic and determined men. They must be good shots and skilled in the use of the bayonet. Their task is to take care of the security of the throwers.

In a frontal attack in the open, they advance on each side of the throwers and protect them with their fire.

In the boyaux they precede the throwers and scout all the traverses and turnings, ready to stop any counter-attack from the ennemy. They try to report the **bursting boints** of the grenades, help to correct the fire, and **warn the chief of their group as soon as it is possible to advance.**

When progression becomes impossible, they warn their chief. Without waiting for orders, they build a barricade of sand bags immediately and place themselves behind it, ready to fire.

In street fights, they watch the doors and windows especially.

MARCHING AND FORMATION
OF THE DETACHMENTS GOING IN TO FIGHT.

These detachments use the normal method of advance of patrols and reconnoitring parties.

The chief of the detachment occupies the place from

which he can best conduct his men. The assistant grenadiers are arranged ahead and on the flanks to scout and to protect the other grenadiers in case of an encounter with the enemy.

While marching in the open, these groups advance in skirmishing order. The assistants are distributed in the line and particularly on the flanks, so as to support the grenadiers. In case of an encounter with the enemy, the assistants scouting ahead fall back into the line.

In the boyaux the group advance by file and in the following order : assistants, throwers, carriers.

GROUP EXERCISES.

Group exercises take place on a prepared ground. The men learn how to split rapidly into assistant grenadiers, throwers, carriers, and how to behave in each of the combat circumstances described further on (Part. IV - Chapter V - 3ᵈ).

The men must always work in the **greatest silence** and ask questions or give orders by **signs** and **gestures**.

It is far more important to have groups of ordinary grenadiers, but used to work together, than to have some few remarkable individuals. It is a great fault to be inclined to carry on individual instruction only and to think that group work will naturally follow. Nothing is more difficult than coordinating the action of the same group, and the action of groups in the same fight.

CHAPTER V

ORGANIZATION. — FORMATION. — MOVEMENTS AND DEPLOYMENT OF THE PLATOON.

Organization.

The following are the regulation designations : **Grenadiers** for soldiers specialized in the use of hand-grenades and rifle-grenades (Viven-Bessières rifle grenadiers).

Automatic riflemen for soldiers specialized in the use of the automatic rifle (A. R.).

Riflemen for the other combatants. (The French call them «voltigeurs» because this designation indicates a great activity and devotion in all sorts of military tasks.) These designations by no means modify the internal regulation of the company; grenadiers, automatic-riflemen and riflemen take an equal share in work of all sorts.

The four platoons of the company have an identical composition.

The platoon is divided into two half-platoons.

1st half-platoon....
(sergeant grenadier
or automatic rifleman).
{
1st group (grenadiers):
   1 corporal and 7 grenadiers.
2nd group (automatic riflemen):
   1 corporal and 6 automatic riflemen (crew for two guns).
}

2nd half-platoon....
(Sergeant rifleman).
{
3rd group (riflemen):
   1 corporal and 8 riflemen;
   2 V. B. grenadiers and 1 ammunition carrier.
4th group (riflemen):
   1 corporal and 9 riflemen;
   2 V. B. grenadiers and 1 ammunition carrier.
}

The other soldiers of the platoon not fighting in ranks, such as drummers, buglers, pioneers, first aid man, cyclist, signallers, strikers, etc., are distributed among the groups in order to equalize their strength.

All the soldiers must know how to throw the grenades. Besides, every rifleman is instructed in a speciality; mention of this speciality is made on the record kept by the chief of half-platoons and of platoon.

Vacancies in the first half-platoon are, in principle, replaced by the 2nd half-platoon, according to orders given by the captain and approved by the major.

In this respect it is important not to reduce to excess the number of riflemen with regard to grenadiers and automatic riflemen. An effort must be made to keep one group of riflemen always at full strength.

For drills, specialists of each category may be assembled by company or by battalion, under command of an officer.

Formations of the platoon.

The platoon assembles in **line in double rank** and in **columns of squads (fours)**.

It maneuvers in column: i. e., column of squads, twos, or

files; line of half-platoons or of combat groups in columns of twos or files.

It fights in skirmish line, skirmishers being divided into one or several waves, generally two.

The **line in double rank** has no longer any tactical value. It is a formation, which for a long time has been the basis of close order and which owing to its very frequent use has remained the traditional formation for assemblies and parade (inspections, calls, guard mounting, etc.).

There has been no necessity to abruptly suppress it during field operations but the tendency must be to replace it everywhere by the column.

The column. — Is the most supple and the most adaptable formation for instruction. It answers all requirements: assemblies, marches, movements. It is, therefore, for the platoon, the formation par excellence.

The column of squads (fours). — Is formed by starting from a line in double rank moving «squads right». In this way, regulation distances and intervals between men are established.

It can be formed as well by: «Assembly in column of squads», the men taking directly their positions, which are the same as would have resulted from the preceding movement.

It can also be formed as a line of combat groups in columns of files at close intervals, the men of each combat group forming one **column of files** behind their corporal, this formation permits the most rapid and simplest change from a formation of movement to a formation of deployment.

Among formations in column, the **column of squads** *is never employed on the battlefield or in the zone of action usually covered by the enemy artillery fire.*

The most usual formations in this case are: **line of groups in columns of files,** or **line of half-platoons in column of files,** or **twos,** but in principle, the skirmish line must be formed as soon as troops are exposed to infantry fire.

The group. — A combat, as a rule, is not brought to a finish with regular units. Incidents of the battle and configuration of terrain create **momentary combat groups** the strength and commands of which are extremely variable.

The smallest handful of riflemen must always have a leader, whether he be a N. C. O., or a private, he must spring up voluntarily and assume the command of his comrades, he leads them forward if they hesitate, makes them hold fast to the ground if they tend to drift back.

These momentary groups are deployed, they progress and fire like regular units: this is the reason why the small units must receive the same detailed tactical instruction as the organized units.

The regular unit of combat is the platoon. All that is said hereinafter about platoons is applicable to the group whatever its strength may be or to any one of the sundry fractions of different composition that may henceforth make up a platoon.

Officers and N .C. O.'s. — The platoon is commanded by a **platoon-leader,** assisted by two **half-platoon-leaders,** file-closers. In movements, the platoon-leader keeps the post normally assigned to him ahead of the platoon. In case he leaves his habitual post a N. C. O. takes his place as guide. In combat, during approach, the platoon-leader guides his unit glancing at it in critical moments only, but always keeping a sharp eye on the enemy.

The men are bound to their leader who in all circumstances remains their rallying point, they regulate themselves on his attitude or his gait. During stops, when fire is opened, the platoon-leader keeps his position on the line of skirmishers or a little rear. At close range the platoon-leader must refrain from making unnecessary gestures which may reveal him to the enemy.

Sergeants take position as file-closers.

File-closers are the indispensable assistants of the platoon-leader. — They take position in rear of the platoon in order to assure the execution of orders from the platoon-leader. They are responsible to the leader for the conduct of the men. They assume command, without orders, each time the leader goes out on reconnaissance. File-closers should never be less than two in number. If disabled, the functions of file-closers are filled by corporals or privates.

I. — FORMATION IN LINE IN DOUBLE RANK.

The men are placed in two ranks at 1 meter distance arranged according to height and numbered 1 to 4 from right to left.

The rear-rank man covers exactly his front-rank file.

The platoon-leader takes position two paces in front of the center of the platoon when the distance which separates it from preceding units is 6 paces or less, otherwise he takes position 4 paces in advance.

File-closers take position 1 meter from rear rank, behind the centers of their groups.

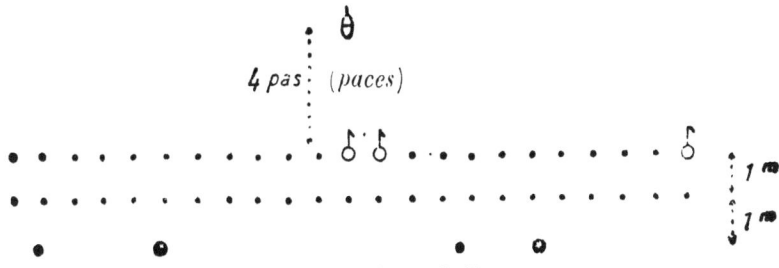

Fig. 17. — Platoon in line.

Conventional signs for formations of Platoon and Company.

⛨ Captain.	R. *Rifleman.*,
ϴ Platoon leader.	G. *Grenadier.*
● Half-platoon leader.	V B. *Rifle grenadier* (*Viven-Bessières*).
• Other N. C. O.	F. *Automatic rifleman.*
⚑ Corporal.	P. *Ammunition carrier of V B grenades.*
⫴ Drummers and buglers.	S. *Other soldier.*

Corporals stand in the front rank to the right or the left of their squad or the flanks of the half platoon.

Platoon is formed in single rank on the same principles.

II. — COLUMN OF SQUADS (FOURS).

The column of squads is composed of elements of eight men in double rank placed one behind the other at 1 meter distance, or of a line of combat groups in columns of files at close intervals.

The platoon-leader marches in front of the leading element whenever the platoon is not immediately preceeded by another unit, otherwise he marches abreast the first element, opposite the side of the file-closers.

The **file-closers** march at 1 meter from one of the flanks.

The column is divided into half-platoons, ocasionally into combat groups. In this case, the sundry elements are abreast or echeloned. The intervals are fixed by the platoon-leader. The fraction leaders march ahead of the leading rank.

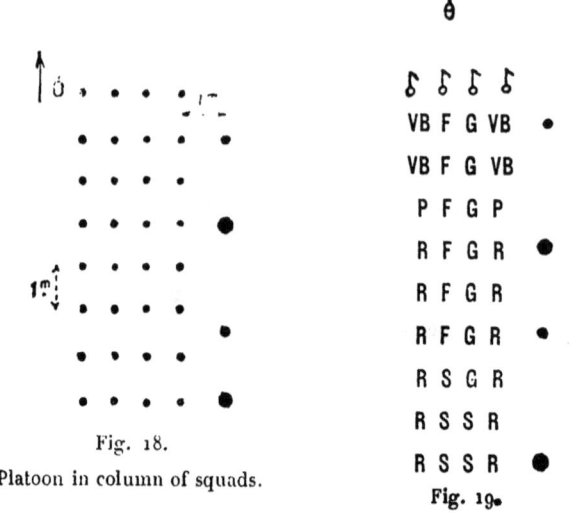

Fig. 18.
Platoon in column of squads.

Fig. 19.
Platoon in line of combat groups in column of files at close intervals.

When the platoon is isolated, the platoon-leader has no particular post, he goes where he thinks his presence will be the most useful.

Assembly, Marching.

(Assembly, march at attention and at ease same as U. S. I. D. R.)

The platoon being in column of squads (fours) to form line of half-platoons or line of combat groups and reform the column of squads.

Line of half-platoons at (30) paces.

MARCH.

The leading half-platoon continues the march until the command HALT the other half-platoon is conducted to its proper position in line to the left of the leading half-platoon, at the interval indicated.

Line of combat groups at (10) paces.

MARCH, HALT.

The leading combat group marches to the front until the command HALT, the second group marches to the right front, the third and fourth groups march to the left front, all taking their position abreast the leading group at the interval indicated. The sergeants and corporals march ahead of their fractions and regulate the gait and direction.

At the command :

Column of squads.

MARCH.

given by the platoon-leader, the column forms again on the fraction in front of which he places himself or indicates.

The preceding movements are constantly executed in the formation for approach.

The line of combat groups is much more easily executed when the platoon is formed in **line of combat groups in column of files at close intervals.**

Formation for approach. — When not under the fire of infantry, the platoon is formed to the best advantage in line of combat groups in columns of files or in line of half-platoons in column of files or of twos.

These formations allow easy marching across broken terrain ; are not vulnerable to artillery fire.

On the battlefield or in the habitual zone of action of the enemy artillery, columns of squads must be absolutely forbidden.

Movements of the platoon in column.

(These are covered in the U. S. I. D. R.)

DEPLOYMENTS OF THE PLATOON.

Formation for combat and combat front of the platoon.

For the same reasons that the **formations for approach** of the platoon under artillery fire are generally the line of combat groups in column of files and the line of half-platoons in column of files or of twos, **the formation for combat of the platoon under infantry fire is the formation in one or in two skirmish lines.**

It is confirmed by the experience of recent combats that the interval at 4 to 5 paces between the men of a deployed line insures the minimum of losses, while maintaining sufficient cohesion. **The interval of 4 to 5 paces between the skirmishers is then the normal interval for combat.**

Consequently, to avoid having a front too greatly extended and on which it becomes impossible to maintain control, the platoon will be formed at the start, **no longer in line but in the direction of depth.**

The habitual front of the platoon is from 80 to 100 paces (65 to 85 yards).

Whether engaged as a **unit of assault** or as a **unit of reinforcement**, the platoon will be formed in two lines, (generally called waves), the first made up of the first half-platoon, the second line by its half-platoon of riflemen or «voltigeurs». The distance between these two waves will be from 10 to 15 paces.

(See *Combat of the platoon*).

Under these conditions, the deployment of an entire platoon in one skirmish line, will be exceptional, so much so, that during the march of approach, the platoon will already have the intervals between its own half-platoon or **its own combat groups progresseing in thin columns.**

On principle, therefore, the deployment as skirmishers is an instruction to be given to the combat group.

Execution of the deployment.

The combat group is deployed according to the principles laid down in U. S. I. D. R. for column of squads, platoon columns and squad columns, the interval desired being indicated in the command.

In the special case, where the half-platoon, or the platoon may not have been already divided into fractions before deployment, the half-platoon or platoon leader gives the necessary indications, especially if the groups are to be deployed in waves.

The corporals, moving rapidly to the head of their units, conduct them to the desired point and, by signs, deploy them on the appropriate direction :

Other deployments as skirmishers. — Skirmishers are also instructed in the deployment without indication of interval, but in such manner as to occupy entirely a line indicated on the terrain, or a space left open on a firing line :

The leader commands :

From such point to such point, as skirmishers.

MARCH.

Guided by their group-leaders, the men deploy rapidly and advance to the indicated line, each one to a point corresponding to his own position in the group, and taking such intervals that the line will be entirely occupied. The line, however, cannot be uniformly filled up because groups and men are given a certain latitude for choosing, where possible, the most favourable posts for firing and resuming the forward movement.

When the fractions of the platoon have been thoroughly trained in rapidly deploying on the drill ground, they are trained afterwards on varied ground, in any direction whatever, starting from any sort of formation, even from an irregular one. A platoon having stacked arms and having fallen out, a platoon resting under arms, one part of it on watch, the other part under cover, etc., should be able to deploy instantaneously at a signal from the platoon leader, without going through any other preparatory movement. The only perfections to be sought after are silence and rapidity.

Finally, groups should be trained in deploying to support a group of another speciality, on both flanks, for instance, the group of grenadiers to support the group of automatic riflemen or a group of riflemen to support a group of grenadiers, etc.

Movements of the skirmish line.

The skirmish line formed of one or more groups and of one or two waves, is trained in marching without cadence or at double time, halting, kneeling and lying down, facing a designated point, extending or closing the intervals by means of the same commands as used in the school of the squad and company U. S. I. D. R.

For a rush, the platoon-leader causes the men to cease firing if necessary, indicates if possible, the cover or the line which is to be reached, and gives the commands of advancing.

The skirmishers repeat the command : «Cease firing», for the benefit of the adjacent men; they cease firing, close their cartridge pouches and hold themselves in readiness for a sudden rise, taking care however not to indicate to the enemy by any movement whatsoever, that a rush is about to take place.

At the command to advance, the skirmishers rush resolutely forward while preserving the alignment as much as possible.

The platoon leader rushes, mingled with his men. If he be in an assaulting platoon, between his two groups of riflemen (voltigeurs); if in a reeinforcing platoon, in the line of the groups of specialists, so as to be able to better conduct his platoon according to the circumstances resulting from the combat of the preceding assaulting platoon. He should not hesitate to rush ahead of his men, if he finds it necessary to lead them on or to attract their notice.

The group leaders rush with their men and set the example.

The file-closers follow the line and see that no one remains behind; they repeat the commands of the platoon leader.

When the indicated cover or line has been reached, the skirmishers halt there on their own accord and take post.

Otherwise : the skirmishers are halted at the command : HALT.

They all lie down at the same time or continue to rush at full speed the few remaining paces which still separate them from a cover, or from the alignment necessary for firing.

In open ground, there is always more danger in crawling slowly toward a cover than in rushing to it suddenly exposing the whole body for a very short time.

The soldier who does not advance immediately at the command, the soldier who lies down before he has reached the alignment of the halted line, commits grave faults which deserve the full rigor of the file-closer.

The wave must also be trained in executing the rush in the following manner : the platoon-leader with the aid of his non-commissioned officers having designated one man out of two, or out of every three for advancing first, the men thus designated rush forward at the command, and, without closing intervals establish themselves in the indicated line. The second numbers, and afterwards the third, if necessary, dart off likewise and fill up the open spaces in such manner that the movement being completed, the platoon is formed on a front of the same density as before having exposed to the hostile fire only very diluted successive lines.

Application of the preceding movements for the progression of the platoon in combat. — Before the combat, the leader indicates the point of direction to the entire platoon. During the course of progression, he regulates the length and frequency of the rushes so as to keep his unit always in good order and in good condition to fight. He profits by all possible shelter to reorganize his platoon and to get it again well in hand (using close order movements, if necessary).

Progression into the combat, is executed :

1° Marching without halting,
2° By long rushes at double time,
3° By short rushes at full speed,
4° By infiltration.

1° et 2° So long as the movement is protected by powerful rafales of artillery fire, at long or medium ranges, the skirmish line marches without halting, otherwise it executes long rushes at double time (50 to 100 meters). File-closers maintain it then in **strict alignment**, particularly in critical moments (artillery fire).

During halts, all consideration as to intervals and distances must disappear in face of the urgent necessity of utilizing the ground to the best advantage.

3° Under fire of hostile infantry, the crossing of open spaces is executed by short and rapid rushes (20 to 50 meters). In combat at close range, avoid making rushes before the point to be reached has been well determined upon and previously indicated to the skirmishers.

4° **When the movement can be executed under cover,** the skirmish line may creep into the new position by infiltration, nearer and nearer.

In open ground, on the contrary, skirmishers moving one after the other **from the same place,** if within good rifle range, are likely to be spotted and shot, by one or two well posted sharp-shooters.

Assault.

The deployments and marchings of the platoon in skirmish line must always be concluded with an assault exercise. Whether the assault be delivered at the beginning of an action, as in the case of a platoon starting from its own trenches to attack the hostile trenches, or is the last act of progression conducted up to within short range of a hostile line, it always preserves the same character.

The assault is usually a combined action of **the whole**, which is executed under the protection of powerful rafales of artillery fire. **The attacking troops should reach the ennemy in a single rush.**

During the struggle which follows, groups of determined skirmishers will also have good occasions to assault. Considerable results may be obtained by the initiative of a handful of braves, sufficient often to cause the advance of an entire line which otherwise would have the tendency to remain immobile.

When a group has succeeded in reaching a cover situated at a small distance from the enemy, the leader gives the command to fix bayonet (without disclosing it); every one makes ready to rush altogether. A volley of grenades is thrown on the enemy; and as soon as they have exploded, the group rises and rushes forward at charge bayonet.

As soon as a platoon has conquered a hostile trench or a center of resistance, if orders are to continue forward, the platoon should previously and rapidly be reformed in good order.

If the platoon is not to continue forward, the conquered point is to be organized immediately. It must not be given up under any pretext even if outflanked. In case of hostile counter attack, it is always desperate resistances of small units that permit the hostile attack to be stopped and the offensive to be resumed.

CHAPTER VI.
ORGANIZATION, FORMATIONS, AND MOVEMENTS OF THE COMPANY.

Organization and officering of the company.

The strength of the company is made up as follows:

1° **Four combatant platoons,** organized as described in Chapter V.

First sergeant, chief of platoon	1
N. C. O.'s (sergeants, half-platoon-leaders)	8
Corporals group leaders	16
Privates	144

2° **N. C. O.'s not included in the combatant platoons.**

1 mess sergeant
1 supply-sergeant   } 3
1 corporal chief of liaison groups

3° **Privates or lance corporals not included in the combatant platoons.**

1 cyclist (liaison agent of captain)
2 buglers (liaison agent of captain)
4 sapper-pioneers
2 mechanics
1 first aid man with battalion surgeon
3 cooks   } 28
2 signalmen
3 observers
4 runners (captain's group)
1 striker (of the captain)
5 runners (1 lance corporal) (battalion group)

TOTAL.............. 200

The assignment of platoon leaders is covered in I. D. R. On principle, a platoon-leader retains command of the platoon to which originally assigned regardless of changes in relative rank.

Formations of the Company.

The company assembles in **close columns of platoons** and in **line of platoons ;** it maneuvers in **line of platoons, in column of squads** and in the formations derived from the above.

The formation in **line** is only used in certain circumstances in time of peace (inspections, parades, maintenance of order, etc.).

Close column of platoons (fig. 20). — The platoons in double rank are formed one in rear of the other, at 6 paces distance.
Front : 20 meters.
Depth : 25 meters.

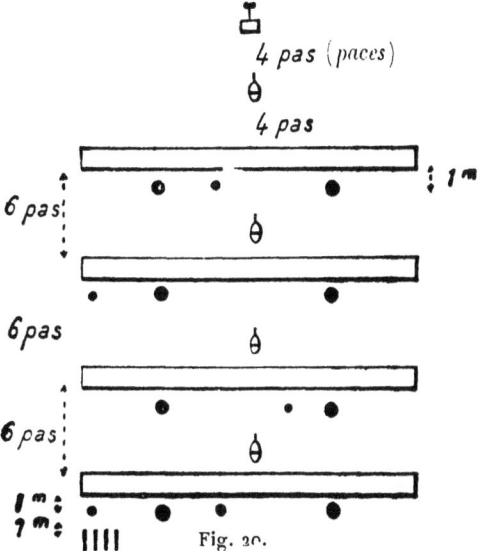

Fig. 20.

Line of the platoons. — The platoons in column of squads are formed abreast, at about four paces (interval resulting when the close column of platoons executes squads right (left). Intervals are varied by giving the appropriate command to extend or close.

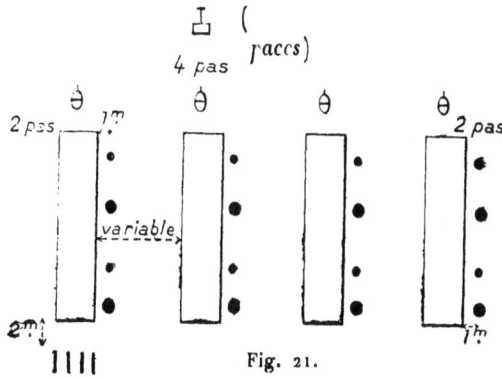

Fig. 21.

Front : 25 meters or variable.
Depth : 25 meters.

— 40 —

Column of squads (fours) (fig. 22). — The platoons in columns of squads are formed in rear of one another at 4 paces distance,
Front: 5 meters.
Depth: 85 meters.

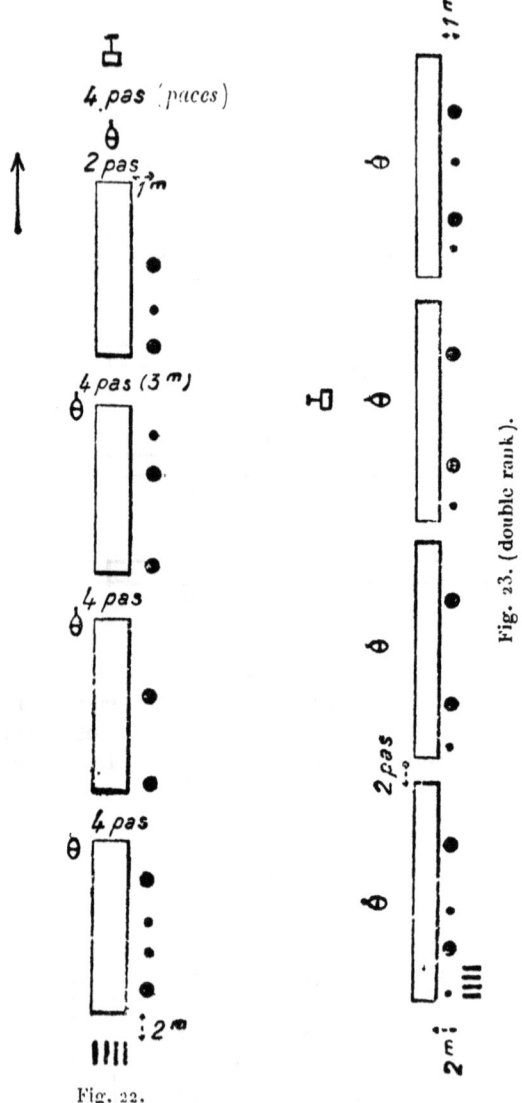

Fig. 22.

Fig. 23. (double rank).

Line (double rank) (fig. 23). — The platoons in double rank are formed in line, at 2 paces interval.
Front: 80 meters.
Depth: 7 meters.

Derived formations. — Besides these four typical formations and the route formation which is described further on, the company may take during the course of its maneuvers and marches of approach, a great number of formations derived generally from the line of platoons, by altering the distances and intervals between the platoons and their formation.

These formations are taken according to indications from the captain who announces the arrangement of the platoons with regard to each other and the **distances** and **intervals** they should take (each platoon being designated by the name of the leader).

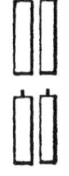

Fig. 24.

Such are :

The column of squads at (so many) paces distances; **the column of linked platoons.** (Fig. 24).

The line of platoons, at (so many) paces, intervals or without intervals.

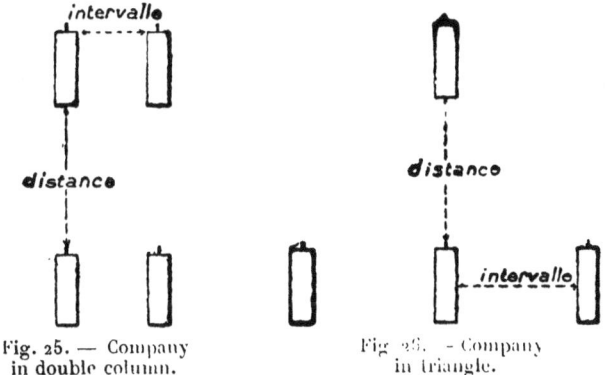

Fig. 25. — Company in double column.

Fig. 26. - Company in triangle.

The line of platoons in column of twos or in column of files.

The line of half-platoons, or **line of combat groups**, in **column** of **squads**, of **twos**, or of **files**.

Fig. 27. — Line of half-platoons in columns of twos at intervals of deployment.

The formations in **double column** (fig. 25), in **lozenge** (fig. 28), in **checker board** (fig. 31), in **echelon** (figs. 29 and 30), in **triangle** (fig. 26), or in **trapeze** (fig. 32), etc.

Notice. — Among these, the **most habitual formation** of approach is the **double column** at variable intervals and distances, the platoons being in line of combat groups (in column of files) or in lines of half platoons (in column of twos or of files). Another formation very often employed is the line of half-platoons (in column of twos or of files, fig. 27).

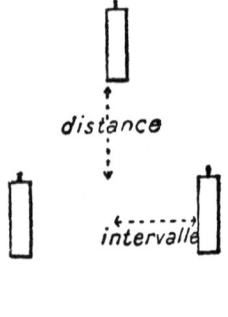

Post of the company commander. — As long as the company is not engaged the captain takes his post at the head.

As soon as the company is engaged he takes his post ahead of his reenforcement platoons, and in any case, close to the skirmish line, so as to be able to follow all its movements, and push it forward, if necessary.

When the platoons are all **engaged**, he takes his post, on the spot from which he can best direct the movement.

Fig. 28. — Company in lozenge.

Liaison for the captain. — The captain has always near to him a « liaison », composed as follows :

1° **Corporal,** chief of the 4 groups of liaison ;

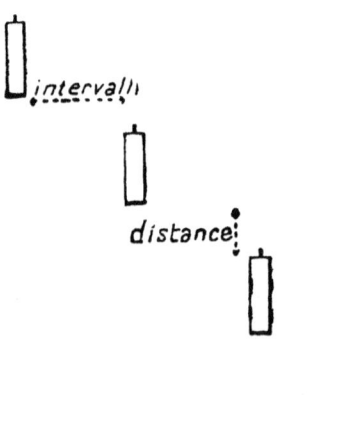

Fig. 29. — Company in echelon left in advance.

2° Group of the agents of liaison : **1 cyclist, 2 buglers.**
3° Group of signallers and observers : **2 signalmen** and 3 **observers** (these later 3 : riflemen).

4° Group of the pioneers : **4 sapper-pioneers;**
5° Group of runners : **4 runners** (riflemen).

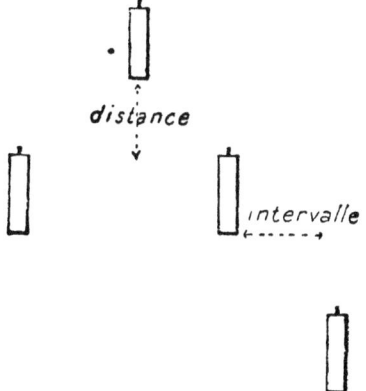

Fig. 3o. — Company in echelon toward the right center in advance.

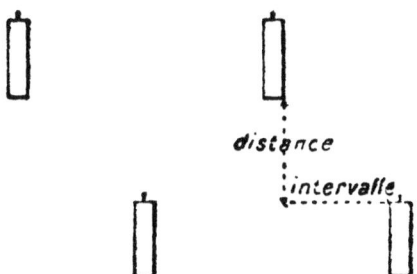

Fig. 31. — Company in checker board 2nd lines overlapping to the right.

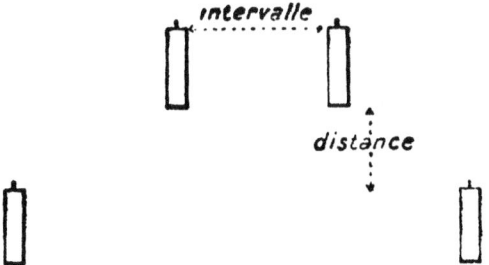

Fig. 32. — Company in trapeze.

The 1st and 2nd elements join the captain without orders as soon as the Company has taken such formation that he cannot command the whole of it by voice. The others join when he calls for them.

The corporal takes care that the personnel does not crowd round the captain and arranges it in a formation.

Movements of the Company.

(In general, as prescribed in U. S. I. D. R.).

The most usual maneuver movements (1) are described as follows. Howewer, if circumstances are such that it is impossible to apply the prescribed formations, it remains with the captain to order such movements as he sees fit, giving to his platoon-leaders all the necessary indications.

To pass from a formation in column of route to an assembly formation.

The captain precedes his company in order to reconnoiter the ground. He indicates which formation is to be taken, the direction in which the company should face, and takes his post eight paces in front of the line to be occupied. The company moves in column of route toward the selected position. Each platoon resumes the attention at the command of its leader, a little before reaching the places where it is to be formed.

If the assembly is to be in close column of platoons, the first platoon-leader conducts his platoon toward the point where the right (left) of his platoon is to rest. If necessary he causes it to change direction a few paces before reaching that point, in such manner that it arrives perpendicular to the direction of the front indicated. When the center element arrives opposite the captain « squads left » (right) is executed. The other platoons take their position in the column by means of the same movements.

If the assembly should be executed in line of platoons, the first platoon-leader conducts his platoon in the direction indicated by the captain, and in such manner that the leading element will be properly faced in that direction before reaching the point which the rear element will occupy when the formation will have been taken. He halts his platoon as soon as the head has reached the line eight paces from the captain. The other platoons take their position, using the same means, the second platoon on the right of the leading platoon, the others on the left.

To pass from an assembly formation to a maneuver formation.

To pass from the close column of platoons and the line of platoons to the column of squads, the captain commands :

« *Column of squads :*
MARCH.

Being in close column of platoons, the leading platoon is formed in column of squads at the command « March », and follows

---

(1) *Note by Tr.* — These movements are not fully covered in U.S.I.D.R. and will serve as an indication in handling large companies.

the captain or the direction which he indicates. The other platoons are formed in column of squads, as soon as they find sufficient room, and follow the movement.

Being in line of platoons, the second platoon moves ahead at the command «March», and follows the captain or the direction he indicates. The other sections march at the command of their chiefs to position in the column, the platoon on the right in rear of the leading platoon.

To pass from the close column of platoons to the line of platoons to the front or to a slightly oblique direction, the captain commands:

« *Line of platoons:*

MARCH.»

At the command « March » the leading platoon is formed in column of squads and follows the captain or the direction he indicates, shortening the step. The other platoons are successively formed in column of squads, and take their position, the second platoon to the right of the leading platoon, the third to its left, the fourth to the left of the latter. The normal gait is resumed at the indication of the captain when all the platoons have arrived on the same line.

To take the same formation in a perpendicular direction or a direction fully oblique to that of the front, the captain may, if he disposes of a space large enough, simply execute « squads right » (left).

To pass from a maneuver formation to an assembly formation.

The company passes from the column of squads to the close column of platoons or to the line of platoons, by the same means as prescribed to pass from the column of route to an assembly formation.

To pass from the line of platoons to the close column of platoons, the captain first forms column of squads. The movement then completed as in the preceding paragraph.

If the captain has sufficient space, he may reach his assembly ground by remaining in the line of platoons and simply executing a change in direction, he then executes « squads right » (left).

To change formation during maneuver.

Being in march the company passes from the column of squads to the line of platoons at the command:

« *Line of platoons:*

MARCH. »

The leading platoon halts; the other platoons take their positions; the second to the right, the others to the left of the leading platoon.

The captain causes the march to be resumed as soon as all the platoons have arrived on the line.

Being in march, the company passes from the line of platoons to the column of squads at the command :

« *Column of squads :*
    MARCH. »

The second platoon follows the captain; the others are halted by their leaders and take their position in the column, the first in rear of the leading platoon.

During the approach, the captain causes the intervals and distances to be increased and divides the platoons, he echelons them on one or two wings, according to the objects in view. It is always to his interest to employ all the ground available and to take widely extended formations to better utilize the terrain, to obtain more suppleness and diminish the vulnerability,

Formations for combat and combat of the company.

The company is formed for combat in **skirmish lines ;** the number of platoons in the first line and of platoons in support is variable. (A company has no reserves.) The company being at the start **in the direction of depth**, the captain is able to make his action felt.

The combat of the company is described in Part VIII.

CHAPTER VII.

THE COMPANY ON THE MARCH.

March formations. — The company marches generally in column of squads, on the right side of the road, the remainder of which is left free. On narrow roads, the company is formed in column of twos, or of files if necessary, the men closing up as much as possible in order to diminish the length.

If a diminution in direction of depth is desired, the company may, on a wide road, march in double formation by marching two platoons abreast in columns of squads (column of linked platoons).

At a given command, the company may march on the left side of the highway, or on both sides, the middle remaining free.

En route, the captain marches where he thinks his presence the most useful, generally at the tail of the company. The platoon leaders march where they can best survey their unit, on principle, at the tail of their platoons. The leader of the first half-platoon of each platoon marches at the head of the leading element on the free side of the road; he preserves the distance from the preceding platoon.

The other N. C. O's. march as file closers in rear of their platoons. The distance of three meters which separates the two consecutive platoons in the formation in column of squads is thus filled up by the rank of file closers of the platoon ahead and by the incomplete rank made up of the leader of the first half-platoon of the following platoon.

Drummers and buglers march at the head or in rear of the company, according to circumstances, if they are not assembled by battalion.

The gait is regulated by a N.C.O. carrying his knapsack, and marching at the head of the first platoon, under the control of the platoon-leader. He tries to prevent irregularities in gait by gradually increasing or diminishing the step, without being bound however to exactly preserve the 10 meters distance separating companies.

The men march at **route step** rifle slung on either shoulder; they are not required to remain silent or in step but preserve very carefully their position in ranks.

To pass through towns, the **attention**, or the march **at ease** is resumed at the command of the major. The captain causes the route step to be abandoned or resumed only when the head of his company reaches the point where the leading company has executed the same.

For the employment of the whistle, during march, see « Commands with arm signals or whistle ». (Chapter IX, Part IV.)

INFORMATIONS. — *Company* in route column of squads: front 3 m. 5o; depth, 9o meters; to pass a given point 1 minute.

Companies of machine guns on two wheel carts (without combat train): 110 meters.

Battalion : 3 companies and 1 machine gun company, about 4oo meters; to pass a given point 5 minutes.

Complete combat train (battalion 3 companies and machine gun company) 180 meters and 2 1/2 minutes.

Regiment of 3 battalions. Troops only, 155o meters and 19 minutes; with combat train complete: 225o meters and 27 1/2 minutes; combat train only (22 wagons): 210 meters and 3 minutes.

Execution of the march. — **Before starting :** Have the canteens filled up, fires extinguished, the cantonment put in order, the billeting marks erased, papers burnt.

Departure is never delayed : If the commander of a unit is not there at the hour appointed for the departure, the senior officer present marches it off.

Initial point : If an initial point has been designated by the battalion commander (to avoid an assembly) and if a company arrives there ahead of time, let it rest on the road side leaving the road absolutely clear.

Liaison : Every element should keep in touch with the preceding element either by sight or by connecting files, in order not to lose the route.

Any element which breaks out of a column should inform the element in rear, in order that the latter should not follow it.

Hourly halts : *Duration :* 10 minutes ; executed, except in case of contrary orders, 5o minutes after the hour. The head of each battalion is halted and resumes marching at the exact moment, the companies closing to their distance (10 meters) on the head of the battalion.

According to orders given once for all by the major, the companies remain in column of squads or form line to the left to stack arms, as prescribed in school of the soldier for a unit being in either of these formations.

During halt, the men keep on the same side as the stacks, unless this side of the road should be lined with walls or hedges. In this case, they may move to the opposite side; while keeping entirely clear of the road. This movement to be regulated in each platoon.

The hourly halt is not obligatory. A unit about to go into action takes rest according to the situation and in favourable places.

Main halt : Is ordered in a place close to water, two thirds or three quarters of the distance to be covered. It is essential to announce the duration in advance and cause a signal to be made 5 minutes before resuming the march.

March discipline. — The principal object of march discipline is to **diminish lengthening the column,** the longer the column the stricter the discipline. With a company or battalion marching separately, it is possible to give more ease by increasing the distance between companies and platoons, the very small difference in distance that may result between the successive ranks in columns of squads has no great consequence. On the contrary, with a column of a brigade, a division, etc., these differences of distances are amplified and work back until they create delay and disorder at the tail of the column. File closers and officers should in consequence rigorously make every one march in his proper place.

Any shout of command **March** or **Halt** or otherwise is prohibited.

A man **exceptionally** allowed to quit the ranks by his

platoon leader, gives his rifle to his next comrade ; he rejoins as soon as possible.

A sick man cannot remain in rear unless he presents a note from the captain to the surgeon at the rear of the regiment.

The column inclines as much as possible to the right side of the road, not however requiring the right files to march off the beaten roadway. In any case a passage should be always maintained clear and sufficiently wide for a horseman or a cyclist to pass the column at full speed without running the risk of accidents and without being obliged to shout to make room.

Each company furnishes a N.C.O. and a few men for the police detachment which marches in rear of the regiment, to pick up stragglers.

Night marches. — Always keep contact with the preceding element; detach connecting files as soon as the distances increase.

According to the situation, prohibit smoking and talking.

Marching in hot or cold weather. — In hot weather have the clothing modified, increase distances, open ranks · halt more frequently and organize the supply of water.

In cold weather, prevent men standing motionless during halts, augment the ration.

CHAPTER VIII.

SCHOOL OF THE SAPPER
IMPORTANCE TO BE GIVEN TO FIELD WORKS IN TRAINING AND IN FIGHTING.

The present war has put the **tool** on the same footing as the **rifle.**

Nowadays, the soldier is at the same time a **combatant** and a **workman :** one cannot be imagined without the other.

He uses his rifle **sometimes,** his tool **every day.**

When the soldier has conquered the ground at the cost of blood, if he counts only on his rifle to hold it he will be greatly deceived. He must, as tired as he may be, immediately start digging ; he must know that each shovelful lifted, in spite of fatigue, is a check to the counter attack which the enemy is preparing against him **at that very moment.**

For officers and non-commissioned officers to lead their men to the field is a rather easy matter **But to get**

exhausted and decimated troops to work without rest or delay is a far more difficult task. It is however just as imperative a duty as the first : the least counter attack may turn an apparent victory into a defeat, if the « digging to hold » energy does not immediately follow the energy to conquer.

Non-commissioned officers will make their work easier if they impress upon their men beforehand such ideas ; ideas which do not always appear to them quite obvious. Non-commissioned officers must never miss an opportunity of explaining to them how in various combats carelesness has been severely punished and how very worth while working tenacity has proved to be.

Two great principles must always be present to everybody's mind :

1° **Never delay starting a work because the necessary time for its complete achievement may be lacking.**

This principle is true under any circumstance : in fighting or in position.

2° **In the fight, after an advance, the best means of reforming the troops consists in showing the work to be done and obliging the men to start it at once.**

The surviving chiefs must be energetic enough to immediately assemble and coordinate the efforts after a fight and **they must think at once of the subsequent operation, preparing the ground for it.** Otherwise, every soldier or small party wastes its strength and time on individual undertakings, they dig where they find holes and bits of trenches which are of no use for resuming the forward movement and in that way a battalion looses sometimes two or three days which could have been improved to the benefit of the following progression.

To thoroughly inculcate the second principle it is necessary in training exercises to order that every infantry **maneuver must be closed with a staking out of the lines and commencing work on the final position occupied.** Officers and soldiers will get into the habit of considering maneuvers and entrenching one and same thing, both of which are to be executed with similar means and commands.

It is wrong to have separate maneuver and entrenching exercises. Entrenching is part of the maneuver to the same degree as extended order or assault drill. And whether on the offensive or defensive, there is no maneuver without entrenching.

Division into chapters relating to fieldworks. Field works as considered in this manual. — Field works

regulations, approved dec. 21st, 1915, have replaced all the previous Regulations. All parts of these regulations are interesting for infantry officers and N. C. O., s.; they cannot study them too diligently. Only the length of these Regulations prevent us from inserting them in full in this hand book. The elementary information selected from them refers to two different leading ideas.

1° In Part II (Elementary Training of the infantry man) have been gathered all the elements of entrenching which every soldier must be able to carry out, mechanically and thoroughly, without having to know the reason therefor. It is the « **manual of arms** » for field works; it has to be taught just as minutely.

2° Chapter VI of Part IV (Field fortification principles) deals with the manner of utilizing these different elements in an organization to accomplish a definite purpose.

Normal types of field works. — To place the infantry pioneer instruction on a solid basis one standard type only of the following works will be given herewith :

1° Skirmisher's trench ;
2° Standing trench ;
3° Traverse ;
4° Ammunition recess ;
5° Communicating trench (boyau)
6° Deep sap ;
7° Russian sap ;
8° Machine gun epaulment ;
9° Deep dug-out.

Non-commissioned officers must know thoroughly by heart these fundamental types : shape, dimensions and regular method of execution.

An order to construct one such element (communicating trench, epaulment, etc.), when given without any further explanation implies the exact construction of the normal types by means of the regular methods.

These normal types are taught to the men before any thing else.

When they thoroughly know them, it is easy to have them execute any other type taken from the « Field Works Regulations » or modified on account of the ground, materials, time, etc.

Nomenclature of the firing trench and of saps. —
The ditches used in field fortification to fire from or to

circulate in under cover have two different names **according to the way they are dug:**

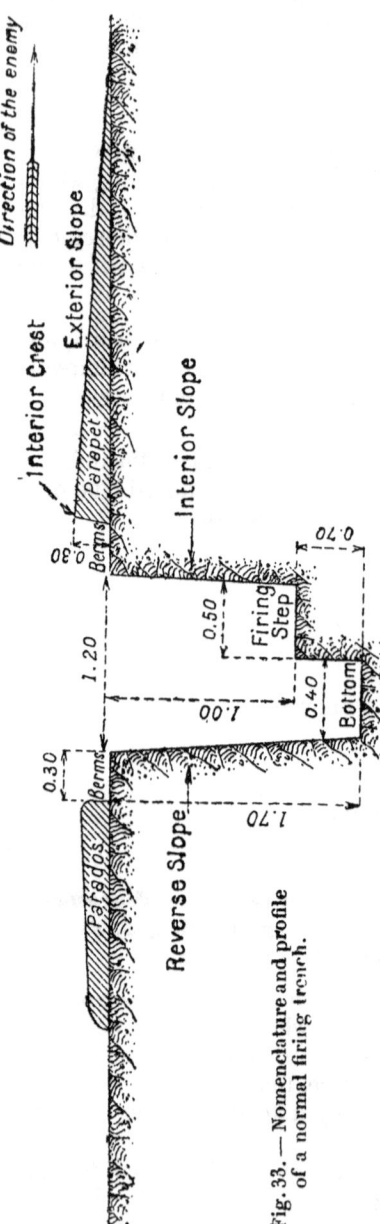

Fig. 33. — Nomenclature and profile of a normal firing trench.

Sap is the name given to ditches dug by sappers pushing forward slowly and progressively in the open.

Trench is the name given to ditches dug simultaneously on a more or less extended front.

In the colloquial language the custom has grown of designating by the word:

Trench a firing trench, **parallel** a communication trench parallel to the front line, **boyau** a communication trench perpendicular to the front line.

The words **sap** and **trench** keep nevertheless their meaning to indicate the method of work to be used. For instance it will be said with a very accurate meaning: a boyau dug like a trench or a boyau dug like a sap, a firing trench to be constructed like a sap, etc.

Lastly, among the excavations dug in the sap system there are:

The **simple sap,** now called boyau;

The **deep sap,** which is a boyau, without parapet, the loose earth having been carried to the rear in proportion as the digging is pushed forward.

The **deep covered sap** or **covered trench,** which is similar to the preceding one except that it is concealed by a light earth bed supported with hurdles or logs.

The **Russian sap,** an underground gallery without sheeting, the roof is cut as a vault 25 to 30 cm. under the ground.

The **armored sap** is a covered sap, the timbered roof of which is bullet and splinter proof.

The **sand-bag sap,** without digging, the two parapets of which are sand bag walls 1 m. 80 to 2 meters high.

It is wrong to use the word **sap** for underground works. The underground works are **mine-works,** they are called galleries or branches.

It is important to keep closely to these terms.

Qualities of a trench. — *Width.* — Cover is better in a narrow trench, circulation and inspection are easier in a wide trench.

Depth. — A deep trench gives better cover and is more difficult to reverse if the enemy happens to take it. It necessitates a higher firing step and special means to keep the step in shape and to reach it.

Slope. — Vertical slopes do not hold as well but increase the security in lessening the width. They enable men to take shelter close to the parapet.

Command. — If too low, it does not give a sufficient view; if too high it is too visible.

Parapet. — A superior slope with a good gradient smoothly joining the natural ground, ives more complete concealment, especially when it is possible to make it resemble the foreground; all sharp angles and hard lines should be avoided as they are detected in the distance on account of the difference in lighting.

Normal types.

1° Skirmisher's shelter trench.

This is a protective parapet which the riflemen are compelled to construct to protect themselves from the assailant's fire.

Fig. 34. — Skirmishers shelter trench.

Riflemen lying near one another protect themselves at the beginning of the work with their knapsacks; they dig the ground so as to gather in front of them a light parapet: they work and fire as well as circumstances allow.

2° *Standing trench.*

The **trench for a standing rifleman** is the only one which under the conditions of modern warfare secures to the soldier a sufficient protection, and enables him to use his arms with the maximum fire effect.

Fig. 33 shows the profile and dimensions of the normal trench.

Interior crest in 1 m. 30 (52 inches) above the banquette which is 0 m. 50 (20 inches) wide.

The bottom of the trench is 1 m. 70 (68 inches) below the ground level and 2 m. (80 inches) below the top of parapet.

The width of 1 m. 20 (48 inches) at the level of the ground permits a good slope.

The width is sufficient to temporarily put two assaulting lines in the trench.

Berms are uniformly 0 m. 30 (12 inches).

If the excavation is stopped at 0 m. 70 (28 inches) from the level of the ground, **the kneeling trench** is the result.

If in addition a banquette 0 m. 40 (16 inches) high × 0 m. 50 (20 inches) wide has been provided the result is a

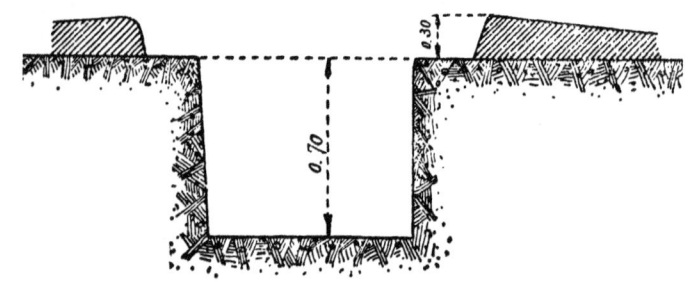

Fig. 36.

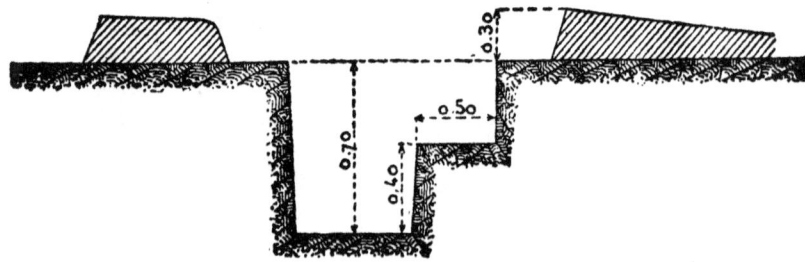

Fig. 37.

sitting trench. These two kinds of trenches must be considered only as intermediate stages in the standing trench construction, which is always the final object.

3° *Traverses.*

Traverses are essential parts of the trench. They are intended to secure protection against very oblique or enfilade fire; they limit the destructive effect of projectiles.

Further, they facilitate a fight against an enemy who may have gained a foot-hold in the trench.

Therefore it is most advantageous to dig loop-holes in the traverse.

Distance between traverses. — meters as a maximum, 4 meters as a minimum.

Dimensions. — Traverses are levelled so that the crest of the traverse is not higher than the interior crest of the parapet. To secure a sufficient protection, the normal traverse is 2 m. 50 thick at the level of the ground and 2 m. 80 at the bottom of the trench. It has to be 1 m. 50 long on the surface of the ground so that the back of the traverse extends farther to the rear than the line of the back wall.

Never make recesses, cavities and, more especially, shelters, in a traverse.

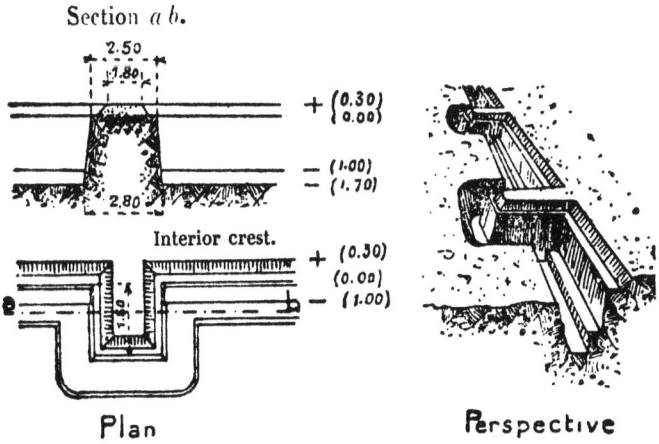

Fig. 38. — Traverses.

REMARK. — If the trench has not been dug with traverses, the same result may be obtained with **splinter proof shields** which are elements just thick enough to give cover against splinters without greatly reducing the length of the interior crest; they are made with fascines, sand-bags, gabions or gravel between planks.

A « traverse », properly speaking, is a part of the natural ground left untouched, while digging the trench; a « splinter proof shield » is inserted after the trench is finished.

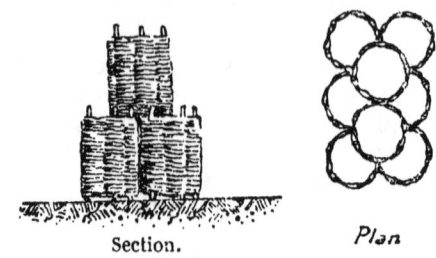

Fig. 39. — Splinter proof shield.

4° *Ammunition recess.*

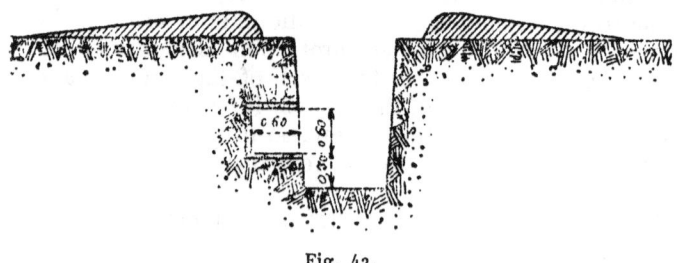

Fig. 42.

5° *Boyau.*

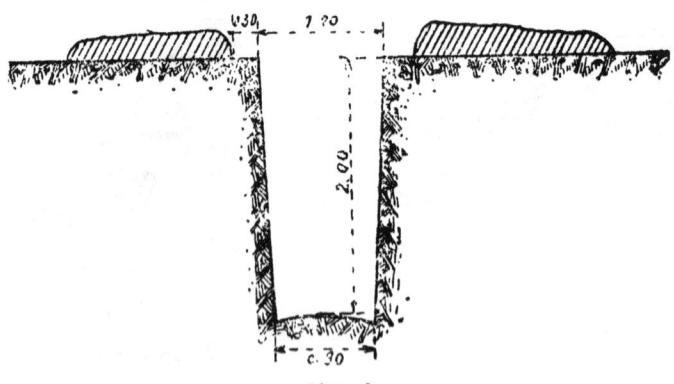

Fig. 43.

Dimension of a passing point in a boyau :
Length : 1 meter (40 inches),
Depth : 0 m. 80 (32 inches).

6° *Deep sap.*

The loose earth is carried to the rear by supernumeraries, by relays of shovellers (4 meters for one relay) or by the use of baskets and wheelbarrows (30 meters for a wheelbarrow relay).

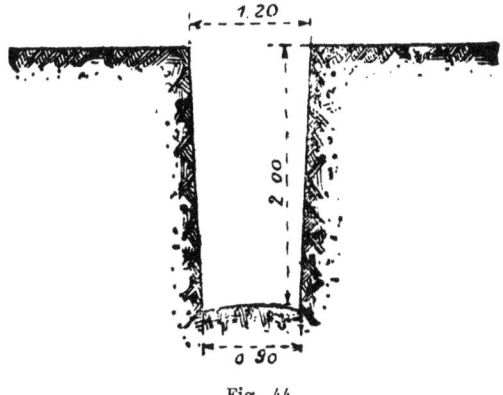

Fig. 44.

7° *Russian sap.*

A gallery without sheetings, the roof of the gallery being a pointed arch. The loose earth is carried to the rear in

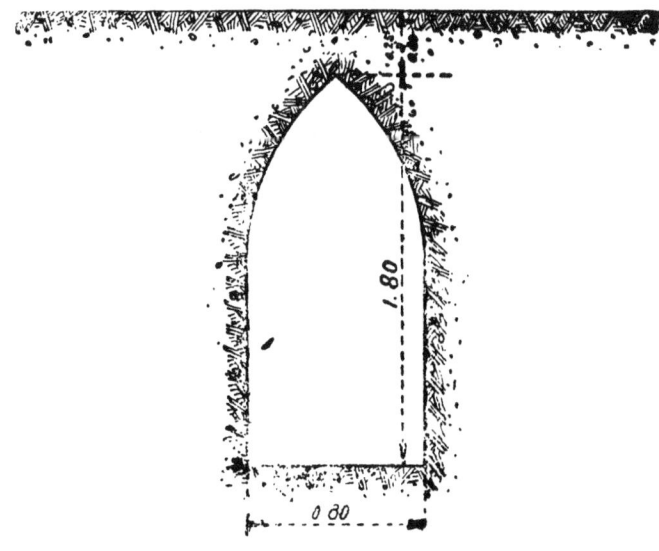

Fig. 45.

the same way as for the deep sap. Ventilating shafts from place to place indicate the direction of the underground work with respect to the surface of the ground. It is delicate work which can be carried out in only very firm ground. Advantages: the advance toward the enemy is concealed; it can be cut open at the last moment and converted into a boyau or trench, the digging of which has been kept from the ennemy's notice.

8° Machine-gun epaulment.

The normal machine-gun epaulment must be quickly dug in the open, during open warfare.

The progress in aerial observation prohibits using it in the parapet of trenches unless it is carefully camouflaged: camouflage is a peremptory condition for its use.

Machine-guns are generally mounted outside of the trench, often in a camouflaged shell crater, with a subterranean access passage.

The excavated earth must be spread or thrown in nearby shell craters.

Under these conditions the epaulment, as shown in fig. 46, gives a good cover to the machine-gun and to the

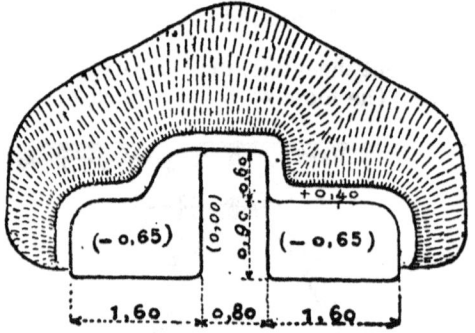

Fig. 46. — Machine-gun epaulment for the lying position.

gunners lying in the firing position; for the normal firing position the platform is lowered 0 m. 30 (12 inches), the nearby trenches are deepened to 0 m. 80.

It is important that any emplacement prepared for a machine-gun should show very plainly **the firing sector** intended for the machine-gun: for that purpose finish the construction by driving three large stakes into the platform. One of these stakes is at the point of the angle, the two others at the sides of the angle inside of which the machine-gun can and must fire. The object of these protruding stakes is not to show the position of the three tripod legs, which would be useless, but to furnish marks easy to find at night and plainly limiting the firing sector.

Throw away any other poorer method or anything which could not be understood without explanation, by the gunners casually occupying the emplacement.

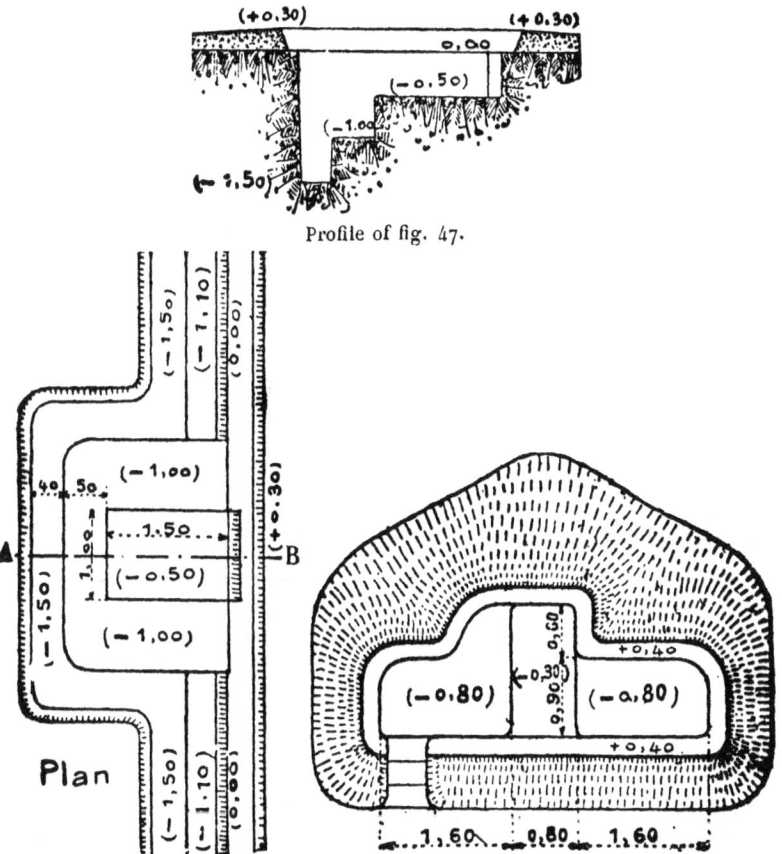

Profile of fig. 47.

Fig. 47. — Projection.

Fig. 48. — Machine-gun epaulment for normal firing position.

9° *Deep dug-out.*

There is no normal type for a **light shelter** or even **reinforced shelters.** Models shown in chapter VI of Part IV of this hand-book and in the Field Works Regulations are only examples in which everything depends upon the circumstances.

A dug-out is said to be **bomb-proof** when it can resist a systematic regulated gun fire of 130's. or 150's. or isolated hits from 210's or greater.

The **surface bomb-proof shelters** i. e. built in the open (a sketch of which will be given later) are never as good as deep dug-outs; the latter must be preferred even if the digging takes a longer time.

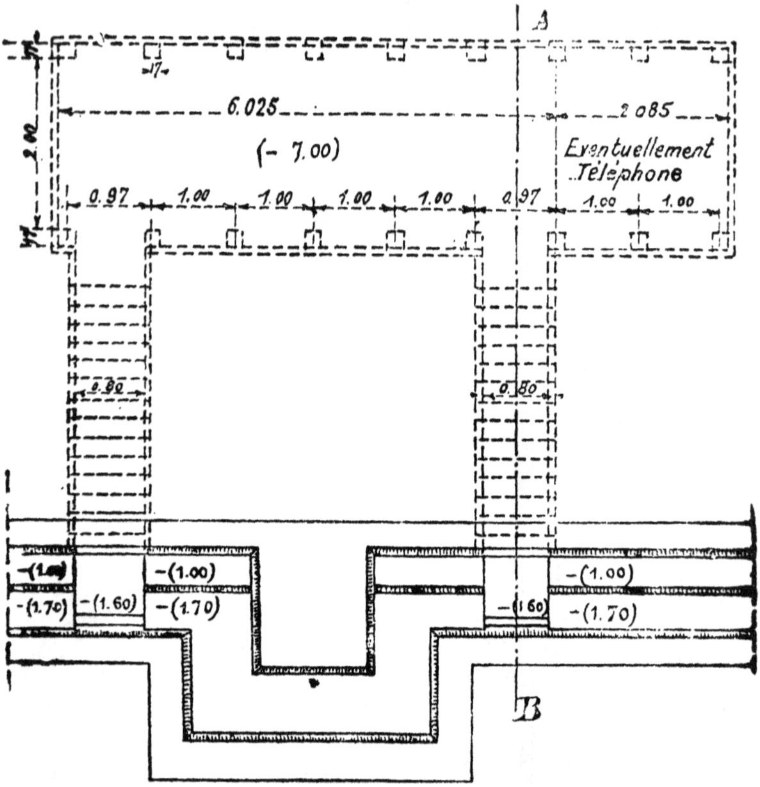

— 60 —

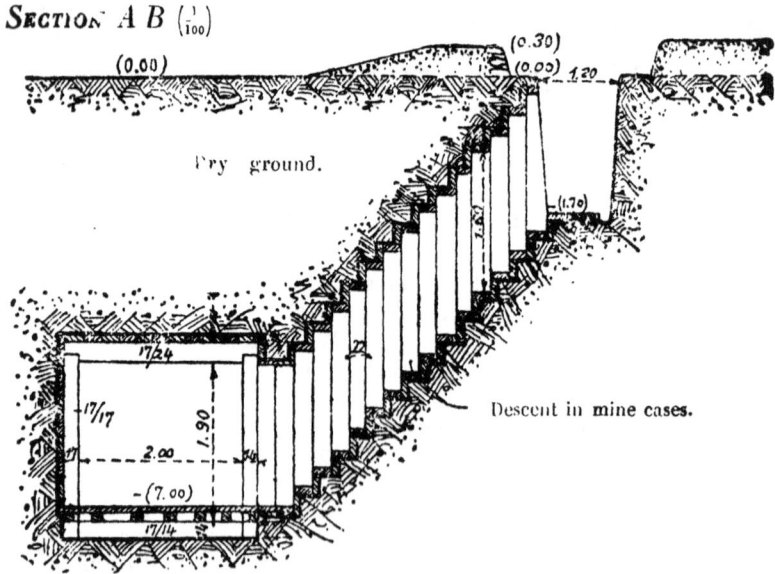

Fig. 52.

The deep dug-out is therefore, except in the case of absolute prevention, the rigid rule. It must be started, **without delay**, by infantry troops themselves under the guidance of regimental or company sapper-pioneers and without waiting for the engineer troops. Every non-commissioned officer must know all the particulars of the normal type as shown in fig. 52.

The characteristics of the normal dug-out are :

1° It is sunken under at least 6 meters of natural ground. 5 m. 20 of hard and solid chalk resist the big aerial torpedoes and the heavy shells with delay action fuse.

Fig. 52 shows a dug-out only three meters deep ; it can easily be imagined deeper.

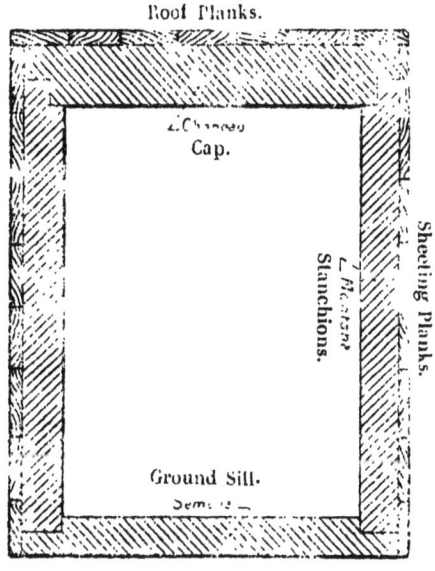

Fig. 52 II.

2° It has two inclined galleries descending on each side of a traverse. These inclined galleries are made with **mine cases** or **in low gallery**.

3° It is a good thing to have a third inclined gallery breaking out in the open ground in rear in a well hidden and camouflaged shell crater, and to have it communicating with the near-by dug-out by means of a low gallery or mine branch.

4° Inclined galleries are connected together with a great gallery which **half a platoon** can inhabit.

5° The dug-out must be constructed with the greatest

care : a **rigid whole** must be obtained ; the lateral bracing is indispensable. All botch work is followed by the crushing and collapsing of the timber casing.

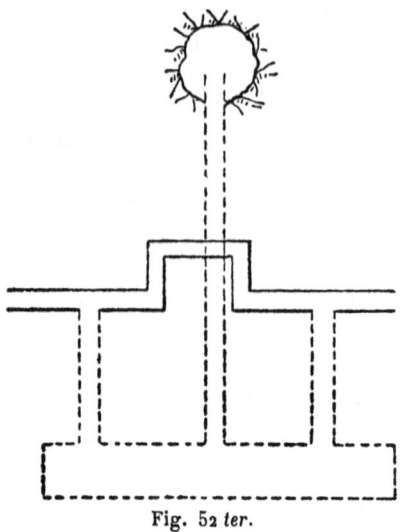

Fig. 52 ter.

Nomenclature of the dug-out. — The inclined gallery in mine-cases is shown by fig. 52, in **low gallery** by fig. 52-V.

Galleries are composed of **frames, roof planks** and **sheeting planks.**

A **frame** is composed of **1 cap, 2 stanchions** and **1 ground** sill. Fig. 52-II.

Roof planks are thicker than the sheeting planks [about 4 centimeters (1 1/2 inch) and 2 1/2 cm. (1 inch)]. Their common width is 22 cm. (8 4/5 inches).

The cap-sill is always the thicker scantling and the ground sill the thinner. Never use one instead of the other.

Dimensions of frames generally used by Infantry troops.

NAME of FRAME.	DIMENSIONS INSIDE MEASUREMENT.		SCANTLINGS.		NUMBER of PLANKS.	
	Height.	Width.	Stanchions.	Caps.	Roof planks.	Sheeting planks.
Low gallery....	1ᵐ30 to 1ᵐ50 52-60 in.	1 meter. 40 in.	11 × 11 4.4 in.	11 × 16 4.4×6.4	12 to 17	5 to 8
Common gallery	2 meters. 80 in.	1 meter. 40 in.	13 × 13 5.2 in.	13 × 16 5.2×4.6	13 to 24	5 to 8
Great gallery...	2 meters. 80 in.	2ᵐ10 84 in.	17 × 17 6.8 in.	17 × 24 6.8×9.6	16 to 24	8 to 12

The **low gallery** is used for inclined galleries only, the **common gallery** to shelter men sitting or a row of men lying lengthwise of the gallery.

The **great gallery** for men lying athwart the gallery or two rows of men lying lengthwise of the gallery, with a central passage; the **branches** (main and small) and the **shafts** are used only by sappers in mining warfare.]

Diverse suggestions. — When scantlings are not a hand, use round logs of equal cross section.

In any construction always use the thickest wood as **caps**: the cap-sill is never too strong. The stanchions, working under compression, may be a little thinner than shown in the table when they are not too long: in an improvised frame they must never be over 2 meters long.

Never omit the ground sill and always bury it so as not to trip against it, otherwise floor the ground sills with planks.

Lateral bracing. — The cross bracing is an arrangement to prevent the different parts of nearby frame work from becoming disconnected and to secure steadiness of framing.

There are always two bracings: a tranversal and a longitudinal. In the peculiar case of a mine gallery the trans-

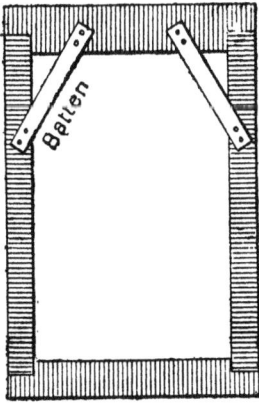

Fig. 52 IV. — Transverse bracing of a frame.

verse bracing prevents the frame from getting out of shape and the longitudinal bracing unites two successive frames; the latter is made with a piece of strip called «batten» nailed as in AB or with a round log strongly wedged up CD.

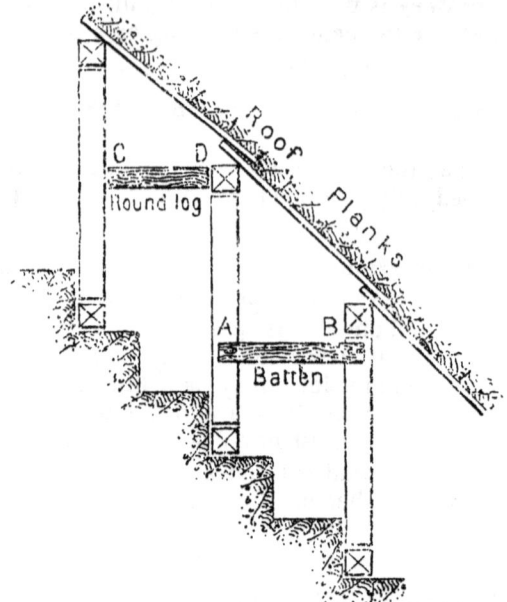

Fig. 5₂ v. — Inclined low gallery. Longitudinal bracing.

Staircase. — The staircase must have the design as per fig. 5₂-V and not the faulty disposition of fig. 5₂-VI.

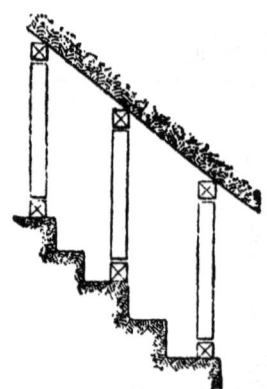

Fig. 5₂ vi. — Faulty staircase.

Tamping. — It is most important to well tamp the earth against the planks and not to leave an empty gap between the cut and the sheetings. A good tamping can be verified by knocking the planks with a stick.

Nota. — Neither the deep dug-out nor staircases should be called saps.

CONSTRUCTION OF A TRENCH.

Trace. — The officer in charge of the work marks on the ground the line of the exterior side of the cutting with tracing-tape, stones, pegs, or by scratching with a pick, etc. and if he anticipates possible errors, marks the other edge also.

He uses white tracing-tape whenever he can obtain it.

Starting the work. — Taking under consideration the duration of the work, the quality of the ground, the number of workers and the number of tools, he determines the composition of the working parties and the length of the task assigned to each party. This length is usually one pace per man in the working party.

Each sergeant has the supervision of the task of several parties. Corporals work like privates except those assigned the function of sergeant i. e. foremen.

With heavy entrenching tools **in easy ground** the party will consist of 2 shovels and 1 pick handled by 3 or 6 men : the length of work will therefore be 3 to 6 paces.

In hard ground the party will consist of 1 shovel and 1 pickaxe, therefore 2 or 4 men and 2 or 4 paces.

When 2 men are detailed to a tool double the length of task may be accomplished in the same time provided the tools are worked without interruption and the men work with an increased energy corresponding to the rest they have during half the time.

The limit of each party's work is marked beforehand by grooves perpendicular to the trace. A non-commissioned officer in rear distributes tools to the men and divides the men into parties. The workers are brought on to the ground in column of two or files on one flank of the intended work, and are then formed into line, each party opposite the particular task assigned to it, facing the enemy.

All must keep silent and undue haste must be avoided. The officer in charge of the work verifies whether everyone is in the right place, then gives in a low voice the command **Commence work.** Only then every worker places his rifle and equipment on the ground 4 paces behind him, finishes marking the limits of his work on right and left (such marks must extend well beyond the side lines of the trenches) and starts digging. The men waiting for work lie down outside the line formed by the knapsacks and equipments.

CONSTRUCTION OF A PROGRESSIVE SAP.

The sap work is explained later on with detailed particulars ; it must be executed with the greatest care.

It is prohibited to change any of these methods as they have proved to be valuable by long experience and give the maximum speed in an approach previous to an attack.

Men left to themselves generally work alternately with the shovel and the pick under the pretext that it is easier and quicker. When the N. C. O.'s have impressed upon them the advantage of following the prescribed method they come quickly into the habit of proper working and will really progress more rapidly.

The first step called the **debouchement** consists in cutting the sap head in the parapet of the departure trench. When the debouchement has been made by one of the prescribed methods of procedure a movable mask is made either with shields or with sand bags closely set together 40 centimeters to the front.

1st METHOD : *In very immediate proximity to the enemy.*

SINGLE SAP.

Personnel and material. — Every sap head working party includes 1 non-commissioned officer and 4 sapper-pioneers. The sap head working party is divided into two equal gangs relieving each other every meter and alternately working in the sap or resting in the trench. Continuous work night and day requires : 1 N. C. O., 1 assistant and 12 men divided into 3 gangs of 4 men with a relief every 8th hour. If practicable there is one supernumerary for every sap head party.

In the working gang sappers are numbered 1 and 2 ; at every relief they change posts, number 1 becomes number 2 and reciprocally. The sapper n° 1 is provided with a pick and a short handled hoe (made out of an ordinary pick mattock) he has besides a rod 1 m. 20 long (for breadth measure at the top) and a 2 meters rod (for depth measurement). The sapper n° 2 is provided with an ordinary shovel and a 0 m. 30 rod (to measure breadth of berm).

The sap head party must be provided moreover with the following implements :

1 long handled wooden hoe ;
2 long handled iron hoe ;
1 bundle of small stakes ;
1 large pick and 2 reserve shovels ;
1 short handled heavy pickaxe ;
1 short handled shovel or spade ;
1 hurdle and metallic trellis to rapidly construct a grenade screen.
A supply of hand grenades.

Construction of the sap. — **The N.C.O. in charge of the sap** marks with pegs the direction of the sap and fixes with the meter rod and the pegs the task of the gang. He posts his 4 sappers. He frequently verifies the dimensions of each part dug and notes the time spent by each gang to do its task.

The sapper n° 1 (with pick) works in at the head of the sap. First kneeling or squatting he digs the ground on the whole width of the sap to the proper depth : 1 m. 20 at the top, 0 m. 90 at the bottom, 2 meters in depth from the level of the ground. He first traces 2 vertical grooves, the depth of the pick head, up to half the height of the excavation, in continuation of the sides of the sap. He then traces one horizontal groove, at the bottom of the excavation, to the depth of pick axe head, to undermine the lump of earth that is to be detached. He then cuts down the lump thus prepared beginning near the bottom. He throws back the loose earth between his legs by means of the short handled hoe, but takes care to clean out the sap in order to always secure a uniform depth of 2 meters. Then standing up he starts digging the superior part of the excavation, making vertical grooves on the right and left up to the level of the ground, he then knocks down with his pick the overhead mass of earth, the limits of which have been thus marked, and throws back the loose earth between his legs. as above explained. He excavates his initial part of the sap advancing 0 m. 40 to 0 m. 50 at a time and verifying frequently the dimensions by means of the rods with which he is provided.

The sapper n° 2 (with a shovel) stands close by n° 1. He throws, first with the short handled shovel or the spade-shovel, then with the ordinary shovel, the loose earth thrown backwards by the sapper n° 1 and heaps it in front to make the mask thicker, then on the right and left to form the parapets. The sapper n° 2 throws the loose earth either above the head of sapper n° 1, or on his left or right tangentially to the top of the parapet. He takes care to throw the earth in the front of the parapet to remedy the breach which is formed every time the head mask is advanced and on this mask itself to keep its dimensions always normal. A berm of about 0 m. 30 is left between the parapet and the edge of the excavation and may be regular if necessary by means made of the long handled hoe.

The sappers n° 1 and 2 may change posts toward the middle of the task assigned to them, the length of which is 1 meter.

Advancing the mask. — When the excavation has reached the mask, the sappers n° 1 and 2, helped if necessary by the other gang and lying as prone as possible to avoid being uncovered, push the head mask 40 to 50 centimeters forward, throwing back the loose earth from the lower part with the hoe obliquely to the axis of the parapet or putting the sand bags on the anterior part o the mask. The sapper n° 1 places his hoe under the earth of the mask. The other sappers push the handle and mov the mask forward.

Changing the gang. — At the signal **Change**, made by the head sapper, when the digging has reached the length of his rod, i. e. 1 meter, the first gang lays down its tools on the ground and the second takes their places.

2ND METHOD : *In immediate proximity to the enemy.*

PROGRESSIVE DOUBLE SAP.

Personnel. — Every sap head working party includes 1 N. C. O. and 8 sapper-pioneers divided into two gangs. A continuous work requires 1 N. C. O. 1 Assistant and 24 men divided into 3 gangs of 8 men with a relief every 8th hour.

In each gang the sappers are numbered 1 to 4; the sappers n° 1 and 3 are provided with picks and n° 2 and 4 with shovels.

Sapper n° 1 is provided with measuring sticks 1 m. 20 and 1 meter long, n° 3 with sticks 1 meter, 2 meters and 0 m. 30 long.

Execution of the saps. — Sappers n° 1 and 2 are provided with short handled tools, they work in the sap head according to the rules explained under the first method and dig a first element 1 m. 20 wide at the top, 1 meter at the bottom and 1 meter in depth from the level of the ground ; they do not necessarily preserve a berm between the parapet and the excavation.

Sappers n° 3 and 4 provided with ordinary sized shovel and pick always keep 3 meters behind the head of the sap; they deepen the first excavated trench to 2 meters and throw the excavated earth tangentially over the upper outline of the parapet of the initial trench to make it thicker. Opposite their work they push back with a hoe the loose earth of the parapet, to secure a regular berm 0 m. 30 wide.

Breaking out the sap from the trench.

a. **Breaking out.** — After having marked with pegs the intersection of the new sap with the trench, the work is pushed forward perpendicularly across the parapet with the progressive sap method.

The excavated earth of the trench parapet is used as a front mask when digging through the parapet and all excavated earth must be thrown obliquely in front to constitute new parapets. As soon as the original trench parapet does not give sufficient cover to the sap head a part of the loose earth is thrown in front to constitute the new mask behind which the sap head progresses regularly, the direction being changed after breaking out of the parapet.

b. **Concealed breaking out.** — The disadvantage of the open cut is that it shows the enemy the breaking out point; in the near vicinity of the enemy that point becomes the target for a continuous shower of hostile grenades.

Concealed breaking out is used when the breaking out place can be fixed while the trench itself is being dug.

It is then sufficient to arrange beforehand on the ground, at the selected point, the roofing materials (panels, beams, logs, railroad ties, etc.) under which the sap will pass.

The roofing materials are at least 1 m. 80 wide; they are brought by a special working party and arranged on the ground at the same time that the workers are put to work on the trench.

The materials are laid at night, horizontally, perpendicular to the trench and close together. They are immediately covered with earth to hide them from the enemy.

Excavation of a covered or protected sap.

Personnel and tools. — Every sap head working party ncludes.

1° 8 sapper-pioneers under a N. C. O. sap foreman and divided into two equal gangs relieving each other every meter of progress;

2° Supernumeraries in sufficient number to carry away the loose earth.

In the working party the sappers n°s 1 and 2 are provided each one with a long handled pick and a short handled hoe. They further have a 2 meters measuring stick (to measure the trench depth), a 1 m. 20 measuring stick (to measure the breadth) and a 1 m. rod (to measure the task of each working gang).

The sappers n°ˢ 3 and 4 are provided each one with an ordinary shovel and they also have a long handled miner's hoe. The supernumeraries are provided with the necessary implements according to the method chosen for carrying the loose earth away.

Method of execution. — The sappers n°ˢ 1 and 2 work alternately in the sap head and relieve each other as often as deemed necessary. They cut the natural ground under the roofing materials and in that direction.

The front sapper cuts first two grooves at right and left up to the full height of the excavation, then another groove at the lower part; when the earth crumbles, he pushes it backwards between his legs with the short handled hoe taking care to clean up the sap so as to always secure a uniform depth.

The sappers n°ˢ 3 and 4 stand close by the front sapper and quickly pull the loose earth backwards with the long handled hoe. According to the way the loose earth is carried to the rear, they throw the earth up to a shovel relay or fill boxes, baskets, wheelbarrows, hand-barrows, etc. which are carried by supernumerary men.

The task of the gang is 1 meter long and measured with a peg set in the left side of the trench by the foreman in charge of the sap, as soon as the working party arrives.

At each relief the sappers change posts; n°ˢ 1 and 2 become n° 3 and 4 and *vice versa*.

The direction of the sap is marked with pegs set in rear, in the bottom of the trench, where they cannot interfere with the transportation of the loose earth.

Evacuation of the earth. — Is accomplished by means of supernumerary men divided in relays of shovellers or who form a chain to carry the earth in baskets.

Working party for sand bag filling.

A gang for sand bag filling includes: 2 shovellers, 1 bag holder, 2 tiers and as many diggers as required by the quality of the ground.

To fill a bag the bag holder kneels, holding the bag straight and open between the two shovellers, shakes it often to settle the loose earth and when filled hands it over to the tiers behind him. A gang fills as an average 150 bags an hour.

A sand bag duly filled weighs about 20 kilos (44 lbs); it should measure: standing 0 m. 50 in height (20 inches), 0 m. 22 in diameter (9 inches); lying on the ground, 0 m. 18 (7 inches) thick, 0 m. 25 (10 inches) broad.

Construction of wire entanglements.

With 2 rows of stakes

aA	bB	cC	dD
a'A'	b'B'	c'C'	d'D'

may be considered as comprising 3 panels:

1° Panel   A   B   C   D
     a   b   c   d

2° Zigzag panel   AA'   BB'   CC'   DD'
       aa'   bb'   cc'   dd'

3° Panel   A'   B'   C'   D'
     a'   b'   c'   d'

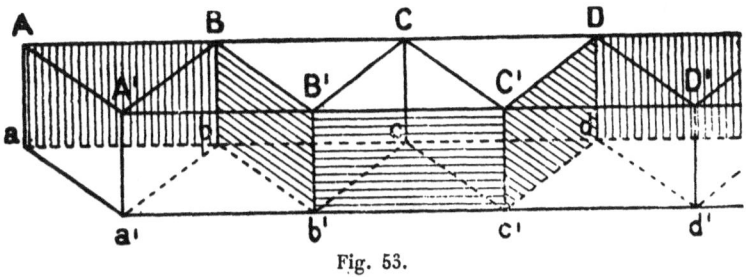

Fig. 53.

Every panel is constituted of 4 wires:
1 high wire;
2 diagonal wires;
1 low wire.

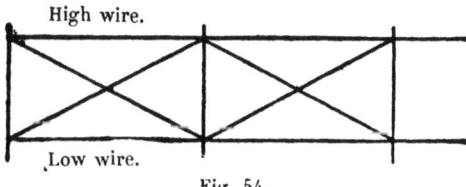

Fig. 54.

From these elements a methodical organization of the work easily follows:

1° Tracing. — A N. C. O. or a guide knowing the direction to give to the entanglement system walks slowly towards the

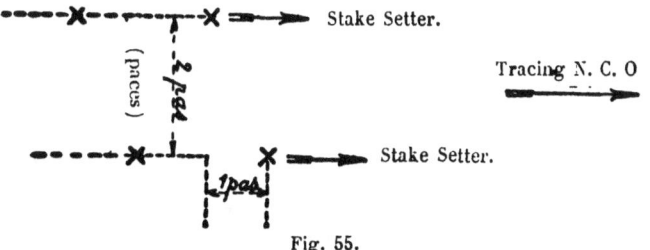

Fig. 55.

desired point of direction. He is followed by two stake men on each side walking in a parallel direction at 2 paces distance

and interval, the pair on one side being 1 pace further advanced than the opposite pair (i. e. in a kind of quincunx order).

These men at every second pace lightly pound down the stakes brought by the supply men.

2° **Driving the stakes.** — The stake men are followed by two drivers carrying mauls. They are accompanied by two helpers who hold the stakes straight and interpose a sack to deaden the noise.

3° **Task of the wire gangs.** — Every panel includes 4 wires and 2 men are required to easily handle one coil of barbed wire.

Panel $\begin{matrix} A & B & C & D \\ a & b & c & d \end{matrix}$ *(1st panel)*: the first gang attaches its wire to the lower part of the first stake, winds it around the lower part of the second stake and so on.

The second gang attaches its wire at the lower part of the first stake, makes a round turn at the top of the second stake then down again to the bottom of the third stake, etc.

The third gang does the same but starts at the top of the first stake.

The fourth gang attaches the wire at the upper part of the 1st stake, winds it around the top of the second and so on.

All together 8 men are needed.

For the *second panel* 8 men are also needed:

 1 gang for the lower wire ......⎫
 2 gangs for the diagonal wire .. ⎬ 8 men.
 1 gang for the top wire ....⎭

For the *third panel* same work and same number of men.

Therefore, all together for the three panels:

  1 N. C. O, 1 guide   2
  2 drivers, 2 helpers   4
  24 wire men 24

     Grand total .... 30 men.

4° **Supply men.** — The number of men needed to supply the markers with stakes depends upon the distance the material has to be fetched.

1 man can carry 3 to 5 stakes according to their thickness.

8 more men are needed, or at least about 2 per panel, to supply the groups with wire.

Characteristics of this method. — All parts of the work progress at the same time.

Every man has an easy task and cannot go wrong even in the dark.

Reels are used up to the last without it being necessary to cut the wire.

Although a large number of men (30) are employed for work this method is not too dangerous because the gangs are always moving; moreover in the dangerous places the workers may be separated from one another by suitable distances as the panels are progressively and independently made.

— 73 —

Remark. — The construction of entanglements with any number of rows of stakes may be easily deduced from the previous explanation.

Special designs made with barbed wires or Brun spirals.

Fig. 56 to 60 show trellis work and chevaux de frise which can be improvised with barbed wire or Brun spirals. The given dimensions are variable.

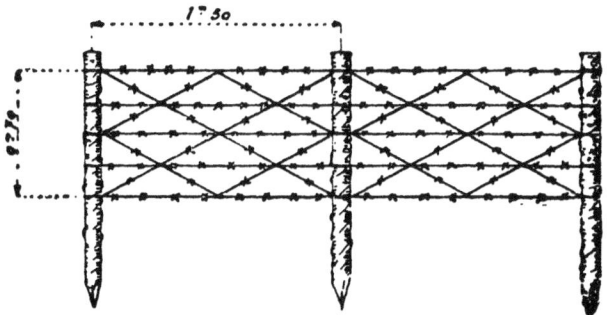

Fig. 56. — Improvised trellis.

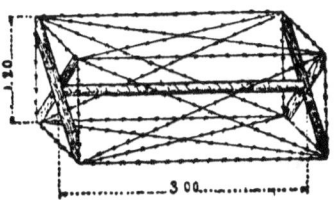

Fig. 57. — Trestle.

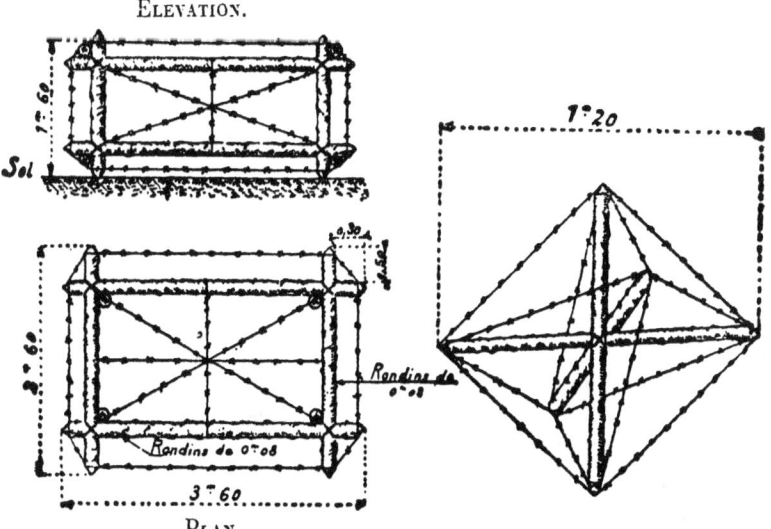

Fig. 58.— Flattened cubes. Fig. 59. — Hedgehog.

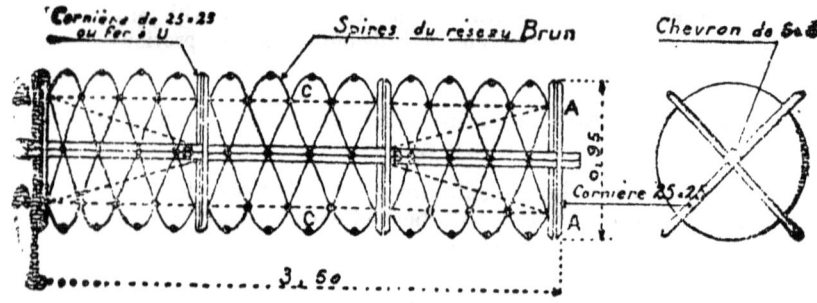

Fig. 6o. — Cornière. = Angle iron. — Spires. = Brun spirals.
Chevron. = Central rafter.

Brun spirals. — Weight of a coil : 8 kilos. To use it, pull it out to 3o meters to break its elasticity and let it go back up to 20 meters. Fasten it to the ground with 4 or 5 **wire staples** (with equal branches) or **hooks** (with unequal branches). If possible add stakes.

A very good method consists in laying two coils extended side by side and a third one on top, the whole bound together with **binding wire**.

The smooth Brun spirals have nearly everywhere been replaced by barbed spirals, they have different names according to different Armies and according to improvements made in them (**Riband** sausages, etc.).

Fascine and hurdle work.

Troops constructing fascine work must keep absolutely to the given dimensions and not forget that these fabrications are to be assembled like bricks in a wall; they must be therefore interchangeable.

Fascine works are made of branches or wattle, stakes and withes.

Stakes. — They are made from the strongest and straightest poles, constituting the lower part of the branches or with strong wattles or with split wood, they are sharpened habitually at small end, by two strokes of a bill-hook.

Withes. — They are used to bind fascines, gabions or hurdles. They are chosen amongst the thinnest and most flexible wattles stripped of leaves and branches.

They are made by twisting the small wattles by one of the following process :

1° Place the butt under the foot, twist progressively with the right hand beginning with the small end holding the withe with the left hand and roll it under the foot.

2° Place the small end of the withe in a slit made at the top of a stake o m. 10 to o m. 15 diameter and driven in the ground ; at first twist the small end keeping the withe straight and rolling it progressively around the stake.

The twisting effected by one of these methods up to o m. 20 (8 inches) or o m. 30 (12 inches) from the butt, make a loop at the small end.

A man can make 20 to 30 withes per hour,

Wire binders are also used: they measure 2 mm. 4 (1/10 inch) in diameter for fascines and 1 mm. 6 (0.64 in.) for gabions and hurdles.

Infantry troops must know how to build fascines, gabions and hurdles.

Building a fascine. — A fascine (Fig. 61) is a cylindrical bundle of brush closely bound, it measures o m. 25 (10 in.) in diameter and 2 m. 50 (8 1/3 ft) length and weighs from 16 to 20 kilos (35 to 44 lbs).

Fig. 61.

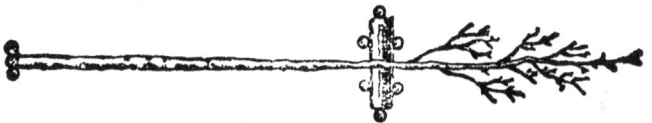

Plan.

Length profile

Fig. 62. — Block to cut off brush.

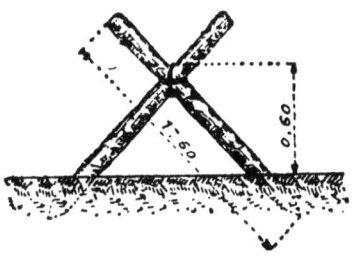

Fig. 63. — Trestle to make fascines

The brush is cut off on a block and put together in a rack or between stakes, the better brush outside. When the cradle is filled the bundle is compressed or choked with fascine choker (rope with loops 1 m. 10 long and levers); the thickness is checked with a gauge (cord 63 cm. long [25 in.]). The binders are then put on: the fascine choker compresses the bundle successiv vely at 5 centimeters from the place of each binder. The binder with a loop is tied like a running-knot; for the binder without loop an ordinary knot is strongly tied. The free ends are twisted between the binder and the fascine and then hidden in the interior. Put the knots on the same line. Smooth the fascine by cutting off projecting twigs.

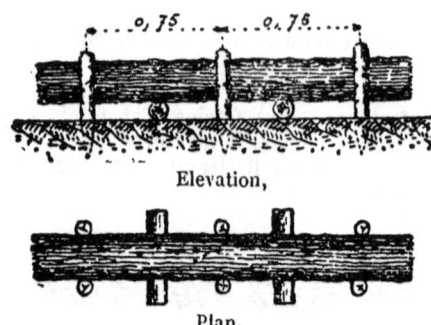

Fig. 64. — Constructing fascines between two rows of stakes.

Gabion making. — A gabion is a cylindrical basket with open ends made of branches woven on stakes. The branches are called wattles and the whole (branches and stakes) is called wattling. The weight of a gabion varies from 18 to 22 kilos (40 to 48 lbs.).

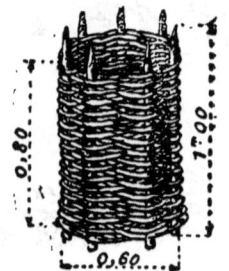

Fig. 65. — Gabion.

To make a gabion 7 stakes are needed as well as 80 to 100 branches and 8 withes.

Fig. 66 shows how the stakes are driven; they are slightly inclined towards the center, two men standing on opposite sides successively weave two branches, braiding them with the stakes and with each other. The successive rows are compressed with a mallet. When the wattling is finished it is fastened by means of 4 binders each binding the top of a stake with 5 or 6 bran-

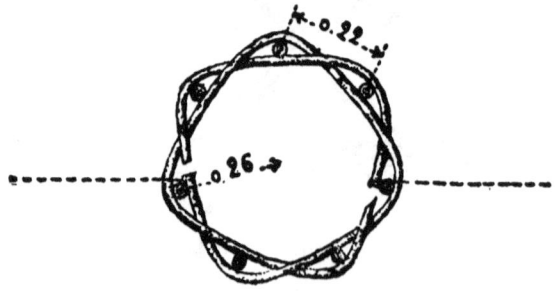

Fig. 66 — Butt-end of rod.

ches; then the gabion is inverted and the wattling is secured with 4 binders (in similar manner). The outside of the gabion trimmed but the twigs on the inside are left

Hurdle making. — A hurdle is a wattling with a plane surface 2 meters long × 0 m. 80 high (80 inches × 32 inches). The weight varies from 15 to 20 kilos (33 to 44 lbs.).

To make a hurdle 6 stakes are needed as well as 80 to 100 branches and 8 withes. Stakes are planted in a straight line and used

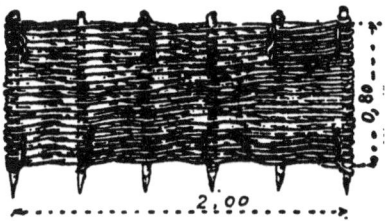

Fig. 67. — Hurdle.

as in making a gabion. The branches are cut off at both ends, except 5 to 6 at each end of the hurdle, which are twisted around the end stakes to bind them with the wattling; 4 withes are used for the 4 corners, then 4 at other stakes (2 above, 2 below).

MEMENTO.
Dimensions to be remembered.

Epaulment. Heights.

Kneeling rifleman	1ᵐ00 (40 in.)
Standing rifleman	1ᵐ30 (52 in.)
Machine-gun lying position	0ᵐ40 (16 in.)
— «standing» normal	0ᵐ80 (32 in.)
Width of firing banquette	0ᵐ50 (20 in.)
Width at the level of the ground of the excavation for firing trench boyau or sap	1ᵐ20 (48 in.)
Bottom of firing trench (without banquette) boyau or sap	0ᵐ90 (36 in.)
Berms (trench or boyau)	0ᵐ30 (12 in.)

Traverses.

Thickness	2ᵐ50 (8-1/3 ft.)
Length (perpendicular to the front line)	1ᵐ50 (60 in.)
Average distance between traverses	5ᵐ00 (17 ft.)
Platform for machine-gun	1ᵐ50 × 0ᵐ80 (60×32)

Ammunition recess.

Opening	0ᵐ60 × 0ᵐ60 (24×24)
Depth	0ᵐ50 (20 in.)

— 78 —

Dug-out.

Dimensions of cases for inclined galleries	$1^m60 \times 0^m80 \times 0^m22$
	$64 \times 32 \times 8.8$
Dimensions. Inside measurement of a low gallery frame	$1^m50 \times 1^m00$
	(60×40)
Dimensions. Inside measurement of a common gallery frame	$2^m00 \times 1^m00$
	(80×40)
Dimensions. Inside measurement of a great gallery frame	$2^m00 \times 2^m10$
	(80×84)
Mine branch connecting 2 dug-outs	$1^m00 \times 1^m00$
	(40×40)
Fascine	$2^m50 \times 0^m25$
	$(8\text{-}1/3 \times 10)$

Gabion.

Diameter	0^m60 (24 in.)
Height pickets	1^m00 (40 in.)
Height wattling	0^m80 (32 in.)

Hurdle.

Length	2^m00 (80 in.)
Height (same as gabion).	

PART III.

THE MATERIAL.

. . . .

CHAPTER II.

THE AUTOMATIC RIFLE MODEL 1915 (C. S. R. G.).

This rifle is an automatic arm, worked by the force of recoil (long recoil of the barrel). The rifle is supplied with cartridges by means of semi-circular clips containing 20 cartridges each. A good adjustment of the extractor affords the possibility of using ordinary small arm ammunition (D cartridges) as well as the machine gun ammunition (D. A. M. cartridges).

Detachment: 1 gunner, 2 ammunition carriers.

Notes on armament and equipment.

a. Gunner:

Automatic rifle with case.........	9^{k}100	(20 ^{lbs})
2 Cartridge pouches (4 clips)......	4^{k}000	(8, 8 ^{lbs})
Special haversack (4 clips and a cleaning kit)........................	4^{k}700	(10,34 ^{lbs})
Automatic pistol and 3 clips and belt.	1^{k}700	(3,74 ^{lbs})
	19^{k}500	(42, 9 ^{lbs})

b. First ammunition carrier:

Special knapsack (8 clips and 1 bundle of 8 packets of 8 cartridges-224).	10^{k}900	(23,98 ^{lbs})
Cartridge bag (containing 4 bundles of 8 packets each-256).........	8^{k}100	(17,82 ^{lbs})
Automatic pistol and 3 clips, belt..	1^{k}700	
	20,700	

c. Second ammunition carrier:

Rifle and ordinary equipment, 60 cartridges in the belt.............	6^{k}000	
Ordinary knapsack and 5 bundles of cartridges-320.................	13^{k}200	(29,00 ^{lbs})
	19^{k}200	

The men of the detachment carry besides : ration haversack, anteen, blanket, shelter half, and a pick-mattock on the belt.

Length of the rifle................ 1^m05 (42 in)
Length of the barrel............... 0^m45 (18 in)
Weight of the rifle without clip..... 8^k750 (19 1/4 lbs)
Weight of a clip.................... 0^k850 (1,87 lbs)

Cartridges carried :

By the gunner............................. 160
By the first ammunition carrier............. 480
By the 2nd ammunition carrier............. 380
                                         _____
                                         1,020

Summary nomenclature. — The automatic rifle is divided into two portions : 1st The *fixed part*, 2nd the *mobile part*.

1° The *fixed portion* consists of :
a. The guide sleeve ; b. Receiver ; c. The firing mechanism ; d. The fittings.

2° The *mobile portion* consists of :
a. Barrel, breech casing and barrel recuperator spring ;
b. The mobile breech and breech recuperator spring ;
c. Feed mechanism.

Action of mechanism. — To perform all the mechanical operations necessary to the proper working of the rifle (extraction, ejection, introduction of a new cartridge into the chamber), the separation of the barrel and the breech must be automatically produced.

In the movements of these two parts, three different phases may be distinguished :

1° Under pressure resulting from the explosion of the cartridge, *the whole mobile portion, barrel and breech, is carried to the rear*.
The rifle is cocked.

2° Under the action of the barrel recuperator spring, *the barrel is carried forward to its firing position,* the breech is held back by the sear.

3° Under the action of the breech recuperator spring, *the disengaged breech moves forward.*
For firing one must draw back the breech by means of the maneuvering handle, i. e. *cock the rifle*, then set the clip under the rifle, then pull the trigger to release the breech which flying forward inserts the cartridge in the chamber and explodes it.

The firing and safety lever has a cam which may be given different positions, — thus permitting automatic fire or single shot fire, — and may be used besides as a safety catch.

To fire automatically place cam horizontal (position marked M), maintain pressure on trigger ; by releasing the pressure, fire is stopped, the barrel being at its forward position and the breech held back.

To regain the aim on the objective, suspend fire and aim again.

Three classes of firing: Short bursts of fire: 2 or 3 rounds (fire for adjustment).
Longer bursts of fire: 6 or 8 rounds (fire for effect).
Rapid fire: 20 rounds (in case of crisis).

For single shot fire, cam vertical and pointed down (position marked C); pull the trigger and release it aiming anew at the target after each shot.

Safety catch. — Cam vertical and pointed up (position marked S). The firing mechanism is thus locked.

Whenever the loader is empty, draw the breech back so as *to cock the rifle*, manipulate the clip stop lever and catch the clip as it falls under the pressure of the support spring.

Incidents of firing. — The most frequent stoppages in the automatic action of the piece can be overcome by the gunner on the battlefield. They are as follows:

1° The breech does not engage with the nose of the sear. To continue firing draw the maneuvering handle as far back as possible.

2° The barrel does not return to its firing position; manipulate the maneuvering handle, in case it should not be sufficient, knock the butt on the ground.

3° The empty case is not extracted; extract it with the Hotchkiss hook or the ramrod, which are found in the cleaning pouch.

4° The rifle is not fed or the cartridge is in a wrong position to enter the chamber: lose no time and change the loader.

Instructions for keeping the rifle in working order. — Keep the rifle in its case up to the moment of firing (in order to protect it from rain, dust, etc.).

During firing: Take advantage of the shortest suspension of fire to clean all visible working parts that can be got at without dismounting the rifle.

After firing: Examine with great attention the barrel screw nut, the chamber, the breech and breech casing, the clip and its spring.

Contemplated inprovements. — A *flame concealer*.

An emergency adaptable cartridge-carrier, permitting the rifle to be fired shot by shot at a rate of 40 shots per minute in case the clips should be broken or missing;

A *sling enabling* the men:
To carry the automatic rifle as a rifle is ordinarily slung;
To carry it in front of the body during the advance of the skirmish line;
To carry it under the right arm for firing while walking.

Duties of the automatic rifle detachment. — *Position of the gunner*. — The position taken by the gunner has a capital influence on the good working of the rifle. Normal position: prone. Body at an oblique angle to the axis of the rifle, forearms used as props; right hand at the pistol grip, left hand grasping the carrying handle. Place the right cheek in front of the washer nut of the plug to avoid the recoil blow. Facilitate the placing of the cheek by refusing the right shoulder and advancing the left. In such a position the eye of the gunner is close to the rifle and easily falls in the line of sight.

Notes on the aiming position. — The rifle has three points of support : the folding fork, the left forearm, the right shoulder. Both hands by continuous traction press the rifle firmly against the shoulder, which retains it directed at the mark during long bursts of fire and avoids temporary stoppages.

Division of duties. — *Duties of the gunner.* — To determine the objectives, estimate the ranges, execute the fire, control the rate of fire.

Duties of the 1st ammunition carrier. — To stand on the right of the gunner, so as to ensure that the mechanism is working smoothly ; to carry the Hotchkiss hook in his hand, to regulate the upward movement of the follower, to warn the gunner whenever the clip is empty, to watch the ejection slot, to overcome temporary stoppages.

Duties of the 2nd Ammunition carrier. — To act as scout during the advance, to refill the empty loaders at the firing position, to assure the ammunition supply and to be prepared to intervene with his rifle and bayonet at the delicate period when clips are being changed and in case of stoppages.

Marching fire. — The possibility of marching firing results from the fact that the automatic rifle fires automatically low and that fire is almost naturally sweeping on account of the movements on the march.

Fire may be delivered shot by shot in short or long rafales and even by whole clips during crises of the combat.

This sort of fire becomes much more effective when the rifle is kept in position by a makeshift sling going from the left shoulder to the end of the barrel.

Manner of carrying the automatic rifle in marching fire. — Press the butt firmly to the body with the right arm, grasp the piece with the left hand at the carrying handle and rest the left elbow against the body so as to give a firm support to the rifle. The left hand must maintain it in position by a continuous pull in such a way that the left arm becomes a sort of clamped firing rack.

Principles of marching. — Go straight toward the objective. Bend the body well forward conforming all movements to the fire of the rifle.

The quick time step will be found convenient for firing shot by shot. The trigger should be pulled every time the left foot strikes the ground.

The flexion step at a rapid cadence agrees well with automatic firing. The gunner must succeed in making himself harmonize with the rifle to such an extent that during the delivery of fire the gunner should not seem to carry his rifle, but it should appear that the rifle itself is advancing and the gunner simply adapting his body to its movements.

One cannot reach such results except after uninterrupted training, including gymnastic exercises such as the Hebert method for physical training, a gradual increase of the load carried by the gunner, marches over broken ground, rushes from shell holes to shell hole, and finally assault practice. The gunner must be trained to change the loaders while advancing.

To obtain the maximum fire effect of the automatic rifle, the detachment must necessarily be well instructed and properly trained. A high standard of knowledge of the mechanism must be reached not only by the men of the detachment but by all non-commissioned officers and as many corporals and men as possible. It is never justifiable that an automatic rifle should become useless if the gunner is disabled. Whenever an automatic rifleman becomes a casualty, the piece must be picked up and put in action again. To carry an automatic rifle must be considered and sought for as an honor.

CHAPTER III.

MACHINE GUNS.

The machine guns in use in the French army are the St-Etienne machine-gun model 1907, transformed; and the Hotchkiss machine-gun, model 1914.

All non-commissioned-officers must have sufficient knowledge of the mechanism to fire either of these machine-guns in critical moments. Theoretical and practical instruction must be given them. Each must have fired at least one or two belts. (The description of the Hotchkiss machine-gun only will be translated here. Tr.)

Hotchkiss machine-gun model 1914.

This gun is an improved type of the Hotchkiss machine-gun model 1900. The Hotchkiss machine-gun is worked by the pressure of the gas resulting from the explosion of the charge. To that effect a hole is bored through the barrel to allow the gases to pass into the gas chamber. The guns has a simple sear and no speed regulator to vary the rate of fire. Its rate is about 450 shots per minute.

Firing the gun. — 1° COCKING : Open the breech by drawing the cocking lever fully back. Move cocking lever forward to its former position.

2° LOADING : The bolt being open, place the belt at the entrance of the feed mechanism, cartridges on top, and push it to the right till you hear the click of the ratchet wheel.

3° FIRING. . *Intermittent fire* or fire by short bursts : Pull the trigger, then rapidly release it.

b. *Automatic fire:* Pull the trigger and maintain the pressure.

4° *To suspend fire:* Release pressure on the trigger.

Regulating the pressure of the gas. — Pressure must be decreased if the vibrations-produced in the gun are too pronounced and if the empty cases are ejected too violently and too far from the gun. Pressure must be increased if the ejection is irregular and too weak.

Screw or unscrew the 'regulator to vary the capacity of the gas chamber. At o (zero) the pressure is maximum; at 4 minimum. The gas regulator is usually well placed when between 3 and 4 at average temperature.

Tripod. — Hotchkiss tripod model 1914, consisting of a pivoting support and tripod. Height of trunnions o m. 70 or o m. 35. Constructed to give 10 degrees elevation and 15 degrees depression.

Hotchkiss guns may be mounted on Saint-Etienne tripod by using the special intermediate clamp.

Ammunition. — Same as for St-Etienne machine-gun, avoid using cartridges 1886 D, as they frequently misfire.

Metallic cartridge-holders or clips containing 24 cartridges or articulated steel belts containing 250 cartridges are used. The number of articulated belts is 3 per gun at the present time.

Ammunition boxes carry 12 clips or 1 articulated belt. The two types of boxes are easily distinguished by their shape. They may be carried in any position.

Disposition of ammunition: Distributed between the ammunition carts, the caissons of the combat train and the artillery park (small arms ammunition section).

Miscellaneous information.

For important repairs or spare parts, machine-gun organizations apply directly to the repair section of the Corps or Division artillery park.

Belts are always filled by that section, never by the men of the M. G. Compagnies.

Disabling of the Hotchkiss machine-gun — Take away breechblock or the pin of the breech cover; batter the steel tongue that raises the cartridges from the belt, or the gas cylinder.

CHAPTER IV.

GRENADES.

Classification of grenades. — All grenades now in use are **time fuse** grenades.

They include a time fuse i. e. they burst a certain number of seconds after the igniting device has functioned (generally 5 seconds). There are **offensive** and **defensive** grenades.

Offensive grenades or **assault petards** can be used for close fighting in the open field, and particulary during an assault, without risk of the grenadier being struck by dangerous splinters. The killing radius of such a grenade, consisting solely in the effect of an explosion, does not exceed a distance of 8 or 10 meters.

Defensive grenades burst into many deadly splinters, which are to be feared up to more than 100 meters. They ought to be thrown from such points as are well protected against the back fire of the fragments.

As regards the means of throwing, grenades are divided into **hand** or **rifle** grenades.

Rifle grenades are thrown by means of a special apparatus adapted to the rifle and called « *tromblon* » or « *mandrel* ».

Lastly there are **suffocating, incendiary** and **smoke** grenades for special purposes.

Igniters. — The igniters now in use are:

The metallic fuse plug ;

The automatic fuse plug model 1916, B.

The latter is intended to eliminate the first.

The metallic fuse plug (see fig. 71) is a **percussion igniter:** after having taken off the protection cap, the igniter is struck sharply against a hard object, heel of the shoe, butt of the rifle, etc.; the primer igniter in contact with the striker sets fire to the time fuse, which causes the explosion of the detonator and consequently of the whole explosive mass.

The cap acts, to a certain extent, as a safety contrivance in preventing the primer holder from being driven down by accident.

In any case every grenade, as soon as the igniter has been struck, must be thrown immediately without waiting to ascertain if the ignition is or is not accomplished.

The automatic fuse plug (fig. 69 and 70) is based on an entirely different principle. An inside percussion spring resembling a pair of tongs strikes two primers at the same time as soon as freed by the removal of a lug. This lug flies out automatically when the safety lever is released. This is effected first by pulling out the safety split pin, then by letting go the hand that grasps the lever and the grenade.

Throwing a grenade having an automatic fuse plug.

1° Take the grenade in the right hand and **grasp it well**, the fuse plug uppermost, the ring turned towards the breast and passing near the base of the thumb (fig. 69).
The safety lever is thus pressed against the palm of the hand and strongly maintained without effort.

2° Insert the forefinger of the left hand into the ring and pull upon it so as to tear out the safety pin (fig. 10 *bis*).
From that moment the grenade is cocked and it is necessary to grasp it firmly to prevent the safety lever from flying off.

3° Aim at the objective with the extended left arm and throw the grenade as it is prescribed in the instruction on grenade fighting 7. April, 1916 (fig. 11 to 15).

Fig. 69.

N. B. — The grenade must be grasped as much as possible round the fuse plug so as to firmly hold the safety lever. The safety pin should not be taken off until the precise moment when the grenade is going to be thrown. Once the safety pin taken off the hand must be well shut, but without effort ; a moderate pressure is sufficient to maintain the safety lever, but that pressure must be continuous from the moment the grenade has been cocked.

It is strictly forbidden to ignite the grenade before throwing it under pretext that the time fuse burns too slowly.

Grenadiers should avoid keeping cocked grenades long in their hands and particularly walking with them, as the grenade may drop at a false step. The normal functioning of the grenade is produced as a rule when the end of the lever is raised 1 inch (25 mm.); but owing to a certain tolerance allowed to manufacturers the release of the spring strikers may be caused by a much smaller raising of the lever. Consequently it is advisable to keep the hands well shut and not to try to make the lever play, for instance, to make sure of its good working order. Grenadiers will acknowledge freely that such a system is easy to handle and not dangerous if managed with care. **If by accident a grenadier happens to let fall a cocked grenade he must not lose his coolness but pick up the grenade and throw it away before it bursts.**

The instructor by means of developing the initiative of his pupils will avoid many accidents to be feared in case of deficient skill.

During an exercise for instance he may suddenly let fall a dummy grenade and count loudly the seconds. The grenade should be picked up and thrown away and all the personnel sheltered before « five » has been uttered.

Precautions to be taken with grenades that have not burst.

Every grenade which has not burst must be considered as dangerous just as a primed and unexploded shell in the same situation. Such grenades therefore must not be left on the ground. Owing to the time necessary for the slow fuse to burn, there is no danger in picking up a grenade which has not burst provided all precautions are taken to throw it away if it happens to become ignited.

If troops come to encamp in a place where such grenades have been left, it is necessary to have them carried away as soon as possible.

Accordingly every body is sheltered and a single man picks up the grenades the place of which may have been marked before hand with twigs.

Generally the non-explosions come from non-ignition of the slow fuse, sometimes from an error in the mounting of the ignition plug and more rarely from primers which do not work.

When the groove of the striker lock is not filled with

mud, it is easy to see if the primers have worked for, in that case, the groove is blackened. Then the grenade is as safe to handle as an ordinary one. If on the contrary the sides of the groove and its bottom look white and brilliant, the primers have not worked. In this case the percussion springs are touching the primers and it may be feared that a shock will ignite them. In fact when an exercise grenade the primers of which have not functioned is struck against a hard object, the plug is broken before the primers will ignite. The small mass of the striker accounts for that. At any rate, when one is not sure that the primers have ignited, it is advisable to carry off the grenades one by one by hand, watching them carefully so as to throw away those which might happen to start burning. The grenades which have not burst are heaped together and blown up by means of a petard.

It is advantageous to use such grenades for charging fougases.

It is strictly forbidden to unscrew the fuse plug of a loaded grenade without a special unscrewing apparatus that protects the operator against explosions.

In the case that more than 6 o/o of the grenades do not explode a report should be made indicating the factory marks found on the plugs.

Grenades now in use (French).

The principal grenades now in use are:

1° The **O. F.** grenade model **1915** (offensive time fuse grenade);

2° The **F. I.** grenade model **1915** (defensive time fuse grenade);

3° The citron grenade C. F.;

4° The **suffocating** grenade model **1916**;

5° The A. B. grenade model 1916 (incendiary and smoke grenade, time fuse);

6° The rifle grenade **V. B.** (Viven Bessières time fuse);

7° The rifle grenade **D. R.** (percussion fuse);

1° **The O. F. Grenade, model 1915.** — (Offensive time fuse grenade).

Oval body made of tin, 3/10 mms. thick, 150 grs cheddite (fig. 70).

Automatic or metallic fuse plug.

Conveyance to the armies. — Separate boxes containing 200 loaded bodies or 50 fuse plugs. After **mounting** in

special places in the armies the complete grenade is sent to the troops.
Total weight : 255 grammes.

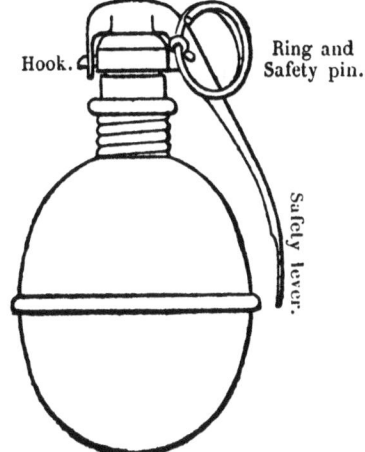

Fig. 70. — O. F. grenade and automatic igniter.

2° **The F. I. grenade model 1915.** — Defensive time fuse grenade.

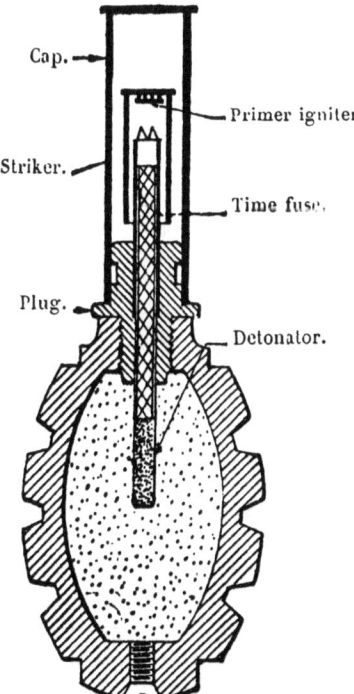

Fig. 71. — F. I. grenade and metallic igniter.

Oval body made of cast iron with fragmentation grooves outside.

As for the O. F. 1915 grenade, automatic or metallic fuse plugs can be used (fig. 69, and 71).

Conveyance to the armies. — Separate boxes containing 100 bodies or 50 plugs. Loading, priming and mounting are effected in the armies before delivery to the troops.

Cheddite load : 60 grs.
Total weight : 600 grs.

3° *Citron grenade C. F.* — Defensive time fuse grenade.
A variety of the F. I. grenade.
Special percussion igniter resembling the metallic fuse plug. This grenade is not adapted to the automatic fuse plug.

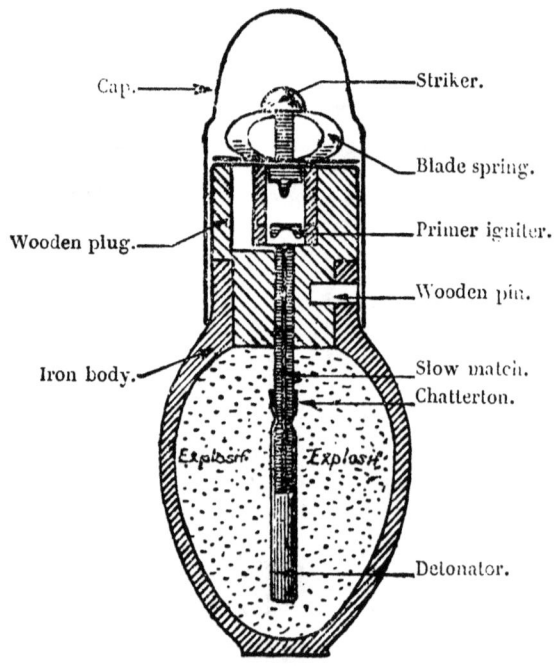

Fig. 72.

4° **Suffocating grenade**, model 1916 pattern. Time fuse grenade.

Oval body, made of iron and lead. Special percussion igniter like the metallic fuse plug. This grenade is suffocating and lacrymatory but very lightly, if at all, toxic.

It can make breathing impossible in closed or badly ventilated places. They therefore are useful to oblige the enemy to abandon dug-outs or cellars, etc. This grenade contains no explosive except a detonator and may be thrown without danger at 15 meters in the open field. It is necessary to **avoid throwing it against the wind** which would carry back suffocating vapours.

Conveyance to the armies. — In boxes containing 25 grenades loaded and with primers.
Load : 200 grs of a special liquid.
Weight : 400 grs.

5° *The A. B. grenade model 1916.* — Offensive time fuse incendiary and smoke grenade (fig. 74).
Spherical body made of tin, metallic fuse plug, used as the F. I. grenade. Does not produce dangerous splinters but sends burning material 15 or 20 meters round the bursting point.
One should not remain on the lee side. This material produces a thick smoke. 20 grenades produce an extensive cloud.
A grenade which has not burst may be picked up without danger and thrown again after the fuse plug has been changed.

Fig. 74.

Conveyance to the armies. — In boxes containing 50 grenades ready to be used.
Load : 500 grs. active material.
Total weight : 715 grs.

Rifle grenades. — They are projected by means of the infantry rifle having a «tromblon» (Viven Bessières grenade) or «mandrel» (D. R. grenade) fixed to the muzzle.

The rifle may be put to the shoulder (V. B.) but it is better to place the butt on the ground or to fire in the position of «ready» or on a rack.

Maximum range (190 meters and 350 meters) is obtained with an angle of fire of about 45 degrees. The angle of fall is very great, permitting plunging fire into the trenches.

6° **V. B. Grenade.** — Cast iron body with inside fragmentation, with two longitudinal interior tubes : a lateral tube carrying primer the fuse and detonator and a central tube which permits the bullet to pass. The bullet hits the striker which ignites the primer while the gases from the rifle cartridge expand in the tromblon and project the grenade.

DIRECTIONS FOR USE. — Push the tromblon well home on the muzzle.

Introduce the V. B. grenade entirely, its bottom lying on the truncated conical base of the tromblon. Load the rifle with the **regular cartridge**. Fire.

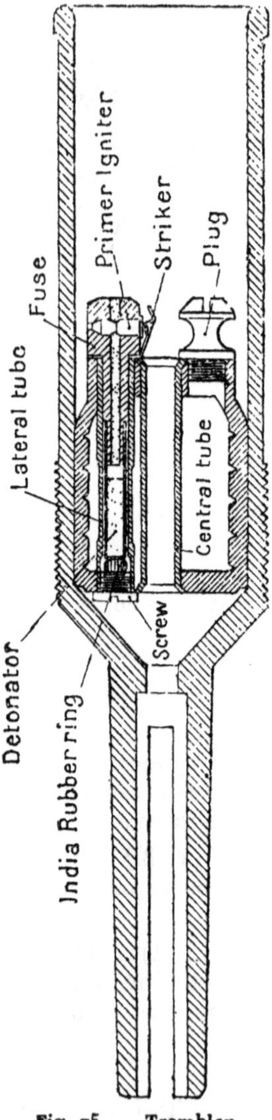

REMARKS AND INFORMATION. — The inside of the tromblon should be very clean and lightly oiled.

Clean off completely all spots of rust from the grenade body.

It is not well to have the striker shut the central tube too completely as it would be broken off by the bullet and carried away without igniting the primer.

Conveyance to the armies. — In boxes containing 100 grenades ready for use.

Weight of a box : 70 kgs.

A box with handle for 20 grenades has been adopted.

Average weight of tromblon : 1 kg. 500 (3, 3 lbs).

Interior diameter : 50 m/ms.

Weight of loaded grenade : 475 grs.

Weight of the explosive : 60 grs.

Time during which the slow fuse burns : 8 seconds with an additional second tolerated.

The rifle becoming hotter by degrees during the firing, the range is lengthened (20 meters for an inclination of 45 degrees).

The following range table is an average one and may imply errors of 10 or 15 meters.

This table shows that if the grenade bursts 8 seconds after the shot the explosion is produced as soon as the ground is reached for the minimum range, and 2 1/2 sec. afterwards for the maximum range.

Fig. 75. — Tromblon and V. B.

RANGE TABLE.

ANGLES OF FIRE.	RANGE IN METERS.	TIME OF FLIGHT in seconds.
45°.	180ᵐ	5.2
50°.	177	5.6
55°.	169	6.
60°.	156	6.3
65°.	138	6.6
70°.	116	6.8
75°.	90	7.
80°.	62	7.2
85°.	31	7.3

7° **D. R. Grenade.** — This grenade is different from the V. B. Grenade on the following points :

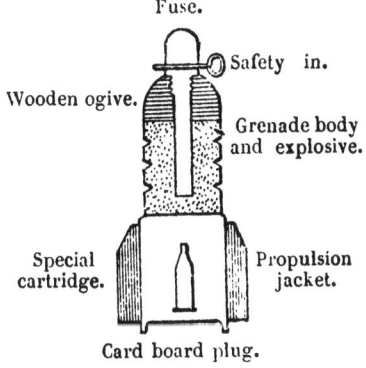
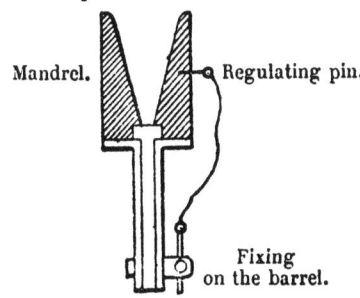

Fig. 75 bis. — Grenade and mandrel D. R.

It is placed on a mandrel instead of being put into a tromblon.

It includes a percussion fuse.

It is fired with a **special cartridge without bullet** instead of with an ordinary cartridge.

It is more cumbersome but its range is twice as long and its effects more powerful.

Cast iron body prolonged in front by a wooden ogive and a fuse; in rear by a jacket made of stamped sheet iron with 4 wings.

This jacket is used to enclose the special cartridge which is held in by a cardboard plug.

Firing is effected with the butt on the ground or at the position of «ready» or on a special metallic rack.

The range is obtained :

Through variations in the inclination of the rifle; or preferably by giving the rifle a constant inclination of 45 degrees and varying the volume of the expansion chamber. Consequently a regulating pin is struck into the hole corresponding to the range to be obtained, this pin limits the sinking of the grenade round the «mandrel».

METHOD OF EMPLOYMENT. — Fix the mandrel on the rifle;

Regulate the inclination of the rifle and the position of the regulating pin;

Take off the cardboard tampon, take the cartridge;

Sink the grenade round the mandrel;

Take off the safety pin of the fuse;

Load the rifle with the special cartridge; fire.

REMARKS AND INFORMATION. — Never fire with a ball cartridge ;

Oil the contact surfaces;

Straighten the wings that happen to be bent.

Conveyance to the armies.. — In boxes containing 24 grenades, ready for use.

Weight of a grenade : 585 grs. including 85 grs. of explosive.

Maximum range : about 350 meters obtained with an angle of 42 degrees, the grenade being entirely down on the mandrel.

8° **Exercice grenades.** — Distinctive colours.

Grenades painted **grey** : loaded for war.

Grenades painted **white** : ballasted with sand, **active detonator.**

Grenades painted **red** : ballasted with sand, inert detonator or no detonator at all.

Fuse plugs with cross mark, active, but only to be used for exercises with inert grenades.

Fuse plugs pierced throughout: inert.

The active V. B. grenade is fired during the exercises with a wooden bullet, it is advisable then to incline the striker at 45 degrees so as to secure the ignition. 45 degrees inclination is never necessary when firing with an ordinary ball cartridge.

CHAPTER V.

THE 37 MM GUN.

Organization. — 37 mm gun 1916 (rapid fire). Each piece includes:

1° A **gun** placed on a tripod and capable of being mounted on wheels if required.

2° A **cart** or limber containing ammunition, spare pieces and accessories.

The whole, i. e. gun and carriage is usually drawn by 1 horse.

In the neighborhood of the enemy, limber and gun are separated so as to be transported by the detachment. Several pieces assembled make a platoon the constitution of which is described in the organization of a regiment (Part. IV - Chap. II).

The six cannoneers of each piece (1 gunner, 1 loader, 4 ammunition carriers) are as a rule specialized. But each one must be able to take the place of any other in case of emergency. If necessary the gun may be manipulated by a single man.

The 37 gun being an infantry weapon its management must be known by all the officers and a sufficient number of additional N. C. O.'s and soldiers.

Equipment of the gunners. — The chief of piece, gunner, loader and ammunition carriers are armed with an automatic pistol; the rest of the personnel with a rifle and a bayonet.

The chiefs of platoon and piece are equipped with a *micrometric field glass*. The gunner carries the *telescopic sight* and the *apparatus for indirect firing*.

Handling of the gun. — The cannoneers are trained to perform the following movements:

To separate the gun from the limber.

To draw the gun on wheels: The two ammunition carriers of the piece pull with a breast-collar; the gunner and loader carry an ammunition sack each and help in case of need.

To carry the gun by hand: Gun, gun-carriage and wheels are separated. The chief of piece carries the shield, the two ammunition carriers carry the tripod and an ammunition sack each; the gunner and loader carry the gun by means of the sponge staff; an ammunition carrier from the echelon takes back the wheels and hooks them on to the limber.

To go into battery on wheels or on tripod: to change the position by hand without dismounting.

Pointing in direction and elevation, by means of a telescopic sight well screwed on its support, the zero of the direction drum being in front of its mark.

Cocking loading and firing. To suspend and cease firing.

Remounting on wheels: uniting gun and limber.

Firing emplacement for a piece. — (See fig. 76).

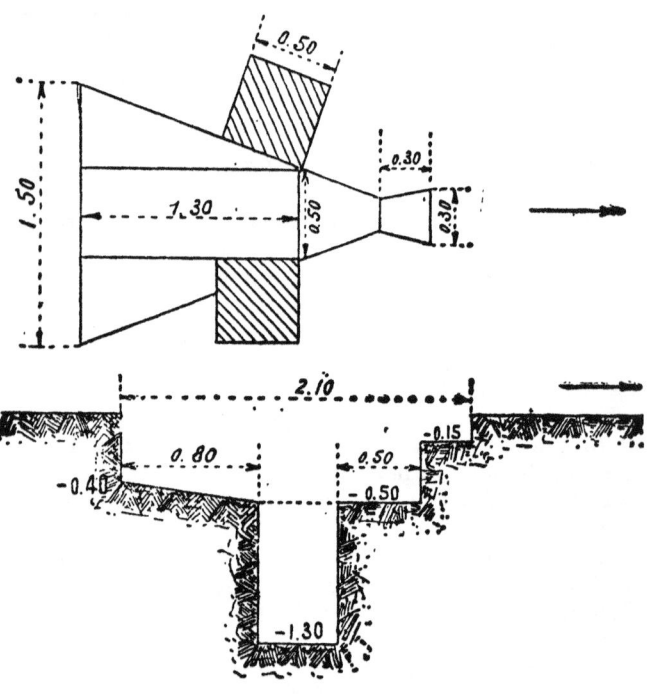

Fig. 76.

Firing. — 1° *Direct fire.* very rapid registering and effective fire in the shortest delay.

2° *Indirect fire:* aiming at a conspicuous target, chosen in the neighborhood of the objective,

3° *Masked firing:* objective visible to the chief of piece only, firing at an aiming point chosen in the direction of the objective.

Adjustment in direction: In direct firing, move the *direction drum;* each division on this drum corresponds to one mil. The angular errors reckoned in mils are observed by the chief of piece by means of the micrometic field glass.

In indirect firing the chief of piece measures the angular error between objective and aiming point and adjusts the direction drum to that error beforehand.

Adjustment in elevation: Try to get two bracketing shots (one short and one over) starting from short or long elevations according to the possibilities of observation.

Begin with varying ranges by 200 meters, then lessen the variations. It is not necessary to get less than 25 meters between two bracketing shots for the ranges over 800 meters and less than 12 meters 50 up to 800 meters. When lessening the variations to 50 meters, 2 shots at least must be observed for each elevation before it is settled if it is short or long. When lessening to 25 meters, 4 shots are necessary.

As soon as possible use *the fire for effect.*

The apparatus for masked firing enables the measurement of the minimum elevation to be used to make the shell pass over the screen. If that elevation happens to give long shots it will be necessary to get further from the screen or lessen its height

Ammunition. — Two kinds of shells.

Cast-iron shell, 450 grs., loaded with black powder, percussion fuse.

Steel shell, with base fuse, weighing 510 grs.

Information. — Initial velocity: about 400 meters;

Range: 2.400 meters.

Average errors: Range: between 14 and 18 meters for all distances.

Direction: 1 meter at 1.400 meters, 2 m. 50 at 2.400 meters.

Height: less than 1 meter up to 1000 meters and less than 2 meters up to 1.600 meters — 4 m. 50 at 2.400 meters.

CHAPTER VI.

EXPLOSIVES AND DESTRUCTIONS.

Allowance of an infantry regiment. — 108 melinite petards of 135 grammes (in one of the tool wagons).

1 box containing 20 meters of detonating fuse, 15 fulminating primers and 46 detonators (in the other tool wagon).

This distribution in the two wagons is an application of the principle of always keeping the explosives separated from the r primers and detonators. (They must never be carried by th same man, or be put in the same ammunition pile.)

The explosives are handled by the sappers. However every officer must be able to recognize and when necessary handle the following explosives and accessories :

Melinite cartridge and petard;
Detonating cord;
Fulminating primer;
Slow fuse (Bickford fuse);
Igniters.

The following notions must be completed by the study of the « Field Fortification Regulations » (Instruction sur les travaux de campagne).

Explosives.

Black powder. — Hard grains of slate colour and of various diameters.

Weight composition : $\begin{cases} 75 \text{ of salpetre.} \\ 12,5 \text{ of sulphur.} \\ 12,5 \text{ of charcoal.} \end{cases}$

The powder explodes by means of a violent shock, or by means of fire. It is a *propulsive explosive* to be employed with tamping (loading mines).

A good powder burns without leaving residue.

Use containers as tight as possible to keep it sheltered from moisture.

Barrels or wooden cases lined with zinc. Weight 5o kilograms.

Precautions must be taken for repacking (to be avoided) and for transport (copper tools, no smoking, etc.).

The artillery grenades M^1 1882 and 1914 were loaded with black powder.

Melinite. — Melinite is a high explosive, advantageously employed for ruptures by means of superficial charges, that is to say simply brought into contact with the things to be broken with light tamping, and even without any tamping.

Molten melinite appears as a compact straw-colored mass.

Melinite is very slightly sensitive to shock or friction; the electric spark does not set it on fire. Its explosion produces a very poisonous gas.

The contact of melinite with alkaline matters (soda, potash) and also chiefly with lead and its compound white lead is to be avoided. Humidity decreases its explosive capacity : when wet melinite is of a vivid yellow color, instead of a straw yellow.

Melinite petard : Rectangular box envelop made of brass supplied with a soldered cover with a priming socket. Contains 135 grams of melinite (fig. 77).

The priming socket has three small brass projections destined to hold the detonator when introduced into the socket. It is shut by means of a pasteboard disc and a strip with a ring that is to be pulled off to uncover the socket.

Weight of the petard : about 200 grams. 7 petards end to end 1 meter long and contain 1 kilogram of melinite.

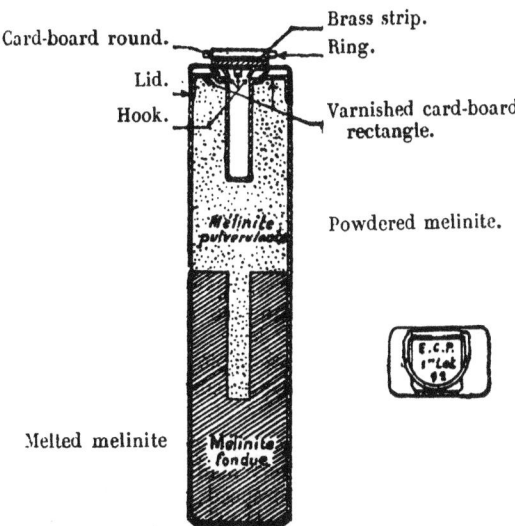

Fig. 77. — 135 gr. petard.

Melinite cartridge : Cylindrical; 85 cm diameter; charge 100 grams of pulverized melinite; same closing as for the petard.

Petards and cartridges being water tight they may be kept in any kind of box.

60 gram petard M¹ 1904 for relays and joinings.
10 and 20 kilograms petards.

Chlorate explosives. — Generally employed for loading grenades and bombs. They belong to high explosives.
The principal are :

Cheddite : Yellowish powder that hardens after some time, based upon chlorate of potash and castor-oil; in bulk or in cartridges (wrapped up in paper).

Perchlorate of ammonia : Blue coloured explosive, based upon perchlorate of potash and inert paraffin.

Common properties : Does not take fire spontaneously; inflammable when brought into contact with ignited matter; inflammation can be propagated through the mass. If the mass is sufficient, inflammation can be transformed into explosion.

They detonate by shock (even light) or by rubbing between two hard surfaces. Take precaution for warehousing and transport. Have many depots of small capacity, separated from detonators and black powder, sheltered from humidity and heat.

Manipulation of chlorated explosives requires great care. The cavities of the grenades that are to be filled must not be rough but varnished or paraffined.

Ignition contrivances.

Contrivances used for igniting in order to provoke or transmit the detonation.

Fulminating primer M¹ 1880. — Detonators. — Load of 1 1/2 gr. of *fulminate of mercury* contained in the black varnished part of a small tube of copper (length: 45 millimeters; diameter: 5 1/2 millim.).

Violent explosive, very sensitive to shock, friction and fire.

To be handled **with the greatest precautions.**

Detonators found in commerce are not painted with black varnish.

Primers and detonators are employed for provoking the detonation of explosives and detonating cord.

Slow match (Bickford fuse). — Thread of fine powder three millimeters in diameter, held in two envelopes of tarred cotton. Burns slowly at the speed of one meter in 90 seconds (about 1 centimeter per second). That speed is to be verified with a sample.

Lighting with an igniter (see fig. 83), or by prepared tinder or any burning material after having uncovered the powder thread with a knife.

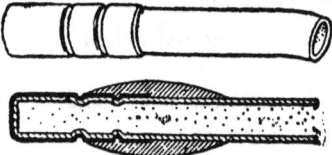

Fig. 78. — Cap for detonating cord.

Cordeau ou Slow fuse.

Fig. 79. — Junction of fuse and primer.

Slow fuse.   Fulminating primer.

Fig. 80. — Untightened priming.

Slow fuse.

Fig. 81. — Priming detonating fuse.

a. Part painted red.
b. Part to be held tight between the fingers.
c. Vent.
d. Lanyard loop.

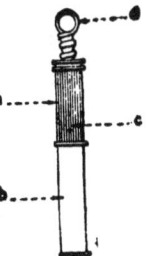

Fig. 83. — Friction primer.

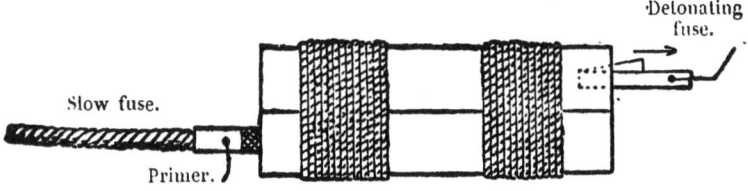

Fig. 84. — Priming with petards.

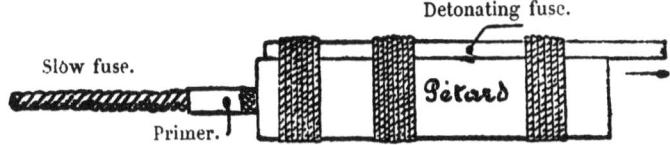

Fig. 85. — Priming with one petard.

Fig. 86. — Spanish twist joint.

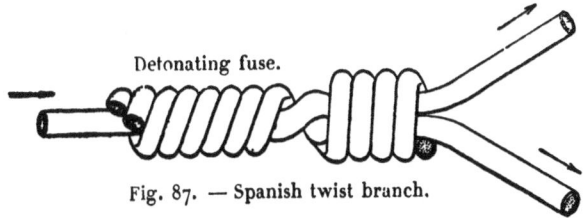

Fig. 87. — Spanish twist branch.

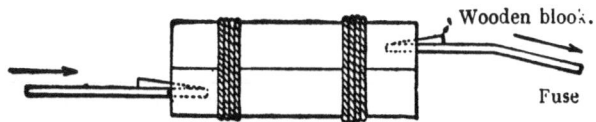

Fig. 88. — Joint with two petards.

5.

Detonating cord. — Thin tube of about 5 millimeters diameter, filled with pulverized melinite compressed by drawing out the tube. Explodes under action of fulminate or melinite and transmits the explosion at the speed of 6000 to 7000 meters a second.

Weight : 90 grams to the meter. When used must not be bent at right angle or pulled. The traction would produce hollows and missfires. Called sometimes instantaneous fuse.

For using great lengths of instantaneous fuse it is necessary to establish relays with one or two 60 grams petards every 200 meters.

Before using it freshen 10 centimeters of the end. May be replaced by trinitrotoluene.

Connections by Spanish twist or by two petards (fig. 86 and 88).

Double or multiple **branchings** (fig. 87 and 89) to secure the simultaneous explosion of several distant charges.

The primed cord is called the master cord.

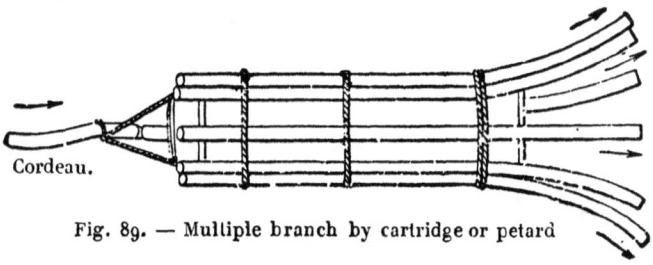

Fig. 89. — Multiple branch by cartridge or petard

The derived fuses are branches from the master cord.

Never place more than two derived fuses ; or make a multiple connection with a 60 gram or other petard.

Tie the derived fuses with a string to the wall of the petard.

Friction igniter M¹ 1913. — Time fuse. Working by pulling out a friction wire by means of a lanyard (fig. 83).

Seize the tube of the igniter by the part not covered with paint between the thumb and the fore-finger of the left hand, taking care not to stop the air holes ; lean that hand on a firm object, leave the fuse free, work the lanyard in the ring of the friction-bar and pull it out freely with the right hand by a sudden shake. Instead of holding the igniter with the fingers, one can tie it with a string on a firm point.

Making the primings.

Simple priming. — Join the slow fuse to the primer ; introduce the extremity of the cut fuse squarely into the bottom of the tube, *without forcing or turning.* Set with pincers (fig. 79) or by pinching the primers (fig. 80) at the part which does not contain fulminate.

Priming with detonating fuse. — Prime with a fulminating primer (fig. 79) if to be fired at once. If not, cap the detonating fuse with a primer, as well as the Bickford fuse and fasten the two primers together (fig. 81).

Priming of the melinite petard :

1° With slow fuse and one primer as shown in fig. 85.

2° With detonating fuse as for the lower petard shown in fig. 88.

Make the assembly firm by turning down socket claws with a small wooden wedge, or by making a ligature.

Chatterton. — Plastic coating put on hot to make the joints tight when explosives are employed under water.

Making up charges of melinite.

1. Concentrated charges. — (fig. 91). Packet of petards tied together, sockets on the same side; section as square as possible.

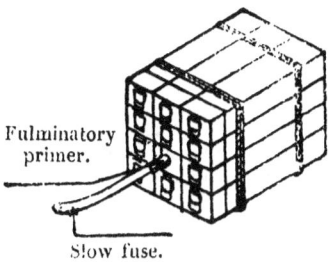

Fig. 91.

2. Elongated charges (fig. 92). — File of petards joined rod.

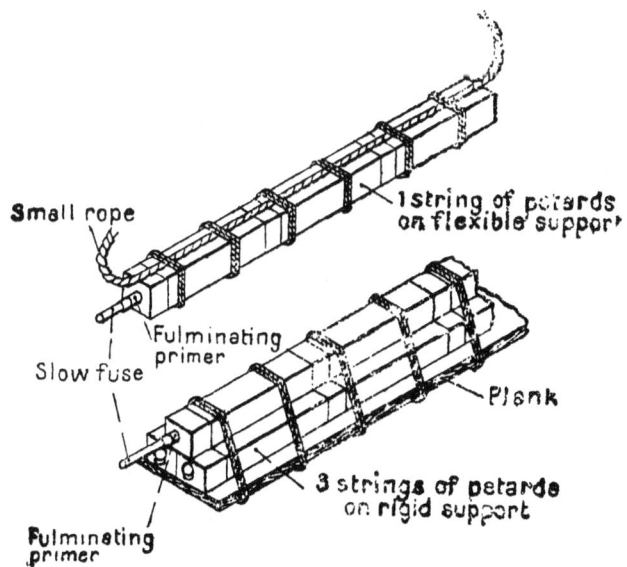

Fig. 92.

The charges are placed so that the largest surface is brought into contact with the object that is to be destroyed.

A light tamping of earth, sand, sod, etc., increases the effect of the explosion because it assures contact.

Never tamp a primed petard. — Tamp first, then prime.

Execution of destructions.

It is important to reserve the explosives for difficult destructions for which they are indispensable, and not to spend them when the purpose can be obtained with tools.

Consequently most of the destructions with explosives will be carried out not by Infantry but by the Engineers of the Division.

It is sufficient that officers have a notion of following cases that may arise unexpectedly.

1. Blowing off a door. — Place charges of 2 petards on each hinge of a wooden carriage-gate and on the lock. Make them explode simultaneously by means of a detonating fuse. If the hinges or locks of the door are not apparent one can use concentrated loads of 3 kilograms of melinite which are brought ready and primed and are placed against the middle of the door and fixed on it by means of a strong nail or heavy stick.

2. Ruining guns. — A charge of 4 or 5 petards exploding in the bore near the muzzle of a field gun ruins it completely. To increase the explosion plug the muzzle with a clod of earth or clay or some sods through which protrudes the slow fuse.

When the fuse is lighted go 400 or 500 meters away to the front if the gun has not previously been covered with fascines to prevent flying fragments.

With 7 or 8 petards a heavy gun can be put out of service.

Another method consists in sliding an **incendiary hand grenade A B M^1 1916** into the bore ; the breechblock being closed and the gun being inclined upwards. The breech block is soldered to the tube and the bore is deteriorated.

At last, in default of a better method one can explode a primed petard or hand grenade in the muzzle of the gun or against the half shut breech block but the gun is not surely and definitely put out of service by this method.

3. Destruction of ammunition :

1° Cartridges. — Set fire to the boxes by means of an incendiary hand grenade.

2° Projectiles. — The best proceeding consists in exploding charges of 2, 3 or 4 cartridges of melinite (according to the calibre of the projectiles) in contact with the projectiles.

With incendiary hand grenades, 3 being placed on a pile of even unprimed shells provoke the explosion of some of them, the others being ruined.

When shells are primed, they can be exploded by an incendiary grenade placed against one of the fuses (take care that the burning liquid does not run away from the pile). Finally the efficacity of these methods can be improved by burning boxes of cartridges placed against the piles of projectiles on the side of the fuses.

3° Explosive hand grenades. — Set fire to the boxes as in the case of cartridges or provoke the explosion by igniting on the top of the boxes some incendiary hand grenades.

The hand grenades that do not explode are thrown in all directions.

4. Destruction of railway track. — To destroy a railway track quickly, break the rails and cross ties.

Chiefly choose points where damage will be the most considerable and where derailments would have the greatest consequences; for instance: curves, embankments, bifurcation, crossings.

Fig. 93 to 97 show the weak points and the way to place the petards.

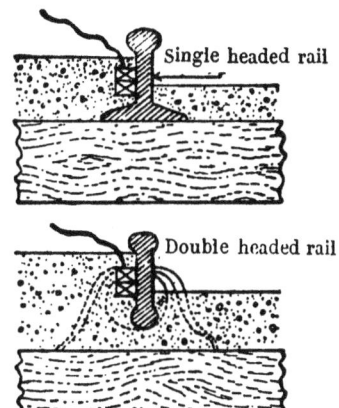

Fig. 93. — Simple rupture.

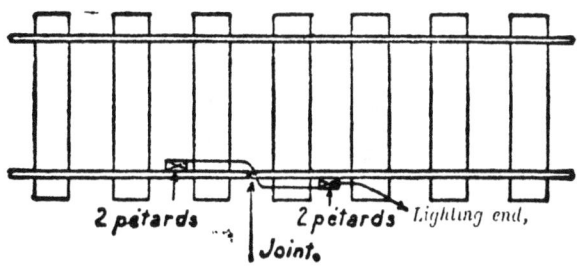

Fig. 94. — Double rupture.

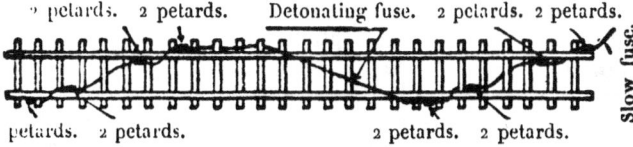

Fig. 95. — Extended rupture.

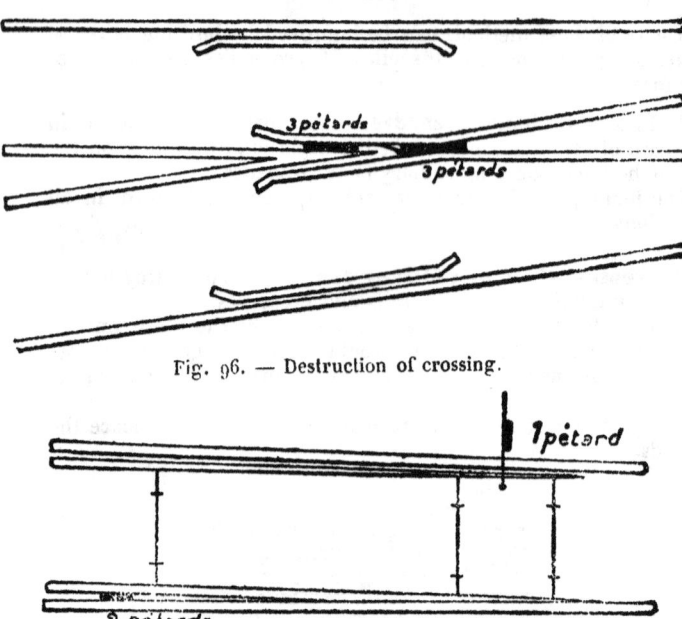

Fig. 96. — Destruction of crossing.

Fig. 97. — Destruction of switch.

5. Destruction of an unexploded shell. — Put a concentrated charge of 1 to 3 petards of melinite (according to the calibre of the shell) in contact to the shell ; make a slight tamping (tamping is necessary with cheddite).

For other destructions : walls, trees, iron fuses, palisades, stockades, etc., see the annex n° IV of the Instruction on field works.

. . . .

CHAPTER VIII.

THE WAGONS AND HORSES OF THE COMPANY.

1° The wagons.

Loading tables. — The commanding officer fixes the contents ot the load and publishes the disposition, the weight and the volume of the articles, and has the list stuck on a board and hung up, inside each wagon.

The company commander is responsible for the proper stowage of the wagons of the company ; **any overweight**

is forbidden. as being a cause of the rapid wearing down of horses and wagons. In the course of the marches he assigns a non-commissioned officer (a mess-sergeant or a supply sergeant) to daily oversee the loading or unloading. He takes special interest in the condition of the horses and in the state of the equipment, as it is often very difficult to replace a lame horse or a damaged wagon. On principle, any driver whose horse becomes unserviceable is relieved.

When the wagon trains are assembled for the march, the officer in command and the non-commissioned officers strictly forbid that anything be added to the load of the wagon, which should remain of its original weight as it came from the company.

In case the commanding officer has authorized an auxiliary driver, the latter places his haversack on the wagon, **but he is forbidden to ride,** as the weight has been calculated for a single man.

Rolling kitchens. — Several models are in use.

The two wheeled kitchens are difficult to drive, as thier balance varies according as they are empty or full. The weight of the driver on the box keeps the balance with the boiler when it is full, but when the boiler is empty, he must walk so as not to bring excessive weight on the horses.

On rest days, have the meals prepared in the individual outfits, in order not only to let the troops become accustomed to them but also to allow the kitchen to be thoroughly cleaned.

The output of the rolling kitchens is very much improved if the cooks are not allowed to follow their own routine and if precise orders are given according to each particular case that one has to deal with (marches, camp, trenches). Consider also the hour at which the distributions arrive and decide if the meat has to be cooked all at the same time or at intervals, if two hot meals will be distributed each day, or if the soldier will keep half a ration to eat it cold at the next meal : in the latter case it is easy to give him a hot soup made out of provisions which have been put aside for that purpose.

The place which the wagons occupy in the column. — The 3 wagons of the company form part of the combat train.

During the marches towards the enemy, the combat trains follow immediately behind their regiments, or else are assembled by division or army corps, behind the fighting columns and ahead of the rearguard.

The combat train may also be divided in two echelons,

the first echelon advancing as has just been described, and the second marching with the regimental wagon train.

In this case the ammunition wagon goes with the first echelon, the two others with the second.

The regimental wagon trains follow the movements of the column at a distance which varies according to the situation.

In each group, the wagon trains are placed in the same order as the corresponding regiments.

II° The horses.

Rules for the care of horses. — *Before saddling* (harnessing or packing) : brush strenuously the back of the horse. Clean out the hoofs with a wooden scraper and not with an iron one. Verify the shoeing.

Saddling : Unfold the blanket and beat it; fold it carefully into four thicknesses; place it on the horse above the withers, the thickest fold forward, the border on the near side, move it to its place by sliding it back the right way of the hair.

Fit the pack-saddle (aparejo) very straight at two fingers distance from the shoulder. Free the blanket from the withers and from the loins by lifting it at the same time as you fit the saddle. Do not cinch too tight. Verify the girths at the first stops; tighten the girths if necessary.

Rules on arrival in camp. — Unsaddle and rub lightly the right way of the hair so as to reestablish the circulation of the blood where the saddle lay. Cover the horse if hot.

Grooming : Wash if possible the eyes, the nostrils, the sheath, the anus, the legs. Dry the pasterns with great care in order to avoid cracked heels. Rub the fleshy parts with the currycomb; brush all over.

Watering and feeding of the horses. — A horse must be watered at least once before each feed, more often if possible, but never during his feed time or during his digestion.

At the watering place let the horse drink freely. If he is sweating, interrupt his drinking several times.

Don't allow a horse that has just been watered to trot. Give him his grain feed. Immediately after his feed don't ask a horse to do any strenuous work.

Kicks. — Take notice in camp of the horses disposition; some horses kick each other and yet remain indifferent towards others. Always put the same horses next to each other. Separate the vicious ones from the others. Some horses become nervous when alone.

Sores on the back. — Verify the padding, have it hollowed out where required; readjust the saddle. Never wash sores on the back. Treat them with picric acid, bickmorine or else charcoal powder.

Galled withers and sores on the back, make the horse unfit

for work for a long period. For the horses harnessed to a two wheeled cart, the wounds come always from negligence of the driver to properly balance the load. In a properly loaded cart the shafts must naturally remain almost horizontal, a small pressure of the fingers being sufficient to move them upwards or downwards. If they weigh upon the saddle, the horse gets a sore back. If the shafts are too high, the girth of the horse becomes sore.

Colics. — A horse with colics gazes at his flank, then rolls; he often is covered with sweat. Cover him and walk him immediately.

Care of saddlery and harness. — To keep the leathers soft, those which have been impregnated with sweat, dust or mud must be washed daily with a damp sponge and then dried and rubbed with a woollen rag or a piece of cloth.

Dry the blankets and the leathers in the open air and not in front of a fire.

Monthly or every two months «nourish the leathers» by rubbing them energetically with Dubling grease, Mironde, vaseline, etc.

Hang the leathers on wooden horses or on supports, placed in such a way that the air may circulate and they will not get creased.

CHAPTER IX.

ILLUMINATING FIREWORKS AND SIGNALLING APPARATUS.

Illuminating fireworks.

1° Illuminating rockets. — 2 calibers : 34 millimeters and 27 millimeters (internal dimension of rocket). No difference between them except in range and intensity of light.

To attach the rocket stick. — A stick 1 m. 30 in length with a square section 13 millimeters (1/2 inch) thick. Fastenings of iron wire, very tightly bound as per figure 124. The stick has to be quite parallel to the rocket.

To uncap the rocket. — When the rocket is about to be fired, pull out smartly the string loop fastened on the side of the rocket, so as to tear off the metallic cap and its pasteboard plug.

To ignite the rocket. — The rocket being placed on the rack, pull out the small brass plug which covers the igniting fuse; with one of the friction blocks which accompanies each case of rockets, rub smartly but very lightly on the igniting substance of the fuse. The operator must at once retire a few meters backwards and sideways. The fuse will go off within five or six seconds after ignition.

In case of misfire, disengage the Bickford fuse from the copper tube, cut it on the bevel and bring it within the wire loop which holds the copper tube and ignite it.

The rocket throws out the parachute and star after having gone over a distance of 250 meters (rocket of 27) or 450 meters (rocket of 34) about 10 seconds after its ascent.

Duration oi llumination : 30 seconds.

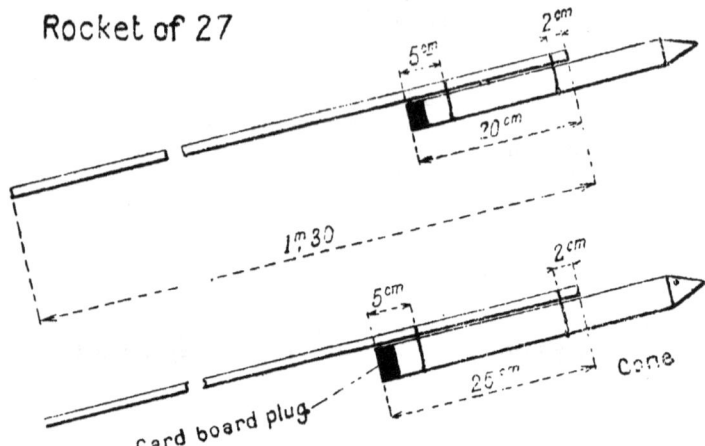

2° Firing racks for rockets. — The handling of that apparatus is easily understood when seen. A fixed quadrant graduated in degrees gives the inclination of the guide tube, when the pivot is in a vertical position. The most favorable angle is 50 degrees.

The guide tube measures 1 m. 50; the stick must be entirely inserted and the rocket must be placed underneath the stick.

An improvised firing rack can be made by fixing two collars of thick wire to a sufficiently long stake (fig. 125). It is even possible to fire rockets by simply driving the stick into soft soil and with a slight inclination, but in that case it is not possible to fire them at an angle of 50 degrees. Considerable deviations in range and direction are observed.

Fig. 125.

3° Illuminating cartridge of 25 mm. with parachute. — A long brass case, shotgun caliber N° 4 i.e. 25 mm. 7, which throws out at 125 meters a star to which is affixed a parachute and which burns 30 seconds.

The illuminating cartridge is fired with an *illuminating cartridge gun of 25* weighing 2 kilogr. 600. It is a breech loading weapon breaking at the breech. It must be kept well oiled. It is brought to the shoulder at an angle of about 50 degrees so as to obtain the proper height i.e. a height such that the star will not reach the ground until it is entirely burnt out.

The star has also incendiary properties.

4° Illuminating stars of 25 mm. — An illuminating cartridge of 25 minus the parachute; same caliber as the illuminating cartridge. It is fired with the same gun or with a special pistol which takes up less space. It is the rapid illuminating apparatus which is fired at the least alarm; it illuminates *immediately* and takes the enemy by surprise.

The cartridge measures about 10 centimeters in length, the star takes fire at about 50 meters from its starting point and in falling illuminates for 6 seconds.

5° Illuminating grenade. — A pasteboard ball about the size of a tennis ball, provided with a Bickford fuse and filled with an alumino-thermic composition. The end of the Bickford match is ignited in the same manner as an ordinary Swedish match, with the aid of a special friction block. The ball is thrown by hand and illuminates for a minute the ground around the spot where it has fallen.

6° Illuminating bomb. — An apparatus recently devised, to take the place of the illuminating rocket, over which it has the advantage of being invisible until the star is ignited, whereas the luminous train of the rocket reveals its starting point and warns the enemy that he is about to be illuminated.

The illuminating bomb is a winged metallic cylinder containing the parachute and star. Diameter: 50 millimeters.

The star is ignited by means of a special percussion ignition placed beneath a diaphragm, which allows no light to show through the bottom of the bomb.

The bomb is fired with a special rifle or with a Viven-Bessières tromblon but *with a special blank cartridge.*

Duration of illumination: 20 to 25 seconds.

Signalling fireworks and apparatus.

1° « Bengal » lights. — There are «white Bengal lights» in 3 sizes, which illuminate during 3 minutes, 1 1/2 min. or 1/2 minute, and *red, green* and *yellow* Bengal lights of the smallest of these sizes (1/2 minute). They are ignited in the same manner as the illuminating grenades.

Other lights (Ruggieri, Lamarre, Coston) are also used.

2° Signalling rockets. — Signalling rockets are operated like the illuminating rockets. They are of two kinds, the *signalling rockets* M. 1885 (13 white stars or 14 red stars which burn for 10 seconds) and the *rockets with large stars* (white, red and green) which contain only 6 stars, but which are clearly visible by day light. These rockets have painted heads, the same color as that of the star; the rockets with large stars have in addition a band of color about midway on the body of the rocket.

Other varieties are in course of preparation. These include : «worm» rockets, red smoke or yellow smoke rockets and flag rockets.

3° Signalling cartridge of 25. — Also called «military telegraph star».
The star is either *white*, *red*, or *green* and lasts eight seconds. The color of the wad indicates that of the star.

These fireworks must not be confused with the *illuminating star cartridges* described above, although the cartridges are similar in appearance, being of the same length (10 centimeters) and of the same caliber (caliber 4).

The latter owe their illuminating properties to the brilliant combustion of aluminium, whereas the signalling cartridges throw out a star of a color visible from afar but unable to illuminate the ground. They can therefore be fired vertically to indicate one's position, or fired in the direction of the post to which the signals are made.

A breech loading **signalling pistol of 25,** made of bronze and weighing about 1 kilogram with a diameter of 26,5 mm. is also used.

This same pistol can fire :

1 cartridge containing 3 stars,
1 cartridge containing 6 stars,
1 red smoke cartridge,
1 yellow smoke cartridge.

4° Signalling cartridge of 35 for the use of the infantry. — A cartridge of 35 millimeters made up of a cartridge base and a case of sheet steel. 3 models :

Cartridge N° 1 : 1 white light star which lasts 10 seconds,
Cartridge N° 3 : 3 white light stars which last 8 seconds,
Cartridge N° 6 : 6 white light stars which last 5 seconds.

Distinctive markings : 1, 3 or 6 large dots which stand out in relief on the end of the cartridge opposite the base, and a circular label with the inscription : « Signal N° 3 for Infantry » stuck on the base.

Weight : cartridge N° 1 : 115 grams; cartridge N° 3 or 6 : 290 grams.

Charge of F 3 powder : 4 1/2 grams.

Range : fired vertically, the cartridge works at about 100 meters high at the end of 3 seconds.

Packing : six small cases of 24 grouped in a case of 144 cartridges (2 of each series].

This cartridge is fired with **a signalling gun of 35 mm.** a breech loader weighing 4 kilogr. 300.

Cartridge N° 1 can also be used as an illuminating or incendiary apparatus. Maximum range : 200 meters.

5° Signalling cartridges of 35 for the use of aircraft. — The same as the preceding but with a charge of only 2 1/2 grams and fired with a **signalling pistol of 35** of a model special for aircraft. In addition to the three models described, the following series will be prepared : 2 stars, worm, red smoke, yellow smoke.

6° Fireworks for use with Viven-Bessières tromblon.
— The V. B. tromblon using a special blank cartridge, will be able to fire the following fireworks: white, green and red stars with parachute; 1 star, 3 stars, 6 stars; worm; red smoke and yellow smoke.

° **Signalling lanterns.** — Former allowance : two to a company. Will be gradually replaced by the *14 cm. portable searchlight*.

Description. — The lantern is made up of a sheet metal box containing :

A *searchlight apparatus* made up of a lacquered silvered mirror and an electric light bulb affixed to an adjustable socket.

A *sighting tube*, the axis of which is parallel to the axis of the parabolical mirror.

A *manipulator* with a folding handle.

An *electric battery* (4 volt) and four spare lamps.

A *spare battery* is also supplied in a case.

Direction for use. — 1° Bring forward the knob of the manipulator after having opened the side shutter. Close this shutter.

2° Take aim at the corresponding signaller so as to bring him in the middle of the field of the sighting tube.

3° Manipulate with the thumb or the forefinger of the right hand. See that during the transmission of the signals the sighting tube remains exactly aimed at the correspondant.

Care and adjustments. — *To replace the battery :* Open the side shutter and unscrew the nuts of the two terminals situated beneath the spare lamps;

Remove the worn battery;

Lay bare the ends of the wires of the spare battery and slip the latter into the lower division of the lantern, the longer wire starting from the bottom. Pass the bare end of the wires through the terminals and screw down the latter tightly. To replace the lamp : remove the mirror by revolving it gently so as to bring the notches opposite the hooks. Unscrew the lamp and replace it by a spare one well screwed down.

Replace the mirror in its socket by revolving it so as to fix the fittings in the hooks.

Adjust the lamp so as to bring the filament within the focus of the mirror. To do this, point the lighted apparatus to a wall about 5 or 6 meters away and turn the regulating screw at the back of the lantern until the projected light becomes as brilliant and as reduced in size as possible.

Range : by day = 500 to 1000 meters,
by night = 1 to 3 kilometers.

8° Portable searchlight apparatus of 14. — Supply : 2 to a company, 3 to a battalion, 3 to a brigade, and 3 to a division.

— 114 —

The 3 apparatus of the battalion are packed in the same case which also contains :

12 spare batteries,
6 spare lamps (3 white and 3 red),
2 packets of wadding.

The 14 centimeter searchlight apparatus is, except in dimensions, similar to the 24 centimeter apparatus described hereafter.

It is used, adjusted and taken care of in the same manner.

Range : by day 1 to 3 kilometers,
    by night 2 to 6 kilometers.

9° Portable searchlight apparatus of 24. — Supply : 4 10 a regiment, 3 to a brigade, 4 to a division.

This apparatus is designed for signalling between either 2 posts on the ground or between the ground and an aircraft or balloon.

Fig. 126.

Description. — The apparatus comprises :

A portable searchlight fitted with a lid, a sighting tube, an insulating connecting wire to which is attached an electric connection plug (fig. 126);

A belt fitted with shoulder straps or braces; carrying two battery cases (each of which holds 4 batteries) and a central pouch or case which holds :

The manipulator;
The socket which receives the connection plug
2 spare lamps;
The case of the searchlight apparatus also carries 8 batteries and three spare lamps.

Directions for use. — Insert the connection plug into its socket, open the lid and take aim at the corresponding post by means of the sighting tube.

The signals are made by pressing on the manipulator with the right hand.

It is very important that the sighting tube remain constantly aimed at the corresponding post during the transmission of the signals.

The apparatus can be held in the hand or placed upon a stand or other support.

To signal to an aircraft the searchlight apparatus is held upon the left shoulder with the left hand.

To correspond with a ground post, the apparatus can be held in front of the body with the left hand.

For a lengthy communication it is better to rest the apparatus on a stand or any other support.

Maintenance in repair. — When the apparatus is not in use the lid must be kept closed, so as to protect the mirror.

Avoid pulling the electric wire which is fixed to the bottom of the apparatus especially when removing the latter from its case.

The mirror must not be handled more than can possibly be helped; it must be cleaned with either gauze or wadding, and if necessary washed with a little pure water.

Adjustment. — The apparatus is supplied adjusted, but it may happen that when a lamp is changed the light may be out of focus.

To remedy this, point the apparatus toward a wall a few meters away and gently move the screws which fix the edges of the mirror until the projected light becomes as brilliant and as reduced in size as possible.

Range : by day, 1.500 meters to 6 kilometers,
       by night, 3 to 10 kilometers.

Red light. — Searchlight apparatus (24 to 14 cm.) are able to make use of red lights so as to distinguish if necessary between the signals of different apparatus. Red lights are as a rule mainly employed by the apparatus for the use of artillery. They reduce to a great extent the range of the apparatus.

Important notice concerning lanterns and searchlights.

The light is supplied to these apparatus by means of batteries which become exhausted very rapidly when used for continuous lighting.

It is expressly enjoined never to use the apparatus for continuous lighting (fixed lights).

The use of signalling apparatus as a means of illumination is absolutely forbidden.

10° The square signalling flag. — Supply : 64 to a regiment.

Size : 5o centimeters.

The inside frame can be taken to pieces and folded for carriage.

Both sides are half white and half red diagonally. This disposition affords the best conditions of visibility against any background.

Flag signals must be observed through field glasses.

11° Panels. — The panels used for corresponding with air craft are of different models, and their meaning varies so as to remain secret.

A. *Indentification panels.* — The white circular panel of 3 meters in diameter is used to identify the division and the brigade.

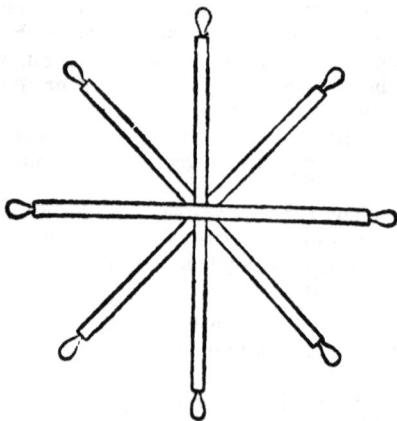

Fig. 127. — Frame work of circular panel.

It is made up of 4 laths of 3 meters in length, joined together in the center by a bolt and provided with a hook at the extremities.

The cloth or canvas panel has 8 rings which are slipped over the hooks.

The *semi-circular white panel* of 3 meters indicates the command post of a regiment.

The *triangular white panel* of 2 meters side indicates the command post of a battalion.

B. *Shutter panels*. — These panels supply the means of causing to appear or disappear a white rectangular figure measuring 1 m. 50 by 2 m. 80. By pulling a tag, either the white surface or the neutral surface made up of seven strips of white canvas measuring 1 m. 50 by 0 m. 40 lined with grey or khaki is shown.
Supply : 1 to every division, brigade and regiment.

C. *« Marking out » Panels*. — Panels made of oil cloth and measuring 0 m. 50 by 0 m. 40. One side white, the other neutral color.
Supply : 64 to a regiment.

These must be unfolded in the first line only. They must remain unfolded until the aircraft signals «**Understood**», **but in any case not longer than 15 minutes.**

Recapitulation table.

	SIGNALLERS.		SEARCHLIGHTS		PANELS.		
	N. C. O's.	Squad of 2 signallers.	of 24.	of 14.	Identification.	Shutter.	Marking out.
Regiment......	2	4	4	–	1	1	64
Battalion.......	1	2	2	3	1	–	–
Company.......	–	1	1	2	–	–	–

CHAPTER X.

THE TELEPHONE.

Infantry telephone :

2 types. — 1° One type of 1908 pattern, with buzzer call. Light, strong, works over badly insulated lines. Needs special boards for vibrated call.

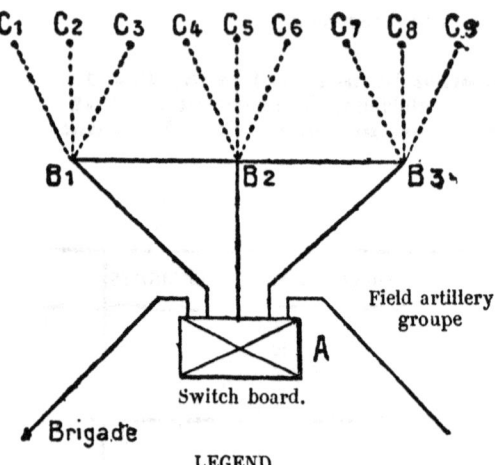

LEGEND.

A. Command post of colonel.
B. Command post of chief of battalion.
C. Command post of captain.

Fig. 128. — Infantry telephone system.

2° Type 1909 or 1915 pattern with magneto and buzzer call. Rather heavy. Enables calling the artillery men, who use shutter boards, and working a bell call.

Batteries. — Dry cells are used which are not re-loaded.

To have them last long it is necessary

Not to place them in a damp corner;

Not to use them uselessly by lengthening the calls or pressing the telephone pedal when not speaking;

To avoid the short circuits produced by metallic wires touching two terminals of the same cell.

A single short circuit lasting a few seconds spoils a cell irreparably.

When the cells are new a single one is sufficient to keep the telephone going. When its power weakens, another one is to be added.

All telephones are in wooden boxes that deteriorate in the damp; accordingly telephones should not be placed on moist ground or grass. In the dug outs they should be carefully fastened on a table or a board.

Conductors. — Infantry uses : the enamelled wire, the light cable ;

Exceptionally the field cable, the cable with two conductors, the «armed» cable or the cable with a lead jacket.

The enamelled wire is kept for the short lived communications of offensive actions (bronze wire of 15 mm.)

The light cable is the normal conductor in the trenches. It must be laid with care and insulated from the earth as much as possible (strung on pulleys or on wooden sticks).

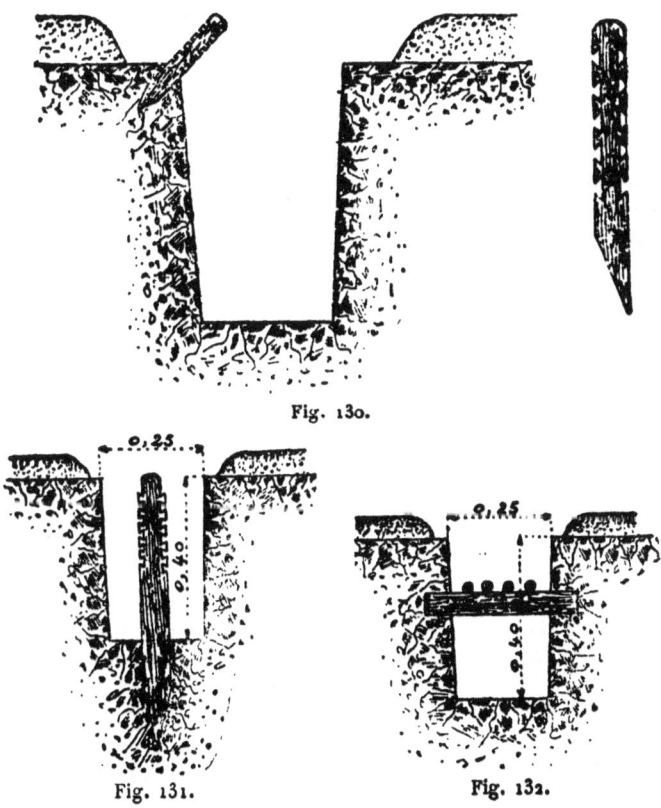

Fig. 130.

Fig. 131. Fig. 132.

The field cable is used for important communications. It is advisable and often necessary to bury it against shells (gutters at the bottom of the trenches or under the macadam of the roads; small special trenches 40 centimeters deep covered with a light camouflage).

The cable with two conductors serves to prevent the enemy from tapping communications. It should be used in the first lines or for the important communications in offensive actions.

Regimental personnel and material.

A telephone squad includes as a rule : 1 N. C. O. or corporal, 5 telephonists, 2 telephones, 1 switchboard with four directions, and 2 kilometers of light cable.

In a regiment with three battalions, there is a telephone officer, and 8 squads, and besides 4 spare telephones, 2 switchboards and 14 kilometers of cable.

Precautions against the enemy tapping communications.

All telephonic liaisons in the zone near the enemy up to 2,000 meters **have double wire**, i. e. they include no earth return; this is an **absolute** rule.

Moreover it is strictly forbidden in the first lines to hint by telephone at any event or situation the knowledge of which might be useful to the enemy (hour of the attacks and reliefs, number of the regiment, of the neighboring regiments, of the brigade, etc.).

In general the telephone is always too much used in quiet periods.

The use of the **message** instead of **conversations** must be enjoined to all : the officer who writes down a message is more terse, weighs his terms more, and better avoids an unwise piece of information : lastly, there remains a record of the communication.

Questions of « priority » should also be settled with perfect clearness.

Precautions to assure the preservation of communications.

Telephonic liaisons are of vital importance for the first line units. Every body whatever his office may be, must try to work for their preservation. So it is a strict duty for any man who sees a broken line to mend it or at least to warn quickly the nearest telephone squad.

Fatigue parties and reliefs of troops coming and going by night, must take great care : they should carry their rifles slung barrel downwards.

The arrangement seen in fig. 130 is suitable only when the trench is two meters deep. If it is not, it is better to drive notched pickets at the bottom of the trench and very close to the sides.

The crossing of a trench must be made with particular care. The best process is to make the line pass under the trench in a conduit made of planks and to use for the crossing the lead jacketed cable. If the crossing is aerial, the line should always be well stretched. It should run along a pole.

To mend a line it is sufficient to uncover the metallic wires at the cable ends, to tie them together and to insulate this knot from the earth by means of a rag or a piece of wood or cardboard. Then, and as soon as possible, the knot must be covered with tarred ribbon that will insulate it entirely.

Labelling and classing the lines.

It is very important that the lines passing in the same trench be identified.

Therefore it is always necessary to avoid placing a line upon those which exist already.

Besides, every 5o meters a label strongly tied to each ine should indicate its origin and its destination.

Every useless line should be rolled up on the same day it is no longer needed.

CHAPTER XI.

MEANS OF OBSERVATION AND OF RECONNAISSANCE.

FIELD GLASSES. — PERISCOPE. — COMPASS. — MAPS AND PLANS.

1° Field glasses. — For reference.

Strong field glasses which magnify to a great extent are not always the most advantageous for an infantry officer. For unless the object glasses are considerably increased in size, which renders the instrument cumbersome, the enlargement is always obtained at the expense of field and of illumination. If two field glasses have object glasses of the same diameter and one magnifies twice as much as the other, the illumination is four times less.

An enlargement from 6 or 7 diameters, a field of 100 to 130 mils and the corresponding illumination give in prismatic field glasses the best balance between these contradictory qualities.

2° Periscope. — An ordinary periscope is composed of two mirrors, M_1 M_2 or two total reflective prisms of which the faces *parallel to each other* are inclined at 45° to the tube. Fig. 133 shows that everything takes place as if the eye, placed in O^1 instead of O could see through an opening which has the same dimensions as the one placed in front of M_1. The conclusion of

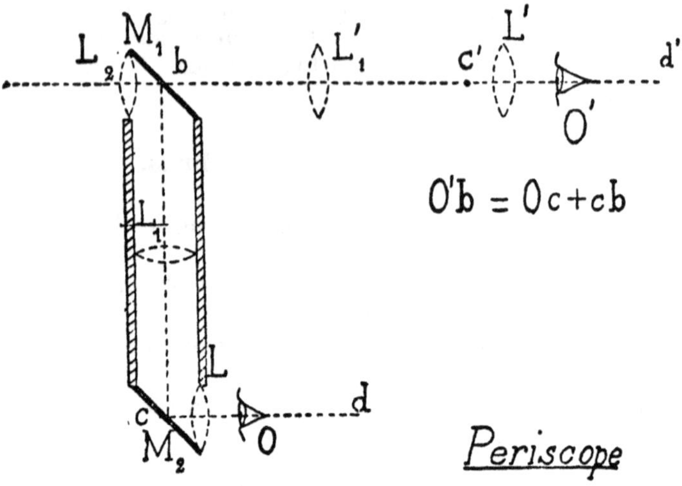

Fig. 133.

this is that for two identical mirrors the longer the periscope the narrower will be its field. Therefore one cannot lengthen a periscope indefinitely. 70 centimeters is a good serviceable height.

On the other hand, the mirror cannot be much more than 7 centimeters wide, or else it runs the chance of being seen and destroyed by the enemy. Under these conditions a periscope 70 centimeters high can at a distance of 100 meters see a stretch of ground only 10 meters wide. The height of the field is on the contrary nearly always sufficient.

If one looks through a periscope with a field glass the scenery is magnified, the clearness is increased, but the field is no greater.

In the folding or sliding periscopes it is imperative to recover the exact parallelism of the mirrors.

The Carvallo periscope which is represented on fig. 134 is held at an angle and with one's back turned to the objective.

As in the ordinary periscope the direction is not reversed that is say that one can read any inscription placed in the field of vision

There are also some precise periscopes which have a field of 85 meters at a distance of 100 meters. They are made with the lenses (fig. 133) L, L_1, L_2; and work the same way as the telescope L', L_1, L_2; they are quite costly.

An other application of the periscope. — When one can observe in open ground, the periscope affords some means of exaggerating the relief of the terrain ; for that, one has only to hold the periscope horizontally in front of oné eye, and look straight at the landscape with the other eye. By very slight rotations of the periscope around its axis one can by degrees superpose the two fields : the relief becomes then suddenly quite extraordinary and the different view planes stand out very distinctly one from the other. One can in this way distinguish any object moving in the distance.

Fig. 134. — Periscope Carvalho.

3° Compass. — The blue needle of the compass indicates the *magnetic north*.

The compasses are graduated from o to 360 degrees (or else from o to 400 grades, or else from o to 6400 mils) in the same direction as the hands of a watch. The line 0-180 (or 0-200 or 0-3200) which is marked generally N. S. takes the direction of the true (geographical) North, whenever the blue part of the needle is made to point 13 1/2 degrees (for Paris) at the left of the o of the compass. (15 grades or else 240 mils.)

The compass which is usually employed is the one which has a needle four centimeters long; the dial twists on the compass case and has a large black arrow-headed directing needle, which is concentric with the animated needle. A small protractor in copper is added to it.

The precision of the angle measurements taken with a compass is proportional to the length of the needle.

The compass is made untrue in the neighborhood of iron articles (helmet).

In order to orient a map of the scale of $\frac{1}{80,000}$ place the compass on the map, the line 0-180 on one of the meridians. Revolve the map which supports the compass, until the blue point of the needle marks the declination. The map is then oriented.

To orient a map which is divided in squares place the compass in such a way that the line 0-180 should be on the arrow marking the true north on the map, and direct at the same time the blue point of the needle towards the declination. One can also place the line 0-180 of the compass, on the arrow which points towards the magnetic north and bring the blue point on the o. This is the best way because it exempts one from reading on the graduation of the compass the declination which varies according to the different regions.

To determine the direction of the azimuth of a far distant object (fig. 135). — Place yourself facing the object, place the arrow towards it as accurately as you can and turn the dial around so that the blue point of the needle is on the 0. The object is then at 138° from the magnetic north, counting it in

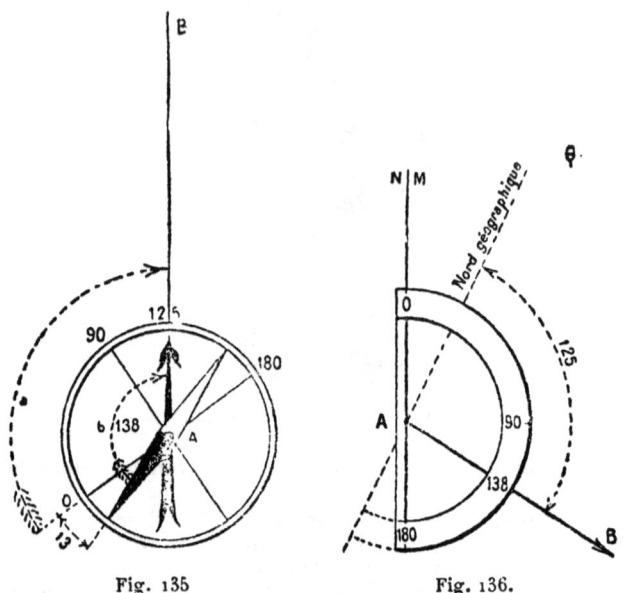

Fig. 135.   Fig. 136.

the same direction as the hands of a watch. If you want more precision place the compass on a fixed support, make several estimations and take the mean.

Angle b is called the magnetic azimuth of B.

If one had brought the blue needle to such a position that it would have pointed towards the declination (which is supposed to be of 13 degrees) one would have read 125 degrees instead of 138. This angle a is called the geographic azimuth of B.

Knowing the station point, locate on the map the sighted point (fig. 136). — Let us suppose A to be on the map the station point. Trace through A a line parallel to the magnetic meridian, measure with a protractor from that line an angle of 138 degrees in the direction of the hands of a watch, B will be somewhere on the line A. B.

One could have traced through A a line parallel to the true meridian and worked with an angle of 125 degrees.

Knowing the station point, to determine the line passing through the point and the station point (fig. 137).

Suppose B to be the sighted point on the map. Trace the

magnetic meridian passing through B, place the protractor along the meridian, with its limb towards A, trace the line B-138, A will be somewhere on that line.

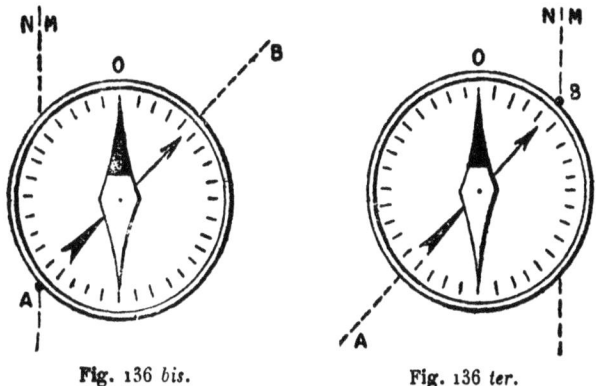

Fig. 136 *bis*.   Fig. 136 *ter*.

One may operate in the same way with the true North and an angle of 125 degrees.

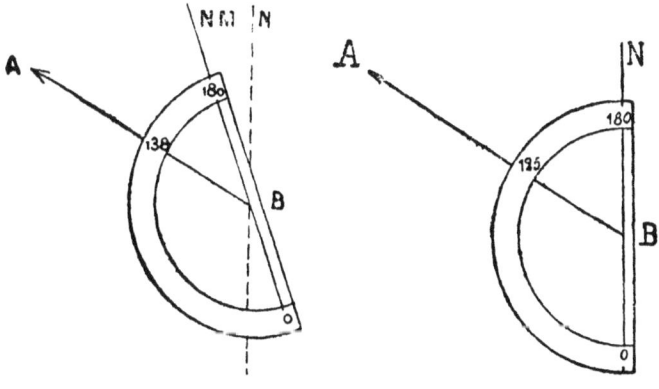

Fig. 137.

Notice. — The two above mentioned operations can be carried out without the protractor and using only the compass.

Let us suppose the map to be oriented. Place the compass on the map in such a way that the edge of the compass which is in the prolongation of the feathered end of the black arrow should be fixed on A (fig. 136 *bis*), make the compass pivot round that point (and not round its centre) so as to swing the needle and bring its blue point on the 0; at that moment the compass is located on the map in the same position as it was in the field when the azimuth was determined. It is therefore sufficient on the map to mark the point in prolongation of the end of the black-arrow and to draw a line between that point and A to determine the direction A B.

By doing the same thing in the contrary way, that is by placing the arrow on B which is supposed to be a known point one is able to determine the unknown point A in the direction of the feathered end of the arrow (fig. 136 *ter*).

This latter method has a double advantage, as it dispenses: 1° with having to read the angle; and 2° with having to use the protractor which is a delicate instrument easy to put out of order.

Second notice. — If one should hesitate between the two positions in which the protractor can be placed lengthwise of B's meridian (fig. 138), the only thing to do would be to determine

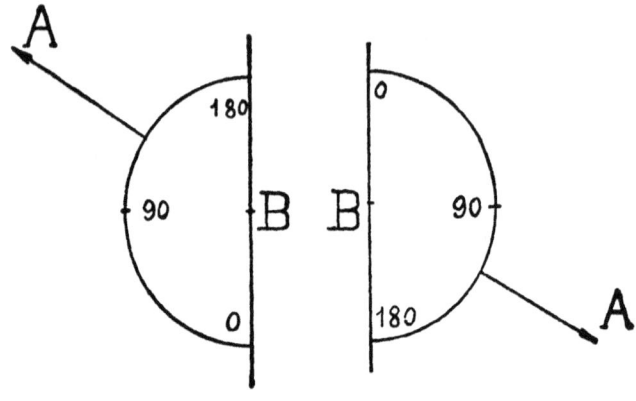

Fig. 138.

whether A has to be located to the E. or to the W. of B. In both positions moreower the line 0-125° determines either BA, or its prolongation.

These operations are the only two into which enter the handling of the compass and protractor.

All the following, such as using polar coordinates from a central station, intersection, bearings, resection, are only one or the other of these two operations repeated once, twice or three times.

Sketching with a compass. — It is rather beyond the limits of this manual to insert into it a summary of topography.

We shall only mention the four operations which, in combination with pacing or the measuring tape will enable any non-commissioned officer, who has elementary notions of geometry and of drawing, to make a passable topographic sketch.

Any sketch has to proceed from the known to the unknown. The known is a triangulation which has been prepared beforehand by enlarging a number of points or of lines which have been chosen on a good map of a small scale; it may be also a rough sketch which one has made with the intention of completing or extending it; if one has no previous document a base line must be chosen arbitrarily on the terrain (on a straight road possible) and its length and azimuth very carefully measured.

Subsequently, when one has determined at least two points of the terrain, their place on the sketch and the direction of the North, it is easy with one of the four operations mentioned below, to determine a certain number of others, between which may be sketched in any object that lies between them.

System of polar coordinates. — Knowing A, to locate B : being stationed at A, measure the azimuth of B, transfer it; measure AB, reduce it to the scale, it gives the distance A. b. (fig. 139).

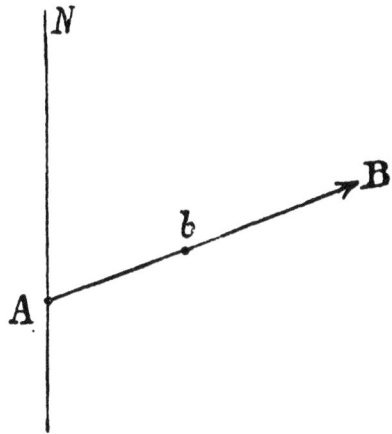

Fig. 139.

Intersection. — Knowing A and B, from these points take the azimuths of AC and BC, lay them off to scale on the sketch, the intersection determines c (fig. 140).

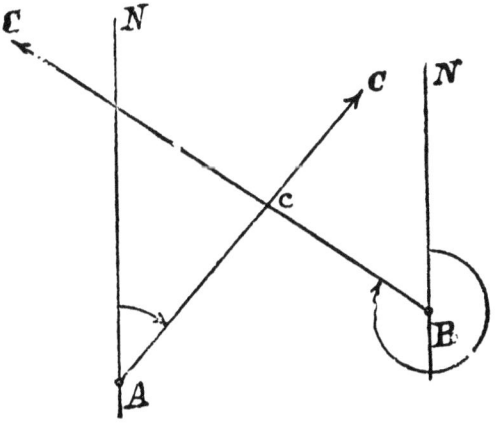

Fig. 140.

Resection. — Knowing A and B, but being stationed at C, determine the azimuths of CA and CB, lay them off on the sketch, their intersection determines c (fig. 141).

Intersection (2^d case). — Knowing that C is somewhere on the straight line AB and knowing D, determine D's azimuth, lay off DC, the intersection with AB will determine c (fig. 142)

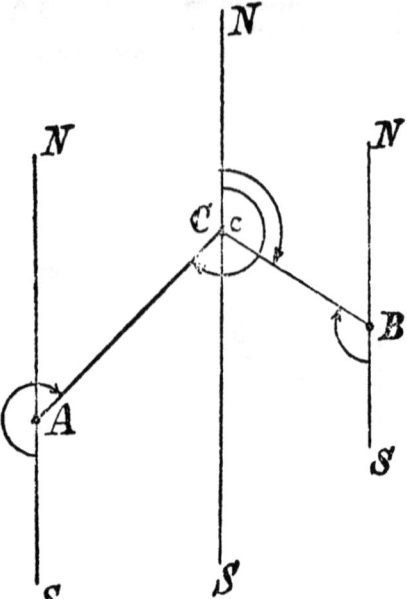

Fig. 141.

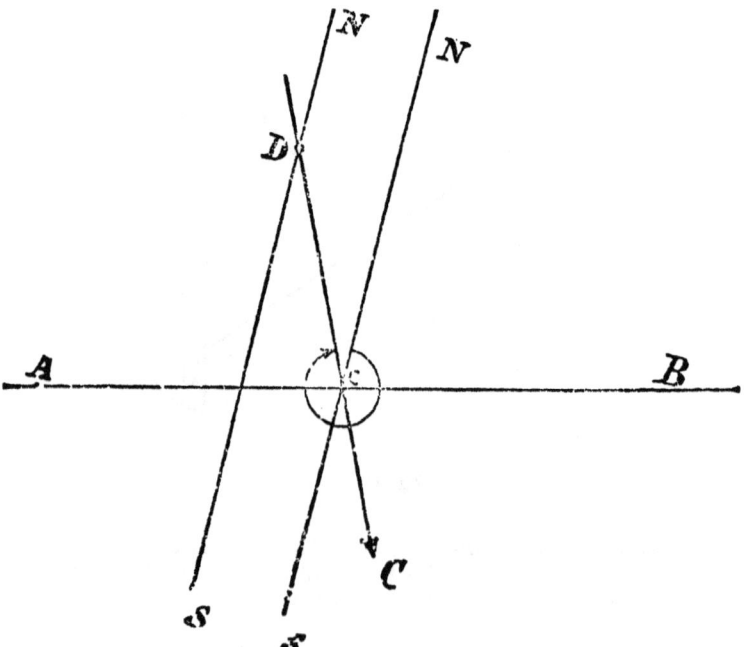

Fig. 142.

These operations have a certain precision only if the construction lines cross one another at wide angles : choose the sighted points accordingly; verify often by performing a supplementary sight or else by measuring a supplementary distance, so that you have three known quantities instead of two to locate the point which you want to determine.

As soon as the sketch is finished and as soon as you have made a fair copy of it :

Place the oriented arrow (Magnetic or true N. S.).
Draw a scale, or else state in writing the scale of the sketch.
Write down the date the sketch has been made;
the name and the rank of the author;
the conventional signs, if any unusual ones have been employed.

An additionnal note may be recorded indicating which process has been employed for the plotting of the sketch, in order that the person who makes use of it should have an idea of its precision. For instance : sketch made without measurement; distances measured by time; distances taken by pacing and with the 5 centimeter compass; or else : from the 1/80,000 map enlarged and completed at sight, etc.

If it concerns an old sketch which has been corrected, so state: date of the most recent correction, the...

Write very legibly and do not exaggerate the proportions of the conventional signs which are always large enough, if legible (width of the roads, houses, etc.). Bear in mind constantly while you are drawing or writing that you are not only working for yourself but for other's benefit.

5° Maps and plans. — The difference between a map and a plan is that the scale of a map is too small to represent objects of any interest at their real size reduced to the scale, for they would be imperceptible : a road of 8 meters on a scale of 1 to 80,000 would only be one tenth of a millimeter wide.

Use is then made of *conventional signs*, the dimensions of which correspond in no way with the true dimension of the roads, houses, bridges which they represent.

The scales which are most frequently used for maps, are described by the following representative fractions : 1 to 320,000, 1 to 200,000, 1 to 100,000, 1 to 80,000, 1 to 50,000. 1 to 20,000.

On the contrary, on a plan which for instance has a scale of 1 to 2,000 a 7 meters road will be marked by two lines 3 1/2 millimeters distant, which is in fact 7 meters at a scale of 1 to 2,000.

The 1 to 10,000 scale is the intermediate scale between maps and plans.

Maps and plans are drawn with system and accurate methods.

A sketch is any drawing of the landscape which has been made rapidly by rough means, sometimes even by recollection or else by information and which is submitted without any guaranteed metrical exactness.

Map reading can only be taught during practical exercises which take place on the terrain.

Orientation. — To orient a map consists in putting one of the meridians or else the N. S. line of the map towards the true North. It consists also in directing the magnetic north line, traced on the map in the direction taken by the magnetised needle. When the map is oriented all the objects figured on the map are parallel to the corresponding objects on the terrain.

One can find one's bearing either by observing the sun (with possible errors of 10 degrees) or by knowing one's own position and by locating another point which is at a distance visible and marked on the map and lining oneself in. Or by the polar star. Nothing however is equal to a good compass.

Scales. — One should immediately recognize the scale of a map, a plan or a sketch, by the following rule.

One unit on the map represents as many units on the ground as are expressed in the denominator of the representative fraction (R. F.)

Examples : $\frac{1}{20,000}$: 1 milimeter equal to 20,000 millimeters, 1 foot equals 20,000 feet.

$\frac{1}{375,000}$: 1 millimeter equal to 375,000 millimeters, 1 foot equals 375,000 feet.

$\frac{1}{2,500}$: 1 millimeter equal to 2,500 millimeters, 1 foot equals 2,500 feet.

$\frac{1}{400}$: 1 millimeter equal to 400 millimeters.

On the 1 to 80,000 scale, 1 millimeter is equal to 80 meters, 1 kilometer is equal to 12 millimeters and a half, The diameter of a 5 centime coin is exactly equal to 2 kilometers.

Finally, in order to make rapid measurements everybody ought to be able to estimate 1 kilometer, by means of the width of a finger, of the length of a finger nail, etc., after having previously recorded these measures.

Compulsory conventional signs to be used on the 0 to 5,000 ratio scale or at any other larger one.

(For sketches and reports, etc.)

— — — — — — Trenches or boyaus which are proposed.

─────────── The same which have been begun, partly usable.

▬▬▬▬▬▬▬▬ The same completed and kept in good order.

• • • • • • • • • • • • • The same dilapidated and become useless (same sign as the preceding one partly scratched out).

Trenches : traced with red or black ink.

Boyaus : traced with a green or a black lead pencil.

⁝⁝⁝⁝⁝⁝⁝⁝⁝⁝⁝⁝ Underground communication.

▆▆▆▆▆▆▆▆▆▆ Raised trench, trench built with gabions.

⟵───── Compulsory traffic direction.

⌐ Small outpost; barricade, defensive traverse.

⟶⟵ ▥▥▥ Footbridge, sortie steps.

× × × × × Wire on pickets.

ℓℓℓℓℓℓ Brun wire entanglements (French wire).

⁓⁓⁓⁓⁓⁓⁓⁓ Any other kind of accessory defence.

☩
⊠ Btn   Commanding post of the chief of battalion (or of a colonel or a general).

☩ Command of the captain.

⌐ Telephone station.

▬ ▬ ▬ ▬ ▬ Telephone line.

⌂ Optical signal station.

⌇ Runner's relay.

♆ ♆ ♆
cart. Gr. Tr.   Depot of cartridges, of grenades, of bombs for trench guns.

✗ Material and tool depot.

⊻ Supply depot.

— 132 —

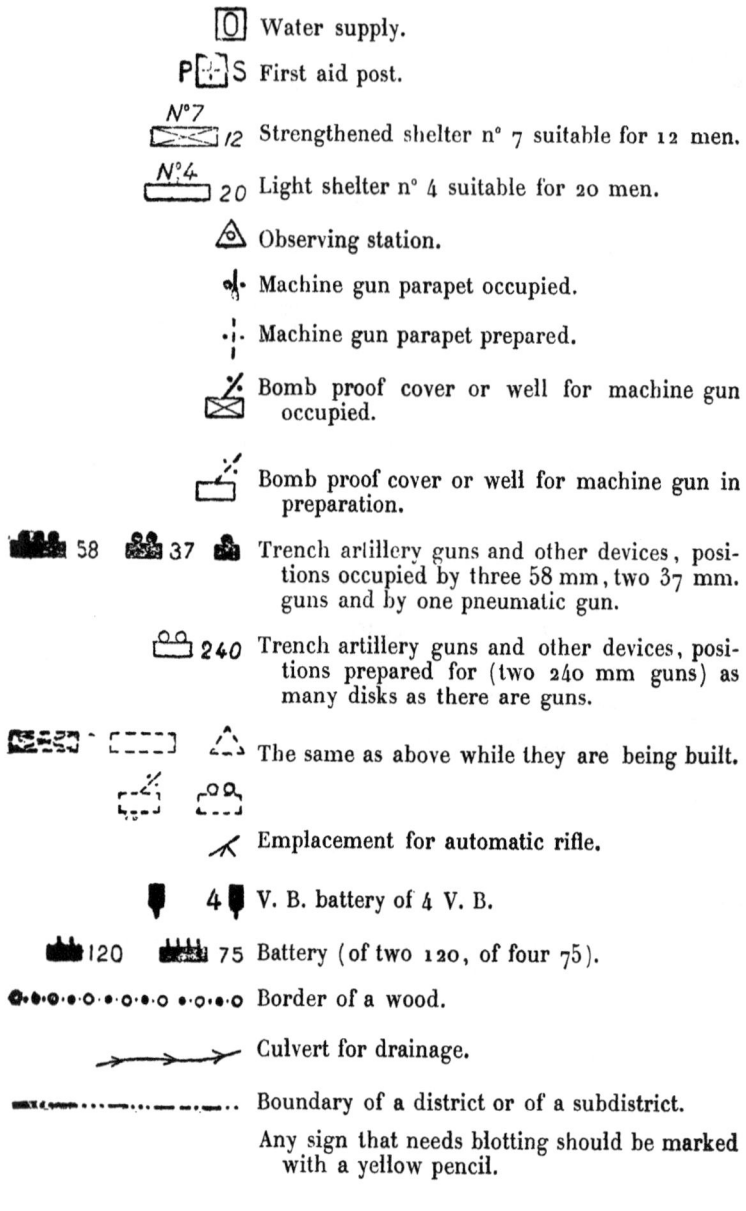

	Water supply.
	First aid post.
N°7 /12	Strengthened shelter n° 7 suitable for 12 men.
N°4 20	Light shelter n° 4 suitable for 20 men.
	Observing station.
	Machine gun parapet occupied.
	Machine gun parapet prepared.
	Bomb proof cover or well for machine gun occupied.
	Bomb proof cover or well for machine gun in preparation.
58 37	Trench artillery guns and other devices, positions occupied by three 58 mm, two 37 mm. guns and by one pneumatic gun.
240	Trench artillery guns and other devices, positions prepared for (two 240 mm guns) as many disks as there are guns.
	The same as above while they are being built.
	Emplacement for automatic rifle.
4	V. B. battery of 4 V. B.
120 75	Battery (of two 120, of four 75).
	Border of a wood.
	Culvert for drainage.
	Boundary of a district or of a subdistrict.
	Any sign that needs blotting should be marked with a yellow pencil.

Designation of objectives on maps marked in squares. — The battle maps and the maps at the scale of 1 to 50,000 which are found in the observing stations and command posts are cross sectioned each square having a dimension of one kilometer, the initial point being common to the whole region.

The abscissa is the distance measured along of the axis of the X, reading from left to right (fig. 144) and the ordinate is the distance measured along the axis of Y upwards.

In order to designate a point of the map in reference to the squares, the following process is required. Begin by designating the square according to the coordinates of its S. W. angle, abscissa first, 33-28; determine afterwards the objective by adding to each of these coordinates the decimal coordinates always in the same order; abscissa-ordinate, 335-282. When errors of 10 kilometers are impossible, one may suppress the first figure of each group. The objective O is determined in this case by the number 3582. This is merely the designation of a region which

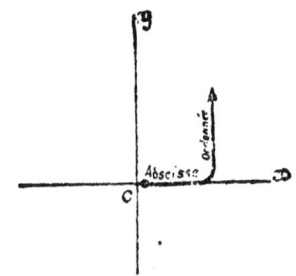

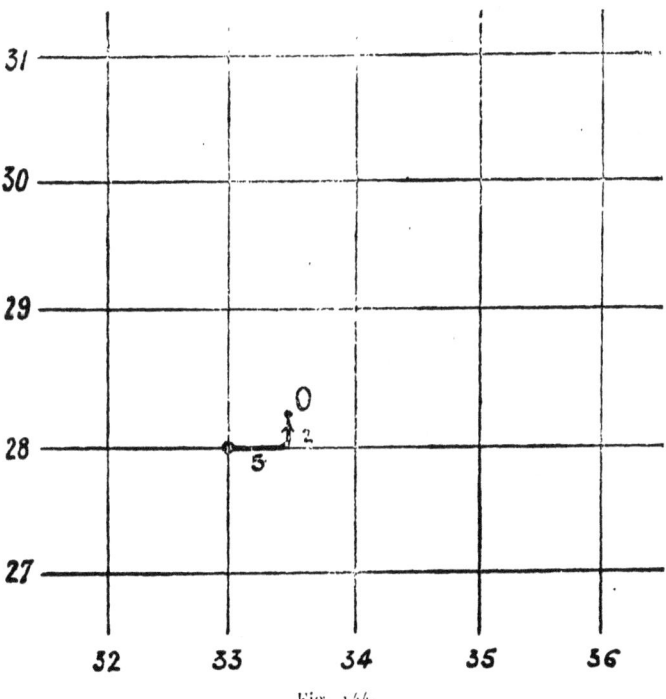

Fig. 144.

is 100 meters square, in which the point is to be found and it enables one to locate it easily on a battle map. This designation is not sufficiently precise to enable the artillery to locate a position which is not yet placed on the map and which an infantry observer has been able to reconnoitre accurately. In that case it is necessary to refer to a large scale plan (1 to 5,000 and above) on which the position of the observed point can be marked with a pencil.

Any officer should be capable : 1° knowing the coordinates of a point, of locating it on the battle map;

2° Of finding the coordinates of any point which is not yet numbered on the battle map. As a rule it is the only way that he will have to locate with a certain amount of precision the position to which he wants to draw attention.

. . . .

CHAPTER XIII.

DEFENSIVE AND OFFENSIVE WAR MATERIAL.

(Miscellaneous notes).

1° Filloux wire cutting device.

2° Individual parapet shield. (fig. 150). — Made of special sheet steel, used in trenches, either as loophole and head cover, or as overhead cover by driving its two feet into the mass of the parapet.

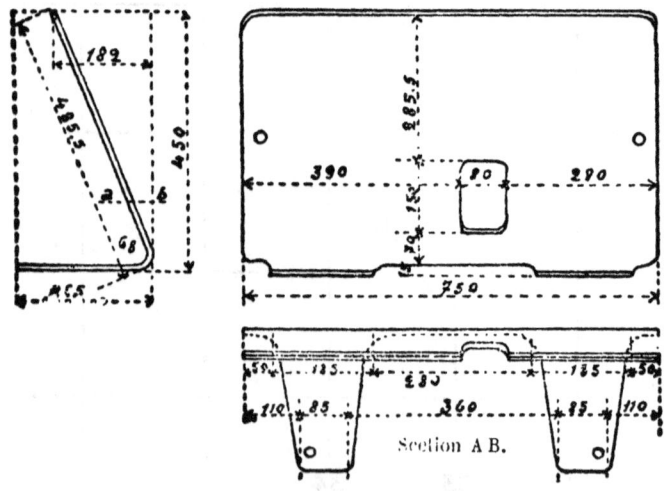

Fig. 150. — *Individual parapet shield.*

The type most frequently used is 11-1/2 $^m/_m$ thick and weighs 30 kilos.

It is proof against the S bullet at any distance, against the same bullet reversed at 30 meters. It is not proof against the

S. M. K. fired perpendicularly to the shield at 30 meters, but such bullets are stopped as soon as the angle of incidence exceeds 15 degrees.

3° Individual offensive shield (fig. 151). — Made of special sheet steel, less heavy than the above.

Though designed for use in open warfare, is often used like the former.

Moreover, a continuous screen made of such shields may serve to start a trench.

Proof against the S bullet at any distance; against the S bullet, reversed, at 50 meters. Weight: 15 kilos. Thickness: 7 $^{m/m}$.

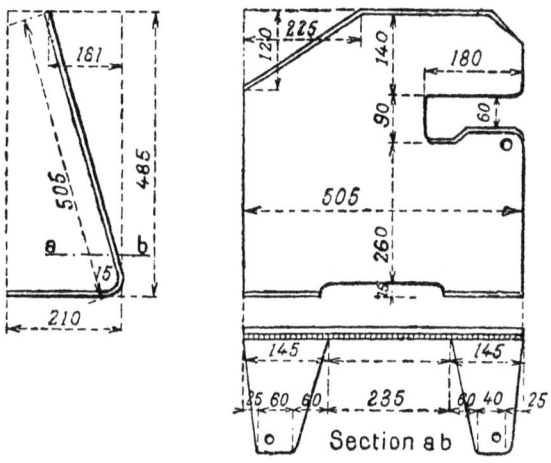

Fig. 131. — Individual Offensive Shield.

4 Sheet iron and sand shield (fig. 152). — Proof against the German bullet at 20 meters and upward; used to protect men firing behind a parapet.

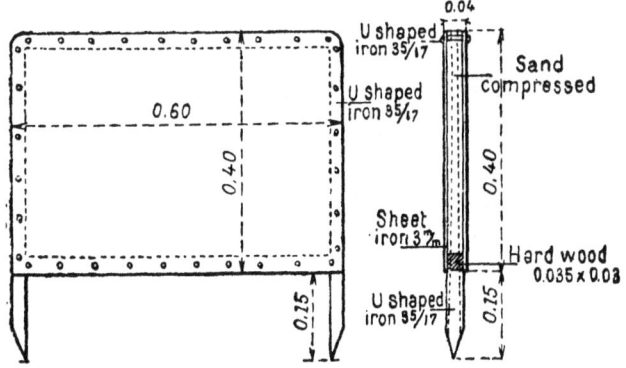

Fig. 152. — Shield of sheet iron and sand.

5° Individual rolling shield (Walter shields). — Narrow armored shelter, mounted on two wheels; may be directed from inside by a man in a kneeling position, thus allowing him to approach under shelter wire entanglements or trenches, to fire or spy through 2 loopholes supplied with moving iron lids.

May be completed by a windlass which enables the man to get explosives from the trench he started from or to help him to get back. The armored plates that protect the head and chest are proof against the K (perforating) bullet; the rest of the shield (wheels, cheeks, roof) is proof against S bullets even when reversed and K bullets provided their angle of incidence does not exceed 5o degrees.

Transported dismounted by two men for the folded armor and one man per wheel.

6° Blazeix shield. — Made by fitting together two machine-gun shields and one individual shield ; sufficient to protect one machine-gun and two gunners. Total weight : 54 kilos. Completed by a machine-gun sled weighing 16 kilos.

Will probably become the normal shelter for machine-guns.

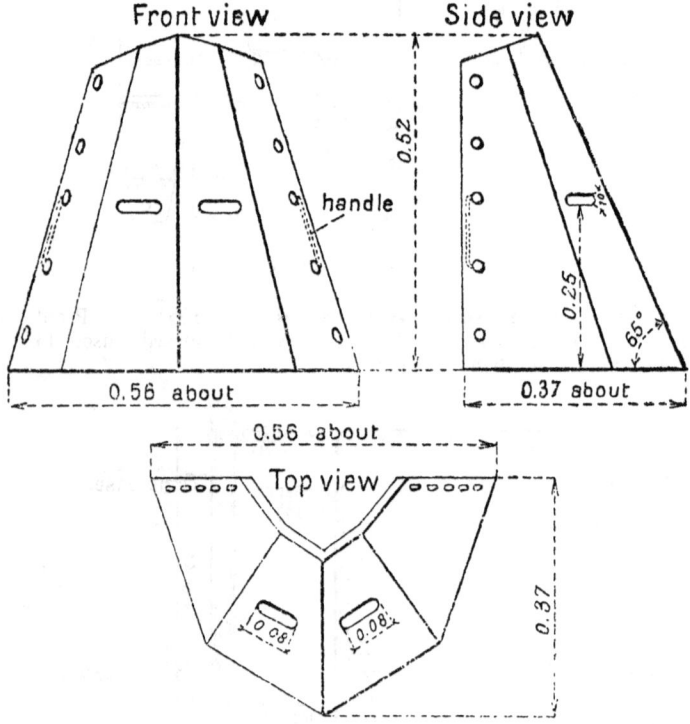

Fig. 153. — Armored shelter (type Girod).

7° Girod spying shield (fig. 153). — 2 models weighing 16 and 32 kilos; made of sheet steel, 8 or 12 $^m/m$ thick.

8° S. T. G. spying shield (fig. 154). — 3 models weighing 25, 32 and 40 kilos. Affords a protection equivalent to that of the parapet shields.

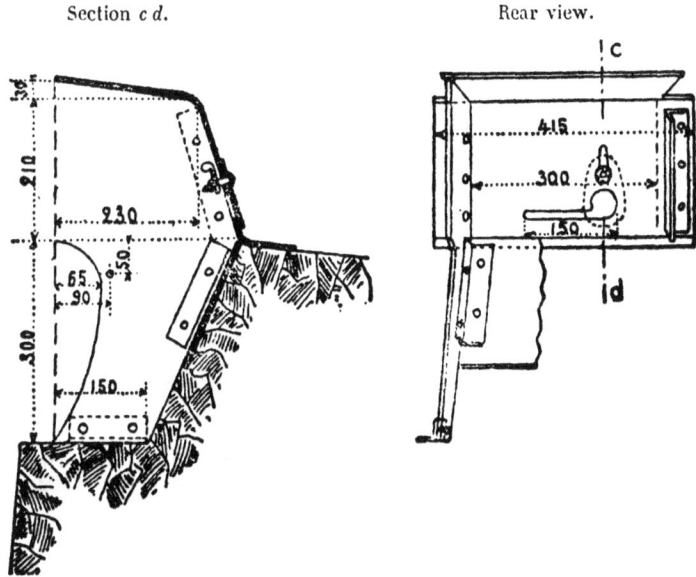

Fig. 154. — Armored shelter for sentry (type S. T. G.)

9° Armored observing station. — 3 different types:
S. T. G.
St. Jacques.
St. Chamond.

The first two are armored shelters in the shape of a truncated cone, consisting of a series of crowns and rings that fit in one another. Each part weighs less than 70 kilos and is proof against armor piercing bullets at 30 meters and against single 37 $^m/^m$ gun shots at 100 meters.

The St-Chamond armored observing station is a truncated quadrangular pyramid, the parts of which are joined by their edges. Each part weighs less than 70 kilos and is proof against armor piercing bullets at 30 meters.

10° Browning pistol. — See " Automatic Pistols ", Part III, Chapter I.

11° Shot-guns. — The shot-gun caliber 12 firing buckshot N° 0, is as dangerous a weapon as the infantry rifle up to 35 or 40 meters. Moreover, on account of the greater dispersion, it may be used with more chances of hitting. It proves a very good weapon for night patrols and raids.

CHAPTER XV.

EFFECTS OF PROJECTILES.

EFFECTS OF PENETRATION OF GERMAN BULLETS.

The Germans use:

1° The S bullet, either direct or reversed; reversed bullets (bullets with nose faced away from enemy) are particularly effective for short range firing at homogeneous steel armor;

2° The perforating steel core SMK bullet, specially for firing at armor.

Table I shows the thickness that ordinary substances must present to efficaciously protect the man against an isolated S bullet (direct or reversed), at any range [1].

TABLE I.

SUBSTANCE.	THICKNESS.
Clayey earth	0m70 (28 in.)
Wet earth (not tamped)......................	0m50 (20 in.)
Wet earth (tamped)..........................	0m40 (16 in.)
River sand..................................	0m30 (12 in.)
Oak wood	0m50 (20 in.)
Pine wood...................................	0m70 (28 in.)
Brick or rough stone wall	0m22 (9 in.)
Manure.....................................	1m to 1m50 (5 feet)
Piled snow	2m50 (8 feet)

[1] Against a prolonged and accurate fire a greater thickness is necessary. Thus, one cannot expect to be completely safe behind a parapet which is not at least 80 centimeters (32″) thick nor behind a wall made of bricks or rough stones which is not a least 35 to 40 centimeters thick (14 to 16 inches).

Table II gives the thickness and composition of some simple armors or protections resisting the direct or reversed S bullet, even at short range.

TABLE II.

KIND OF ARMOR OR PROTECTION.	TOTAL THICKNESS.
Ordinary soft steel, one or several sheets in juxtaposition (direct S bullet only)..................	14$^{m/m}$ (1/2″).
Ordinary soft steel, three 4$^{m/m}$ sheets (3/20″) separated by intervals of 20 to 30$^{m/m}$ (8/10 to 1-1/10″).	60 to 70$^{m/m}$ (2-1/3″) of which 12$^{m/m}$ (1/2″) of steel.
Iron sheets and wood, oak plank of 45$^{m/m}$ (1-8/10″) between two 4-1/2$^{m/m}$ (1/5″) sheets.............	About 55$^{m/m}$ (2″).
Pine plank of 60$^{m/m}$ (2-1/3″) between two 4-1/2$^{m/m}$ (1/5″) sheets................................	About 70$^{m/m}$ (2-2/3″).
Two oak boards 27$^{m/m}$ (1″) thick between a front sheet of 2 1/2$^{m/m}$ (1/10″) and a back sheet of 4$^{m/m}$ (3/20″).	About 60$^{m/m}$ (2-1/3″).
Ordinary iron sheets and sand, 4$^{c/m}$ (1-1/2″) of sand or fine gravel between a front sheet of 2-1/2$^{m/m}$ (1/10″) and a back one of 4$^{m/m}$................	About 50$^{m/m}$ (2″).
Wood and sand, 10$^{c/m}$ (4″) of sand filling between two oak boards of 27$^{m/m}$ (1″) or a front pine board of 25$^{m/m}$ (1″) and a back plank of 60$^{m/m}$ (2″)	16 to 20$^{c/m}$ (1/2 to 2/3 feet).

NOTE. — When an armor is composed of several sheets, with or without filling, it is always necessary to place the thinest sheet in front.

Firing trials on special steel armor have shown the following results:

DIRECT S BULLET:

5$^{m/m}$ shield (1/5″): can be perforated at short distance up to 150 meters.
7$^{m/m}$ shield (1/3″): resists from 25 meters up.
8$^{m/m}$ shield (1/3″): resists at any distance.

INVERTED S BULLET:

7$^{m/m}$ shield (1/3″): can be perforated up to 50 meters.
8$^{m/m}$ shield (1/3″) can be perforated up to 25 meters.
10$^{m/m}$ shield (2/5″) can be perforated up to 20 meters.

PERFORATING SMK BULLET:

To resist the SMK perforating bullet at a distance of 50 meters with normal incidence, special steel, 14$^{m/m}$ (1/2″) thick, is necessary. But the resistance of the shields increases quickly with the angle of incidence of the bullet, table III shows the angle of incidence after which protection is obtained for varying thicknesses with perforating bullets fired from a distance of 30 meters.

TABLE III.

THICKNESS OF SPECIAL STEEL SHIELDS.	ANGLE of INCIDENCE.
$7^{m/m}$ to $7^{m/m}5$ (about 1/4 inch).................	40°.
$8^{m/m}$ to $8^{m/m}5$ (about 1/3 inch)..-...............	30°.
$10^{m/m}$ to $10^{m/m}5$ (about 2/5 inch)................	20°.
$11^{m/m}$ to $12^{m/m}$ (about 2/5 inch)................	15°.

These conditions are substantially fulfilled with the different types of individual or parapet shields.

EFFECTS OF ARTILLERY FIRE.

Time fuse firing.

a. **Shrapnel.** — The cone of shrapnel bullets is dense and narrow (15 to 20 degrees). The penetration of shrapnel bullets in various materials is very inferior to the penetration of rifle bullets.

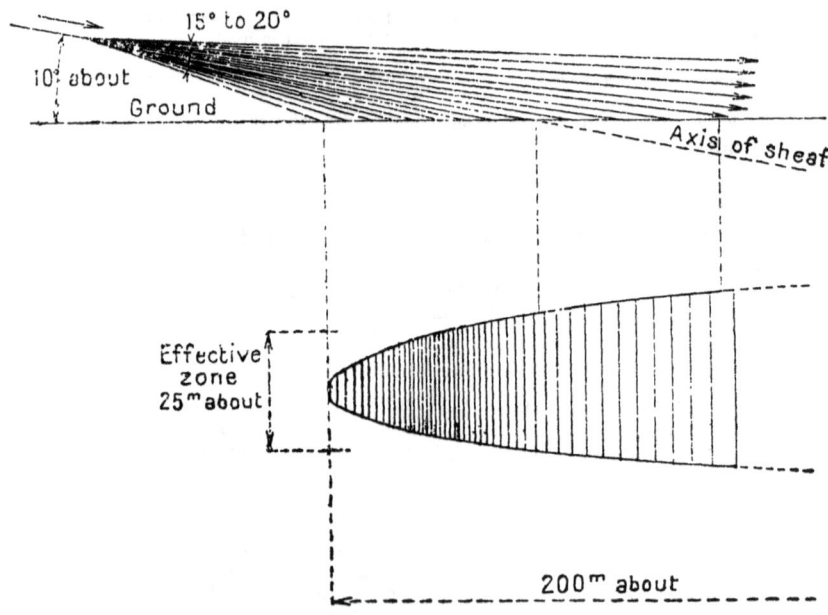

Fig. 155. — Sheaf of shrapnel explosion.

While the defenders are waiting leaning against the interior slope they are completely safe.

In the firing position, the upper part of the body is exposed. To be able to use rifles under shrapnel fire it is necessary to place on the parapets special devices to protect head and shoulders. These devices must not betray the trench.

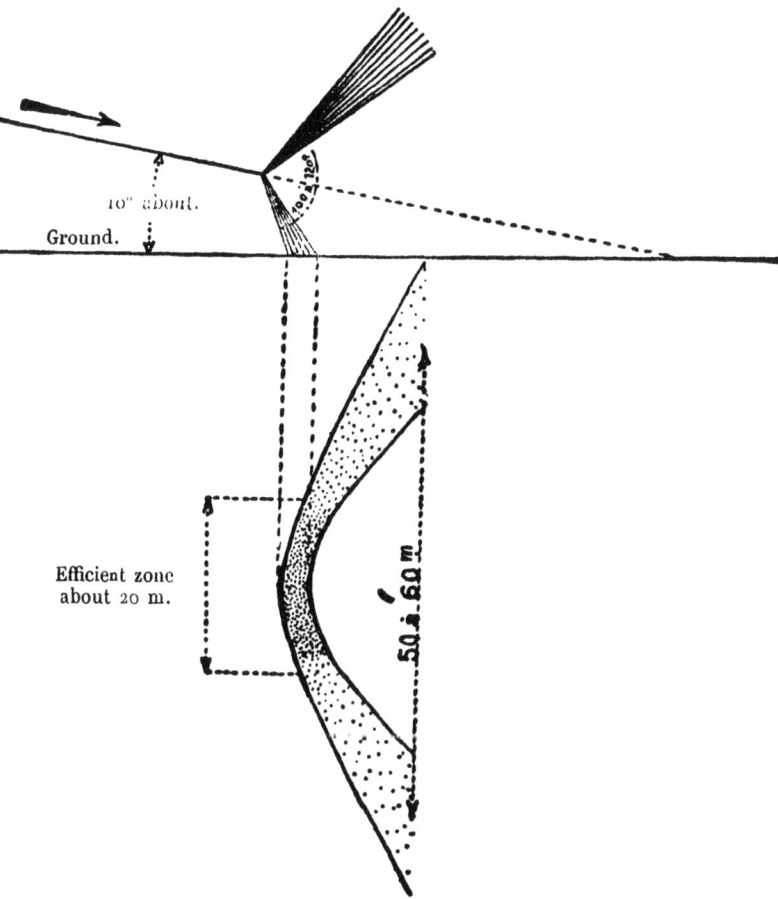

Fig. 156. — Sheaf of shell explosion, German field gun.

b. **High Explosive Shells.** — Such shells give a hollow and very wide cone. The fragments are very numerous and irregular; propelled at first with great speed, which decreases rapidly; their penetration is slight.

The result, when the shell explodes at a good height, is a sort of vertical « axe-stroke », the effect of which is considerable but over a small area.

The high explosive shell of the German field gun can reach men behind a cover at less than 60° (fig. 156).

The 105 light howitzer shell has a wider cone and more curved trajectory, and projects fragments even backwards.

The result is that the defenders, though not in firing position, can be hit unless they are protected by special shelter overhead.

Moreover, every trench must be supplied with a parados to protect it from fragments being projected from the rear.

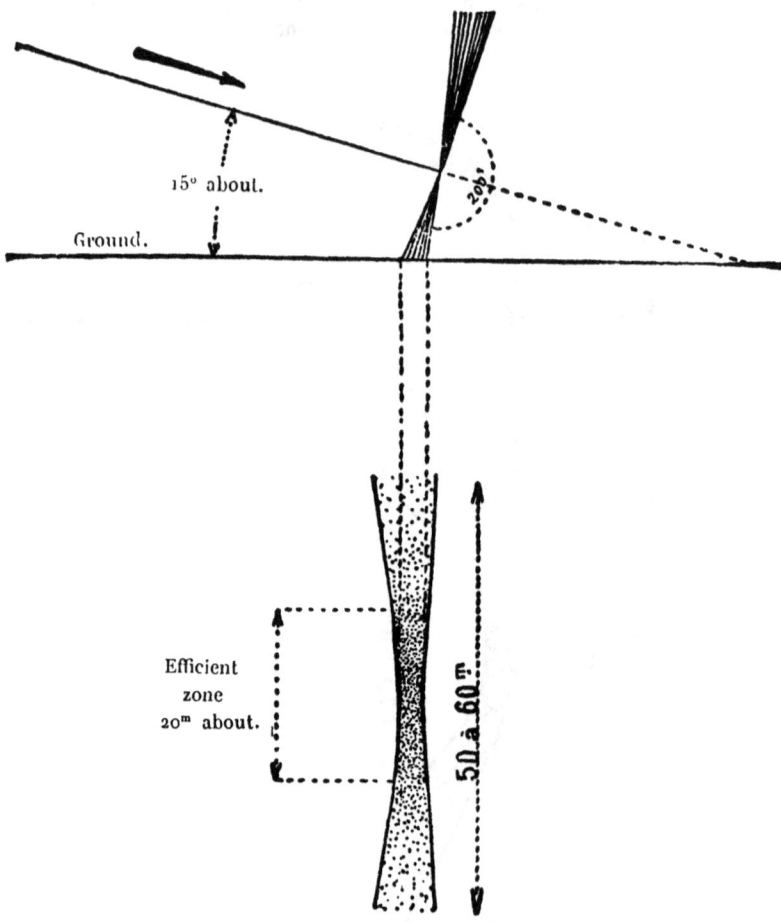

Fig. 157. — Sheaf of shell explosion of light howitzer 105 ᵐ/ᵐ.

To be effective, the fire must be very accurate in range and elevation, and consequently, needs good observation, in default of which appreciable results require great expenditure of ammunition.

Percussion shell firing.

A thickness of 2ᵐ50 to 3 meters (8 to 10 feet) of ordinary earth is sufficient for resisting a prolonged fire of percussion shells of the German field gun. Field artillery can certainly open breaches in the parapets of the trenches; but complete reduction of an important length is possible only by using an excessive amount of ammunition.

The effect of the $105^{m/m}$ and the $150^{m/m}$ shell is more powerful: up to 2,000 meters (1-1/4 miles) it is sufficient to perforate a light shelter (layer of round logs $20^{c/m}$ thick (8 inches) surmounted by a stratum of earth $30^{c/m}$ (12 inches) thick, but this effect is not attained against the roof of a strengthened shelter composed of two layers of logs $20^{c/m}$ (8 inches) thick and of two strata of earth (12 inches) $30^{c/m}$ thick.

Table IV shows the thickness necessary to resist field artillery fire.

TABLE IV.

KIND OF FIRE.		EARTH.	BRICK MASONRY.	WOODEN ROOFING.
Field gun.	Shrapnels and fragments.	0^m40 to 1^m ($16''$ to $40''$).	0^m22 ($8''$).	0^m08 ($3''$).
	Percussion shells.	1^m to 2^m ($40''$ to $80''$).	1^m60 ($40''$).	"
Light howitzer.	Shrapnels and fragments	1^m00 ($40''$).	0^m22 ($8''$).	0^m16 ($6''$).
	Percussion shells.	3^m to 4^m (9 to 12 ft.)	2^m ($6'$) [1]. 0^m90 ($3'1''$) [2]	" "

[1] Direct fire.
[2] Plunging fire.

Artillery fire against walls and houses.

Percussion shrapnel and high explosive shell make holes about 0^m40 (16 inches) in diameter in walls of common thickness and burst after they have passed through the wall. The first does much less harm than the second because of its narrow sheaf. Men behind a second wall are safe.

The destruction of a wall of considerable length requires a great expenditure of ammunition and an accurate fire.

The heavy 15 centimeters howitzer and still heavier guns cause considerable damage to houses. Beyond material damage, produced by the shock of the projectiles or their fragments, their concussion destroys the upper stories of houses, but cellars are generally left intact.

Artillery fire against wire entanglements.

About 150 high explosive shells of a field gun suffice to make a breach of 5 to 10 meters (15 to 30 feet) wide, in an entanglement 20 to 25 meters (60 to 75 feet) thick, at the range of 3,500 meters (2 1/4 miles).

The same effect is obtained by 75 shells of the 155 gun.

At the range of 6,000 meters a double quantity of ammunition is necessary.

A high explosive 75 shell clears 10 to 12 square meters (90 to 110 sq. ft.) of Brun spirals.

CHAPTER XVI.

INFORMATION ON THE 75.

75 mm., rapid fire gun, for field and horse batteries.
Piece served by six cannoneers.
Carriage with shield, immovable during fire, hydropneumatic brake with recuperator, returning the piece into battery.
Weight of the cannon, 460 kilos.
Weight of the piece in battery, 1,140 kilos.
Weight of caisson (96 cartridges, 1,200 to 1,300 kilos, according to the nature of the cartridge (shell or shrapnell).
Contents of limber, 24 cartridges.
Ammunition allowance for each piece of the battery 312 rounds.
Limit of the range scale, 5,500 meters.
Maximum range, 8,500 meters.
Front covered by one battery at medium ranges :
 Time fire without sweeping, 100 meters.
 Time fire sweeping 200 meters.
 Percussion fire «largeur d'obstacle», 25 meters.

Abattre et relever. (To seat and raise the piece.) — During fire the carriage is fixed to the ground by the trail spade and the wheel brakes. The wheel brakes consist of two solid metal shoes having a central spine parallel to the axis of the carriage. Before firing, these shoes are allowed to slide to the ground, the piece is then recoiled upon them by means of a ratchet which functions by raising the trail and again lowering it. The shoes are clamped to the wheel and the carriage seated upon them. This operation is called «abattre la pièce», or seating the piece. It is then fixed to the ground at three points and is ready to fire.

When a piece has been seated it is necessary in order to move it that its trail should be raised and the brake shoes released, this is called «la relever».

It is necessary to know these facts since an infantry N.C.O. may be called upon to move a piece by hand or even to limber it up, or attach it to some sort of conveyance. He cannot do this if he does not know how to raise the piece from abattage; the piece would resist all these efforts and remain fixed,

Each officer should profit by the neighborhood of a battery for practical instruction :
 1° To raise the piece from abattage;
 2° To release the recoil lug and to put the 75 mm. material out of action.

To release the recoil lug. — A strong steel lug called a recoil lug unites the piece to its recoil system. If this lug is detached the weapon becomes unusable. If a projectile is then fired the barrel being no longer attached to its recoil system leaves the carriage under the influence of the recoil and is thrown to the ground some distance in the rear.

An officer or N.C.O. in the infantry may be obliged to execute this operation under critical circumstances.

Further information upon putting material out of action is contained in the chapter on explosives.

PART IV.

MISCELLANEOUS INFORMATION USEFUL TO PLATOON LEADERS.

CHAPTER I.
GENERAL PRINCIPLES.

The military training of a leader, whatever be his rank, rests on a few general principles, which every one has to know. These principles are the following ones:

Energy.

Energy is the chief fighting quality. From it originate courage, tenaciousness, abnegation, sense of duty and discipline. It is the energy of the leader and of the men that affords the possibility of carrying on the combat to the end under all circumstances and causes the first acts of gallantry.

Whenever a decision has to be taken, one may be sure not to err in choosing the more energetic course.

Teamwork.

To get the better of the enemy, all must strike hard, as hard as they can, and consequently all together. A troop is never too strong when the victorious issue of attack or defense is at stake. A good platoon leader will bring all his men to the battle and will cause every one to act in such a way that no force remains unemployed. If he has lost connection with the neighboring unit, if he receives no orders, he will at once join the nearest troops engaged with the enemy and place himself at the disposal of their commander.

Surprise.

Any troop that is engaged, will obtain results so much the greater, as its action is more sudden, and unforeseen by the enemy. Surprise is thus to be sought under all circumstances.

Surprise effect is the outcome of two essential conditions : secrecy in preparing the movements, rapidity in carrying them out.

Security.

Consequently, one must avoid being surprised. An elementary duty of troop leaders is to provide security for their commands and guard against attempts of the enemy in any direction.

PART IV.

MISCELLANEOUS INFORMATION USEFUL TO PLATOON LEADERS.

CHAPTER I.

GENERAL PRINCIPLES.

The military training of a leader, whatever be his rank, rests on a few general principles, which every one has to know. These principles are the following ones:

Energy.

Energy is the chief fighting quality. From it originate courage, tenaciousness, abnegation, sense of duty and discipline. It is the energy of the leader and of the men that affords the possibility of carrying on the combat to the end under all circumstances and causes the first acts of gallantry.

Whenever a decision has to be taken, one may be sure not to err in choosing the more energetic course.

Teamwork.

To get the better of the enemy, all must strike hard, as hard as they can, and consequently all together. A troop is never too strong when the victorious issue of attack or defense is at stake. A good platoon leader will bring all his men to the battle and will cause every one to act in such a way that no force remains unemployed. If he has lost connection with the neighboring unit, if he receives no orders, he will at once join the nearest troops engaged with the enemy and place himself at the disposal of their commander.

Surprise.

Any troop that is engaged, will obtain results so much the greater, as its action is more sudden, and unforeseen by the enemy. Surprise is thus to be sought under all circumstances.

Surprise effect is the outcome of two essential conditions: secrecy in preparing the movements, rapidity in carrying them out.

Security.

Consequently, one must avoid being surprised. An elementary duty of troop leaders is to provide security for their commands and guard against attempts of the enemy in any direction.

Infantry brigade. — The infantry brigade has no general headquarters. It includes the brigadier general, his staff and 2 infantry regiments. It does not exist in divisions of 3 infantry egiments.

Infantry regiment.

The infantry regiment includes :
1 regimental staff,
1 regimental company,
3 battalions (as a rule),
1 platoon of 37 mm. guns (as many guns as there are battaions) assigned to the 1rst machine-gun company for pay and subsistence.

Regimental staff. — 1 colonel, 1 lt.-colonel or cavalry major detailed to assist the colonel.
1 captain assistant,
1 signal officer,
1 lieutenant commanding the pioneers,
1 lieutenant color bearer,
1 officer in charge of combat trains and details,
1 subsistence officer (in command of the field train),
1 surgeon, head of the medical service,
1 bandmaster.
(The intelligence officer is detailed from a company.)

Battalion. — A battalion includes a staff, a N. C. staff, 3 companies and 1 machine-gun company. The 4th infantry company is detached to form the divisional depot.

Combat train. — Field train.

Combat train. — The combat train, under the orders of the officer in charge of details, includes :

For the regiment: light tool wagons, material wagons (carrying telphone wire, barbed wire, sandbags, grenades), water-carts, ambulance, medical cart (carrying first aid packets, respirators, stretchers, etc.), field forges, 2 ration-and-baggage wagons, 1 rolling kitchen, led horses.

For each battalion : medical cart, ration and baggage wagon ammunition wagon carrying 25,000 cartridges and 48 knapsacks of the automatic rifle detachment.

For each company : ammunition wagon, ration and baggage wagon, rolling kitchen.

For each machine-gun company : ammunition wagons, ration and baggage wagon, rolling kitchen (add the 37 mm. gun ammunition wagons).

The combat train may be divided into two echelons :

The first echelon includes the medical carts, the ammunition wagons (when loaded), the tool and material wagons, the led horses.

The second echelon includes the ration and baggage wagons, the water carts, the rolling kitchens, the field forges, the ammunition wagons (when unloaded).

Field train. — The field train under the control of the subsistence officer, is divided into three sections :

2 sect'ons of 5 wagons each, which are alternately sent forward to the distributing points, where the day's rations are issued. Each section is under the orders of a sergeant.

1 reserve section (3 wagons), under the orders of the field train sergeant major.

The fiel l train includes, besides, 2 forage carts, 2 wagons or 1 siege wagon (to carry the grain ration), 3 meat wagons, and 6 spare horses.

Posts usually assigned :

a) **The sanitary personnel :** with the medical cart of their battalion (or with their company when it is operating independently);

b) **The litter-bearers :** with the company they belong to, up to the moment when combat is imminent; they are then grouped under the orders of their corporal, who marches with the battalion medical cart;

c) **The drummers and buglers :** act generally as orderlies to the company commander;

d) **The battalion ammunition sergeant :** in charge of the battalion ammunition-wagons, when they are loaded. When the vehicles are unloaded, and sent back to the rear, he assists in getting them refilled from the small arms ammunition sections (See Ammunition service. Part IV, Chapt XI);

e) **The orderlies of mounted officers :** grouped with their horses in rear of a designated unit.

Men trained in special duties. — Apart from those already mentioned, a few men in each company may be detailed to be practised in the following duties :

a) **Liaison with company commander** (See Part II. Chap. VI.) under the head « Formations of the company »;

b) **Liaison with battalion commander.** — Each company sends to the battalion commander a non-commissioned officer and generally a detachment which includes 4 runners. The machine-gun company sends a sergeant.

For conveying messages by carrier-pigeons, the company commanders detail the necessary men, when required.

For observing and signalling. — There are two signallers in each company, who are usually assisted by two observers; all are trained by the regimental signal officer. Moreover in every company, **1 officer, 2 non-commissioned-officers, the orderlies and 6 other men at least must be able to send and receive Morse code signals.**

Specialized officers. — The officer in charge of the battalion grenadiers, the officer in charge of the automatic rifle detachments and the regimental intelligence officer still count in the total strength of the infantry company. The first two retain their duty as platoon-leaders. A non-commissioned-officer is sent to the battalion headquarters for the intelligence service.

CHAPTER III.

TACTICAL QUALITIES OF THE INFANTRY.

The main characteristics are as follows :

1° **The infantry has in itself no offensive power against intrenched positions protected by fire action and strengthened by obstacles.**

When a firing line is stopped by intrenchments **unimpaired by artillery fire and occupied by the enemy.** reinforcement of the skirmish line gives no additional chance of penetrating the adversary's position: **it will but make losses heavier.**

Troops must never be launched to the attack, when such attack is not **prepared and supported by an effective artillery action.**

It is impossible to fight with men against material.

2° **The infantry is very efficient in holding terrain.** — With entrenching tools, troops may quickly protect themselves against fire.

The power of modern armament (rifles, automatic rifles, hand and rifle grenades, machine guns) makes any attack unprepared by artillery fire absolutely impossible.

The extensive use of obstacles which keep the enemy under frontal and preferably enfilade fire makes even a limited field of fire quite sufficient.

The infantry may thus occupy at a short distance from the enemy, positions which might at first appear unfavorable. If time permits the digging of trenches and placing of obstacles infantry may feel sure of holding the ground already gained.

3° **The infantry is very rapidly used up.** — The attack in trench warfare is subject to difficulties of all sorts. First, advancing across broken ground (across fire and communication trenches shell, craters, etc.) is extremely difficult and it is not easy to keep the attacking line in hand, then surprise efforts are frequently made by the enemy (artillery « barrage », machine-gun oblique, or enfilade fire, grenades, etc.) and these contribute heavily to the disorganization of the units.

Excessive density in the firing line must therefore be avoided as much in the earlier as in the latter phases of an offensive action. Whenever gaps develop in the line, they must be judiciously filled, but crowding must be guarded against because its only effect is to increase disorder and losses.

When a troop has incurred particularly heavy losses, it is better, when possible, especially if a further effort is necessary, to have it relieved by fresh troops. This is the only means of avoiding complete disorganization.

4° **The infantry must not maneuver in dense formations.** — In the zone reached by artillery fire, columns of squads, lines of platoons, etc., are not to be employed.

6° **The morale of the infantry is extremely impressionable.** — Military operations are not only materially, but also and to the greatest extent, morally prepared. Such preparation depends upon the leader, who must avail himself of all opportunities in the daily visits he pays to his men.

CHAPTER IV.

RIFLE FIRE.

The execution and accomplishment of the fire varies according to the tactical situation of the troops firing :

Whether the latter must defend their trench when attacked;

Whether they are partaking in a general offensive against a fortified position;

Whether when in open warfare they remain on the defensive or assume the offensive.

Neither the different nature of the objectives, nor their various appearances, nor their vulnerable points can be compared, therefore, the conditions, under which the fire is to be conducted, differ in each instance and each case is suited by a different solution.

Nevertheless there are a certain number of points in common and these constitute **the characteristics of rifle fire.**

1° The fire is always executed **by groups.**

The platoon is too numerous and the armament of the men is of too great a variety to enable the authority of the chief to be efficient from one end of the line to the other. Some intermediate agents must be placed between the chief and riflemen, and so it is necessary for those who are in charge of half-platoons or groups to take the actual command and follow the instructions of the chief.

2° **The magazine mechanism** is always employed for the fire.

On the battlefield the objectives are visible only during a very brief interval, during which time it is necessary to obtain the maximum effect by means of the densest possible fire that can be delivered.

3° **Fire discipline** is of first importance.

It permits the concentration of fire and enables one to surprise the enemy; it avoids the waste of ammunition and allows the combat **to endure**; it elevates the spirits of the troops and prepares the men to yield to discipline in view of future efforts.

The principal object involved in fire discipline is that the fire should begin and cease at the exact command of the chief, a thing which all officers and non-commissioned-officers, especially the file closers should endeavor to obtain.

Ordering volley fire is an excellent method of disciplining troops whenever their firing begins to show nervousness and irregularity.

4° Finally, good results depend essentially upon :

a) **The calmness of the commanding-officer.**

It is **his calmness** that will enable him to obtain the very best results from the disciplined fire of his men, that is, if he is able to open and suspend it at the opportune moments. **Fire discipline** can only be obtained by a chief who is master of himself.

b) **The coolness and skill of the troop.**

Collective fire can be efficient only on condition of the precision and good adjustment of the aiming of the individual skirmishers.

Fire of the platoon, defending its trench during an attack.

The chief of the platoon organizes beforehand the groups of men which he puts under the command of the non-commissioned-officers and places them in those parts of the trenches which are most favorable for the defence; the instructions in case of an alarm foresee all these dispositions.

During the day, the usual fire is the fire-at-will.

Volley-fire, however, is often used : it acts strongly on the morale of the enemy's troops and gives confidence to the men.

During the night volley fire is the rule.

Platoon engaged in a combined offensive action against a fortified zone.

Generally speaking, in an action of this kind, the plaoon fires very little inasmuch as its object is to reach the assigned objective as soon as possible.

It may happen, however, that the advance is impeded by local resistances concentrated at various points (groups of enemy skirmishers, machine-guns, etc.).

These resistances must be broken as soon as possible, the commanding officer ordering the **platoon to fire together** and with such vigour as to enable it to resume progress.

Rifle firing in open warfare.

Defensive. — When on the defensive in the open country the platoon fires at **long range** in exceptional cases only; the automatic rifles and machine-guns being more certain to reach distant objectives.

On the other hand, it is often profitable to withhold the opening of fire in order to produce a more certain effect upon the advancing enemy.

The fire is all the more efficient if it takes the enemy **by surprise.**

In order to obtain this, the preparation of the fire (instructions concerning the sight and the objective) must be as complete as possible, so that the first rafales will bear certain results.

The chief of the platoon gives orders that rifles be prepared, if necessary brings his group forward on the firing line, and fire is opened only when the skirmishers have recognised the objective and have had sufficient time for correct aiming.

Sighting. — The officer in command of a platoon on the defensive ascertains during the waiting interval the range of the different parts of the terrain, in order that once the objective appears, too great a mistake be not made in indicating the elevation of the sight. He consults the map, measures the distance by pacing, or he demands the distance of the different points from the nearest troops provided with instrumental range finders.

Designation of objectives. — In order to designate an objective not self evident, an aiming point which is clearly visible and can give rise to no confusion is pointed out. Thereupon the number of finger widths, or handbreaths, at which the objective is found to the right or to the left of the given mark, is indicated.

Offensive. — As a rule, objectives are not very obvious, the presence of the enemy is more often estimated than actually detected by sight. To detect the enemy one must be extremely attentive and particularly watch anything that moves in the direction of the assigned objective. It is an absolute rule in the offensive to alternately fire and march. The platoon fires only for the purpose of protecting the advance of an adjacent fraction or to prepare for its own advance.

However favorable the opportunities may be, there is no reason for firing if at the same moment advance is possible.

If the immediate advantage of the fire is not utilized the fire is useless.

The fire is generally performed by a half-platoon, seldom by a group.

The opening of fire must be instantaneous.

Rapidity of fire. — The normal rapidity of the fire is eight shots a minute.

Influence of the terrain. — A single sheaf G will beat the zones AB, AC, and AD differentiy according to their

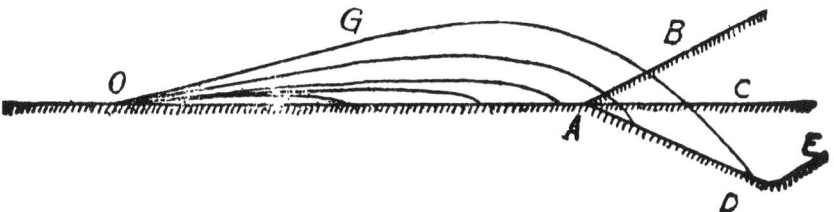

Fig. 158.

inclination to the horizontal. As regards the zone AD, the grazed surface will be more extensive than in the case of AC and AB. It is also conceivable that if the reserves can be concealed, it will be less dangerous for them to occupy the ascent AB than the slope AD although the latter be not visible. The occupation of the other side of the slope E will combine the advantages of both positions if the enemy fires from position O.

Particular case : Firing on aircraft.

Firing on aircraft is forbidden to :

Detached men,

Troops already having an objective to attain or beat which must not be lost sight of.

It is always ordered by a commissioned-officer.

Only begin firing if it is certain that the aircraft is hostile and that there are no friendly troops assembled within a range of 1,000 to 4,000 meters (zone in which the bullets are liable to hit the ground) in the direction of the fire.

The fire is conducted by platoon and without haste. These platoons, when in column or in the first line supports, must be notified beforehand and are constantly on the look-out.

It is possible to formulate simple rules only in the case where the aircraft passes directly overhead.

Firing regulations. — As the aircraft is flying towards the riflemen, set the sight at 2,400 meters. Face the approaching aircraft and begin to fire as soon as it appears at an angle of 45 degrees. Aim straight at it and continue to fire until the aircraft passes vertically overhead.

Thereupon, the riflemen face to the rear toward the departing aircraft, and sights are laid down.

As the aircraft departs, set the sight at 250 meters aiming to begin with 10 lengths in advance for approximately 30 seconds. Then aim directly at the aeroplane and continue to do so until it reaches an angle of 45 degrees.

The application of these rules assures that the aircraft crosses the cone of dispersion once during the approach and twice during the departure.

It is useless to fire on an aeroplane the spread of whose wings is under 8 mils.

It is forbidden to fire upon landing aircraft.

Estimating distances.

Pacing. — Each one must know how many strides he takes in covering a distance of 100 meters. Error is less liable in counting off the strides (i.e. count each time the left foot strikes the ground) than the single pace.

Having counted the number of strides which cover 100 meters (62 for instance) make a mark on a piece of paper or place a pebble in your pocket, and begin again to count 1, 2, 3... strides. To translate into meters the excess over the last hundred strides it is only necessary to add half that number to the total.

Example : 6 pebbles + 36 strides = 600 + 36 + 18 = 654 ms. (the result of 36 multiplied by 1.50 meters or 1 1/2 equals $36 + \frac{36}{2}$). This method is used in sketching.

Estimating by sight. — By personal observation one acquires the knowledge that although the human face for example is not visible at 400 meters, the arms can still be seen, that at 600 meters one can still count the files and that at 1,000 meters a horse can be distinguished from the cart, etc. Be careful of the grave errors arising from the conditions of light, background, dust, or from an intervening hollow. The method is not very sure, but can be improved by allowing several good observers to make their estimations and then taking the mean.

Estimating by sound. — Sound travels 333 meters a second, that is to say 1 kilometer in 3 seconds. Learn to reckon time by mental calculation, for example, so as to be able to count to 10 in 3 seconds. If in keeping such time one starts counting 1, 2, 3... as soon as the flash of a discharged gun is seen, the number articulated at the moment of the report will be equal to the number of hectometers (100 meters) to the gun.

CHAPTER V.

TACTICAL USE OF MACHINE GUNS, AUTOMATIC RIFLES, GRENADES, TRENCH WEAPONS, AND 37 MM. CANNON.

The chief of platoon has under his immediate command automatic riflemen and grenadiers. He works in intimate connection with the machine gun platoons and batteries of low power weapons in his neighborhood. He may even have under his command one of these batteries or platoons to perform some defensive or offensive mission.

It is consequently necessary that he should be well acquainted with the best manner of using these means of destruction.

1° *Machine guns.*

Properties. — The machine gun will be used in preference to infantry when it is sufficient to act **by fire alone.** The infantry again becomes indispensable when it is necessary to act **by fire and movement combined.**

The machine gun produces a very effective grazing fire up to 800 or 1,000 meters; this fire is also effective beyond 1,000 meters against large objectives, **providing the distance is registered very accurately**

Two methods of use :
FLANK FIRING AND FIRE BY SURPRISE.

The sheaf is dense and deep but narrow; the maximum of effect will therefore be obtained against an objective having a narrow front and a great depth as for instance a **thin line taken in flank.**
Machine gun fire parallel to the probable front of the enemy, i. e. on its flank, will therefore be the rule.

The sweeping fire must be used against a thin line which appears in front, but as the depth is insufficient, the effect produced is of small importance (See Fig. 280).

The machine gun is easily hidden; it must remain out of sight and take no notice of objectives which are not worth while, the firing will then be suddenly opened **by surprise** with considerable effect.

Consequently the commander who has a machine-gun at his disposal and who uses it only to reinforce his firing line employs only part of what is given him. He makes a full use of it when he uses it in **flank firing** and when he has chosen beforehand emplacements in which it is possible to play several roles according to circumstances.

The use of machine guns in trench warfare. — In trench warfare the machine-gun is generally employed by sections with the Infantry companies.

The enemy who prepares an attack will particularly endeavour to destroy them.

Therefore :

They must be placed under shell-proof shelters.
They must be made invisible.
They must be echeloned in depth.

Open emplacements on the parapet are absolutely condemned unless they have been skilfully «camouflaged» from the time of their construction.

Shell proof casemates cannot be used owing to their relief above the ground unless their invisibility is assured by favorable circumstance (such as counterslopes, woods, coverts). Failing these, emplacements with no relief and well «camouflaged» must be constructed with near-by deep shelters out of which the men will be able to emerge rapidly with their materiel. These **emplacements** can be holes dug out in the shape of shell craters in front of the trench and connected to the shelter by an underground passage.

The emplacements must be as numerous as possible and their access assured by covered invisible saps. Avoid firing every day from the emplacement set apart for use in case of attack.

The machine-guns must not all at the same time run the risk of being destroyed in the advanced line : they must be **echeloned beforehand** and divided **for the greater part** between the line of support and the line of strong points, against which the enemy who has penetrated in the first trench following the bombardment and poisonous gas, should be broken.

It is preferable to allot to each gun a strip of ground within which it will be able to mow down by flank fire any enemy wave coming upon it, than to use it to «sweep» the front of an extensive sector.

The firing sector of each machine gun must be bounded by three wood stakes, as is explained in Chapter 8 (fig. 47).

Under no circumstance must the machine gunners abandon their position. If necessary they must allow themselves to be besieged and fight to the last man. Very often the doggedness and heroism of a few machine gunners have afforded the means of rapidly retaking a lost position.

To bring about this result more easily, the machine gun should be placed in the center of a sort of small field work, surrounded by barbed wire entanglements well out of sight and provided with several firing emplacements, a store of provisions and water and an abundant supply of ammunition.

Concerning the ventilation of a machine gun shelter see Chapter XIV, Part III, 8°.

Use of machine guns in the war of movement. — In the war of movement the **machine gun company** will often fight with all its platoons grouped together and will frequently be advanced to the head of the column behind the protective elements, so as to spare the infantry at the beginning of an engagement.

When the company has no special or independant mission to fulfill it must be placed at the disposal of a battalion commander who may in the same way place one or more sections under the command of the captains.

It is in the war of movements that the machine gun is liable to make use of open air earth works as illustrated in figures 46 to 48.

Principal tactical roles of machine guns. — **In the offensive :** They will deploy with the head of the troops and cover the deployment of the main body.

They will reinforce a temporarily stopped front and provide the length of time necessary to prepare a further advance.

They will add to the artillery preparation by a fierce and concentrated fire and even replace the artillery in the pursuit of the enemy or in the organization of a success

They will march on the flank of an attacking body of troops so as to protect it from any counter attacks which are liable to be made against its flanks.

They will sweep with their fire any interval whether intentional or accidental which may have been left between two attacking units.

In the defensive. They must provide along the front a number of « barrages » of flanking fires ready to be opened in succession at any time day and night.

To sum up :

1° Machine guns must be used to a great extent **to spare the infantry.**

2° Always endeavor to use them for flanking fire.

3° They must always be well concealed so as to act by surprise.

4° They must be echeloned in depth and sheltered so as to prevent their premature destruction.

2° *Automatic rifles.*

The characteristics of the automatic rifles are the following :

1° They are extremely easy to transport.

2° They are very efficient at short distances. **Their fire is automatically low.**

3° They are efficient to a lesser extent at longer distances; the automatic rifle is as accurate as the machine gun up to 6 or 700 meters; beyond that a considerable dispersion is observed.

4° The fire is very supple. A sweeping fire is easily obtained and the change of objective is instantaneous.

5° **It can be fired while marching** and this obliges the enemy to remain under cover during the final rushes of the attack and allows the grenadiers to approach and fulfill their office.

This rifle has neither the rigidity nor the rapid fire of the machine gun and therefore cannot completely take its place. Its fire, however, has the same moral effect.

Moreover, it is at the disposal of the smaller infantry units and at such times and under such conditions that the installation of a machine gun would not be possible.

The automatic rifle is therefore par excellence the weapon to **accompany the infantry,** to maintain conquered ground and to **stop counter-attacks.** This is due to the density of the fire which it can open **instantly**, after the conquest of an objective, and also to the mobility of that fire.

It also affords the possibility of bringing up **at leisure**, after reflection and reconnoitring, the machine guns to the most favorable points, principally with view of delivering a flanking fire.

To sum up, **the automatic rifle is the advance guard of the machine gun** which latter really becomes a defensive weapon.

To obtain the maximum of efficiency with automatic rifles, they must be manned by well instructed and well trained squads necessarily made up of strong men owing to the weight there is to carry. The mechanichal parts have the necessary strength, and if the automatic riflemen have thoroly studied the working of the rifle and the reasons why the mechanism sometimes fails to work, good results are obtained. Good care must be taken that it is well protected from mud and water which are its chief foes. To this effect, **never remove the weapon from its case except when it is about to be used.** In addition, an oblong shaped piece of oiled canvas will be fixed by its four corners to the left push button of the cartridge stop and to lower band; this canvas covers the charging clip and the aperture of the ejector. When firing, two corners are unhooked and the covering remains hanging by the two other corners.

The automatic rifle is not as bulky as a Lebel rifle but it is heavier. It is best to fit it with an improvised strap which allows it to be slung or carried in front of the body when advancing, or which will support the end of the barrel when a marching fire is opened; for this last purpose the sling is passed over the left shoulder.

Firing power. — When firing **shot by shot** a well trained rifleman can fire from **60 to 80 rounds per minute**, and take good aim. This is the most efficient fire and it can be kept up some time. Series of 20 cartridges are fired shot by shot, the rifle remaining at the shoulder. 1000 shots can thus be fired with no fatigue when the rifle is well placed at the shoulder.

The shot by shot fire of the 8 automatic rifles of a company produces a density equal to that produced by 60 or 80 ordinary rifles.

Machine gun fire, by short rafales (2 or 3 rounds) or long rafales (7 to 8 rounds). A well trained rifleman can thus fire **140 rounds per minute**, but this fire is not well regulated and rapidly fouls the weapon, which fails to work after 300 or 400 rounds, or at the end of 2 or 3 minutes. The rifle must then be taken to pieces and cleaned.

Marching fire. — An automatic rifleman can, when walking, successively fire a number of clips; the clips are changed without stopping.

In the offensive, automatic riflemen and grenadiers make up the first wave of attack. They also make up the contact patrols which are sent out after the last objective is gained with a view to the exploitation of the success.

On conquered positions, the A. R. becomes the first essential part of the new line.

It provides the means of sweeping the boyaus leading to the enemy and of those probably used by the reserves for their approach.

At such a moment it is important to use it as a preventive means to act upon the moral of the enemy and frustrate any counter attack.

A simple shell hole is sufficient to hold it.

It must be used to a great extent for flanking : *on a broken line the grenadiers should be posted at the salient angles and the A. R. in the recesses so as to flank the salients.*

Grouping. — It has been found necessary to place an N. C. O. in command of two gun crews (A. R. group). The use of *coupled* crews is the only method which makes it possible to fire continuously at a given point, for a given time, the two A. R.'s firing alternately.

The group thus formed can have a «barrage» sector allotted to it. The captain arranges the overlapping of these sectors so as to obtain a continuous barrier of fire.

Groups of 4 and 8 rifles can also be formed with a view to offensive or defensive plans. It is important that they should be under good command. Larger groups run the risk of forming good objectives for the artillery and so of being destroyed.

COMPARISON OF THE POSSIBILITIES OF THE LEBEL RIFLE, AUTOMATIC RIFLE AND FRENCH MACHINE GUN.

	WEIGHT.	NUMBER of cartridges per minute.		WEAPONS.	DISPOSING of in cartridges.
Machine-gun..	24^k 000	300	27 men......	1 section of two machine-guns	10.800
Machine-gun with stand..	55.000
Automatic rifle	9.100	140
Rifle with loaded magazine and bayonet.........	4.900	11		9 A. R...	9.200
				27 rifles..	3.240

3° *Grenades.*

Properties. — The distinctive qualities of hand grenades, offensive and defensive have been described in Chapter IV, Part III.

An efficient grenadier can throw a grenade 30 or 40 meters with a maximum deviation of 2 to 3 meters. The rapidity varies; it depends upon whether it is only necessary to ignite the primer before throwing the grenade (metallic primer) or whether there is some safety arrangement to remove, (automatic primer). Under the best condition, a speed of about 10 grenades per minute can be obtained.

The O F grenade is more generally used for attacks on flat or open ground.

The F I grenade is a **parapet grenade** dangerous for unsheltered men within a radius of 150 meters and even more.

The O F grenades are often preferred to the F I, because they are really very efficient, and a double amount of them can be carried for the same weight.

Rifle grenades can be fired from 30 to 200 meters. Their rapidity of fire is considerably less than that of hand grenades, and therefore, their tactical use is different.

Organization. — **1° Hand grenades. Equipment of the grenadier.** — The first group of each platoon is made up of : 1 corporal grenadier and 7 grenadiers. In an engagement it fights either as a single group (1 corporal, 2 throwers, 2 ammunition carriers, 2 assistant grenadiers, 1 grenadier in reserve or for the «liaison») or in two groups (1 group commander, 1 thrower, 1 carrier, 1 assistant). In addition, every man individually must know how to throw a grenade.

In every battalion an officer chosen from a company is charged with the instruction and the training of the grenadiers. He must always be prepared to take command eventually of the different groups of the battalion in view of a combined action.

The groups are assembled for instruction, work or action under the command of the captain or battalion commander. Apart from that, the grenadiers remain with their platoon.

The equipment of the grenadiers includes the rifle and bayonet, the dagger and automatic pistol.

The throwers will not necessarily take their rifles with them when the engagement is not to be continued, as for example in the execution of a raid.

Apart from this exception, **it is imperative to combat the tendency which grenadiers have, of wishing to** be rid of their rifle or of getting rid of it themselves in the course of a fight. The grenadier must be proud of his special work, of his rôle of soldier in the advance guard, and of the fine results he alone can obtain when the rifle would be useless.

He must remember also that a grenadier who has used up his grenades must not consider his task as ended and that he must fight with his rifle until the arrival of abundant supplies. Attacks on limited objectives can give no idea of what will be the supply of grenades after successive advances of several kilometers and particularly after numerous stages. It would be the greatest of mistakes not to foresee that supplies may be deficient after several days running; and to deprive the grenadier of his rifle at such a time, when it becomes necessary to push through an attack with or without grenades.

Groups of grenadiers are supplied with baskets for carrying grenades or equipped with a grenade carrying belt.

A grenadier can carry in addition to 48 cartridges 10 F. or 20 Q. F. grenades.

2° **Rifle grenades.** — Grenadiers must also be familiar with the use of rifle grenades.

The V. B. tromblons are supplied to 2 men in each group of riflemen. They are carried at the belt in a leather case. The V. B. grenades are carried by the rifle grenadiers themselves and by one carrier for each group of 2 grenadiers. They have the advantage of requiring very little space. The supplies, which are comparatively easy when on the defensive, will become more difficult in the offensive until the boyaux are established. It will therefore be advisable to supply the men armed with the tromblon and their carriers, with the greatest possible number of V. B. grenades they can carry.

Tactical use of hand grenades.

A hand grenade engagement can have the following aims :

1° To defend a trench and keep up a « wearing out » struggle between the trenches.

2° To advance foot by foot in a trench or « boyau » in possession of the enemy.

3° To prepare the attack of a trench.

4° To fight inside the enemy's positions and to « clean out » the trenches and shelters.

5° To make a raid.

1° The defence of a trench. « Wearing out » struggle. Barrage.

Emplacement of the grenadiers and grenade depots must be allowed for in the **plan** of **defence** of company and battalion sectors.

The grenadiers are divided up into small groups all along the line; their number is increased on the more exposed fronts (salient angles, points nearest to the enemy trenches). It is advisable in such a case, to second these trench elements by others placed quite near to the first so as to form, as it were, two lines of grenadiers at these points.

Every soldier, unless clumsy, must be able to execute a barrage at 25 meters at the rate of 1 man to every 10 meters with O. F. grenades, and with F. 1 grenades at the rate of one man to every 25 meters.

So as to avoid daily losses at the points where the trenches are nearest to each other, a marked superiority in the throwing of the grenades must be attained so as to **make it impossible for the enemy to remain in his trench.**

Emplacements for grenadiers and grenade depots must be allowed for in the cover trench at the entrance of the boyaux all along the boyaux of a certain length and in the dugouts so as to provide means of issue for them, should the trench be overrun by the enemy; and also behind the barricades.

The various fractions of groups should be well trained in the rapid organization of counter attacks with grenades made in order to regain any lost part of the trench.

2° Advance foot by foot in a trench or in a boyau.

The arrangements in view of a fight in the boyaux must above all things be made so as to **avoid crowding.** Only the smallest possible number of men must be exposed to the enemy grenade fire and they must have ample room to move.

This mode of fighting is very strenuous. It is therefore necessary to arrange frequent reliefs; in addition, the group commander must immediately be able to replace every man who is disabled and to reinforce, if necessary, the forward group with fresh riflemen or throwers.

Strictest silence must be observed so as to hear any sound which might indicate the enemy's intentions. Consequently as far as possible all orders or communications should be given by signs or signals.

Figure 159, given as an example, shows the arrangement of the men.

The grenadiers who are uninterruptedly supplied, continuously throw grenades some on the nearest enemy group and others as far as possible so as to impede the supply in grenades. Sand bag «barriers» are as far as possible destroyed with blast-charges.

When the forward group is satisfied that the enemy is overwhelmed (slackening or stoppage in the throwing of grenades, or indication supplied by sound) the assistant grenadier slips into the smoke, looks rapidly at the turning and beckons to his comrades; in this manner progress from turning to turning and from traverse to traverse is made.

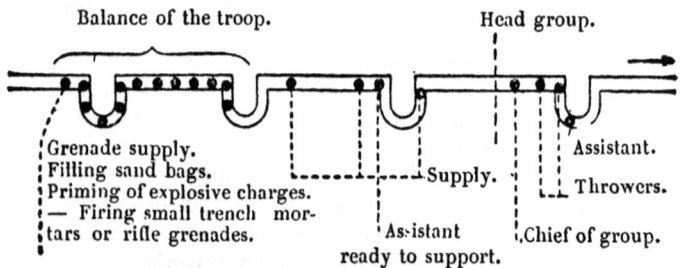

Fig. 159.

When the assistant discovers the mouth of a side boyau he signs to the throwers, who throw grenades into this boyau which is then explored in order to prevent any surprise.

Should the progress not be continued in this new direction, a «barrier» of sand-bags is established and guarded beyond grenade range from the main boyau.

A group is specially detailed to fill earth-bags in order to provide the rapid construction of «barriers».

It is advisable to use rifle grenades, or low power mortars, to impede at a great distance the enemy's supply in grenades.

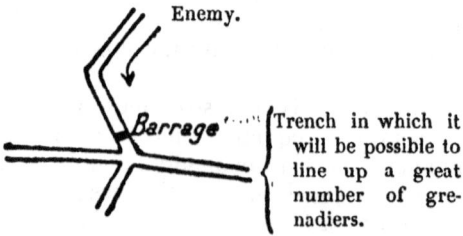

Fig. 160.

When the enemy has managed to become momentarily superior, the ground must be defended foot by foot until the advantage is regained. In this case the «barriers» will be increased in number so as to slacken the progress of the enemy; the trench should be obstructed by piles of sand-bags, or « crumbled in », order to oblige the enemy to show himself in the open in front of the rifles.

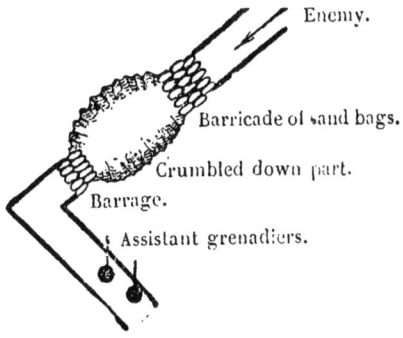

Fig. 161.

The enemy should be drawn to a point where it will be possible to organize a greater number of grenadiers than he (fig. 160).

Simulate the cries of wounded so as to draw the enemy under rifle fire and take him by surprise.

3° Grenade preparation of an attack of a trench.

Assault is generally a combined action which is executed under the protection of powerful artillery rafales. But sometimes in the course of an engagement it happens that a fraction of the troops manages to become lodged quite near to the enemy and the artillery preparation cannot take place.

One then tries to overwhelm the enemy with grenades and afterwards rush him with the bayonet.

Throwers approaching the enemy take advantage of all the features of the terrain. In the meantime the rest of the group remains sheltered and awaits the moment of attacking.

The grenadiers overwhelm the enemy with a continuous hail of well directed grenades and oblige him to either quit the place or get into his shelters. At this moment, the assault is made.

4° Struggle inside the enemy's positions. Cleaning out of trenches and shelters.

The assault is followed by a struggle inside the enemy's position. This struggle can previously be prepared thru the knowledge possessed concerning the enemy's defensive organization.

It is therefore possible to set apart for certain groups of grenadiers, well determined missions, such as:

Progress in the boyaux towards the intermediate and second positions:

« Cleaning up » of the trenches and shelters.

The groups which have these missions allotted to them must have been previously trained.

The «cleaning up» of the trenches comprises two distinct parts which must not be executed by the same groups: viz.

1° The destruction of enemy groups which continue to resist at certain points.

2° The «cleaning up» proper, which consists of making sure that no enemy is left in the conquered trenches and shelters.

The groups which are to break any eventual resistance are mainly if not exclusively made up of grenadiers. They advance with the first or second wave; continually on the alert, they immediately rush against any resistance, running as far as possible along the trench so as to attain the least defended side.

The groups allotted the «cleaning up» proper of the trenches, follow a fixed route. They rapidly skirt the trenches and boyaux, and their progress is so arranged that no part of the enemy trenches is forgotten.

To avoid any loss of time, the men who «clean up» the trenches must not go down into the trenches or boyaux. they will strew grenades in passing and particular attention must be paid to the shelter openings, which are often obstructed as a result of the bombardment, and are not always visible. The prisoners are assembled and rapidly taken away by order of the N. C. O.'s in command, or by special groups previously told off for that purpose.

5° Carrying out a raid.

The grenade is continually used for carrying out raids.

Raids are attempted by:

Either small groups of picked men, having full confidence in each other and particularly versed in the handling of grenades;

Or by a unit also picked, sometimes reinforced by N. C. O.'s, and which has before hand eliminated doubtful elements.

The aim of a raid is to throw grenades into an occupied part of the enemy trench, to attack a sap head, to occupy a crater, or take a small post with a wiew to capturing prisoners.

The success of such an operation depends essentially upon the care with which it has been prepared, by particular reconnoitring and by the rehearsal at the rear of all the phases of its execution under conditions as real as possible.

PREPARATION.

The preparation must be carried out with scrupulous care.

The particular part of the officer who has to carry out a raid is:

1° To make and have made all the necessary reconnaissances (terrain, auxiliary defences, enemy trenches).

The terrain must be studied from a double point of view: means of approach and cover for the grenadiers who must be placed within grenade range of the enemy's position.

The enemy defensive organization is best studied with photographs taken from aircraft.

2° To study the conditions under which the raid will be carried out (day, hour, etc.)

3° To allot a clearly defined mission to each squad or group of grenadiers.

4° To seek the best method of supply.

5° To well inform the infantry and artillery units which are to second him, on the manner in which he intends to carry out his mission,

The officer who carries out the raid is personally in command of the group in charge of the main operation. He must specially appoint one of his subordinates to see to the supply of grenades.

ATTACK ON THE TRENCH.

The group which is to carry out the raid silently approaches the ennemy trench; if there has been artillery preparation, the approach must be extremely rapid.

When the group is near to the points chosen for the passage over the auxiliary defences (which are supposed to be destroyed in front of the point of attack), a volley of grenades is thrown into the enemy trench, and immediately after the explosion the grenadiers leap into the trench.

Such an operation must generally comprise two groups which when they have arrived in the enemy trench will procede to the " clenaing up ", one group towards the right and the other towards the left.

Every precaution must be taken to avoid falling under the fire of the enemy grenades. A position situated a few meters to the rear of the attacked trench may have been prepared by the enemy.

Sometimes it will be advisable to act on a specially dark night or in very bad weather.

An arrangement can then be made between the garrison of the departure line and the group of grenadiers. A few shots fired under the prearranged conditions will warn the grenadiers that an illuminating rocket is about to be sent up. The grenadiers then lie down and take advantage of the light to study the lay of the land.

As soon as the rocket is extinguished they make their rush and await if necessary another rocket.

During the «cleaning up» of the trench, the assistant grenadiers keep watch, according to instruction received before their departure.

Supply. — The supply of grenades must be one of the chief thoughts of commanding officers of every echelon. The most scrupulous measures must be taken to prevent the grenadiers running short of ammunition. These precautions must be based upon the fact that out of every two grenades sent up from the rear, only one reaches its destination.

Every necessary indication is given in chapter XI, part IV Supplies of ammunition and of material.

Tactical use of rifle grenades.

The use of rifle grenades when well understood demoralises the enemy and inflicts upon him losses far more considerable than the bombardment.

The enemy trench must be carefully studied, and it is necessary to be acquainted with the points where it will sometimes be possible to seize an enemy (observation post, the immediate neighborhood of the shelters and the boyaux cross roads, etc.)

The rifles must remain on the firing racks and continually aimed at these points so as to be able to immediately fire a grenade at the least indication of movement.

The fire of the rifle grenades is continued day and night on the registered points.

Although the enemy is out of sight, and in spite of his low density, and the fact that he is hidden in his shelters, it will be possible to inflict considerable losses upon him by a continuous rain of rifle grenades upon carefully chosen spots.

The V. B. grenades.

The Viven-Bessières rifle grenade is a part of the infantry's equipment. Every man must be trained to its use.

The number of «tromblons» in use is limited by the weight of the apparatus, and the necessities of supply.

The V. B. grenade has the advantage of requiring very little space and of being fired with ordinary ball cartridge.

Use when on the defensive. — The V. B. grenade is used in the course of the defence, **either for wearing down fire**, or for inflicting daily losses upon the enemy, to prevent him from continuing his work, **or in barrage fire**, to repulse an attack.

The 16 «tromblons» of the company can fire on its front 150 grenades per minute and can make impassable barrages at distances between 80 to 150 meters.

It is very often an advantage to group together the tromblons of the company into batteries of 2 to 4 tromblons under the command of an N. C. O.

Wearing down fire. — The use of these fires is based upon the knowledge of the enemy's habits. It is indispensable to have a specially well organized observation service. When observation studies of air-craft photos, and of the battle map, and of all kinds of information are combined it will be possible to indicate with a degree of accuracy, upon which objectives, and at what time, the fire will be the most efficacious.

Choosing the emplacement of a V. B. battery.

Barrage fire. — These fires combined with grenades, are intended to stop any enemy attack. They become of considerable importance when communications are interrupted, or the nearness of the adverse defences cause the artillery «barrage» fire to be ineffective.

Example of organization. — Figure 161 *bis*, being a portion of the battle map at 1/5,000, the captain draws the line of «barrage» K. K. (shaded line) which he intends to obtain by means of the V. B. tromblons. When this is done he notices that the part A. B. of the enemy trench would be well enfiladed by a battery of V. B., which could be placed in the cover trench at C. The map shows that C is 40 meters distant from R, a known junction. It happens that from C, trench D. E. is also enfiladed; this will be a second «wearing down» fire. The other batteries of the company will be placed accordingly.

On the other hand, that part of the «barrage» allotted to the 4 «tromblons» of C battery and which is gauged according to the company's front is G. J., at the rate of 30 meters for each tromblon. Points G, H, B, J are then marked at 6 millimeters from each other.

8

The measurements to scale of the distances CG, CH, CB, CA, CJ, CD and CE are taken, and with a protractor the azimuth of these directions are calculated.

It is then easy to set up a **range scale** for C battery.

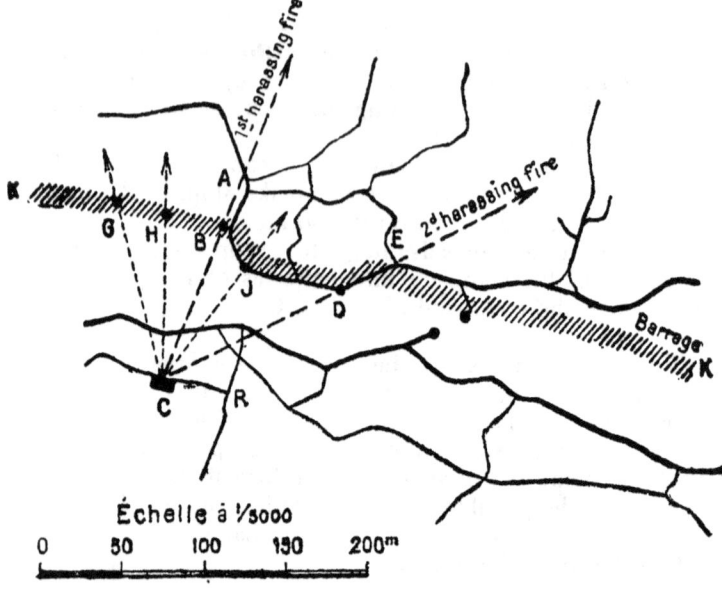

Fig. 261 *bis*.

This scale will give the following information :

1° For all the tromblons — first « wearing down » fire. Common azimuth CA; **distances** : every distance between 90 and 140 meters — so as to « sweep » the whole of BA;

2° A second « wearing down » fire; common azimuth CE; distances : every distance between 110 meters and 160 meters, so as to « sweep » the whole of DE;

3° For each tromblon, an individual barrage fire at a fixed distance : — for the left hand tromblon azimuth CG — distance 100 meters.

For the others :

Azimuth CH, distance 90 meters.
Azimuth CA, distance 90 meters.
Azimuth CJ, distance 75 meters.

The weapons are placed on racks and registered accordingly, in direction and inclination, by means of a compass and plumb rule.

Every « tromblon » rifleman must know without hesitation what to do when the indications : « wearing down » fire n° 1, « wearing down » fire n° 2, or « barrage » are given.

se in an offensive engagement.

In an offensive engagement, the V. B. grenade furthers the action of hand grenades by making it possible to reach at a fair distance, the enemy earthed in his shelter.

In numerous local fights where it is not possible to obtain the support of the artillery, it supplies this support by bombarding with accuracy the enemy resisting groups.

It isolates the enemy groups attacked with hand grenades, by preventing their retreat, or by impeding the arrival of reinforcements.

Lastly, the V. B. grenade is of great efficiency against enemy counter attacks.

Whatever the situation, but more particularly in offensive engagements, it is advisable to use the V. B. grenade in concentrated fire.

D. R. Grenades.

As compared to the V. B. grenade, the D. R. grenade or shell has a range double that of the V. B., and its effects are greater — but it is a bulkier projectile, and its supply requires a greater number of men, for the same number of projectiles carried.

It cannot, therefore, take the place of the V. B. in offensive work; it is only used to hold an occupied point.

In the defensive, the D. R. makes it possible to do without the artillery. It is fit for harassing fire and rapid concentration fire upon any indicated group.

In the offensive, it strengthens a conquered front. It takes the place of the artillery for any preparation against an isolated knot of resistance which has been left behind in the course of an attack. It adds to or takes the place of the destructive effects of field artillery. It is used with advantage in the execution of a raid, in the « cutting off » or « boxing up » of a small objective, in the protection of an attacking troop when it retires after having obtained a given result, etc.

6° The 37 mm. cannon.

The tactical properties of the 37 mm. cannon are :

Its mobility, the small space required for its ammunition which allows it to follow the infantry in any part of a fight.

The ease with which it can be hidden behind a parapet, or sunk into the soil in constructing unimportant works; the possibility of delivering a masked fire.

The great ease with which it is adjusted or regulated.

Its great accuracy which allows it to make direct hits upon embrasures up to 1.200 meters; and a useful range of 1,500 meters.

The rapidity of its fire which for a short « rafale » can attain 20 shots per minute.

Its percussion high explosive shell is used against troops and material, its steel shell against armour. Its effects can be compared to those of a grenade which before bursting could pass through either three rows of sand-bags, or wooden protection, or a steel plate.

It has little effect upon earth shelters.

It has been designed to destroy by direct fire any machine gun within sight.

It also gives appreciable results against troops taken under an enfilade fire.

Use in offensive engagements. — The 37 mm. cannon is a battalion weapon. In certain cases, the colonel can retain the use of it.

It is used :

To prepare and follow up an attack.

To break any enemy resistance in the course of an assault.

To cooperate in the occupation of a conquered position.

Preparation and accompanying of the attack. — Before the attack starts, the 37 mm. cannon is installed in an emplacement whence it can act efficiently, either by :

Demolishing machine gun emplacements which might reveal themselves at the last moment;

Sweeping those parts which are dangerous for the flanks of the attack;

Firing upon the second and third enemy lines.

To prevent them being destroyed too soon, it is advisable to put them into action only at the last moment.

Use during an assault. — The 37 mm. gun is taken forward as soon as it is no longer of use in its initial place, or when the infantry needs it to destroy an enemy resistance.

Its movement must be foreseen in the plan of engagement. The 37 mm. gun is never used in the first waves, because of its vulnerability. It is sufficient that it should follow up the battalion or regimental reserves.

It s used either to destroy a machine gun shelter or to

clean up a trench or boyau that it can reach with enfilade fire.

As far as possible never use it at too short a distance from its objectives. Cause it to open a masked fire every time it is possible.

Occupation of a conquered position.

The 37 mm. gun contributes to maintain the hold upon a conquered position under the same condition as the machine-gun.

It is so arranged as to be able to act upon the probable issues of the enemy counter-attacks by seeking an oblique or slanting action.

It is always advisable to prepare a number of masked emplacements, which supply the means of avoiding easy registering by the enemy's artillery.

Use in defensive engagements. — Endeavor to always place shells into every small window, embrasure, spying post, etc. indicated by the observation service.

Prepare numerous emplacements on the front of the battalion and in the rear.

During the violent bombardment preceding an enemy assault it is not necessary to keep it in the first line. Installed towards the line of support, or a little to the rear, it might cooperate in the **barrage** fire especially by enfilade fires, It will «sweep» those parts of the terrain where the barrage fire of the artillery will be less efficacious (very broken up ground, dead angle).

Lastly, the 37 mm. gun can be used for **masked fire**. It can be registered on the main boyaux, the important cross roads, etc. But the range adjustment must be examined after every fire; for although very accurate, in the course of the same fire this gun has important variations in range according to the atmospheric changes.

CHAPTER VI.

PRINCIPLES OF FIELD FORTIFICATION.

Field fortification is to preserve, as far as possible, troops engaged in battle from the murderous effect of the enemy's fire, and, on the other hand, to afford small effective means to hold strongly a defensive position.

The latter is possible if it is intimately connected with the increased power given to infantry by abundant machine-guns, rifles, hand-grenades and other trench weapons.

— 174 —

During the battle, effectives in action are so numerous and the efforts of all so great, that nothing else can be conceived but **continuous** lines of fighting men', occupying trench lines equally **continuous**.

These trench lines are multiplied necessarily from front to rear, in as great a number as necessary for giving shelter to the firing line, supports and reserves during the main halts in their manœuvres. They are connected by a system of communication trenches **as perfected as possible**.

The continuous line is not without **strong points** (points d'appui). But the latter should be hidden amid a network of trenches, connecting trenches and dummy trenches. Isolated «points d'appui» once registered by photography, become «bomb nests.» On the other hand, the lack of a continuous line may permit «infiltration» by the enemy between the strongholds.

A continuous line also keeps the defender from feeling isolated in his «point d'appui».

After the battle, on the contrary, on a front which becomes stationary, the question is to hold the ground very firmly, although manning it with effectives much less numerous than required for a lively action. That is the usual system. It does not require the constant occupation of a continuous line.

Lastly, to such a defensive organization, may be added all devices necessary for offensive action on one part of the front.

It follows therefore, that a new problem arises for the organization of each particular sector. the solution of which depends upon the military situation, the terrain (Flanders, Champagne, Vosges, etc.), and also upon the available time, forces and material.

The following principles are to be observed for the defensive organization of a position under the most usual circumstances :

1° **The firing-line need not be continuous** if the foreground is entirely swept either by **frontal fire** or by **flank fire**; better still, by both together. Most generally the line with intervals will be used.

Fig. 163 shows how ground may be entirely swept either by a continous firing line A B, or by a line with intervals made up of T, T 1, T 2.

2° However, a line with intervals must be essential by a continuous obstacle and, besides, the intervals must look like neighboring elements so that the enemy is not able to discover the occupation plan of our positions. To accomplish this, trenches belonging to the different strong-points are connected by communicating or dummy trenches. Everything should be so designed that a photograph taken by air-scout should be quite unreadable by the

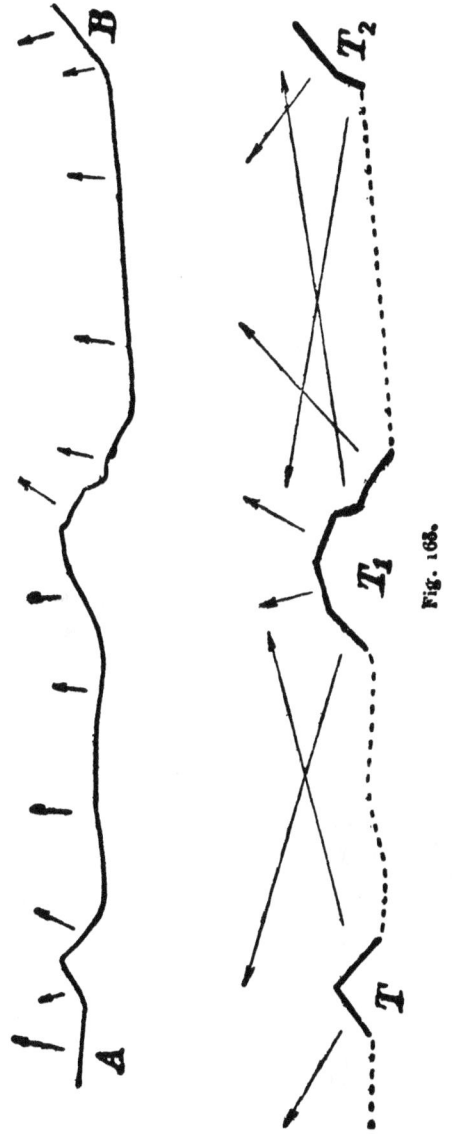

Fig. 168.

enemy and give no information whatever of our occupation plan or of our intentions.

3° The rapidity of fire of modern arms allows a **short field of fire**.

4° **Location of good flanking positions is, on the contrary, of capital importance and should first be considered when tracing the fortifications.** Flanking insures convergence of heavy fire on attacked points. It permits the use of lines with intervals, from which results economy of men exposed to fire in the first line.

5° The best way to lessen casualties among troops is to **keep in line only the strictly indispensable effective;** the solidity of a position rests in the accuracy of **trace**, in the excellence of **flanking-devices**, and in the **stubbornness** of small groups of defenders who, sticking to their own earth-work, know exactly their own role in the general scheme.

6° With the men thus saved, strong reserves are formed and are set to work **improving and increasing communications** with the rear (approach trenches). Communications enabling the rapid and sure arrival of **supplies** and **reinforcements,** and, eventually, **counter-attacks,** are the **vital elements** of the position and can never be too highly developed.

7° All kinds of works must be concealed, and troops given **bomb-proof** shelters, in order to escape premature destruction.

8° Lastly, measures must be taken to avoid **surprise,** and all means foreseen to enable the defenders, sheltered during bombardement, to reach their firing-posts in due time.

Active and passive segments. — Very seldom have the trenches in close touch with the enemy's trenches been traced theoretically, and very seldom do they answer the scheme of a line with intervals, provided with flanking devices; rather they present very entangled continuous lines located, as they probably were, by the ups and downs of the struggle.

They should nevertheless be occupied according to the expressed principles.

The task of cutting up such continuous trenches into **active segments** and **passive segments** belongs to the higher authority, the former alone being provided with a garrison and acting as distinct elements in a line with intervals; the latter being held merely by **flanking-fires** from adjacent active segments, or by frontal fires from active segments or the trench in the rear.

Such passive segments always serve as **communications** between active segments. In case of attack they may, according to the **plan of defense,** either be manned by supports, or be used as **routes for counter-attacks,** as will be explained later.

Active segments can be imagined as small segments of resistance extending from 20 to 50 yards; passive segments as lines from 40 to 100 yards.

Fig. 164 illustrates an example of such a system.

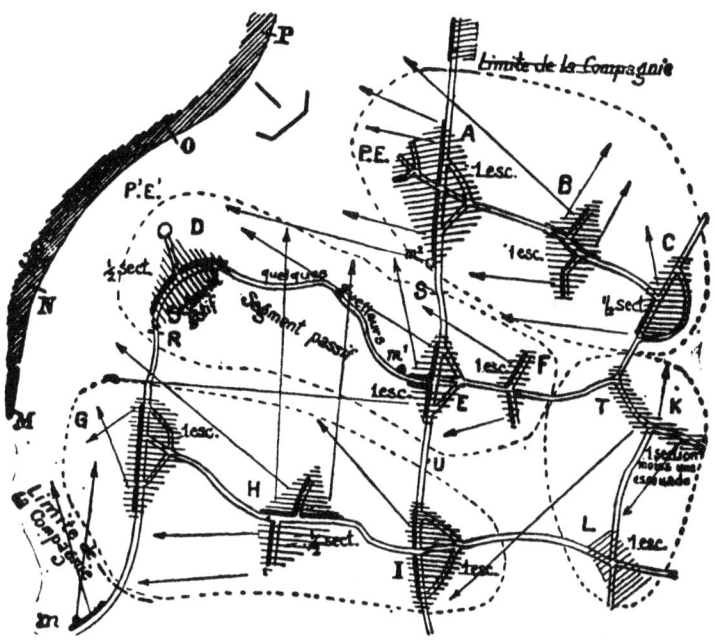

Fig. 164.

Limite de la Cie = limit of company's sector; Section = platoon; Escouade = group; 1 section moins une escouade = 1 platoon less 1 group; Segment passif = passive segment; Quelques guetteurs = several sentries; P. E. (poste d'écoute) = listening post.

Definitions.

Element. — The term **active elements**, or **segments**, may be given to the most simple of distinct «islets» generally made up of a small knot of trenches and barricades. They are manned by a **complete unit**. This garrison receives special orders. Its strength varies from a group to a platoon.

Points d'appui (strong-points). — Several of the above-described elements grouped together in a single body, extending along the line or towards the rear, constitute a «**point d'appui**» or a **work**; the garrison is a company or a fraction of a company. It may include a **redoubt**.

Behind the **first-line strong-points**, others are designed to limit any progress of the enemy.

Centers of resistance (Supporting points). — The grouping of several strong-points, in width or in depth, takes the name of **center of resistance**. Such a grouping is manned by a battalion or by several companies under command of a single officer. The officer in command is responsible for providing the **strong-points** with garrisons, and besides, for keeping **reserve troops** ready for giving counter-attacks. A center of resistance always includes a redoubt; sometimes artillery is attached to it

Sector. — Lastly, a **sector** is the combination of several centers of resistance under the same command. Generally a sector is manned by a division, and divided into **sub-sectors** given over to brigades or regiments. A sector possesses its own reserves, distinct from the reserves of centers of resistance. The names «sector» and «sub-sector» should be exclusively given to organizations such as have been described; the names of «**quarter**» and «**sub-quarter**» can therefore sometimes be given to the ground ascribed to a **battalion** or a **company**.

Position (Intrenched zone). — The first position is constituted by a **line of centers of resistance** grouped into sectors for command.

Any defensive organization includes at least two positions, the second one being at such a distance from the first one (6 to 8 kilometers, i. e., 3 to 5 miles) as to prevent its being shelled at the same time as the first by the enemy's heavy artillery or artillery using asphyxiating shells.

Between these two positions «intermediate positions» are organized in such numbers as appear necessary, and as are allowed by the ground and the means available.

Partitioning the terrain. — A position should not be imagined as a cluster of centers of resistance located side by side, and forming an uninterrupted defensive organization.

Successive lines of trenches (first line, supporting lines, redoubts, intermediate trenches) divide the ground into compartments in the direction of the front. Likewise, the centers of resistance often show groups of active elements (small works, resistance «islets» etc.) forming segments perpendicular to the front and separated by less well defended segments of ground. Such strongly held segments complete the partitioning of the ground. They must generally result from the features of the ground and the strong-points provided by nature (ridges, crests, woods, villages, etc.).

Fig. 165 illustrates in a general way one of the sectors of a position and shows an example of partitioning the ground.

The resistance zone encircling the sector has for its object to prevent the enemy from reaching the interior of the sector. This zone contains the line of observation, first line, and support line.

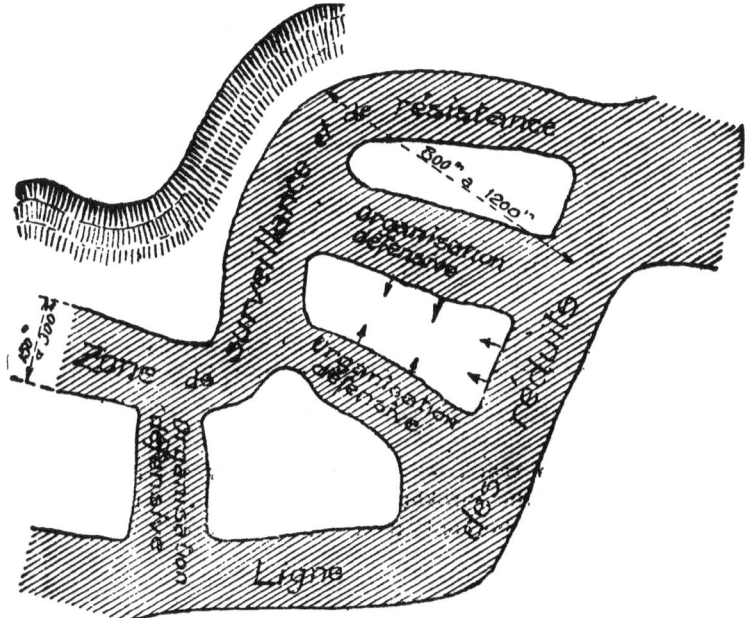

Fig. 165.

The line of redoubts and the defensive organizations, the latter supported by the redoubts and the lines of resistance, are intended to round up any hostile offensive that has broken into the sector, and to expose it to frontal and flank fires, and to counter-attacks delivered from redoubts and defensive organizations still in our possession. The enemy's rush across our resistance-zone should only result in his loss.

These explanations are necessary for a sound understanding of the plan of defense and of the mechanism of counter-attacks. (Part VII).

Principles of the different traces.

The following notions are given on the classical types of works (cutting, redan, bastion, redoubt); geometrical shapes of such types are seldom realized but make explanation and argument clearer. Fitting their individual peculiarities to any trace is then easy.

Straight line trace. — Cutting. — Advantages and disadvantages. — The most simple trench is the straight line trench, named **cutting** (special case : barricade).

It is the quickest to make and the one that is instinctively made during the course of an action by a skirmish line hurrying to dig itself in.

Its disadvantage is to allow only frontal fire, or oblique fire not exceeding 30 degrees. If attacked on a flank the cutting is enfiladed, and the defense rendered impossible.

The angle of 30° is not invariable; it is theoretical.

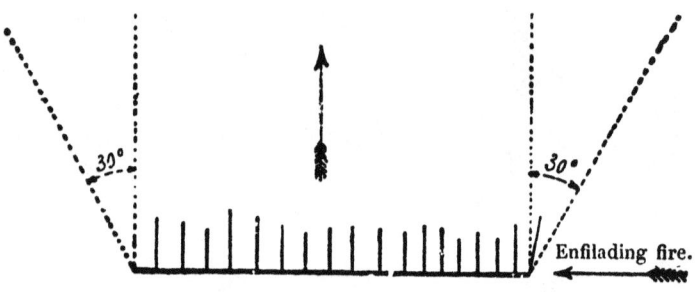

Fig. 166. — Limit of oblique fire.

Broken-line trace. — The above disadvantage gives preference to the broken-line trace which, moreover, applies better to the contour of unlevel ground.

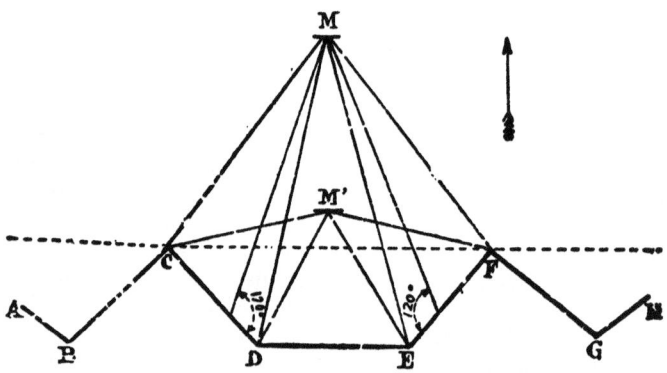

Fig. 167. — Intrenchment in broken line.

Salients and re-entrants. — When a line of intrenchments is traced thus its plan presents **salient angles** and **re-entrant angles.**

The salient angles are turned towards the enemy; the re-entrant angles towards the defender.

Such a succession of salient and re-entrant angles places the parapets obliquely, enabling the defenders to **open cross-fires** on the ground to be crossed by the enemy.

— 181 —

For instance, if the enemy, M, is trying to penetrate into re-entrant CDEF, he is fired on full-face from DE, and obliquely from CD and EF. This fire becomes more murderous as M approaches M' and the moment comes when the whole line M' is in the sheaf of a single machine-gun located in the whereabouts of C or F, flanking DE. Direct fire from DE will no longer be necessary to stop M'.

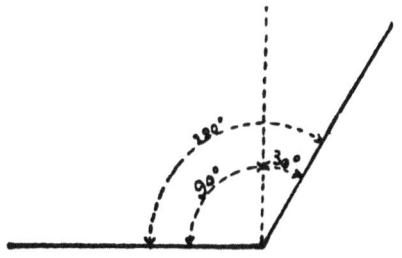

Fig. 168. — Limits of re-entrant angle.

From what precedes we must conclude:

1° That **re-entrants constitute the strong part of a broken line** on account of the cross-fires delivered in front of them, these cross-fires growing more murderous as the attack approaches.

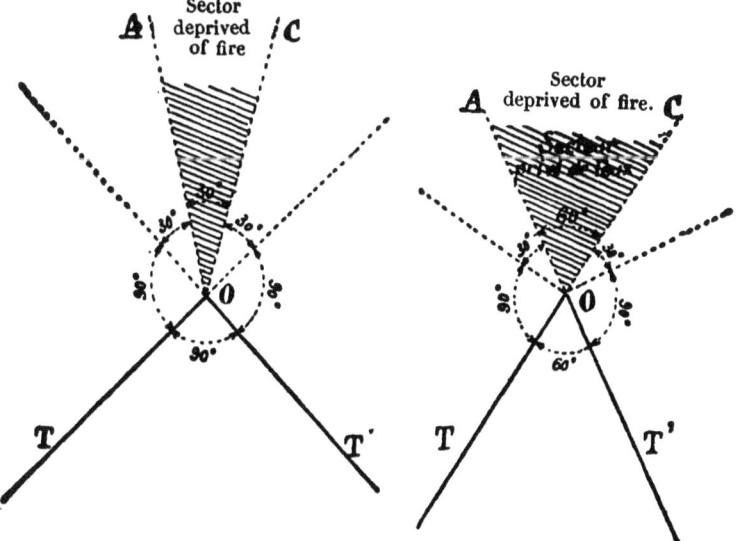

Fig. 169 and 170. — The greater the salient angle the smaller the sector cut off from fire.

2° That the defenders may be few on DE, provided that all or a part of CD and EF can keep up a sustained fire.

The minimum limit of a re-entrant angle is naturally 90°, because if it were less the defenders of one side of the angle would be in the range of the defenders of the other side.

If it is necessary that the ground be swept by fire from both sides the angle should not exceed 120°.

On the contrary **a salient is a weak part of the line** because assailants can crush it under **converging fire** and, if it is **isolated,** the defenders of the salient can reply only with **diverging fire.** Still more, there may be no firing possible.

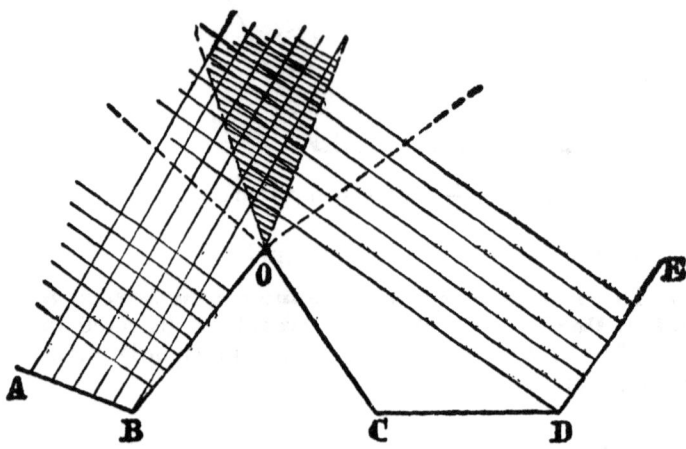

Fig. 171. — Flanking.

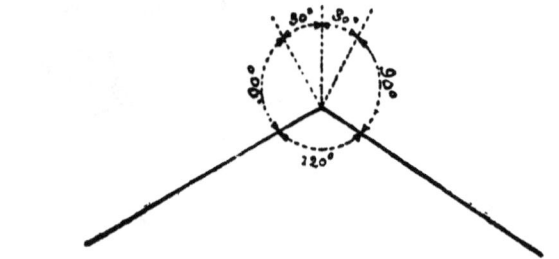

Fig. 172. — The sector cut off from fire disappears with a salient angle of 120°.

Sectors cut off from fire. — Let us imagine a salient angle O less than 120° (fig. 170). Trench T can fire as far as OA, trench T' as far as OC. Angle AOC, cut off from **direct** fire, is called the **sector cut off from fire.**

Fig 171 shows how this serious defect is remedied by **flanking:** AB and DE flank the salient O.

Fig. 173 shows that the broken-line trace, although sweeping the nearby ground better than the straight-line trace, creates dead space on the ground farther off. This disadvantage is counter-balanced by the efficacy of rapid-firing arms.

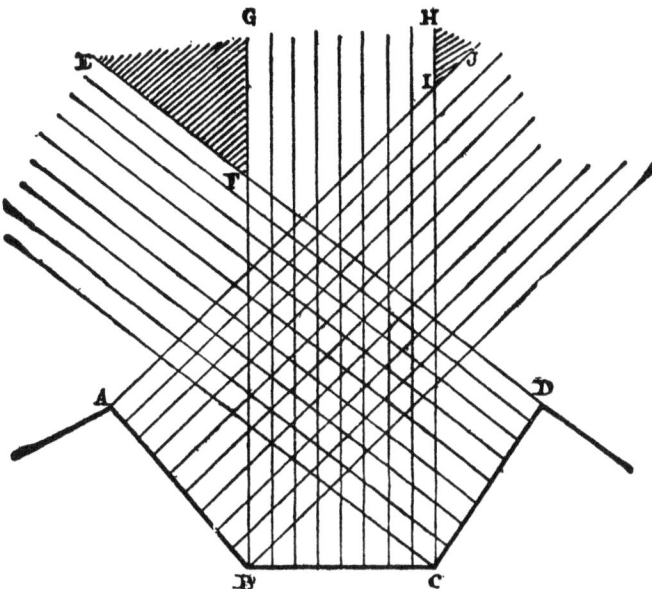

Fig. 173.— Advantages and inconveniences of the broken line trace.

The following are different types of broken-line traces

1° **Indented trace**. — Parts BC, DE, running parallel to the main line, and the flanks AB, CD, always succeed one another in the same order. Such a trace gives good protection against enfilading fire.

Fig. 174. — Indented trace.

2° **Tenailled trace**. — The firing line is broken up so that two adjacent parts, BC, CD, flank each other.

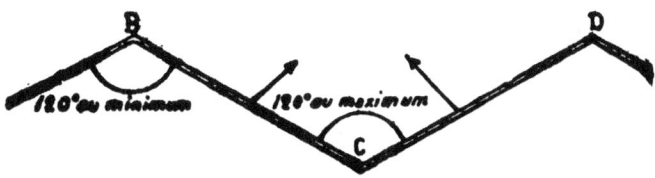

Fig. 175. — Tenailled trace.

3° **Redan trace.** — A redan is nothing other than a salient angle, considered as an isolated work. The sides of the angle are called **faces.** If impossible to give the angle

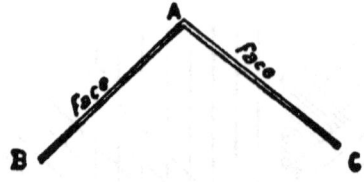

Fig. 176. — Redan.

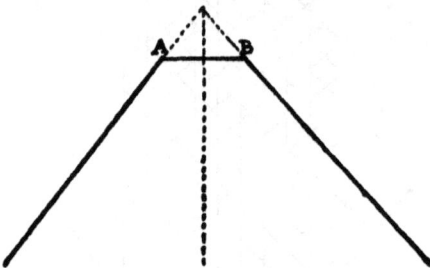

Fig. 177. — Redan with pan coupé at salient.

an opening wider than 120° a **pan coupé** a few yards long may be constructed to bring the dead space under fire. It is the proper place for an automatic rifle.

The **double redan** flanks its face by its own means.

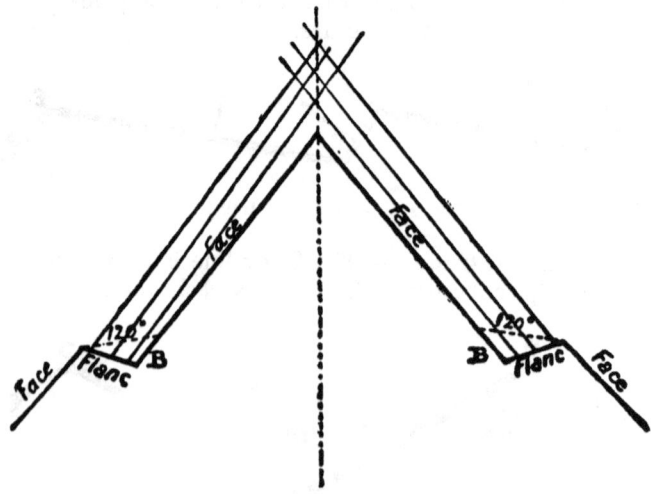

Fig. 178. — Double redan or redan with flanks.

A **redan trace** is a broken line including redans connected by **curtains**.

Fig. 179. — Redan trace.

4° **Bastioned trace.** — If two **flanks** are added to the faces of the redan a **lunette** is **obtained,** which is called a **bastion** when it is part of the scheme of a polygonal trace.

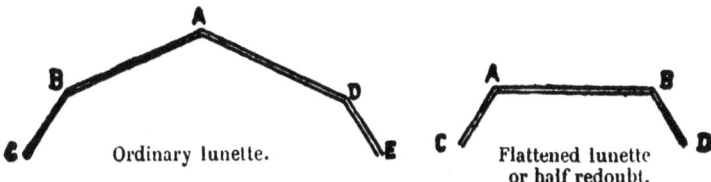

Ordinary lunette.   Flattened lunette or half redoubt.

Fig. 180. — Lunette.

In the **bastion trace** (fig. 181) the **flanks** of each bastion cross their fire in front of the **curtain** and flank the **faces** of the neighboring bastion.

The salient is the weak part of a lunette as well of as a bastion. If you withdraw it, bringing the two faces in a straight line, a **flat lunette** or **half-redoubt** is obtained.

All these works: redan, lunette and half-redoubt, are said to be « open ». Their defense would be very difficult were they turned.

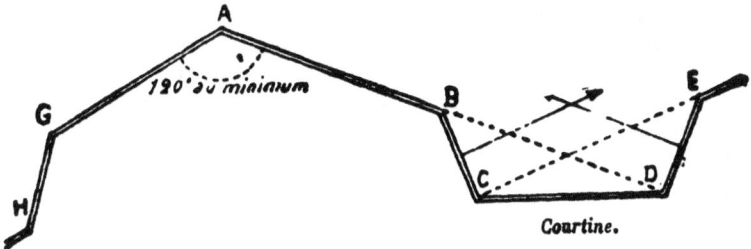

Fig. 181. — Bastion trace.

Redoubt. — **A redoubt** is a closed polygon, able to offer stubborn resistance, and to favor a counter-attack.

A redoubt should be divided as much as possible by

traverses and **parados** to afford shelter from fire from any direction.

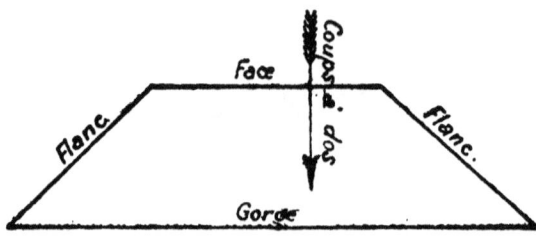

Fig. 182. — Four sided redoubt.

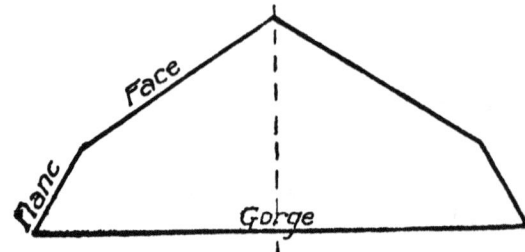

Fig. 183. — Five sided redoubt.

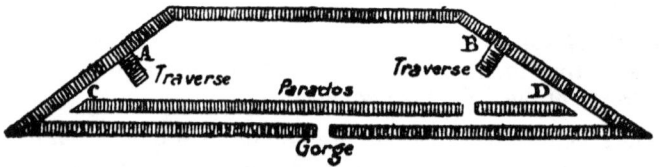

Fig. 184. — Traverses and parados.

Use of preceding traces. — **Trenches and works in reality are never as regular or precise as the above, they being theoretical traces for teaching the names and principles of such works.**

Any trace must, first of all, comply with the contour of the ground, which seldom permits straight lines. The firing crests will curve in and out as often as necessary. Nevertheless salients and re-entrants, irregular bastions and redans, and more or less winding curtains will be found in succession, bearing relation to each other according to the preceding principles.

Elements of a position.

All positions, first, second, or intermediate, include, as a general principle, the same elements, and are to be defended in the same way. They are, as has been stated, **lines of centers of resistance.**

The defense of a center of resistance is planned in depth by the organization of:

a) A first-resistance line (first-line trenches).
b) A line of supports (support trenches).
c) A redoubt.

A. Organization of a first-line trench.

The first line trench is the locality where the advance units sustain the first shock. It is a series of well-manned elements (active segments) connected by continuous trenches, the whole covered by uninterrupted wire-entanglements as thick as possible. The trench is always connected with the rear by means of numerous approach trench' (boyaux) (at least one per platoon).

Sometimes this trench is called **firing trench** or **fighting trench**. This indicates its being the zone of « **wearing down** » **fighting**.

There is advantage in having the first line trench less than 100 yards from the enemy for then he is afraid to shell it for fear that he might hit his own trench. It must be located out of range of hand-grenades and flame projectors (40 yards). At a short distance there is also danger of the trench being mined.

Small posts. — In front of the first-line trench small posts, or even **sentinel trenches** are to be found. They are surrounded by wire entanglements. Such posts, although manned by small effectives, offer the enemy a first resistance and thereby permit action by flanking fire parties who sweep the hostile zone. The excavated way to the post may also be used for flanking part of the main front. (Fig. 185).

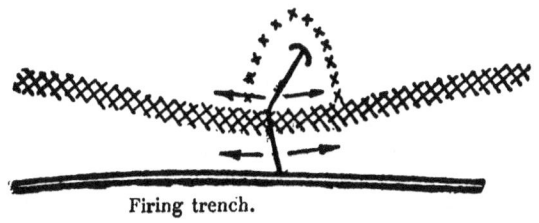

Firing trench.

Fig. 185.

Where no small posts exist sentries and watchmen stand in the first line trench, which is then sometimes called a «sentinel trench»; this is, however, a misnomer.

There should be no abuse of small posts. They immobilize a small garrison and this garrison becomes unavailable for any other duty. Posts should be located in front of the trench only if there is a reason for doing so, such as to obtain outlooks or flank positions which could not be flanked by the first trench.

Cover trench. — The first line trench is sometimes doubled by a so-named cover trench, located from 30 to 40 yards in the rear and allowing immediate counter-attack or, in the case of a very heavy bombardment and of a lack of bomb proof shelters, the swift withdrawal of the garrison which, however, is kept near by.

The cover trench is indispensable and obligatory: a) when the first trench has been pushed very close to the enemy's trenches; b) when only very primitive obstacles can be constructed in front of it; c) when loose earth and repair difficulties render it despite of all rather bad.

The cover trench dug with greater leisure establishes the confidence of the defense.

Profile of the firing trench. — The regular type of **firing trench** has been given Part II, Chapter VIII, School of sap (Fig. 33).

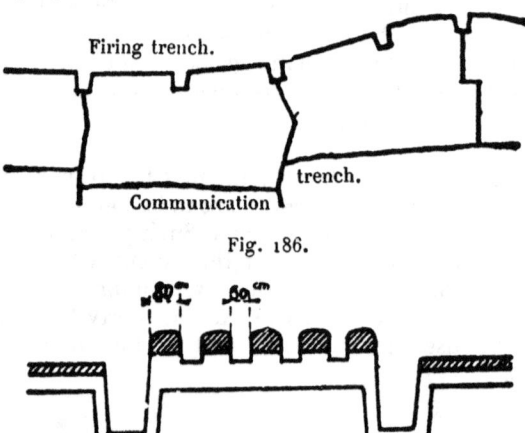

Fig. 186.

Fig. 187.

Narrow and deep trenches are those which afford the best protection against artillery-fire, bombs, rifle and hand grenades. But the circulation is very difficult for relief, for carrying the wounded, etc. So it becomes necessary either to widen the trench and to dig it still deeper, making a circulating passage on a lower level than the banquette, or to dig a special circulating-trench from 12 to 15 yards in the rear. The depth enabling circulation under cover behind firing squads and through the communicating trenches must be **at the very least** 6 feet and frequently 7 feet, better still, 8 feet.

In such parts of the line as are particularly exposed to enfilade fire, recesses for snipers may be dug along the intervals between traverses. This is also the way to make the best of an old trench whose interior slope has given way from place to place.

Up-keep. — Protection against bad weather is provided by revetments of sod, sandbags, planks, hurdles, wire-

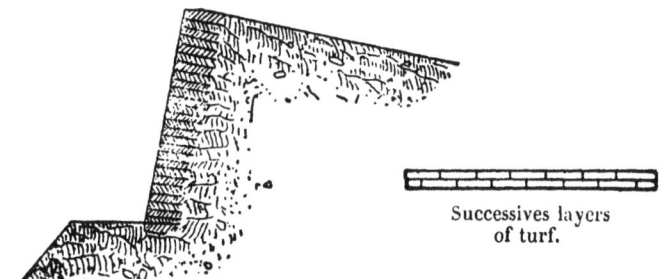

Fig. 188. — Sod revetment.

Fig. 189. — Gabion revetment.

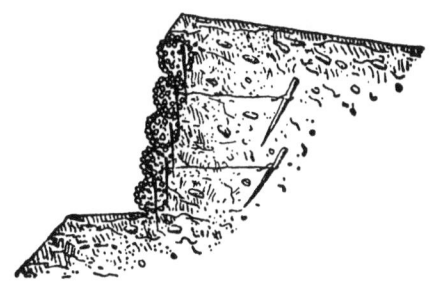

Fig. 190. — Fascine revetment.

netting, etc. The parts of the trench to be kept up in this way are, first of all, the interior slope and the banquette.

In principle, it is forbidden to dig into the interior slope any contrivances that would weaken it. Recesses for ammunition, entrances to dugouts, etc., dug into the parapets, must be reenforced by wooden frames.

Drainage. — When ne ground has a regular slope it is possible to drain the trenches by means of a well elaborated system of gutters. One must be sure the water is directed to lower ground or to natural excavations, and not to other trenches or communication trenches.

If ground is permeable, or if at a short depth a permeable bed is to be found under superficial clay, sump-pits

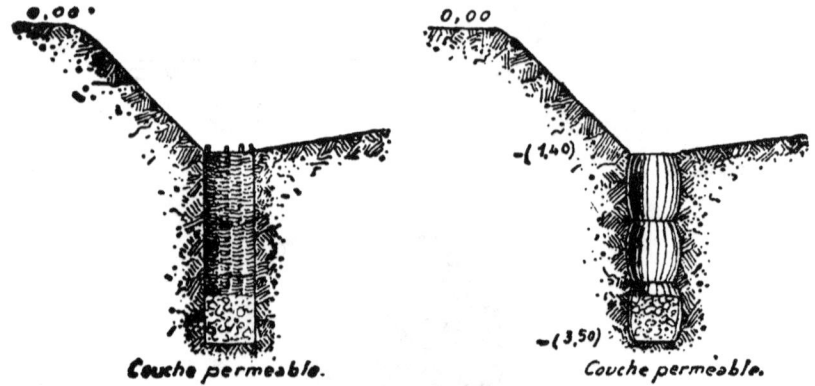

Fig. 191. — Sump-pits.

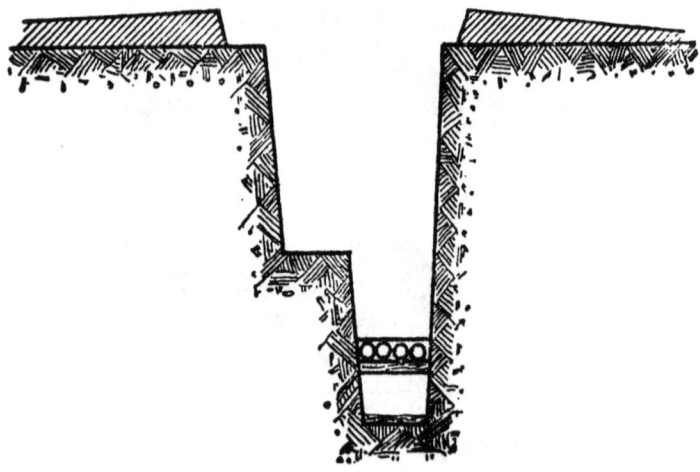

Fig. 192.

are to be dug at convenient distance. The bottom of the sump-pit is paved with stone to avoid its being filled up with mud.

In impermeable ground sump-pits are not sufficient. It is necessary to organize the drainage with pumps, pails, scoops, etc. This drainage must be continuous. The only means of keeping the trenches in walking condition in clay ground is to lay stringers of wood on which rest gratings of planks or split logs. Pits are dug under this corduroy and gutters designed in the middle or along the inside bottom corner of the trench so as to drain the water and mud into the pits.

Sandbag revetment is the best. The sand bags should be well filled and well piled. Other kinds bulge after a certain time and obstruct circulation. They should be immediately pulled down and removed, or else the trench must be turned in another direction. Protection is lessened by **abnormal** widening or by the existence of a « square » **incompletely** covered; but anything is better than the obstruction resulting from a yielding revetment.

Loopholes. — Loopholes are only used in case the enemy cannot discern whether they are manned or not. That is why none are to be found on the greater part of the firing line that is in close touch with the foe.

Use of loopholes is reserved for observing-posts and for well hidden and far-off flanking trenches.

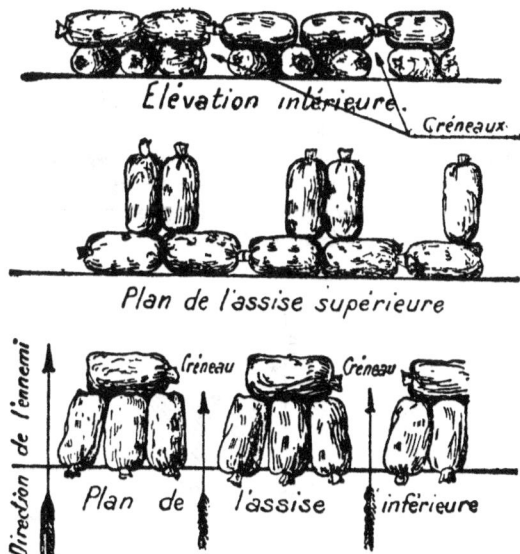

Fig. 193. — Loopholes with sandbags.

The exterior opening should be concealed, usually by a tight string netting stretched over the exterior frame of the loophole but affording passage to the gun-barrel, or by any other method.

The opening should not stand out against the sky nor on a background contrasting with the color of the trench.

Therefore, the loophole must be laid level with the parapet. The parados must be heightened. A piece of cloth may be stretched behind the rifleman's head, etc.

If loopholes have been provided, the direction in which they permit firing is one of the main cares of the platoon commander in the trenches. He must examine them each

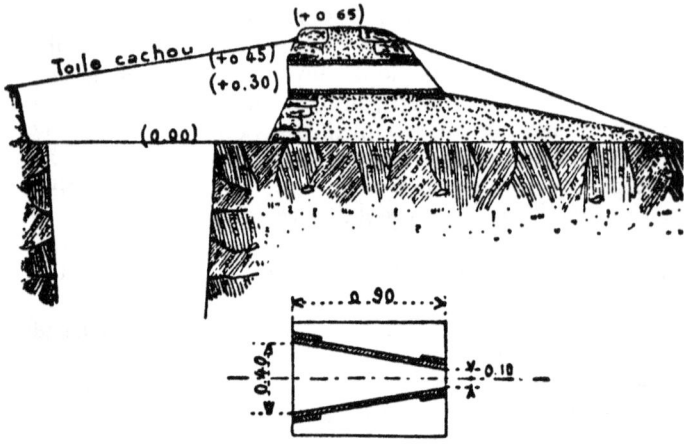

Fig. 195. — Loopholes of wood.

in turn to be sure that the trench segment allotted to him fulfils the tactical purposes ascribed to it. **Each rifle resting naturally on the floor of the loophole must be directed towards the zone to be swept and must assure a grazing fire along the ground, even at night when aiming is impossible.**

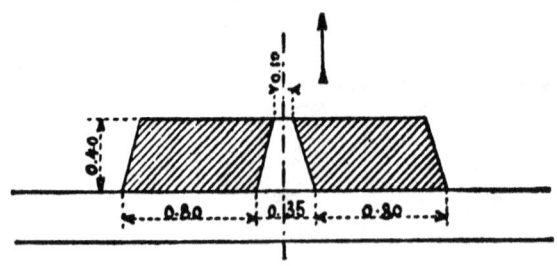

Fig. 197. — Loophole with collapsible gabion.

Such a necessity is evident. Furthermore the officer in command must frequently assure himself that the loophole has not risen slightly and that the rifle does not shoot «into the blue», i. e. too high.

All loopholes have the same drawback; when the foe gets too near all firing must cease so as to get the rifles out of the loopholes and fix the bayonet. If the bayonet is fixed beforehand, it is hard to come to a «guard». Loopholes are also destroyed by artillery fire.

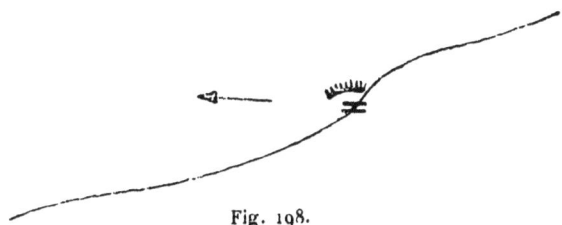

Fig. 198.

So the loophole is only used for «wearing down» fire. All devices should be prepared (firing-step raised between two loopholes on logs, blocks, stools, sods, etc.), so as to check an attack by firing **over the parapet** (barbette firing), which is the only way to give a man the full advantage of his rifle.

Whenever possible (and such is generally the case in flank fire) the loophole will be pointed obliquely in regard to the opposite hostile trench, so that the loophole becomes invisible and the sniper keeps his head entirely protected.

If the defenders of the trench are to fire a little away from the perpendicular to the front it is good to prepare *notches* which are merely grooves made for guiding the soldier's fire and to remind him not to shoot mechanically straight ahead.

When loopholing a wall in defense of a village, it is better to make the loopholes one foot or a foot and one quarter above the ground; and to fire prone. Loopholes are less visible and less promptly destroyed at this height than if they were the height of a man (4 feet and 4 inches).

They should be four feet apart.

Traverses. — Their usual size and the distance between them is given in School of Sap, Part II.

The prescribed breadth (8 feet) is a minimum which one should never fear to increase at the spots where direct hits may be expected. A breadth of 3 or 4 yards may be, in such cases, advisable.

Should such broad traverses be provided it may be advantageous to a prepare, all along the traverse, a banquette or loopholes flanking the inside of the trench. The filling up of the trench behind the traverse is also necessary. Sandbags, chevaux de frise, hedgehogs, etc., should be ready on the berm to be shoved into the trench to form a barricade.

If there is not time to build traverses while digging the trench the latter may at least be provided with elbows. (Fig. 199).

In this way a provisional partitioning is assured, similar to the one given by traverses. Later on splinter proof shields are built of gabions and sand-bags. (Fig. 201).

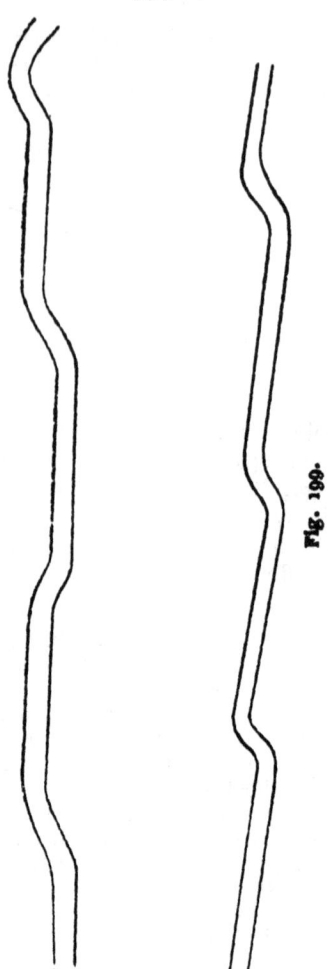

Fig. 199.

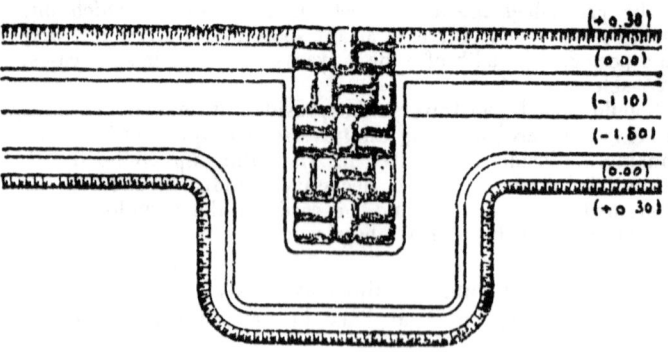

Fig. 201. — Sandbag splinter-proof shields.

Protection against grenades. — For protection against grenades a vertical grille of wire-netting may be erected above the firing crest, or the trench may be covered by a roof with two slopes of wire-netting, or of joined logs with a light layer of earth.

The appliances described in Appendix 4 of «Instructions on Grenade-Fighting» (a pivoting wire-netting cage) is a very good one. It may also be used instantly as an obstruction for a trench.

Field of fire. — In front of every segment there must be a field of fire, but in trench warfare one may be satisfied with a field of fire of **about 100 yards,** and even less, if flanking is well insured and **accessory defense** well established.

Influence of the relief of the ground. — Occupation of a crest. — The locating of firing line depends more often on the events of the struggle than on the deliberate choice of the one who traces it. However, rules must be laid down on how to pick out a firing crest in reference to the relief of the ground when the opportunity to do so presents itself (second and third positions).

On level ground, the view being about the same from any point, there is no choice of a site.

On the contrary, if a crest is to be held on rolling ground, it may be difficult to decide.

One may wish to locate the firing-line along A (Fig. 204), almost at the foot of the slopes. In such a case a good sweeping fire will be possible by the infantry and the foreground is usually sprinkled with artillery fire (thanks to the observations taken from B). But the ground in the rear of the trench is easily made out and swept by the enemy. Movements and counter-attacks thereon are difficult.

Topographical crest is the line connecting the highest points of the ground.

Military crest is the line uniting the points in front of the topographical crest from which the foot of the slopes can be entirely seen.

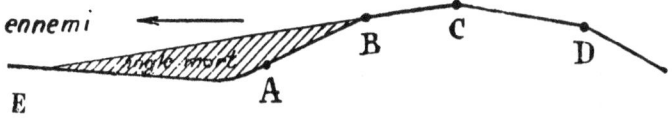

Fig. 204.

While walking from the topographical crest towards the military crest a **dead angle** exists in ABE. From the military crest and on down the dead angle disappears.

The firing line located in B, at the **military crest**, still has a good field of fire, and, above all, a very good view. But the defender will be in view of the enemy and will therefore be exposed to accurate fire from his artillery. Furthermore, help from friendly artillery will often be feeble on the descending slope BA. Movements and counter-attacks are easier than in the preceding case.

On the **topographical crest** C a long view is still available, but in front of the defender a large dead angle will be favorable to the enemy and the field of fire small.

Properties of the reverse slope. — On the **reverse slope** D there is no view and a still greater dead-angle. But there is the advantage of hiding the trench and the wire-entanglements from the enemy. Traffic is facilitated, reenforcements more accessible and the range finding of the enemy's artillery is made more difficult. It is established that the enemy's infantry is powerless against trenches and entanglements that are intact, even should the field of fire of these trenches be restricted.

Such advantages have led many authorities to advocate reverse slope positions.

However, systematic use of reverse slope positions should not be adopted as a general rule.

In fact, the recent progress of air scouting and the use of zone-firing have robbed such positions of part of their previous immunity.

On the other hand, it should not be forgotten that the **possession of observation posts is of the utmost importance**, as well in the trench warfare as in field warfare. However if the crest is not held, observation posts are no longer available.

It is necessary to know the advantages of the reverse slope trenches so as to make use of them, e. g., to double a trench on the crest.

The **line of supports** and the **line of redoubts** will generally be well placed on the reverse slope. However, avoid the hollows where asphyxiating gases accumulate.

In any case, if the first line is on the reverse slope there is immediate neccessity of observation posts in front of the crest or a very active mobile watch (patrols).

Flanking. — **Above all, good flanking is to be effectively obtained along the whole front. A firing line is less defended by direct than by flanking fire.**

Efficacy of flanking is such that it will often be recommanded to **prepare at first only the flanking devices of a position**, and to build the position itself later on.

By breaks in the trace, construction of salients and reentrants adapted to the features of the ground, the various centers of resistance, the strong points and the segments of these strong points will be made to mutually flank each other.

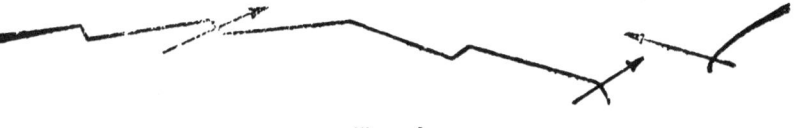

Fig. 205.

As soon as the main site of the firing line has been chosen **close flanking devices** must be traced.

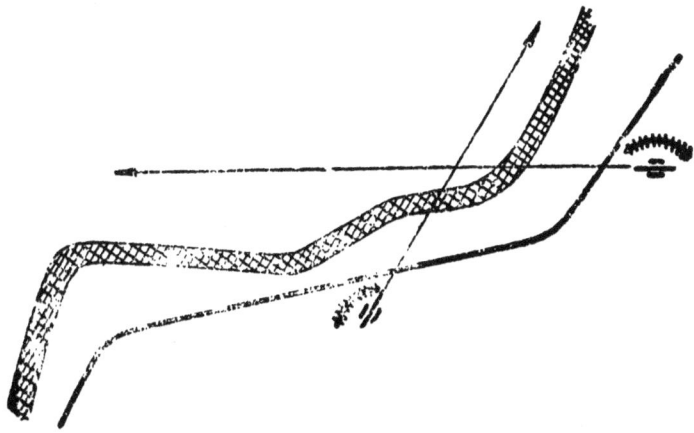

Fig. 206.

These close flanking devices are designed in such a way as to sweep **each element** of the front lengthwise, and as far as possible to sweep the **exterior edge of obstacles.** They must be prepared so as not to accidentally open fire on friendly elements and so as to be protected against front fire from the enemy.

Fig. 207.

The traces giving the most effective flankings are indented and bastion traces. They will be adopted for such part of the ground as can be leisurely prepared (line of supports, line of redoubts of first, intermediate and second lines).

The first line, on the contrary, is generally built during the fight. Officers in command scarcely have control and can not trace the trench. Flanking can be obtained only later on by devices usually designed by officers **commanding companies and platoons.**

For instance, dig a small trench straight ahead with a parados, give it a few rifles or a machine-gun and look out for enfilading fire. (Fig. 207).

Dig out a circular trench-element projecting from the parapet and around a traverse. (Fig. 208).

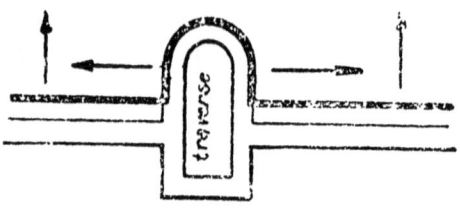

Fig. 208.

Turn the communicating trench leading to a small post into a firing-trench (Fig. 209).

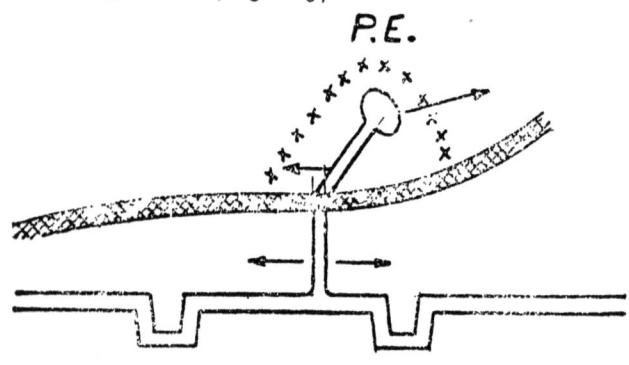

Fig. 209.

If a little earth-work has been pushed forward, in view of sweeping a dead angle or a depression, use the communicating trench leading to it in the same way for flanking the main front. (Fig. 210).

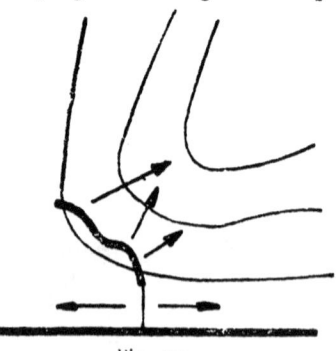

Fig. 210.

The machine-gun is, above all others, the best possible flanking arm. — A machine-gun must be sheltered. The emplacement or the shelter must be concealed so that the machine gun may be intact when a close attack is delivered.

A large number of emplacements should be prepared, either armored emplacements, manned continuously, or emplacements under splinter-proof shelters only manned when needed, by machine guns kept close by under bomb-proof shelters.

Pits in open ground completely seperated from the trace of the trench, and communicating with the trench by underground saps, are also to be advocated (Fig. 212).

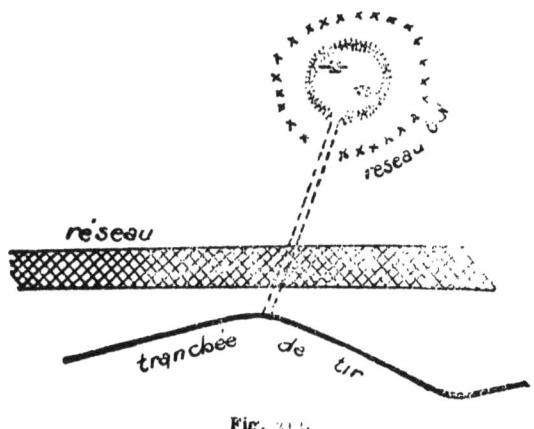

Fig. 212.

The distribution of machine-guns between the first line support trenches and the line of redoubts is explained in Chap. V of Part IV.

Flanking from one center to a neighboring center by means of a machine-gun, a 37 or a 75 gun, is ordered by the superior commanding officer.

Devices for sorties. — Sortie-steps (Fig. 213) enable troops to get up to the open ground either to the rear of

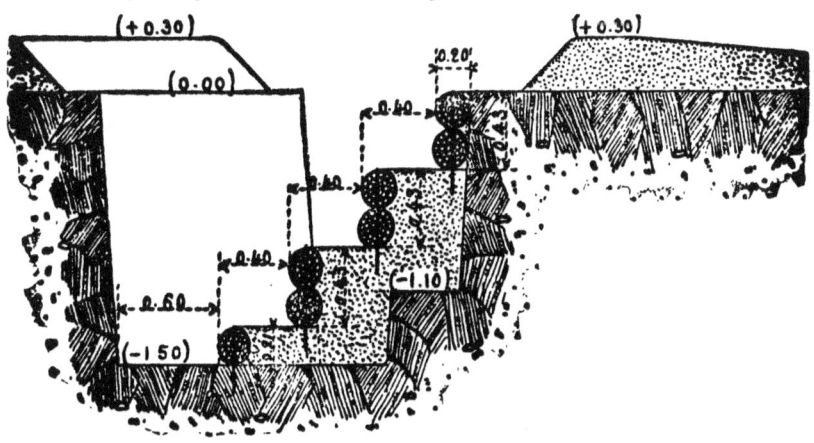

Fig. 213. — Sortie steps.

the trench or along the approach trenches, or even in a paralled of departure, in view of assault.

— 200 —

In the latter case, **sortie ladders** should be substituted for sortie steps for their use does not necessitate widening the trench.

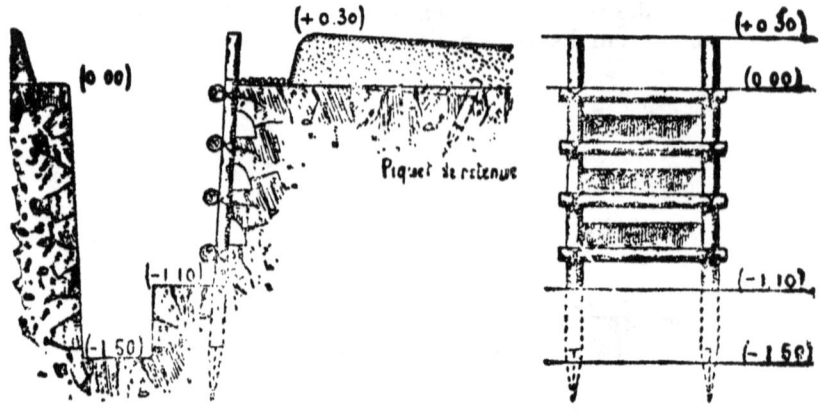

Fig. 214. — Sortie ladder.

Stakes measuring from three to four inches in diameter, may also be used, driven vertically close to the back slope, and better still in the re-entrant angle of a traverse. They should rise some two feet above the banquette. A man puts one foot on the top of the stake, the other foot on the berm, and leaps over the parapet.

Steps are replaced by a ramp if no means are at hand for strengthening the steps. Ramps leave the appproach trenches parallel to the firing-trench.

Obstacles. — The obstacles are described in « School of Sap » (wire entanglements and chevaux de frise). Other obstacles may be added.

Low wire entanglements. — Posts of an average diameter of two inches emerge one foot above the ground.

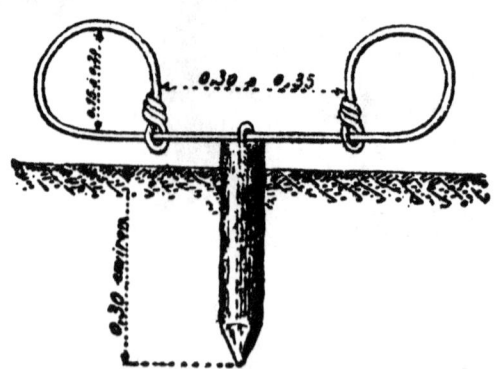

Fig. 215. — Double loop.

They are bound together in all directions by wire 3-4 $^{m/m}$ thick or by barbed wire. Crops render such an entanglement invisible, even at short range.

Loops of fine wire. (Fig. 215, 216, 217). A simple loop is obtained in making a clove hitch, or half hitch, tying both turns together, and fastening to the ground, so as to keep the loop standing erect.

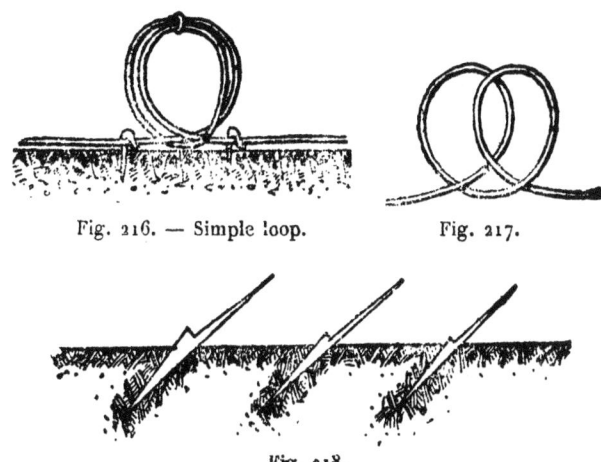

Fig. 216. — Simple loop.   Fig. 217.

Fig. 218.

Crows's feet with four or six points.

Isolated wire on the ground and fixed here and there by posts or staples.

Wire stretched between trees in a wood.

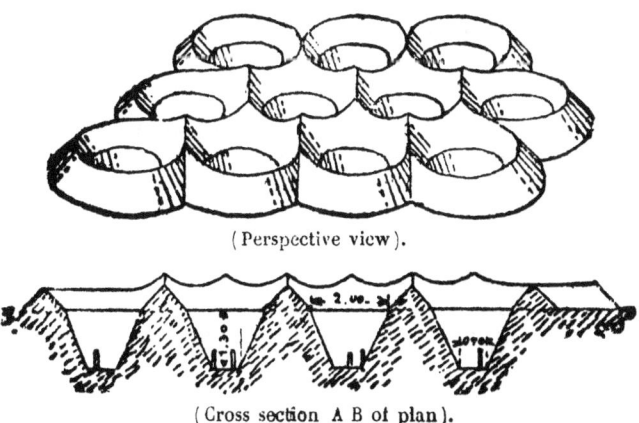

(Perspective view).

(Cross section A B of plan).
Fig. 219. — Trous de loup.

Abatis and slashings. (Fig. 220, 221.)

Sharpened and fire hardened pickets obliquely driven into the ground by pounding on little prepared shoulders.

These obstacles should be placed so as to fulfill the following conditions :

1° Be hidden from observation from the ground or from air scouts, and, if possible, be concealed behind a natural or an artificial embankment giving protection from the enemy's artillery fire.

Fig. 220.

2° Be placed from 30 to 50 yards in front of the trenches **so that** a destruction fire on the trench whould not hit them, and vice versa. The same distance protects from **flame projectors.**

3° Be perfectly and entirely swept by fire from the firing line. **An obstacle not swept by fire has no value.** The enemy comes and destroys it without danger.

4° **Be traced quite independently from the trace of the firing line** so as to baffle the enemy's range finding. Trace all necessary salients so that flank fire will sweep the exterior edge of the obstacles.

Fig. 221.

5° Be so arranged as to form **several lines** 5 or 10 yards apart rather than a single line. For instance, if wire entanglements are to be constructed, make two of them 10 to 15 yards deep, rather than a single one 20 to 30 yards deep. **The most distant entanglement is to**

be constructed first. The depth of the entanglements should be greater in front of the **passive** than in front of the **active** parts of the line.

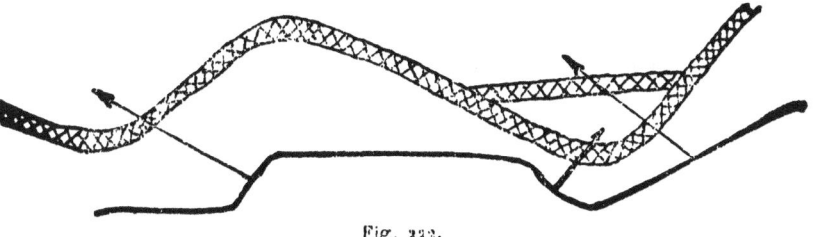

Fig. 222.

6° Provide **passages** for the issue of sentries, patrols, etc. Such passages are established in zigzags across the entanglements and provided with movable obstacles close at hand (fig. 223).

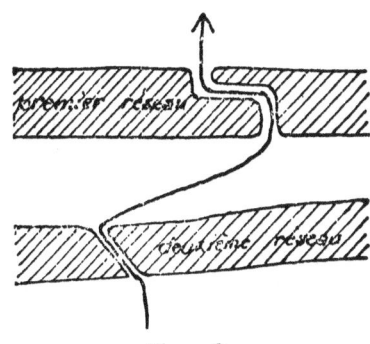

Fig. 223.

7° Be closely **watched** at night by means of listening-posts, dug in on the edge of the obstacles, or beyond it and protected by obstacles. Such posts are connected to the trench by means of communicating trenches dug under the entanglements and are ready to give the alarm by signals, bells, shots, etc.

Before an offensive, obstacles are to be removed to give passage to assaulting waves. Crow's feet, loops, etc., irregularly strewn on the ground, are hard to find, and hinder the attack.

Dummy trenches. — It is always a good thing to dig **dummy trenches,** i. e., extra trenches not intended to be held, so as to deceive hostile observation, whether from the ground or from the air, and to baffle the enemy as to the real occupation of a position and the distribution of the troops.

Often, indeed, a good scheme is to locate them as a trap for the enemy, in case he should try to gain a footing in them. For that purpose dummy trenches may be made out of straight parts, completely enfiladed by the real trenches. Should the enemy get to them he would be wiped out quickly by the fire of rifles or machine-guns properly concealed.

As an example the following arrangement, to be used in the first line, may be given (fig. 224).

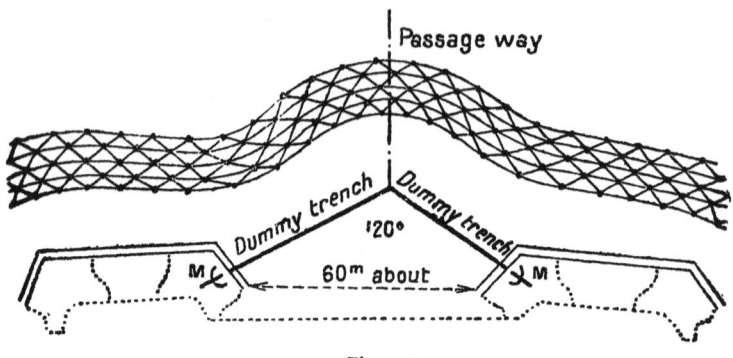

Fig. 224.

In the interval between two trenches 60 yards apart, dig a dummy trench in the shape of a redan, the two flanks being swept by machine-guns. From the salient towards the enemy prepare a bit of sap which will serve as bait.

Dummy trenches can also be prepared as passive obstacles if they are filled with wire entanglements.

The damage inflicted by artillery on dummy trenches should be repaired so as to prolong the illusion of the enemy.

Ground observation.

Company observers. — 1° **In the trenches, when simply holding, observation must be uninterrupted as well as during combat.** Each company must therefore organize **observation posts.** Such posts should be concealed, should not project above the parapet and should look out on the important parts of the enemy's first line assigned to the watch of that company.

Observers should endeavor to see all that is going on, and to perceive the slightest sign. They do not necessarily stand in the first-line trenches or in listening posts. Often points will be found in the rear offering an excellent view and calling less attention from the enemy. Salients, from which a more extended view may be obtained, are also favorable places for observation.

2° In addition to this normal and continuous observation duty, the duty of **watchmen during the attacks** must be foreseen.

During attack, defense has no other security but that given by an observation system able to work under the most intensive bombardment.

As a rule a watchman is placed close to each shelter. He takes his post as soon as a heavy bombardment forces the men to get into the shelter and foretells a probable attack. The latter observation post must be armored and protected by all possible means and must offer sure connection with the shelter for giving alarm. The watchman's duty is to warn when the enemy increases the range and is about to rush the trenches. Officers and non-commissioned officers, when attack is threatening, come and occupy the same shelters as their men. They must be able to keep an eye on the watchman and replace him if he is disabled.

The defense relies entirely on this organization. Should it fail, the men, overtaken in their shelters, could not use their means of resistance.

The same emplacements for the watchmen can, moreover, be used for both missions just explained. Shelters can be dug beside the emplacements for **continuous observation**, instead of being dug anywhere and leaving the observation posts to be looked for afterwards.

Location of watchmen. — Should there be a lack of time or of material means, or should it be feared that shelter posts disclose the position, watchmen will be installed uncovered hiding their heads behind bush-wood or grass clumps.

In day time, observation takes place through loopholes of different shapes (fig. 193 to 198), or by means of periscopes (fig. 138 and 139). For watching certain points it is often sufficient to bore a circular hole through the parapet with the help of a stick or of a metallic tube.

Fig. 125.

Observation with a field glass is possible only if the loopholes are four inches wide.

In order to avoid a changing of light and shadow due to movements behind the loophole, a simple means, in open posts, is to **stretch a piece of cloth behind the watchman and over his head.**

At night the watchman should observe **over the parapet.** If the emplacement is high enough the observation loophole will be placed on solid soil and the banquette

Fig. 226.

will be cut off directly under the loophole. At night the watchman climbs on the part of the banquette that has not been cut off (fig. 225 and 226),

Armored observation posts are metallic recesses or sentry boxes (fig. 153 and 154). They may also be built in accordance with fig. 227 and 228.

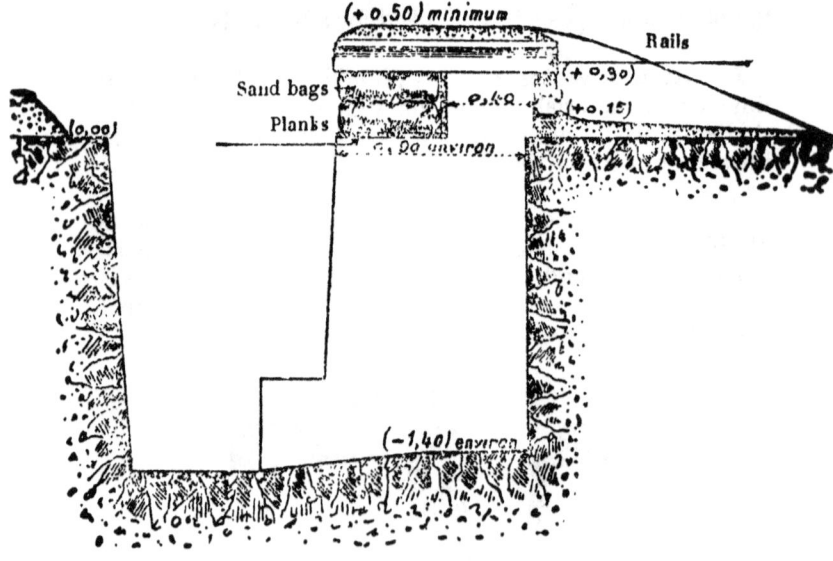

Fig. 227. — Observation post.

Organization of ground observation in a sector. — From a general point of view ground observation is methodically organized in the whole sector of the division so as to complete and to control aerial observation. No matter how complete the latter may be, it is always intermittent (photography, etc.)

— 207 —

Plan of observation, indispensable appendix to **plan of defense**, indicates **commander's observation posts** and **artillery observation posts**.

The latter are in turn divided into **intelligence observation posts**, with very extended views, and **observation post for adjustment of fire** having shorter views.

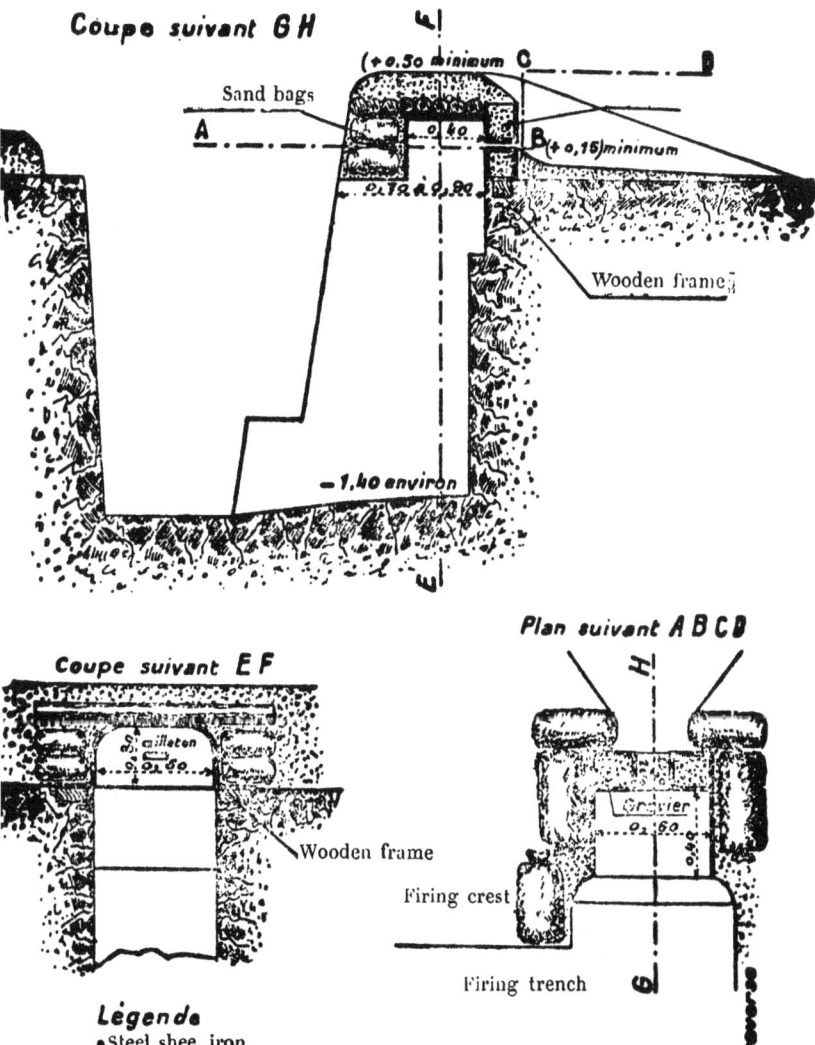

Fig. 228. — Observation post.

Plan of observation includes :

1° A general map of the location of the observation stations clearly indicating the zone observed by each one of them.

2° A panorama of each one of the observation stations.

3° A drawing of telephonic connections between observation stations, and the corresponding posts of command.

4° A general description of the workings of the observation service (the stations which are permanently and temporarily occupied, the personnel of each of them, special regulations of some of the observation posts, contribution of artillery observation stations to the observatories of the commander, transmission of information, etc.)

An observation station should be convenient, sheltered and concealed path leading to it included).

An observation station should be provided with

1° Special instructions (personnel attached to the station, duty roster, sector to be watched, transmission of information, points of the sector which are to be watched with special care, precautions to be taken by visitors **of any rank**).

2° An observation station notebook in which all observations made should be written **immediately.**

3° An up-to-date copy of the battlemap on a 1/5,000 scale, and, if possible, a copy of the 1/10,000 or the 1/20,000 scale, each with German organization only.

4° A map of the ground seen from the observation station.

5° Material for observation.

Observers are trained in reading precisely maps and panoramas, in searching a terrain methodically and in giving complete and precise explanation of their observations.

They **immediately report** any preparation of attack from the enemy. They note all signs of activity, all change in the aspect of the lines, and send every day, at prescribed times, an extract of their " observation-station notebook ".

In each regiment the **intelligence officer** assembles and discusses all reports. He delivers them to the colonel and brings the battle map up to date (scale 1/5,000). Interesting information is handed over to the generals and then to the information bureau of the army corps.

B. *Organization of support trenches.*

Support trenches are located 150 or 200 yards in the rear of first line trenches and **should have them within range** as much as possible.

Such a distance is sufficient for the two " echelons "

of trenches not to be hit by the same destruction-fire. In the case of a rush on the first line the garrison has the time to make use of all the fighting devices foreseen in the **plan of defense.**

The organization of the support trench should be quite similar to that of the first-line trench, the former being designed with a view to replacing the latter in case the enemy should capture the first-line trench.

This rule is general and applies to all successive " echelons " of trenches in the rear of the first line, i. e. cover trenches, support trenches, redoubts, etc. As any trench may at some future time become a first-line trench, it must be prepared **beforehand** to fulfill this role, Moreover, main communicating trenches connecting different lines must be defensively organized and girded with wire-entanglements. Should a momentary withdrawal occur, entanglements, loopholes, flanking-devices, machine-gun emplacements, observation posts, shelters, etc,: can not be built during the course of the struggle, nor can gaps be remedied at such times.

On the contrary, if successive lines are provided with all that is wanted, a real **partition** of the ground will have been realized, further advance of the enemy will be stopped, and strong systems will be held, enabling counter-attacks from the flanks and from the front.

There should be no excuse for not rendering a support trench much stronger than a firing trench, since tracing, digging, constructing wire-entanglements, etc., is much easier in the former trench than in the latter. Likewise, in what concerns its tactical role, the support trench should be better than a mere cover trench which is situated 100 or 150 yards in the rear of the firing trench. The trace of the latter can rarely be planned methodically and is difficult to change. On the contrary, the trace of the support trench must endeavor to realize a perfect system of defense, and, to accomplish this, all the advantages presented by the ground must be carefully considered whether it gets closer or farther from the first line.

Also it is the real defense-trench; the one that is chosen and organized at will under the protection given by the firing trench. Under such circumstances it must be unbreachable.

Like the firing trench, the support trench is not occupied entirely; it contains passive and active portions, the latter lying, logically, behind passive portions of the first line.

C. *Organization of a redoubt.*

When a center of resistance is completed by a redoubt the latter should be entirely closed and girded with wire-entanglements. Its distance from the support line varies greatly. A redoubt is designed for offering the utmost resistance, even when entirely surrounded. Therefore, it must have fields of fire in every direction, shelter, a first-aid station, and depots supplied with such water, food and ammunition as is necessary for several days. The garrison will vary from one to several platoons commanded by an energetic leader.

Each of its faces are ordinary firing trenches but traverses and parados must be increased in number against enfilade and reverse fire.

Occupation of a strong point. — The regular garrison of a strong point is one company. The following distribution is recommanded : a captain may assign three platoons to hold the front, each platoon to be distributed so that part will be in the advanced line, and part in the support-line, guarding one or two active segments in each of these lines.

The support platoon is kept together in the support line or in the redoubt (fig 268). In such a way the advanced line is manned by a quarter or a third of the total effective, which is the regular proportion of outposts.

Details of duty are given in the chapter " Infantry in the trenches " (Part VII).

As for the distribution of automatic-rifles, machine guns and trench-mortars, it is given in the chapters containing the tactical properties of these arms.

Communications. — Communicating trenches (boyaus) constitute the artificial means of communication enabling the fighting line to constantly receive all kinds of supply such as men, ammunition, food, etc., and also permitting the carrying out of the wounded.

In the advanced zone, communicating and approach trenches exist in great numbers, rendering movements of supporting troops, assaulting troops and reserves easier.

To the rear this number is less.

Their number is never too great, but their system remains simple and clear and may be used by troops having made only a summary reconnaissance.

The necessity of tracing communicating trenches, so as to insure rapid circulation by night as well as by day, can not be insisted on too strongly. There should be no obstruction, nothing to catch the clothing. Every obstacle should be levelled and every hole filled up. The secret of holding large fronts with small effectives lies in the ability of supports to hasten **with great speed** to a threatened point. If such speed cannot be relied on, the officer in command does not lessen the garrison of the first line and useless fatigue is imposed on the companies.

In the interior of a position, boyaus are **emergency defense-devices** and are organized accordingly.

The name of the boyaux is more specially given to communications leading towards the enemy (approach trenches); the names of **parallels** or **transversals** to communications parallel to the front.

Profile. — A regular communicating trench is a little over two yards deep, and one yard wide at the bottom (fig. 43). These dimensions fit the **main communicating trenches leading to the front.** They may be reduced respectively to 68 and 32 inches for **secondary communicating trenches.**

To lessen conspicuousness a deep sap is resorted to (fig. 44). It is covered up by some earth on hurdles if it is to be concealed entirely.

The width of the **main evacuation trench** may be greater. A stretcher must be carried along it without difficulty. It must be insisted upon. The width is increased to five feet for passage of columns of twos, and to eight feet for passage of carts, Decauville trucks, etc. In the latter case the depth must be increased to ten feet.

If the soil is soft the interior slope should be less steep and the width at the top increased.

The trace. — Approach trenches lead in the general

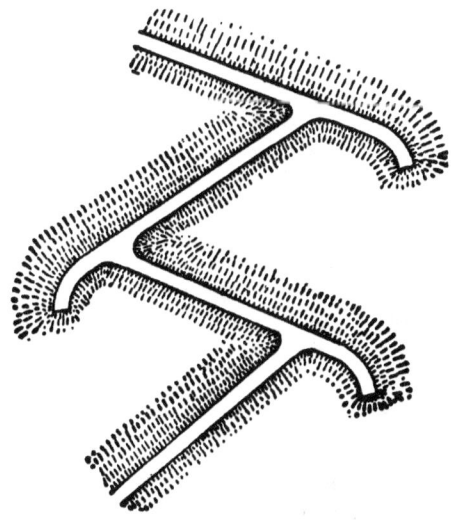

Fig. 229. — Zigzag trace.

direction to the enemy. They are, therefore, greatly **exposed to enfilade fire.**

They can never be too deep and winding, especially on slopes facing the enemy, or when the enemy is on higher ground.

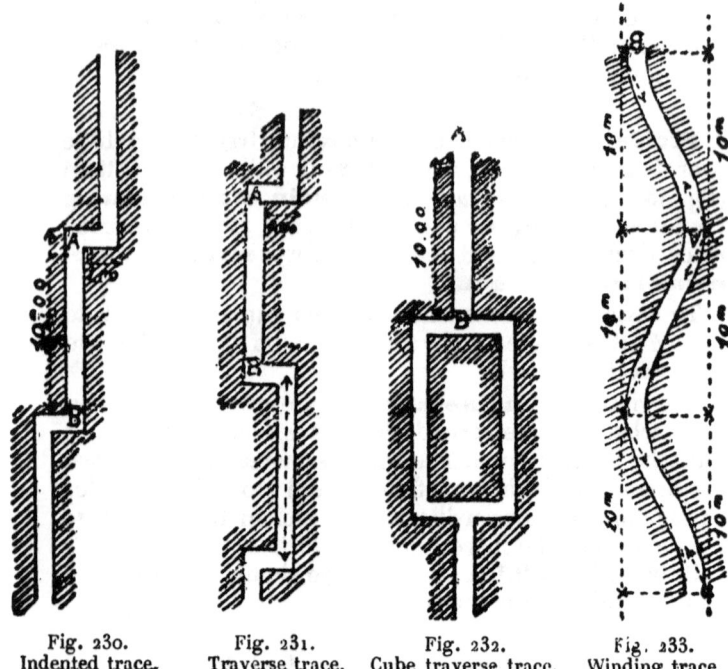

Fig. 230. Indented trace.   Fig. 231. Traverse trace.   Fig. 232. Cube traverse trace.   Fig. 233. Winding trace.

In certain points protection can be expected only in deep, covered saps (fig. 234).

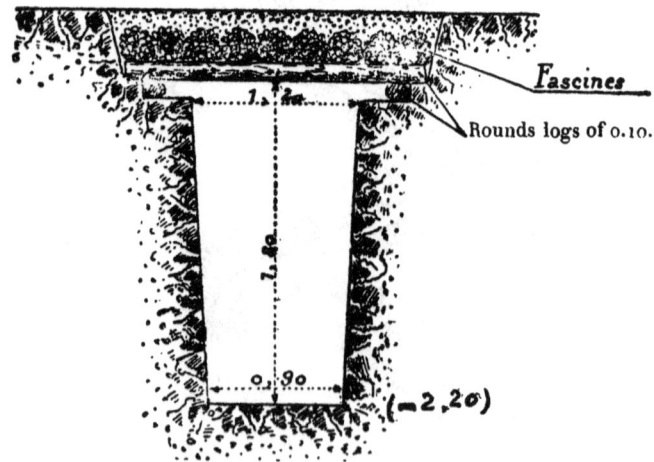

Fig. 234. — Deep covered sap.

The zigzag trace (fig. 229) gives a good protection against enfilade but its length is greatly increased.

When a straight line trace is rendered necessary by the ground, any one of the traces of fig. 230, 231, 232 and

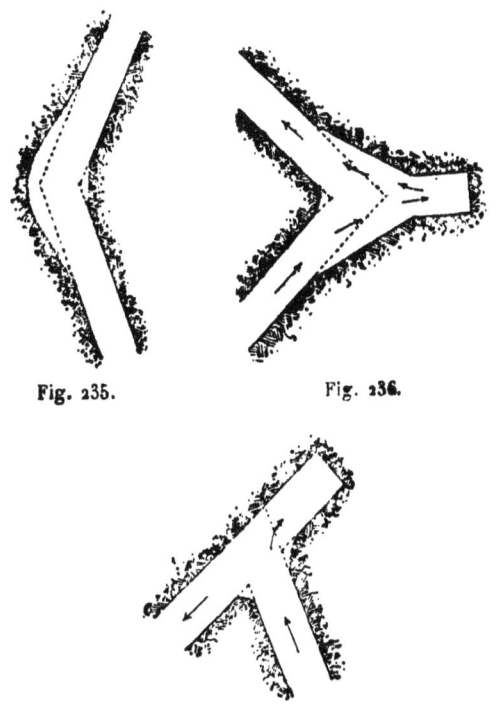

Fig. 235.   Fig. 236.

Fig. 237.

33 is adopted. Circulation must be made easy at the bends as shown in fig. 235, 236 and 237.

Evacuation trenches are always traces without traverses.

Miscellaneous devices. — Every 100 yards **sortie steps** should be provided, and more often, **turn-outs**, long enough to hold a stretcher and both stretcher bearers.

There should be wide sortie steps (fig. 213) at the points where approach trenches are to be used as assembly places for counter-attacks, according to the suppositions made in the "plan of defense".

Give to the approach trenches the same name or the same number, from the beginning to the advanced parallel. Secondary approach trenches and traversals are given names in series differing from the series adopted for main approach trenches.

Crossings receive such appliances as to allow any-one, ouce he has entered the approach trench, to be guided by it to the advanced parallel. A good means is to change the level at the place where a transversal or a branch line runs into the main communicating trench, or to fix a small log across the transversal.

Where a transversal crosses, an overhead passage should be established. Sortie steps should also be built on both sides of the transversal, so as not to block entirely side movement should two colums meet.

Approach trenches and transversals should be marked by means of sufficiently numerous signboards, the shape dimensions, color, etc. being different for the main, secondary, up and down approach trenches and transversals.

These signs are placed at the entrance into the communicating trenches, at every crossing and branch, and at sortie steps. Arrows indicate the direction of permitted traffic.

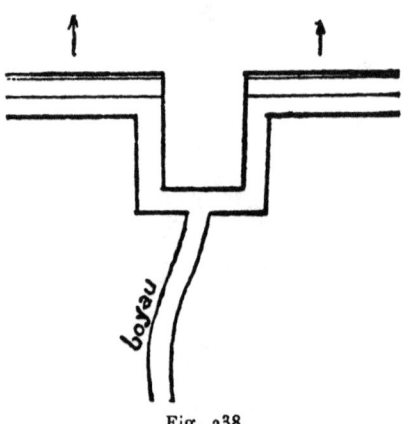

Fig. 238.

In each main approach trench circulation is allowed in one direction only (except for certain authorized isolated men, runners, etc.) A strict policy of circulation is organized.

Berms enable one to jump over approach trenches and transversals, and permit the easy placing of gangways or bridges. It is always a good thing to double each main approach trench, by use of a sufficient number of gangways, with a path in the open, which may be used at night.

When reaching the firing-trench, communicating trenches should always end behind a traverse (fig. 238).

Defensive organization of boyaus. — Approach trenches must contribute to checking at every point an enemy who may have gained a hold on the advanced trench.

They are, here and there, prepared as a firing trench by means of firing steps or sniper's recesses. In this way they flank, by means of rifles or of machines-guns, all the ground between the parallels (fig. 239).

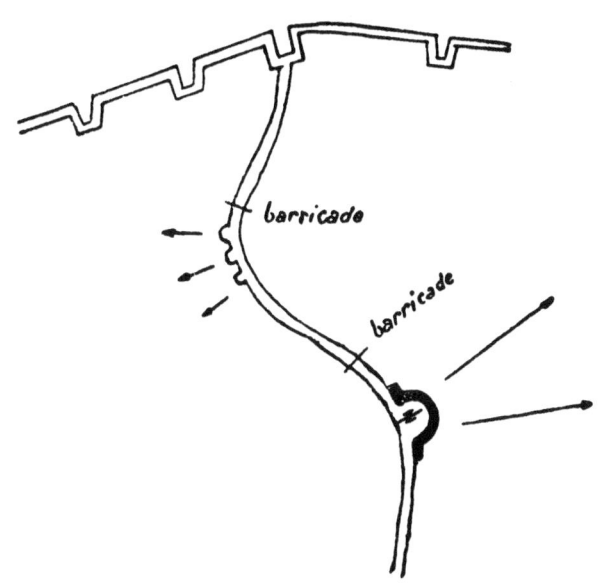

Fig. 239.

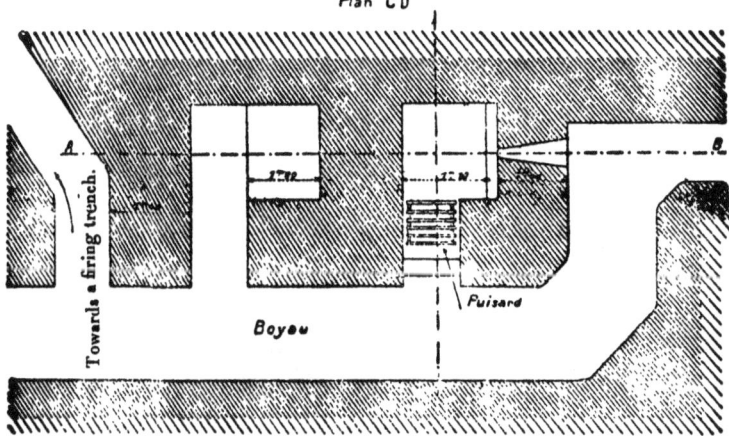

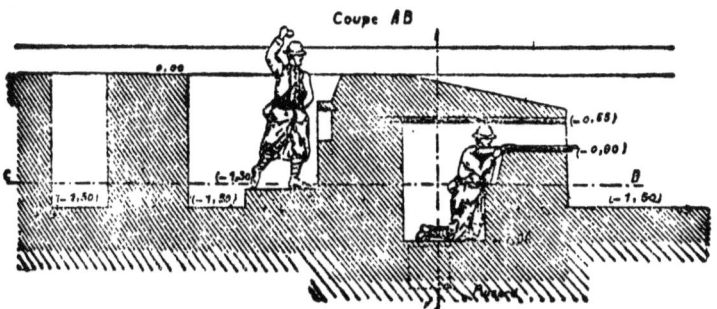

Fig. 240.

Foot by foot interior defense is prepared. Barricades, loopholed traverses and stands for grenadiers, are provided at places enabling enfilading fire on all sufficiently long branches of the boyaux.

Fig. 240 gives an example.

These branches may extend to a length of 50 yards and be terminated in defensive devices. Such a distance keeps them out of range of grenades, even should the enemy have been able to construct a barricade on the other end of the branch.

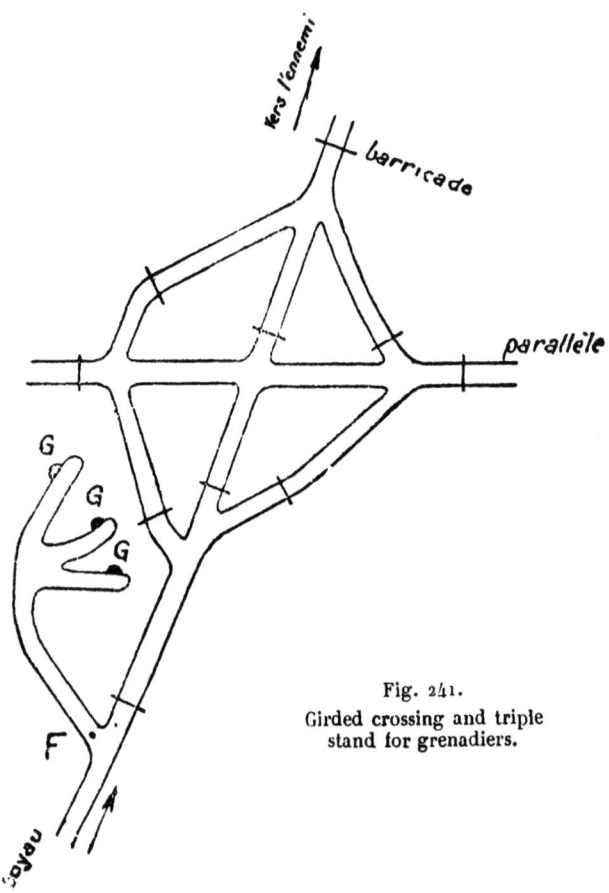

Fig. 241.
Girded crossing and triple stand for grenadiers.

Means of obstruction (hedgehogs, gabions, etc.) are prepared to keep the enemy under the fire of these interior flank works.

An advisable device is shown in fig. 241. It consists in the systematic girding of all crossings. Each center of communication is changed into a veritable earthwork, forming one of the active elements of the whole, and may be confided to a group or a half group. Barricades will provide a passage easy to be filled up in case of attack. The enemy will be obliged to rush them one after another in order to advance.

Double or triple **stands for bombers** may be prepared at any place when a thoroughfare is to be disputed (fig. 241). The small trench leading to it will be defended by the assistant grenadiers.

Recesses for grenades are prepared as illustrated in fig. 42, or by means of a gabion horizontally buried in the side of the slope.

All these devices of preparation and defensive organization are in charge of the company occupying the strong point.

Shelters.

1° Bomb-proof shelters.

Shelter has value only when the men can **hold out in it and get out of it in time.**

The only shelters to be considered in an organization are bomb-proof shelters, and especially dug-outs, under six yards of solid soil, as has been explained in the School of sap (Part II, chap. VII).

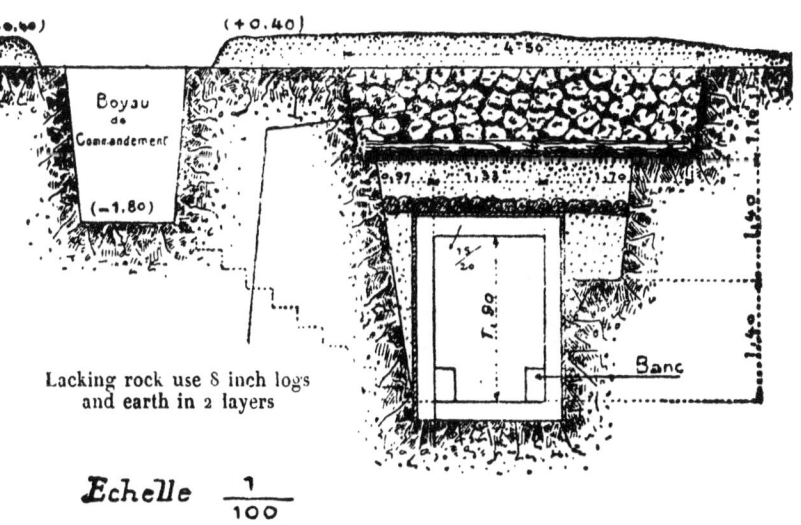

Fig. 241 bis.

Shelters dug in the open in loose ground, with roofs built out of transported earth and logs or rails, should only be used in special cases. If the underground is damp they should be used and also for observations posts, casements for machine guns, etc.

They need more material than dug-outs but are built more rapidly, if they are dug freely in the open. To such shelters must be given the greatest possible strength without visibility.

To provide shelter against a 105 gun (4 inches), they should offer :

One bed of joined rails covered with earth one yard thick.

One explosion layer composed of timber, cement, bags, thick corrugated iron and sand, stones, etc.

Armor for a 150 gun (6 inches) demands :

Two beds of rails separated by one-half a yard of earth.

Two explosion layers, as above described, separated by half a yard or a yard of earth.

Or else one bed of joining rails surmounted by a layer of concrete one yard thick.

The explosion layer may be constituted by one or two layers of concrete flag-stones such as are constructed by the armies.

Generally speaking, one yard of solid soil is equivalent to one bed of logs 6 to 8 inches thick surmounted by loose earth one yard thick.

Fig. 241 *bis* shows an example of a bomb proof shelter dug in the open. Such shelters always give way after a while under the weight of their protection and do not last as long as well-built dug-outs.

Whatever the system, the shelters must be provided with **several entrances** (at least two) facing towards the side opposite the enemy. Precautions against gas must be taken as prescribed (See Chap. XIV, Part III).

It is better to organize a great number of small shelters for squads or half-platoons than a small number of large shelters. During artillery preparation the officers must be divided among the shelters of their men, instead of getting together in the same shelter.

A good arrangement consists in digging two small dug-outs on each side of a traverse, each entrance being located at least two yards from the traverse. They are immediately connected by means of a mine gallery; one yard square. Later on, the gallery can be enlarged so as to constitute a single large shelter (fig. 242).

Each shelter should possess ;

A shovel and a pick allowing one to clear the entrance in case it were obstructed.

Some grenades, to permit the occupants to sally out by force if the enemy has invaded the trench.

Devices for ventilation, heating and bedding.

Devices for observation (long periscope), for connection with the watchman, for defense of entrance to the shelter (see fig. 277).

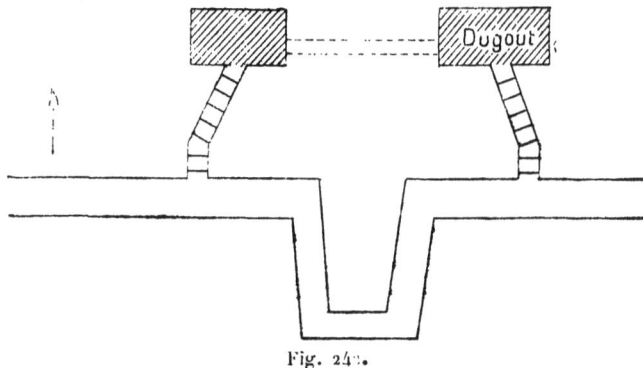

Fig. 242.

Location of the shelters. — Shelters should seldom be constructed in the firing trench; but rather in the circulating trench, or, if the latter does not exist, in small

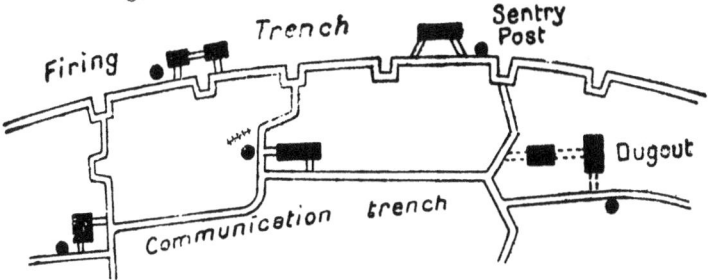

Fig. 243.

special transversals connected with the firing trenches be means of two communicating trenches, or more. Other shelters will be located in the support-trenches, designed for the platoons reserved for counter-attacks. Their location depends upon the location of **sentinel posts**. The most favorable points for locating the latter must first be chosen. The shelter will be constructed in close proximity to one of these posts.

The number of these shelters must be great enough to allow the whole garrison (excluding observation sentries) to find there an **entire refuge and stay there under the heaviest fire**

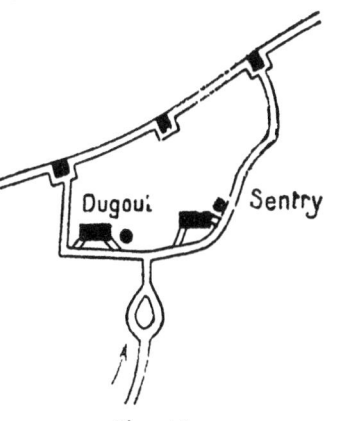

Fig. 244.

of the enemy. Therefore, a company will generally have six or seven shelters for half-platoons, part in the cover trench, and part in the support-trench.

2° Light shelters.

Apart from **bomb-proof** shelters, which are indispensible on the first line and which must be constructed there without delay; the other lines and the emplacements for reserves must have **light shelters.** These will, while awaiting better-ones afford **protection against shell-fragments** and bad weather.

Such shelters are constructed, either in the trench] that is, by using the excavation itself (covered trench), or beside the trench. Fig. 245, 246, 247, 248 and 250 give all

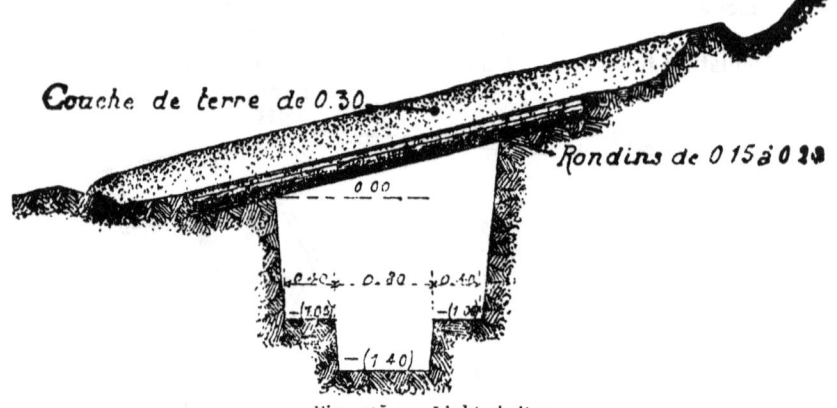

Fig. 245. — Light shelter.

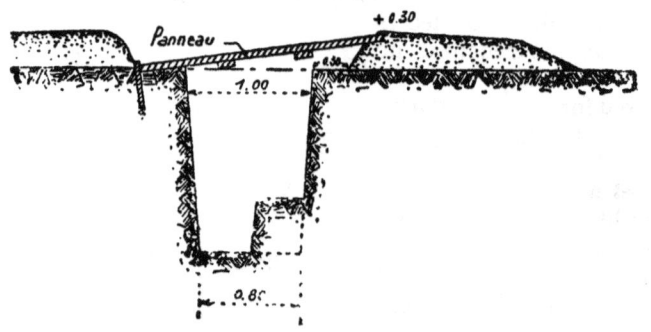

Fig. 246. — Covered trench.

necessary indications. Available time and material should determine which type to use.

They are mere shifts, of a temporary character, because weather rapidly ruins them.

The working parties should avoid forfeiting the solidity of the parapet and diminishing the length of the firing-crest.

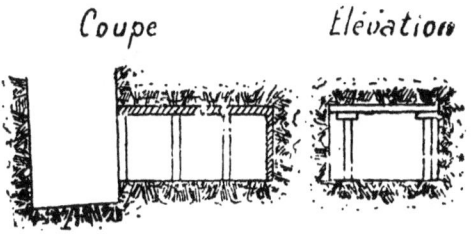

Fig. 247. — Recess for one man with wooden ceiling on supports.

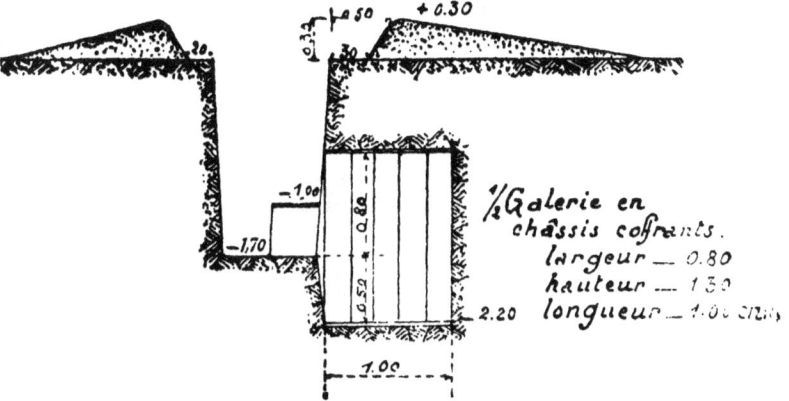

Fig. 248. — Recess for 2 men seated.

Fig. 250.

When the soil is loose or liable to crack by frost, recesses should always be lined.

Sheds, panels, etc , should not be fixed for good but should be easy to remove to make room for riflemen.

For **shell-fragment and shrapnel-proof shelters** a layer of earth one foot thick on a support of light logs or planks must be used.

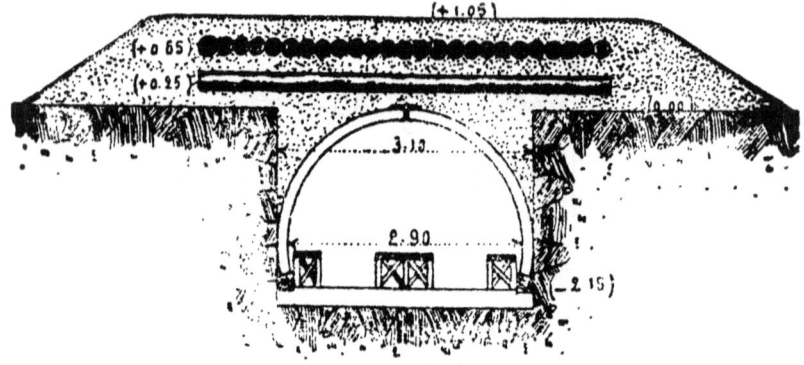

Fig. 252. — Arched iron shelter.

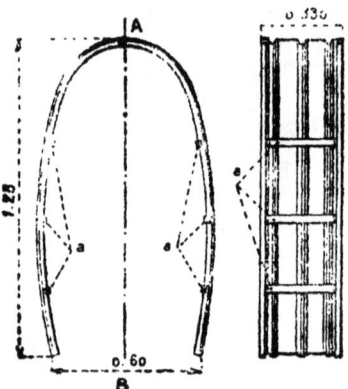

Fig. 253. — Element of light shelter of corrugated iron.

3° Sheet iron shelters.

There are:

1° Arched sheets of corrugated iron, affording construction behind the lines of shelters typified in fig. 252;

2° Elements of light corrugated iron shelters, one millimeter thick and weighing 21 pounds (10 kilogs) [fig. 253]. Strips «a» ending in a hook permits them to be fixed together.

They are covered with earth.

They permit prompt construction of a shelter during an attack.

4° Re-inforced shelters.

So-called re-inforced shelters are to be excluded from any organization. There is no intermediary between light shelter and bomb-proof shelter.

Should it be found impossible to plan the digging out of heavy shelters, it would be better to scatter the men in numerous light shelters, than to assemble them in one insufficient shelter, though re-inforced. Should time be available to construct a so-called re-inforced shelter, the latter should not be constructed, but a deep dug-out should be begun.

Posts of command. — Telephone posts. — First aid stations. — Ammunition depots. — These posts or depots differ from other shelters only by their dimensions and interior.

The choice of the **observing post** for the commander always precedes the choice of his **post of command** which must be close to it. If possible, place it also close to a main communicating trench. Take all necessary precautions (signboards, lanterns, orderlies, etc.), to make it possible for the liaison agents not belonging to the unit to find it by day or by night.

Telephone stations join the observing post or the commanding post. **They are doubled by optical stations, which can be substituted for them immediately.**

In every post of command an incendiary grenade should be provided in order to destroy all the papers in the post, were the latter to be evacuated suddenly.

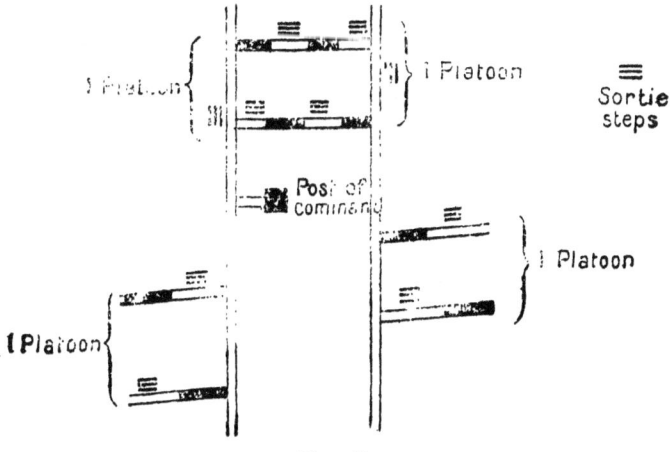

Fig. 244.

First-aid stations and shelters for the wounded are cost by the evacuation trenches.

Avoid establishing in the communicating trench itself, any organization that may oblige men to stop (tool distribution, etc.); and thus make circulation slower.

Places d'armes. — «Places d'armes» are designed to permit the assembly of all the supports and reserves under cover for a relatively short time. They may be constituted by parallels in existence or to be made, on either side of the approach trenches. They are well located, near the line of redoubts where they may be near shelter.

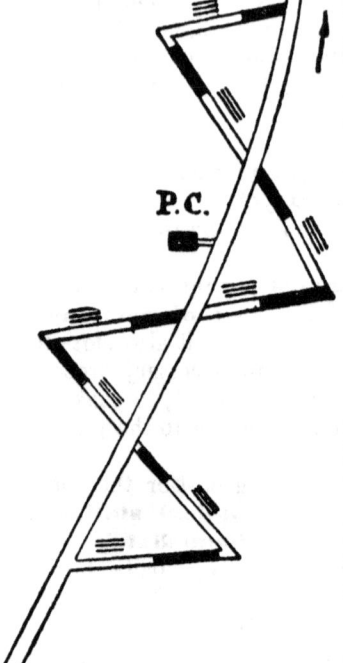

Fig. 255.

They must:

Avoid dividing up the various units.

Have easy access to the open ground (steps), and to the communicating trenches.

Have shelters (covered shelters, command post, etc.) a water depôt and latrines.

Not distinguish themselves by their exterior aspect from the remainder of the organization.

The choice of the location of «places d'armes» depends upon the role given to the units that will occupy them. Manoeuver being slow when marching, in the boyaux and it being important to shorten the distance over swept ground, it becomes necessary to place the «places d'armes» close to the parallels of attack.

Working order. — The plan of the work to be executed is determined by the commander.

When rapid organization on newly conquered territory is necessary the following order of urgence holds :

1° Arrange flanking devices.

2° Begin the digging of the trenches.

3° Construct at the same time wire entanglements, the observing station and shelters (and latrines).

4° Open communications to the sides and to the rear (begin the approach trenches from the front).

5° Finish up the trenches.

CHAPTER VII.

IDEAS RELATIVE TO THE TACTICAL QUALITIES OF THE DIFFERENT ARMS AND OF THE STAFF SERVICE.

Artillery.

The artillery acts exclusively by the power of its fire; its rang allows it to act directly in support of the troops which are in front of it and also to open cross and flanking fires in favor of neighboring troops (concentration of fire).

The artillery cannot by its fire alone drive away the enemy from the position he holds; the infantry takes advantage of the artillery effect to advance. These two sister services must therefore be permanently and narrowly in *liaison*. The liaison is at the same time the resulting work of the high command, of the gunner and of the infantryman.

Different kinds of artillery. — Viz. :

A. **Trench artillery**, which fires at short ranges large amounts of explosives (58, 150, 240, 340 mm. mortars).

B. **Field artillery** (75, 80 and 90 mm.), which can be moved from place to place at any speed on any ground, and which is instantly brought into action. The 75 mm. gun has a range approximating 7000 meters. Field artillery is used against troops, to break up auxiliary defenses and against enemy batteries within its range.

C. **Heavy artillery**, which is not easily displaced and which necessitates a certain amount of preliminary work to bring it into battery before it can begin to fire. When it has means of displacement of its own (horses, motor tractors) it is called *Heavy Field Artillery*. When it has no means of transport it is called *Fixed Heavy Artillery*. Heavy artillery owes its value to the weight of its projectile which has a crushing effect, to the quantity of explosives that it fires, and, for some of the guns, to their long range.

The *long guns* are chiefly intended, owing to their range, to fire at objectives far away (batteries, observation posts, and communication trenches, etc.).

The *short guns*, or *mortars*, owing to their curved fire, can reach depressed objectives (batteries, trenches, or barbed wire entanglements on counter slopes) and owing to their crushing effect upset shelters, casemates or P. C., etc.

The long guns are the 95, '105, 120 and the 155 mm. The short guns are the 155 mm. and the mortars of 220 and 270 mm.

D. **High power artillery** (A. L. G. P. — High Power Heavy Artillery). — It includes guns provided with tractors, or which are displaced on railways. Its work is to fire against and destroy the objectives which other artilleries cannot attack owing either to their lack of weight of ammunition or because they have not sufficient range. Objectives which may be allotted to it are : strongly organized supporting points, railway stations, communication and supply centers, aviation depots.

The most important long guns are the 14, 16, 19, 24, 27 and 32 centimeters, 305 and 340 mm. The most important short guns are the 370 and 400 mm. howitzers.

Projectiles. — Three kinds :

The *shrapnel*, which, when it bursts, throws but the bullets it contains.

The *explosive shell*, which contains only a charge of explosive and the effects of which are produced by the splintering of its case and the shock produced by the explosion.

The special shell.

The projectile may explode *after* having touched the ground (percussion shells) or *before*, on any point of its trajectory (time fuse shells); in either case the explosion is obtained by means of a fuse.

Concerning the effects of the shells, see Chapter XV, Part III.

Adjustment of the fire. — When the distance between the gun and its objective is accurately known, it is not sufficient, in order to reach the objective, to take the range corresponding to that distance. For example : to reach an objective situated exactly 4,500 meters away, it is nearly always necessary to take a slightly different range (4,400, 4,475, 4,550, etc.). The reasons for this correction are : the temperature, the wind he difference in the level between the gun and its objective (site), the difference in quality or quantity of the powder charge or in the weight of the projectiles, which are not always regular.

Adjusting a fire is, therefore, calculating in *a practical way* the range which places upon the objective, the *average* point of fall of the projectiles : this adjustment is of capital importance; a badly adjusted fire is of no value, and is sometimes harmful.

Observation. — To be adjusted, a fire must be observed; it is the artillery observer who adjusts the fire. Generally the observer is an officer.

Artillery can act usefully only as long as it can observe its shots and it can adjust the fire to the movement of the infantry only as long as it sees or knows exactly the positions held by the foremost lines of infantry. The gunner therefore requires excellent observation posts, i. e., posts which provide views corresponding to the mission of its occupants and which can be held there in spite of the enemy's fire. The gunner cannot, however, plead the precariousness of his observation post as an excuse to leave it, should the infantry still require his cooperation. The observation post is connected by telephone, signal, runners, etc., with the batteries it throws into action and with the infantry chiefs it has the mission to support.

Relative to the dispersion of the fire. — It has been explained above that neither the guns of a battery nor the powder charges or ammunition are of regular or even quality and that, in addition, the atmospheric conditions have their effect on the firing.

The shells of a well-adjusted fire do not therefore all fall upon the same point; a certain percentage of their fall is short or over. This the infantry must know so as not to ask the artillery to lengthen a well-adjusted fire should a few shells fall short in the vicinity of the infantry trenches. Infantry that makes premature or unjustified complaints against its artillery spoils the fire of the latter and diminishes, to its own disadvantage, the support which it would otherwise receive.

Duties of the infantry towards the artillery. — The infantry owes the artillery :

Information.
Protection.

Information. — A. **At ordinary times** (trench warfare) the observation service of the infantry, which collects, controls and establishes all information relative to the activity of hostile infantry and artillery, must allow the artillery which supports it to daily benefit by it. It therefore gives it all information concerning the enemy **reliefs** (frequency, time, route, etc.) the same information re the supplies, trench organization, fatigue parties, enemy observation posts, machine guns, bomb throwers, etc. It is by keeping the gunner well informed of what he knows and sees, that the infantry officer, whatever his rank, makes his artillery vigilant and prepared, one which wears down the enemy by well timed intervention and defends the infantry at the least call.

B. **During periods of attack,** the infantry officer must know that without his help the gunner is liable to make mistakes, to delay his intervention or to make it at a wrong moment; briefly, to help him badly and let him suffer.

Therefore, the infantry officer's duty is :

a. To report, not only to his chief, but also to the nearest artillery, concerning the position of his troops. The best way is to trace a small sketch on the map he possesses with the following indications :

My company stands from..... to.....
My neighbors right and left are so and so.
Sign his name and **give the time.**
Insure a rapid transmission.

b. To indicate to the gunner the good artillery observation posts which are discovered by the infantry in the ground it has just occupied, «good observation posts for artillery at such and such point, with a view upon such and such a part of the ground». If possible, a sketch with a cross to mark the position of the proposed observation point.

The two above prescriptions, made for the purpose of an attacking period, are also applicable to a defensive combat when the enemy has succeeded in penetrating into the trenches. The importance of the information is also of value to the gunner, whose mission it is to stop the enemy and protect the infantry.

Protection. — At ordinary times the protection is assured by the fact that the batteries of artillery are covered by the whole of the friendly trenches which are in front of and around them.

During the periods of combat, on a fortified position or in open country, the artillery may be displaced, and brought into action on a ground exposed to an offensive return of the enemy. The infantry in the neighborhood of the batteries must of itself watch and insure their safety. In some cases, the command details a unit to the special mission of **artillery support.** In addition, every artillery chief has the right to ask for support from the nearest infantry chief, who cannot refuse it.

The officer in command of the support gets into touch with the commander of the batteries, studies the position with him and then settles upon his plans, for which he is the only one responsible. On principle, he places part of the troops at his disposal, sufficiently in front of the guns to protect them from the enemy rifles, and places in ambush other fractions on the threatened flank.

In any case the infantry must know that the capture of the guns by the enemy is a trophy for him and a weakening for us and that the infantry which abandons the artillery in its neighborhood commits a dishonorable action.

Composition of a battery of field artillery.

A field battery of the 75 $^m/^m$ guns includes:

The *fighting battery*, which can advance at any speed, and the field train (4 wagons) which can only advance at a slow rate of speed. The fighting battery, when brought into action, is divided into the *firing battery* (4 guns, 6 caissons), *limbers* and *combat train* (6 caissons, 1 forge, 1 battery wagon). The limbers and combat train are sheltered in the rear, at a distance which varies greatly according to the safety desired and whether it is urgent or not, to bring up the limbers or supplies.

In a war in open country these two echelons can be between

500 and 1,000 meters in the rear of the guns; they are guarded by a special support or by a part of the support of the firing battery.

Artillery service.

The artillery is not only a weapon; it is also a *service* which assures the supplies of all the other services as to ammunition and fireworks, also replacing the weapons and the material of the artillery and service transports.

Cavalry.

The cavalry supplies one regiment of cavalry to every army corps. The other regiments are grouped into divisions of cavalry which in turn are grouped into cavalry corps.

The army corps cavalry provides the divisional cavalry (1 or 2 squadrons).

The infantry regiments have, in addition, 12 mounted scouts.

Combat on foot. — When the ground or the situation makes it necessary, the cavalry fight dismounted. Four men in each platoon remain behind to hold the horses. Each one holds 12 horses. The regiment thus musters about 400 men. Every dismounted platoon can fight in the same way as an infantry platoon.

Missions. — The cavalry is « par excellence » the weapon of surprises.

Attached to the infantry it rapidly obtains information for it, and protects it from surprise attacks. The *advance cavalry* scouts for the columns beyond the limits accessible to the infantry, and often up to a day's march in front of the main body of the army corps. The *divisional cavalry* forms the vanguard of the advance guard and sends out in the rear and on the flanks the necessary patrols and «vedettes».

The *army cavalry* (divisions of cavalry) is entrusted whith the *reconnoitering* at great distances; it remains grouped to be able to fight, and boldly pushes forward light elements, *exploring patrols and reconnoitering parties of officers*.

Besides reconnoitering, the cavalry takes part in the battle in the same manner as the troops of other services; either by fighting on the threatened flank, by obtaining the utmost of a success by means of a relentless pursuit or by sacrificing itself to protect a retreat.

It may even become its lot to gloriously bear the brunt of the battle while awaiting the arrival of the infantry (military operations extending from the battle of the Marne to the battle of the Yser).

Lastly, in the war of position, it relieves the infantryman by sharing his trenches.

The cavalry is a service which requires long training and which is very expensive to keep up; it may remain unemployed a long time, but under such circumstances it will repay in one hour all it has cost.

Engineers.

The engineers are intimately attached to the infantry; they devote themselves to perilous work; detachments of engineers accompany the waves of attack and run the same risks.

The infantry must therefore never forget that this service is of limited strength and that the number of its technicians and specialists would be insufficient in the actual mode of warfare if they were not kept for the work which the infantryman cannot possibly do himself.

The infantry must therefore request of the engineers, not work, but advice, and on the contrary, supply them with the men they may require for the war of mines and other special work. The engineers must not be divided up unto small detachments in the different infantry units unless it is to provide them with foremen. It is preferable to employ them «en masse» for a well determined piece of work, but for which will be allotted, however, exactly the number of men required to finish the work in a given time.

The engineers establish and improve the means of communication (roads, railways, bridge trains, searchlight sections, military telegraph, pigeons, etc.). They take part in combat, either by destroying or setting up obstacles or by constructing the delicate parts required in the organization of points of support.

The army corps includes *divisional and corps companies* (which have each a park of its own), *1 company of engineer park* (which supply tool lorries and caissons of explosives), and *1 company of bridge*.

In addition, the **engineer service** has at its disposal, in every army, the *army park* and *telegraph detachment of the engineer park*.

It supplies every service with material.

The aircraft service.

The *aeronautical service* includes the army corps squadrons (reconnoitering, fire adjustment, bombardment), groups of bombarding squadrons and kite balloon sections.

Staff service.

The generals have with them a certain number of officers who make up their staff.

The staff acts in the name of the commander. Its work consists in :

1st. Preparing for the general the different elements required for his decisions.

2nd. Setting out these decisions in the form of instructions and orders.

3rd. Completing the instructions and orders by any neecssary details, which the general might have omitted.

4th. Ensuring the transmissions of the instructions and orders and controlling their execution.

The chief of staff regulates the action of the staff, directs the services and is, in authority, over the whole of the general headquarters.

General headquarters.

The grouping of the staff and the different personnels which are attached to the same commander constitutes the general headquarters. An officer specially detailed and designated *commander of the general headquarters* insures, according to the instructions of the chief of staff, the installation, the service and the guard of the headquarters.

CHAPTER IX.

METHODS OF LIAISON AND SIGNAL COMMUNICATION.

The intellectual activity of a commander must be directed towards the necessity of **incessantly obtaining information.** To give orders a commander must be thoroughly **informed** of the situation. The commander's place is therefore, where he can most easily obtain information concerning the whole front occupied by his troops.

Information obtained by any officer must be **transmitted at once** to his proper superior and if possible to neighboring troops as well.

Information is very often gained at great cost. **Such sacrifice is useless if the information does not reach the proper superior, if it reaches him too late, or is inaccurately transmitted, or written illegibly.**

Transmission of orders and reports. — The transmission of orders must proceed through military channels and no intermediary must be missed except in urgent cases. In the latter case the commander who issues orders informs the intermediary authority and the recipient reports at once to his proper superior.

The commander who as a matter of exception sends a **verbal** order, message or information, always asks the messenger to repeat exactly the order, message or information. The messenger delivers his order or report to the addressee or to his substitute. He waits for the acknowledgement or the answer and never leaves without order or authorization. He then returns to the officer who sent the order and reports; and if there is no answer from the recipient, he simply says: « order transmitted ».

Any **wounded** messenger must call for help at the neighboring unit. The commander of that unit takes measures to prevent any delay in sending the order.

Important orders are carried by **officers** who are acquainted with the situation and know the contents of the despatches they carry. It may be advisable to send duplicate messages by different routes.

An officer on such duty must be ready to destroy his despatches at any moment. To such an officer the commander of any mounted troop is compelled to supply a good horse, should the first mount be too exhausted to deliver the message at the proper time. The borrowed horse must be sent back as soon as possible.

During the performance of his duty the officer tries to gather still more information out of any event he may witness, so that he may be able to acquaint his proper superior and the recipient of the order.

Should any change occur in the situation while the officer is on his way, the order referring to it is brought nevertheless unaltered to the addressee, and the necessary explanations are added concerning the intentions of the higher autority at the time the order was issued.

If the order implies immediate execution he waits for the beginning of the action so as to be able to give a detailed account of it.

Every subordinate receiving an order or report in place of an absent superior, must secure its transmission to the latter, according to directions previously given him. He reads the contents if it does not bear the word « personal »; on his own initiative he takes the measures indicated by circumstances and reports them to his superior.

At the outposts and advance guards and in the first line trenches commanders of the different fractions may read the contents of any message sent to the rear, under the condition that they delay it as little as possible.

Liaison. — The object of liaison between commanders belonging to the same large unit is to provide them with all possible information essential to the successful use of the **combined arms**, especially the artillery and the infantry.

For small commands, liaison may be represented by the four arms of a cross, the first one representing liaison with the advanced fractions, the second with commanders at the rear, the third and fourth representing lateral liaison with right and left neighboring units.

It includes for them as a means of information, **terrestrial observation** and as a means of transmission the telephone, signaling, messengers and **carrier-pigeons.**

The use of the different means of information is always clearly determined by a **general plan** which forms a special paragraph or a supplement to the **plan of attack** or to the **plan of defense.** This does not dispense, however, with frequent and personal liaison with neighboring units.

The fact that under particular circumstances the usual mechanical means of communications have failed to work is no excuse for a commander's remaining unacquainted with changes in the situation of his unit and neighboring units, and not exercising the necessary personal action on the conduct of events.

A small unit will establish its liaison differently according as it may be :

In the first line.

In support,

Or in reserve.

Each particular case must be a matter of mature reflection on the part of the commander.

In the first line lateral connections are the most important.

In support, the mission as a rule is given beforehand and will consist generally in supporting a unit in front of it : hence in knowing the situation of this unit, its emplacement, means of communications, and all that must be known in order to enable the supports to relieve or reinforce the first line units without any loss of time.

In reserve the unit may be called to act in any direction. The troops are at rest but the commander's mind must be all the more active ; foresee all possible events, plan in advance the necessary means of communication to be established; and above all he must have the roads in all directions thoroughly reconnoitered.

1° MEANS OF INFORMATION.

Means of information may be divided into two parts ground observation and aerial observation.

Ground observation. — During the combat every commander of a unit (company or platoon) selects an **observing station** in the place where he may best follow the events in the zone of action of his unit. Permanent observations are made, if necessary, by means of **obser-**

vers whose work is portioned out in such a way that observations are continuous in time and space. Six observers in each platoon must be trained in advance.

Their mission consists as a rule in following the developement of the combat (movement of friendly or hostile troops, activity of both artilleries), in observing signals made by the advanced units and transmitting or repeating these signals in accordance with orders previously received.

The post of command must be close to the observing stations. **The selection of the observing stations precedes that of the post of command.**

In stationary trench warfare observation is continuous as in combat. This part of ground observation is treated in detail in Part IV, Chapter VI, and Part VII, Chapter I.

Aerial observation. — The aeroplane and balloon are employed to obtain information (observations, photographs) and as a means of transmission, thanks to the signals that they can receive and send.

Among the missions that may be assigned to them those concerning the infantry are :

a) **Infantry aeroplane.** — One to each division. Mission :

To follow the progress of advanced units and reserves ;

To observe the signals made from the firing line or from posts of command and transmit them to the division headquarters ;

To inform the general in command of the division of everything that happens in the vicinity of the firing line and in the rear.

b) **Aeroplanes of command.** — One to each army corps, to follow the general development of the combat and observe the movements of the enemy.

c) **Courier aeroplanes.** — To transmit to the generals and colonels any useful information and orders issued by superior commanders (weighted messages with sketches prepared beforehand, photographs, conventional signals, etc.).

d) **Captive divisional balloons.** — Observation of artillery fire and skirmish line, transmission of signals. In short throughout the combat they act as infantry balloons.

e) **Captive balloons of command.** — Same task as the aeroplanes of Command.

Working of the aerial system of liaison.

The infantry iuforms the **infantry aeroplane** or the **infantry captive balloon**, or both at the same time, by signals made :

1° By the firing line.

2° By battalion, regiment, brigade or division posts of command.

1° **By the skirmish line.** — The **skirmish line** marks the front it occupies :

a) **By Bengal lights.** — This is the surest means. The Bengal lights are placed where they are best seen from the aeroplanes and the balloons and where they escape the attention of the enemy.

b) **By panels.** — When requested by the aeroplane, open and fold the panels several times to show the aeroplane that they are not abandoned panels or accidental white spots, and then leave them open until the aeroplane returns the answer «understood» (one-three star-rocket); **in any case panels are not left open more than 15 minutes.**

c) In case Bengal lights or panels are not available, the first line uses all possible means to make its position known to the aeroplane : making calls with the searchlights (— ▪ — ▪ — ▪), waving handkerchiefs, overcoat linings, pocket mirrors, etc.

The line is marked out :

Either on a previously determined line (one of the assigned objectives).

Or at the request of the aeroplane, made by sound signals followed by one rocket (6 simultaneous stars).

Or on the initiative of the company commanders, when the unit cannot go any further or when after withdrawal it has succeeded in holding the ground. In that case it is advisable to use Bengal lights either alone or with panels to more surely attract the attention of the aeroplane.

It is forbidden to use Bengal lights or unfold panels except in the first line.

2° The battalion, regiment, brigade or division, posts of command, show their positions by means of **identification panels.** Each post of command is known by distinct **conventional** signs, which consist of a few letters or figures.

The posts of command secure liaison with the aeroplane :

By using signals of a conventional form (combining panels in the way explained below).

By using **searchlight of 24 cm. diameter** (or 14 cm.).
By using shutter panels.

They correspond with the balloon by means of searchlights, but they open communications by using special post of command calls first.

The balloon answers with searchlights or Morse signals made with the **folding cylinder,** an apparatus which displays and suppresses instantaneously a black surface 1 m. 15 cm. high along the ascension cable. It gives first a special call to tell which post of command it wishes to correspond with. Its answers are limited ordinarily to « understood » or « repeat »,

Identification panels are unfolded at the request of the aeroplane (sound signal) or on the initiative of the post of command.

They are taken away as soon as the aeroplane answers « understood ». (3 stars).

The battalion panel is 2 ms. square.

INFANTRY ESCORT AEROPLANE.

It flies lower than the other aeroplanes and not above 1,200 meters. It is provided with distinctive permanent marks (colored stripes, rows of lights, etc.) and **is further distinguished by a special** signal cartridge.

I am the infantry aeroplane of the 1st division : 1 one star cartridge.

I am the infantry aeroplane of the 2nd division : 1 two star cartridge.

These cartridges are fired two or three times at intervals of a few minutes, before any other signal.

The shape of the aeroplane, its characteristics, its signals must be familiar to all the men of the units for which the aeroplane works.

On their part, the aviators must constantly bear in mind their duty to help the infantry by noting its exact positions and its needs, and by transmitting this information rapidly to higher authority and to the artillery.

It may in certain cases fly low over the lines. But the aviator must not risk the air-craft by flying lower than 800 meters except in case of absolute necessity.

The aeroplane corresponds with the infantry by means of a small number of signals made by signal cartridges and always preceded :

First by a sound signal.
Then by the special cartridge.

It is to be remembered that **any aeroplane which fires white stars is an infantry aeroplane and that its cartridges concern the advanced infantry units only.**

These cartridges must be fired by the aeroplane from a height above 300 meters to avoid any confusion with rockets fired from the ground.

The aeroplane notes the position of the firing line and the posts of command which are indicated to it as explained above. It may note also moreover, as has been explained, conventional signals: Searchlight, signals or shutter panels.

The aeroplane transmits this information :

By wireless telegraphy (T. S. F.) for urgent information, especially concerning artillery fire, to posts of command of the division, brigade and artillery group.

By means of weighted messages for other particulars required by the post of command of the division of infantry or the army corps. The weighted messages allow the aeroplane to give more complete information and especially to mark the exact position of the line on prepared field sketches.

CAPTIVE DIVISIONAL BALLOON.

It is distinguished by several pennants tied to the rear and at night by a row of lights at regular intervals.

The divisional balloon must be familiar to all troops.

Communications from the basket of a captive balloon to the ground post is by telephone. Messages are transmitted thence to division headquarters.

INFORMATION CONTAINED IN OPERATION ORDERS.

The infantry finds in operation orders:

The time at which the aeroplane or balloon may begin to make observations.

The manner of marking out the positions of the line adopted for the operations under consideration.

Conditions of time and place under which signals will be made by the firing line.

Conventional supplementary signals.

Conditions under which observation will cease.

2º MEANS OF TRANSMISSION.

The means of transmission have been described in Chapters IX and X of Part III and are cited below for the sake of completeness :

1° Telephone (Chapter X);
2° Signals by rockets;

3° Signalling cartridges of 25 and 35 mm. Fire works for V. B.;

4° Lantern for signalling;

5° Searchlights of 14 and 24 cm.;

6° Flags for signallers;

7° Panels for identification, shutter-panels, panels for marking out.

To which may be added :

8° Runners;

9° Carrier-pigeons;

10° Wireless telegraphy (T. S. F.) which acts rapidly between air-craft and artillery observation stations (but not inversely.)

None of these methods is absolutely sure.

The employment of all of these methods is necessary, and at same time each one should be prepared as if it, were to suffice alone.

As nothing can be improvised and as troops during a battle will only make use of means that current usage has rendered familiar to them, all these processes of transmission should be compulsory and employed daily if only by way of drill.

Therefore, an officer who has a telephone installed near by should foresee the rupture of his line and establish liaison with his battalion commander by visual signalling and runners.

OFFICER IN CHARGE OF LIAISON.

The telephone officer of a regiment is *chief of liaison* of every kind. Also in each battalion an officer or an N. C. O. is designated by the battalion commander.

PERSONNEL EMPLOYED FOR LIAISON.

The composition of squads of telephone operators and signallers is enumerated in Chapters IX and X of Part III.

The term **liaison agent** should be reserved to designate officers (and exceptionally N. C. O's.) capable of discussing a situation, transmitting instructions and gathering information. The usage has become established to call (also) **liaison** the group of *agents of transmission*, privates or N. C. O's., charged only with writing and carrying orders or with fulfilling simple missions. These men should be chosen with discernement.

In a company they are as a rule, the cyclist, the drummers and the buglers.

Runners.

Apart from these, train by platoon some agile and devoted **runners** to be charged only with transmission of messages. **The liaison by means of runners, especially doubled runners, is that which gives rise to the fewest failures under a violent bombardment.**

The distance between 2 **relays of runners** varies from 150 to 300 meters.

Each **chain** is under the orders of a chief seconded if necessary by some N. C. O's distributed among the relays.

In order that the liaisons by signallers, agents of transmission or runners may work well during an attack they must have reconnoitered the ground in advance under the direction of officers, **not only the system of boyaus, but the open ground,** so as not to be bewildered when they have to leave their usual track. Have this **ground studied** not only on plans of large scale, but on the ground itself. It is indispensable that all posts of command down to include captains should be easily found even by liaison agents not belonging to the unit (routes clearly staked out, large and solid signs, an orderly in the principal boyau if the post of command is somewhat out of the way, etc.

These posts of command should figure on all plans and have a number, a name or a distinctive letter, so as to avoid confusion.

Visual signalling.

Visual signalling should be made the object of a studied plan at every echelon, so that each will understand the probable emplacements of its correspondents and their signs.

As a rule, liaisons are to be assured from the front to the rear. But a liaison is certain only if the receiving post can acknowledge reception of messages, and on the other hand signals sent towards the front are apt to draw the enemy's fire.

It will be prudent to reduce them to brief messages or replace them by the signalling cartridge signifying : « **understood** » or « **repeat.** »

The light of the apparatus is all the more visible when it stands out against an obscure background.

Install posts in front of a hedge or a line of trees, avoid taking for background the sky, a white wall, or open ground, avoid the vicinity of rivers or ponds, which are likely to give reflections.

Do not expose the mirror to the solar rays, which by reflecting give the illusion of a fixed light and prevent the reading of signals. Keep in the shade and protect the apparatus by a screen.

Observe with a field glass of large field and slight magnifying power (X 6 or X 8).

As often as possible two signallers should be attached to each apparatus : one manipulating, the other charged only with directing the rays of light on the receiving apparatus.

SIGNALLING BY FIREWORKS.

The following precautions should be observed :

Choose sets distinct from each other; make use of the most visible for the most important signals.

Limit the code to a few phrases; make it known long enough before its coming into force, that everyone may be sufficiently informed of its meaning.

Determine according to situation, which authority (major, captain, exceptionally chief of platoon) has the right to fire signal rockets : this will avoid alarms without motive and the wasting of ammunition.

Prepare relays for the repetition of signals, make sure that the artillery has located these relays and has them watched effectively from its observation stations.

All officers and N. C. O.'s and the greatest number of men possible should know the conventional signals. If there is danger of forgetting these, write them down in hieroglyphics in a note book, in a manner which will be entirely incomprehensible to the enemy if it should fall into its hands. Frequently assure yourself that you are in possession of the most recent code.

CARRIER PIGEONS.

Carrier pigeons have been used under the most violent bombardments and through clouds of toxic gas. Great confidence can be placed in them, but they should be reserved for cases of importance. They do not fly well at night unless they have been subjected to a special training.

Regimental personnel

1 N. C. O. of the H Q. company.

4 auxiliary pigeon keepers for the regiment and 4 per battalion (infantry soldiers, especially instructed and detached from their companies in case of the organization of a carrier pigeon post).

A post comprises :

2 auxiliary pigeon keepers.

1 team of 4 pigeons and the necessary material.

3 teams called A, B, and C, are assigned to the post at the pigeon cot. The relief team is sent at evening or by night every two or three days. The pigeons relieved are let loose one by one, the following morning, with an exercise despatch. The commander of the unit interested may retain the two teams if circumstances require them.

Messages are written in three copies in a dispatch book : 1 remains on the stub, the other two are entrusted to 2 pigeons that are let loose at several minutes interval. If there is reason to fear a shortage of birds, one copy only is sent and the other is joined as confirmation to the next message sent out.

The pigeon can carry an *aluminium dispatch-tube* on each foot, which allows it to be entrusted with a message and a sketch.

To be let loose the pigeon is placed on the ground at a certain distance from the post of command, its head is turned towards the right direction and it is driven off.

The pigeons should be installed in the post with the maximum of hygiene but *not of comfort;* they should feel themselves in confinement and desire ardently to return to the pigeon loft where there is awaiting them abundance and dainties. It is therefore strictly forbidden to all others but the pigeon-keepers to feed them.

3º MORSE SIGNALS.
MANIPULATIONS AND RULES OF SERVICE.

Troops use two series of signals :

Morse alphabet signals.

Conventional signals generally composed of letters from the Morse alphabet.

Alphabetical signals can be transmitted :

By projectors or lanterns,
By arm signalling with or without flags,
By shutter-panels.

Conventional signals can be transmitted by :

Lanterns,
By searchlights,
By arm with or without flags,
By fireworks or panels.

Morse alphabet (international).

ALPHABET.

a ·—	i ··	r ·—·
b —···	j ·———	s ···
c —·—·	k —·—	t —
ch ————	l ·—··	u ··—
d —··	m ——	v ···—
e ·	n —·	w ·——
é ··—··	o ———	x —··—
f ··—·	p ·——·	y —·——
g ——·	q ——·—	z ——··
h ····		

NUMBERS.

1 ·————	6 —····
2 ··———	7 ——···
3 ···——	8 ———··
4 ····—	9 ————·
5 ·····	0 —————

The study of the Morse alphabet is facilitated by classifying the letters in series presenting a particular character.

See table given below for example :

· e	— t	·— a	—· n		
·· i	—— m	··— u	—·· d		
··· s	——— o	···— v	—··· b		
···· h	———— ch				

——· g	———·— q	——··z	··—··é	·—· r
—·— k	—·—— y	—·—·c	··—· f	—··— x
·—— w	·——— j	·——·p	·—·· l	

SERVICE SIGNALS.

—····—	b r	(Invitation to transmit.)
·—·—·	a r	(End of transmission.)
···—·	s n	(Understood.)
·—···	a s	(Waiting.)
··——··	?	(Repeat.)
—···—	=	(Separation.) [Hyphen].

CONVENTIONAL SIGNALS.

Call for artillery fire................	O	— — — — —
We are about to advance, lenghthen your range.....................	H	•••• •••• ••••
Artillery is firing at too short a range.	S	••• ••• •••
Send up ammunition...............	Y	—•——

Representation of signals.

Morse signals are represented :

Visual. — The dot by a short flash (1/2 second).
— The dash by a long flash (3 seconds).

By shutter panels. — The dot by showing a short white signal about 1 second.
— — The dash by long white signal about 6 seconds.

By flags. — The dot by the appearance of one flag or similar object.
— The dash by two flags or two similar objects.

Interval between two signals of the same letter : duration of one dot.

Interval between two letters or two figures : approximately 4 seconds.

Sending of visual signals : For Morse signals to be legible to the vision it is indispensable :

That the cadence should not be too rapid.
That the dashes and dots should be most distinct.
That the successive letters should be well separated.

The signallers should have their attention especially called to the following points :

To manipulate without haste.
To exaggerate the length of dashes (about 3 seconds).
Leave between two letters a very noticeable interval (4 seconds at least) so as to allow the receiving signaller to dictate each letter after reading of same.

Regulation of light. — It is most important that the light be well directed on the correspondent.

In case the receiver does not see the signals clearly he sends out a series of dots ••••••••••••••.

The sending post makes sure that the apparatus is well directed and that the lamp is sufficiently bright.

* The correspondent indicates the variations of light that he perceives :
* By precipitating the cadence of the dots, if the light becomes worse ▬ ▪ ▪ ▪ ▪ ▪ ▪ ▪▪▪▪.
By slowing it up if the light becomes better ▪▪▪▪ ▪ ▪ ▪ ▪ ▪ ▪.
By sending out ▬▬▪▪▪▪▬▬▪ (b r) if light has become normal.
The use of field glasses is recommended for observation.

Signals of recognition. — By reason of the number of visual liaisons capable of simultaneous use, it is indispensable to attach to each post an **indicative** (call letter) identifying the authority from whom the communication comes.

The indicatives are fixed by the divisional staff.

They are made up of a letter and a number.

Care should be taken to avoid letters leading to a confusion with the conventional abbreviations.

Writing of messages. — They should be as brief as possible.

Each letter economized avoids a chance for error.

Transmission. — There must be as a rule two men per signalling post.

At the station of departure one dictates the message letter by letter, the other maneuvers the apparatus or the flags.

At the receiving post, one signaller reads the signals, then he dictates them, letter by letter, to his assistant.

To call up, the sending post sends out the call of its correspondent several times.

The latter replies by the signal ▬▬▪▪▪▪▬▬▪ (b r).

The message is transmitted, word for word, the receiving post sending out after each word:

(One dot) ▪ if it has been correctly read;

(A point of interrogation, ?) ▪▪▬▬▬▬▪▪, if it demands a repetition.

At the end of a transmission:

The sending post sends the signal ▪▬▬▪▬▬▪ (a r).

The receiving post sends ▪▪▪▬▬▪ (s n) (understood) if it has understood the message, or only ▪ (dot), by special arrangement, when, as it has been stated above, the receiving post should emit the fewest possible signals towards the front.

It sends out the last word correctly received followed by (?) ▪▪▬▬▬▬▪▪ if a repetition is desired.

A post that is changing ground warns its correspondents by sending CL (closing) followed, if possible, by the hour and the place where it intends to take up its next station.

Ex. : CL = 17.00 (5 P. M.) = Hill 140.

The sign = (▬▬▪▪▪▬▬) representing a dash of separation (hyphen).

Example of transmission of a message.

Call of sending post C_3.
— receiving — F_4.
Post C_3 has a message of 4 words for F_4.

Signals transmitted.

POST C_3.	POST C_4.	OBSERVATIONS.
F_4 F_4 F_4	Understood. B. R.	
F_4 from C_3 — separation —		
1st word............	Dot.	
2nd word...........	Dot.	
3rd word............	?....................	F_4 has not read correctly 3rd word.
3rd word............	Dot.	
4th word...........	Dot.	
a r..................	Understood or 1 dot.	

4° SIGNALS FOR LIAISON BY AVIONS AND BALLOONS.

It is necessary to distinguish :

A. The signals made by the avion;
B. The signals made by the balloon;
C. The signals made by the infantry to the avion or the balloon.

A. SIGNALS MADE BY THE AVION.

a) **Signals made by white lights** are always addressed to the units of infantry :

The avion fires first a signal cartridge of one or two stars which is repeated 2 or 3 times and at an interval of several minutes, before any other signal. This is its indicative and means :

I am the avion of the infantry of the first division.
or — — **second division.**

Then it inquires : **Where are you?** by firing a signal **cartridge of six stars.**

When it perceives the panels of identification or marking out panels that are then shown it signals : **Understood** by firing a signal **cartridge of three stars.**

To sum up, 3 signals and 3 only :

1 or 2 stars : Indicative.
6 stars : Where are you?
3 stars : Understood.

b) **Signals made by means of wireless telegraph (T. S. F.) to the post of command** supplied with antenna.

The avion sends its **indicative,** then a message worded according to the abbreviation lists figured in annex II of the Instructions on Liaison december 13th 1916, or the **signals of the conventional signal table** given above, or by supplementary conventional signals fixed by the operation orders.

c) **Dropping a weighted message.** The avion intending to drop a weighted message calls the post of command by a sound signal agreed upon in advance : the post of command shows its **identification panel** (at the most favorable point for the message to fall). The avion descends in a spiral to about three hundred meters and drops its message. The post of command acknowledges the reception by the signal : «Message received.»

B. Signals made by balloon.

The balloon sends out the call of the post it is calling and then signals :

Understood (SN) ···—· ···—·
or **repeat** (?) ··———·· ··———··
by means of a folding cylinder.

C. Signals made by infantry to the avions or to balloon.

a) By **projector** or **shutter panel,** make use of the **table of conventional signals** to which must be added :

I am here (firing line) ·—·—·—·—·—·—
Understood or **message received:** ·· —· ···—·

b) By **Bengal fires :** The firing line will light 1 or 2 Bengals per platoon.

c) By marking out **panels,** 1 or 2 per group.
Bengal fires and panels may be combined.

d) By **Identification panels and rectangular panels :** Annex II of the Instructions on Liaison indicates these panels and the combinations to be spread out on the ground, in order to say :

I am here. (Battalion, regiment, brigade, division).
Demand for artillery fire.
We are about to advance, lengthen range.
Artillery is firing too short.
Demand for supplies of ammunition.
Understood or message received.

This method gives also the means of signalling the nine primary numbers and in consequence a message of any kind that has been agreed upon.

5° AGENTS OF LIAISON OF THE ARTILLERY WITH THE INFANTRY.

The artillery cannot act efficiently unless it is in intimate liaison with the infantry, for whose benefit it i working.

This liaison is established :

By a constant understanding between the chiefs of the infantry and the artillery, whose posts of command should be established in close proximity to each other whenever the case is possible.

By the agents of liaison detached from the artillery with the infantry.

The necessity cannot be too much emphasized of officers of field artillery and heavy artillery (chiefs of group and higher commanders frequently coming into contact with the chiefs of infantry units (chiefs of regiment and chiefs of battalion) for whose benefit they are acting.

Detachment of liaison and observation. — For the execution of an offensive action, each group of artillery charged with the direct and immediate support of an infantry unit (regiment or brigade) will detail to the commander of such a unit an officer, **chief of liaison,** who has under his orders a **detachment of liaison and observation.**

This detachment includes :

N.C.O. observers,

Corporals and soldiers as scouts and liaison agents,

Telephone operators and signallers with the necessary material (telephone, optical appliances, flags).

The liaison officer marches with the commander of the infantry that he is charged with supporting.

His mission is :

To keep his chief of group informed on the situation and the needs of the infantry and to transmit the demands of the same under a formula which can be used by the batteries.

To keep the commander of the infantry informed on the support that can be given him by the group that he represents.

He details when possible an N.C.O. observer to each chief of battalion acting in the first line.

He will keep connected by his own means with his group commander on the one hand, and with the advanced observers detached with the chiefs of battalion in the first line.

The permanent working of good liaisons between these various echelons requires his constant attention.

This liaison installed by the care of the artillery should by no means keep the infantry from joining up with the supporting artillery by their own means as well. By this method the **double liaison** is insured.

During a defensive combat and in a period of stability the liaison between infantry and artillery is organized by taking a suggestion from the above. The object to be followed is always the same : to assure to the infantry at the right time an efficacious support from the artillery. The importance of the means of liaison put on foot varies only accordng to the situation, it may be reduced during a periodiof stabilisation.

Flags, lanterns and arm-bands (French).

Army Corps:
  Tricolor flag without tassel;
  Lantern with white or tricolored lens;
  Arm-band tricolored with thunderbolt and n° of corps.

Infantry division:
  Flag: red with a vertical white band, for the 1st; division of infantry of the Army Corps;
  2 bands for 2nd, etc.;
  Isolated division: horizontal white band;
  Red lantern;
  Red arm-band with grenade and number.

Infantry brigade:
  No flag;
  Blue lantern;
  Blue arm-band with grenade and number.

Infantry ammunition column :
Yellow flag and lantern.

Artillery ammunition column :
Blue flag and lantern.

Ambulances :
2 flags, one tricolor, the other blue with red cross ;
2 lights superposed, white and red.

Establishment for contagious diseases :
Yellow flag ;
The flags of generals of artillery are blue and red ;
Those of cavalry generals blue and white.

On the arm-bands :
Crossed guns for artillery,
Star for cavalry ;
Helmet and cuirass for engineers.

Distinctive colors for battalions and companies.

1st. blue.　　　　　3rd, yellow.
2nd, red.　　　　　4th, green.

Units not included in battalions :
Khaki.

Agents of liaison :
Blue arm-band with letter L in darker blue.

CHAPITRE X.

SANITATION AND ALIMENTATION.

Sanitation regulations.

Sanitation may be defined by these two words : **order** and **cleanliness**.

Most of the epidemic diseases are carried by **water**, by **soil** or from **man to man**.

The prescribed measures must be all the more rigorous in proportion as the camps and cantonments are more numerous and more dense.

Hygiene of the body. — The men must wash from head to foot, without any false modesty, as often as possible : it is not enough to wash only face, hands or feet : a dirty skin infects a wound under its dressing. The officers of a company must organize douches in all places where it is materially possible to do so.

Make use of the tooth brush, keep the hair and the nails short.

Venereal diseases are nothing to be ashamed of; see a doctor as soon as a discharge or a suspicious ulceration appears. Never neglect to wear a flannel belt. The ultra violet rays of the sun disinfect the clothes, the blankets and the straw.

The head lice and inguinal lice are harmless and easy to destroy. The bites of the body lice on the contrary are apt to inoculate diseases. Lice lay their eggs in the creases and in the seams of the clothes. They can be avoided by sewing camphor sachets or else by fixing light compresses of benzine or gasoline under the shirt or inside the drawers.

They can be destroyed by rubbing over the whole body spirits of wine, camphorated alcohol, petroleum or benzine. Soak the seams of the clothes with the same liquids or else iron them with a very hot iron or put them into an oven.

Sanitation on the march. — The advice to be given is : clean feet, greased, soft, and ample shoes, the leggings and the tie not too tight.

Let the soldier eat as he likes, drink moderately, not too cold drinks. Alcohol weakens the legs, sugared food and **good will** stimulate them.

If the feet are particularly tender, grease them with tallow or paint them with formol, or with picric acid. On arrival wipe them with a damp rag but do not bathe them. Do not burst the blisters too soon, they are likely to become infected.

Sanitation of the cantonment. — It is the business of the medical service **to look after the sanitary conditions** of the cantonment, of the bivouac, and of the trenches (drinkable water, latrines, contaminated houses or shelters, incineration, etc.). There must be an understanding between the doctors of the unit and the officers of the company for the fulfillment of all necessary measures.

In each cantonment there is a **sanitary commission** composed of the chief of the cantonment and of the senior doctor.

Latrines. — The officers in command of the sections have latrines dug **within half an hour after the**

instalment and not the following morning; if the platoon is not too scattered have one latrine dug for every platoon, no more nor less, so there will be no chance of overlooking one of them when they are shown to the agent of the medical service whose duty it is to disinfect them **daily**. Ask for that agent if he does not come. The suitable disinfectants are : Sulfate of iron at 10 %, cresyl at 5 %, quicklime or lime water.

The simplest latrine is a narrow deep trench (width and depth of a spade) with a small berm on each side, to stand upon; when he leaves the latrine the man must spread a little earth in the trench, if he does not do so, the latrine will be disagreeable to enter and the men will go anywhere else. Also it is better to have a **latrine** like that in fig. 256, especially if the troops remain more than one night in the cantonment, and if boards four or five centimeters wide can be found.

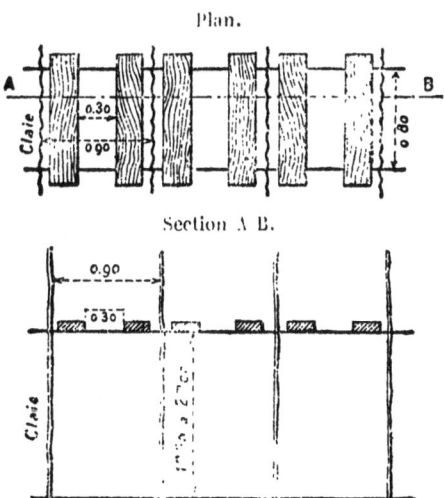

Fig. 256. Latrine for cantonment.

Any place which one tries to keep tidy will certainly be hygienic. Allow air and light to get into it, roll up the straw in the morning, never tread upon it, arrange a central aisle, fold up the kits neatly, improvise insulators, build superposed couches, rifle racks, brush away the dust and the spider webs, do not spit on the floor, protect the bread.

Manure heaps should not be allowed to remain in villages which are permanently occupied by troops, but should be carted outside the village on the farm land of the inhabitants. Sprinkle the places where they were and their surroundings with disinfectants, cover them with a layer of earth, 10 centimeters thick, and forbid depositing any more, cart away or burn the manure accumulated during the day. See that drainage is assured; clean the ditches.

Fetid pools. Clean the approaches and make them as wholesome as possible, pour some petroleum or some shist oil on them.

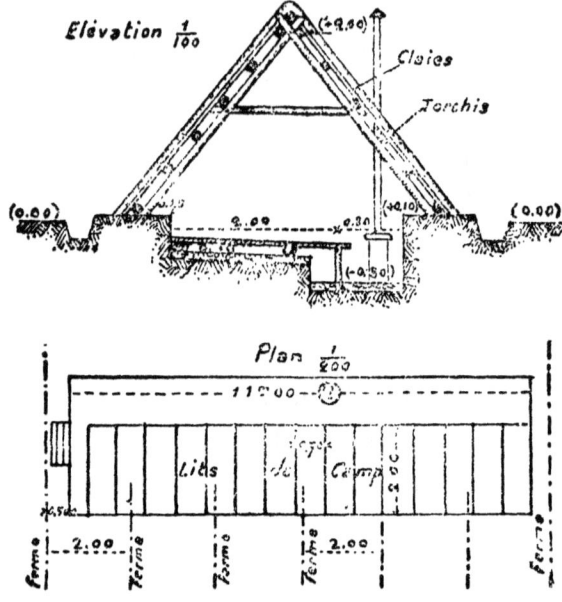

Fig. 258. — Hut for 16 men.

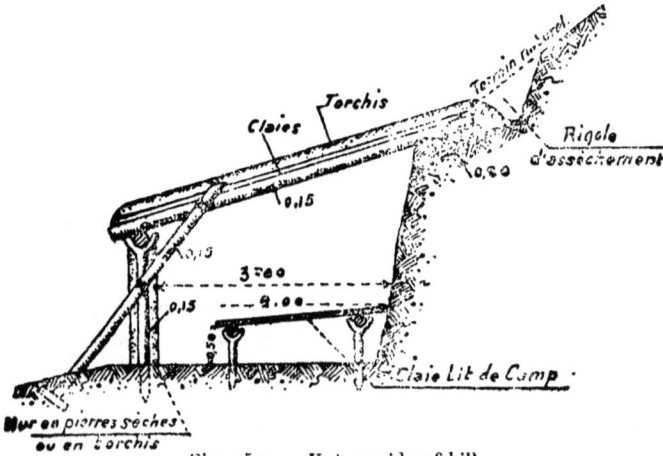

Fig. 259. — Hut on side of hill.

In each village construct one or more **crematory ovens** and burn all sweepings, or, lacking these, bury them deep.

These regulations concerning the incineration and the disinfection are prescribed particularly to destroy the larvae of flies. They pick up disease germs everywhere which they deposit on everything with which they come into contact. One must try to destroy them by every possible means.

In the **bivouacs**, construct huts of canvas or any other material which can be found.

The commonest of all the **huts** is the **Adrian**. It is 8 meters wide, and its height at the ridge is 5 meters. The bays are 2 meters wide and their number is unlimited. A hut 30 meters long and holding 100 men is used frequently.

Food sanitation. — Install clean kitchens, far from manure heaps, and from the latrines; don't allow any scraps to be left lying about such as peelings, bones, canned food boxes, old papers, rags, etc.; it is better to burn them than to bury them. Make some receptacles of wire gauze, or of the wrappings of frozen meat. In any case, keep the meat and the bread from the flies, the dust and the sun.

Clean the utensils with hot water and ashes; never scrub them with earth, (there are certain kinds of earth which have harmful effects, still little known, but which none the less exist). It is better to fire the receptacles with spirits of wine. Wash with soap and water the sacks used for the distribution. Cover the receptacles before transporting them. Wash your hands before eating.

Water sanitation. — Contaminated water spreads typhoid, enteritis, cholera, etc. Very clear water may be contaminated. Water may be purified by **boiling** it, for five minutes (tea, coffee) or by a **chemical sterilization** (3 or 4 drops of extract of Javel water to 10 liters, to be drunk in an hour; or crystals of permanganate of potassium until the water turns slightly pink; a little sugar takes the color away).

The unsubmerged sand filter is also to be advised; one should calculate the flow in such a way that no part of the sand should ever be submerged (fig. 262).

Hygiene against cold. — Keep the blood in circulation. Wear clothes that are not tight; several thin garments, worn one on top of the other are warmer than a single very thick garment (two pairs of socks, newspaper on the back and on the chest). Increase fatty foods; alcohol causes congestion.

Precautions taken against frozen feet. — One may have frozen feet at a temperature above freezing if the feet and legs are damp, if the shoes and socks are too tight, and if one remains too long a time without moving, either standing up or sitting down. Therefore, drain the trenches, grease the feet, loosen the laces of the leggings and shoes, move about, take the boots off at once, rub the feet and ankles for 10 minutes every day, work the joints of the feet, put on dry socks, if necessary russian socks or paper bandages. If there is a sign of chilblains, avoid putting the feet in front of the fire. Rub them and dry them without fire. In intensely cold weather, give up greasing the feet, because the grease might freeze, and increase the danger of frozen feet.

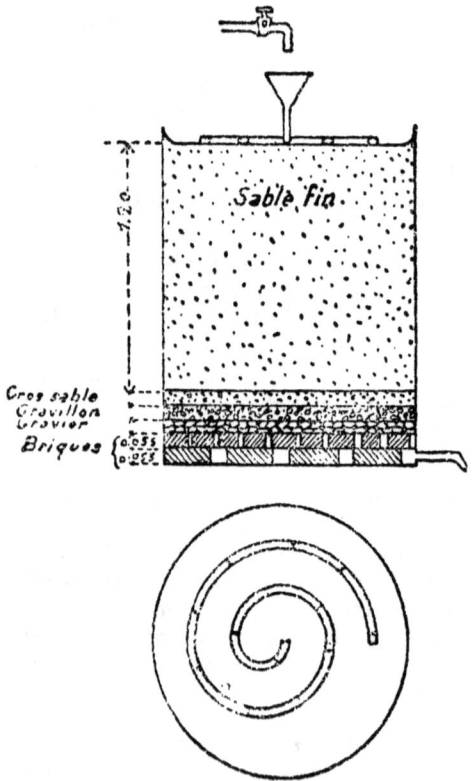

Fig. 262. — Unsubmerged sand filter.

First aid to the wounded. — Keep in mind directions inscribed on the first aid packets. Preferably, have first dressing done by a comrade. Neither the hands nor any other object should come in contact with the wound or with the part of dressing which directly touches the wound.

Never wash the wounds with any liquid supposed to be antiseptic. To reach the wounds, cut the clothes at the seam, do not rip them anywhere else.

Head wounds. — Wear only official helmets of special steel, not those found in the stores. Where there is great loss of blood from head wounds, a tight dressing is always good.
Never tighten a dressing round the neck or round the chin.

Chest wounds. — Do not be too alarmed by the spitting of blood, and by shortness of breath; remain calm; sit down with your back supported; do not move and do not talk. If, while breathing, you suffer, bandage the chest fairly tight with the flannel belt applied as high as possible under the armpits.

Abdomen wounds. — Remain motionless, lying flat on the back or partly raised. Never touch the wound; apply the dressing and be sure not to **drink** nor **eat**, no matter how long you may have to wait for help. Take, if possible, an opium pill. At the dressing station accept no nourishment which has not been prescribed by the doctor, not even milk or water.

Limb wounds. — If there is excessive bleeding of the wound, stop the hemorrhage by a tight bandage or by a tourniquet placed above the wound; it is a proceeding which is apt to be dangerous; therefore, if you have a bandage or a tourniquet, be sure to warn all the attendants of the ambulance or the surgeons, so as to have it replaced as soon as possible by another treatment for stopping the hemorrhage.
Do not tighten the dressing of the limbs, first roll the bandages round the extremity (hands, feet) and then work up towards the root of the limb.

In order to relieve the pain of a **broken limb**, immobilize it immediately.

1. Fracture of the arm. Fix it in the most convenient position, the elbow touching the body, the forearm bent, the wrist passing through a gap between the two buttons of the great-coat at the height of the breast, the whole fixed with a puttee legging rolled once or twice round the chest.

2. Fracture of the leg. Do not try to walk, as that may aggravate the wound, nor try to drag yourself on the ground, as you may infect the wound with tetanus, etc.; wait quietly where you are. Immobilize the limb by tying

it to the other with the straps of the haversack. The bayonet, an **empty** gun or a stick may serve as a temporary splint. If you are wounded in the thigh or in the pelvis, try not to evacuate the bowels, as the contact of fecal matter with wounds is very dangerous.

Regulations concerning the regimental sanitary service. — Emergency treatment is administered in aid stations placed immediatly behind the firing line (the expression «dressing station» is a misnomer): their personnel is designated by the senior medical of the regiment.

The regimental bearers pick up the wounded and carry them to the **regimental aid station :** the bandsmen help them.

The dressing station is established in the rear of the regimental reserves, in a sheltered place, where water can be obtained.

It provides the dressing and simple equipment for the wounded and furnishes them with a tag authorizing them to proceed to an evacuation hospital.

The wounded who are still able to fight have their wounds dressed and are eventually sent back to their units. Those who are only slightly wounded and are able to walk are formed into groups and detailed to some assigned point, where they are collected: they are put under the command of a wounded N. C. O.

Those who are unable to walk are conveyed to the field hospitals by the automobiles of the sanitary section or by division or corps litter-bearers.

No wounded man is allowed to wander to the rear before reporting himself to the dressing station. It is everybody's duty to know where the latter is situated.

If there are many wounded, special arrangements must be made: increase the number of bearers for searching the battlefield ; make use of the prisoners, who should be put under the command of the regimental bearers : send the divisional bearers, reinforced by auxiliary troops and prisoners, as far as the aid stations of the battalions.

CHAPTER XI.

SUPPLY OF AMMUNITION AND MATERIEL.

Organisation of supply of ammunition and materiel. — The development of specialists who for the most part use up heavy and voluminous ammunition renders the good organization of supplies a vital necessity and a most delicate problem.

Whatever be the kind of ammunition concerned, it is best in any case to push the animals as close to the troops as possible so as to shorten the length of the distance for the fatigue parties. Mules and donkeys will be found the most useful in this respect.

The fatigue parties must be under a strong command, such as one guide or corporal in front, an energetic sergeant behind for every 20 men. All defection or slacking is a crime.

It is advisable to calculate that only half of the men sent forward will reach the first line because of bombardment, men going astray, etc.

Another principle is to have the fatigue parties belong to the unit they supply. They are more certain to arrive at their objectives. Then if the front line of the company is not wide, it may be ordered that each of the two platoons of reinforcement shall leave behind its half-platoon of riflemen. The one marching with the reserves will bring the most necessary supplies to the conquered position, which are as a rule **tools, grenades and water**. A little later or perhaps in the course of the evening the other one will bring the **sand bags, Brun wire coils, fireworks, food supplies, brandy, cartridges**, and some more grenades.

All these articles will be drawn from the **depots which were established before the attack, in the most advanced position**, either in the departure trenches or close to the P. C. of the captain or battalion commander.

These objects will be put into **sand bags by loads of 11 to 18 pounds** so that one can be given to a man already loaded, and two, three or four to a supply man who will tie them together and carry them over his shoulder.

It seems convenient to organize beforehand **ammunition lots** consisting of :

Cartridges for rifles (not a very important amount generally speaking).

Cartridges for machine guns and automatic rifles.

Hand grenades.

V. B. grenades.

Signalling rockets or cartridges.

Illuminating rockets.

Sandbags.

Every time troops ask for ammunitions a complete lot will be sent, unless otherwise stated.

It is strictly forbidden to send a man from the front line to the rear for supply purposes, when on the battlefield.

Food supply. — The men will be provided on starting with all the food that they can carry with them, especially 2 or 3 quarts of water.

The rolling kitchens and the water carts of a battalion, under the command of a very energetic officer or N. C. O., will be brought as near the troops as possible.

Avoid food with too much liquid in it, because of the difficulties of transport. It will be some times convenient to make up a meal basket containing the food for the whole course of the next day. Preserved food depots should be placed close to the command posts of the captains.

Men will get a ration of solidified alcohol to warm their food.

Supplying with ammunition in open warfare. — Either in camp or on the march, the men's supply will be ordinarily kept up first by taking the cartridges from the sick or absent soldiers, and only later from the company ammunition cart.

Before the battle. — According to the order given by the chief of the battalion, the battalion ammunition sergeant sends each company its cart with ammunition which is distributed.

Empty carts are sent back to the 2nd echelon of the combat train at the rear of the regiment and are not filled again during the action.

The ammunition sergeant on his part reports to the regimental ammunition sergeant. The latter stays at a certain point, determined by the colonel, behind the available battalions, with some sappers or reinforcements.

In action an infantry S. A. ammunition section (34 ammunition caissons, yellow flag and lantern) or a part of the infantry S. A. ammunition section is designated to supply the regiment. A liaison agent N. C. O. is sent from the S. A. ammunition section and gets his instructions from the colonel and brings back to the regimental ammunition sergeant the number of caissons wanted (generally one for a battalion and machine gun company).

The ammunition sergeant of each battalion and two sappers take the caisson as near as possible to the firing line, distribute the cartridges and take it back to the regimental ammunition sergeant. The liaison agent of the S. A. ammunition section takes back the empty caissons to the section and brings up an equal number of filled caissons.

After the combat. — The S. A. ammunition section completes the necessary supply of ammunition for both men and company ammunition carts.

The supplying of horses for ammunition carts devolves

on the nearest S. A. ammunition section, on an order signed by the general of the brigade. Requisitioned carts may be used if needed, to replace the regulation carts.

During action the S. A. ammunition sections must provide their own troops with ammunition and any troops in the neighborh d who present an order signed by their chief.

The commander of a regiment or of a battalion may also supply ammunitions to the troops of another regiment.

List of armament in rifles in a company.

NOT ARMED. with a rifle.	ARMED WITH A RIFLE, BUT WITH A REDUCED number of cartridges.	ARMED WITH A RIFLE.
1 warrant officer.	10 sergeants.	12 corporals.
1 1st sergeant.	4 grenadier-corporals.	68 riflemen.
8 automatic-riflemen.	28 grenadiers.	15 miscellaneous.
8 first carriers aut.-riflemen.	16 V. B. rifle-grenadiers.	8 second carriers auto-rifle.
1 first aid man.	8 carriers V. B.	
2 field musicians.	1 cyclist.	
3 drivers.		

Various and useful knowledge concerning an organization of supply.

1° Supply to be carried by men.

A supply man can carry :

700 cartridges weighing 50 pounds.
30 grenades O F, weighing 25 pounds (their number being limited by their size).
30 F^1 grenades weighing 40 pounds.
40 suffocating grenades, weighing 35 pounds.
25 A B incendiary grenades weighing 40 pounds.
40 V B grenades weighing 49 pounds.
33 shells of 37 m/m weighing 42 pounds (1 case).
50 to 100 sand bags (according to the thickness of the cloth).
5 wooden or iron stakes.
15 meters of Brun wire coil.
1 stake and roll of wire to cover 2 square meters.
100 signalling cartridges or illuminating shells of 25 m/m.

Water for one group (12 water bottles of 2 quarts each).

It will always be an advantage not to fill the sand bags up to the top and have the weight not exceeding 11 to 18 pounds.

2° *Supply to be carried on mule's back.*

A mule can carry :

3.000 cartridges.
4 cases of 50 grenades O F, that is to say 200 pounds.
2 — 50 — F^1, — 155 —
4 — 33 shells of 37, — 180 —
1 — 100 grenades V B, — 155 —
(to be divided into two side loads).

2 cases of 100 illuminating shells that is to say 180 pounds.

2 cases of 30 illuminating shells of 35 m/m with 1 star, 60 with 3 stars, 60 with 6 stars, 155 pounds.

One machine-gun cart can transport the load of 2 mules.
One donkey the load of three men.

3° *Example of an ammunition lot, for a platoon.*

12 bags of 256 rifle cartridges.
8 — 256 M. G. —
3 — 20 O F grenades.
6 — 10 F^1 grenades.
1 — 10 suffocating grenades.
2 — 5 incendiary.
10 — 10 grenades V B.
1 — 10 Bengal lights, 15 signalling cartridges, 15 star shells.
1 package of 60 sand bags.

Making a total of 44 loads, in 100 sand bags.

Such a lot may be transportable from the depot of the battalion to the firing line.

Either by a platoon of equipped men or by 12 unloaded carriers.

The lot will be completed by :

10.000 cartridges the supply of a machine-gun second
3 sacks of 11 shells of 37 (supply for a 37 m/m gun.)

4° *Supply for a company.*

a) **In cartridges.** — 4 men carrying 3 sand bags of 256 (48 pounds) each, supply the platoon in one trip and the company in 4 trips.

1 man supplies his platoon in 4 trips.

Very often, half of the supply only will have to be replaced, that is 2 men and 4 trips for the company.

b) **In hand grenades.** — The above numbers show that a platoon is fully supplied in grenades by 4 men, and the company by these 4 men making 4 trips : 2 will carry 20 OF, 10 F1, and 5 AB (incendiary); the third 3 bags of 10 F^1; the fourth 1 bag of 10 F^1; 1 bag of 5 AB; he may also carry 1 bag of rockets or signal cartridges of 25 m/m.

c) **In grenades V B.** — By using a man carrying 40 VB in 4 sand bags (42 lbs), the full supply of the company will be obtained with 4 men making four trips. The supplying is often unnecessary at the beginning of the occupation of the objective. The expenditure in VB grenades during a progression is small, if the troops have not come across a center of resistance to break.

And thus we see how the 12 carriers mentioned above are used for the platoon. This proves that two groups of riflemen can easily insure the supplying of the company and will moreover bring up a certain amount of engineering material, according to the information given in the paragraph entitled : « Supply to be carried by men.»

d) **In accessory means of defense and park tools.** — 12 men can carry 180 meters of Brun wire coil (front of the company) or 60 park tools.

25 men making 4 trips will bring the necessary material for 200 meters of barbed wire entanglement on stakes.

2 groups of riflemen will be able to bring to the company either 100 park tools in one trip or in 4 trips the necessary material to make up 100 meters of Brun wire and 80 meters of wire on stakes.

e) **In food.** — One-man will have to be detailed for each group to be in charge of the water, and another one from every half platoon for the dry food, that is a group of riflemen making two trips. The food fatigues can also carry sacks of fireworks.

To sum up, for a battalion in action, supplies between the battalion depot and the companies can be organized as follows :

1° Each company, in first line, details two groups of riflemen taken from the support section, who supply it with ammunitions (cartridges, grenades V B and fireworks).

2° The reserve company details to the depôt of the battalion :

4 groups of riflemen to supply with engineering material the two companies on the firing line; and two groups of riflemen to supply these two companies with food.

2 groups of riflemen remain available to be used by the reserve company for its own supply.

5° Supplying a battalion.

The battalion must have at its depôt an amount of supplies at least equal to that taken away by the companies.

Referring to preceding instructions, it appears that one company of auxiliary troops for each battalion is necessary to insure the conveyance between the depôt of the regiment and the depôt of the battalion.

6° Supplying a regiment.

It is advisable, as a rule, to foresee that a package of 50 sandbags for the distributions is to be put on each caisson or service wagon.

It is impossible to decide about the proportion of grenades O F, F 1 and others which may compose the supply. It is somewhat arbitrary to say that the grenade F 1 must constitute most of the supply, because some combats have been entirely supported and successfully with O F grenades only. The latter is the only suitable one for combats in the open and some of the grenadiers even prefer it in any case.

The following proportion may be admitted on an average of 1/5 incendiary grenades, 3/5 of F grenades and 2/5 of O F grenades or these last two numbers inverted.

The proportion of 1/2 incendiary grenades will be suitable for the groups of trench cleaners.

CHAPTER XII.

RAILWAY TRANSPORT.

A train of 50 cars can transport the third part of an infantry regiment; this is the greatest element that may be moved by rail in a single train.

Length of the train 350 meters. Siding track required 400 meters.

Maximum time allowed to entrain or detrain, one hour and a half either with platforms or with ramps.

It is absolutely necessary that the fatigue party detailed for loading and unloading should be sufficiently trained to avoid any delay.

Officer sent ahead to the entraining point. — An officer is sent ahead, half an hour at least, assisted by a N.C.O. who is supplied with a list of the personnel to be entrained and of the material to be loaded. Duties: To number the cars from the engine to the caboose; note down the carrying capacity of each car, assign the cars to the officers, men, guard, animals and vehicles; mark the contents of each car on the side, and make a written report of inspection and assignment to the commander of the troops. Send the report to him as soon as possible and communicate all useful particulars about the approaches to the train and the most convenient place for dividing the units. This distribution must always take place **outside the station.**

Carrying capacity of the cars. — **Ordinary passenger cars.** — For each compartment, take the usual number of seats, diminished by two.

Transformed freight car. — See the mark painted on the side of the car. «Men 32-40» means 32 men with arms and equipments or 40 without.

Ordinary freight car. — 40 men is the number alloted to cars of that type, whatever be the number indicated on the side.

Flat cars. — The carrying capacity is indicated on the side, say 5 fictitious axles. The **fictitious axle** is the unit which has been conventionally adopted for all army vehicles, the smallest being the limber of the 75 field gun caisson which is rated one fictitious axle.

It thus becomes easy to properly allot the vehicles to a certain number of flat cars.

Guard to be detailed. — 1 officer, 1 N.C.O., 1 corporal, 1 bugler, 15 men; they are placed in the middle of the train, next to the officers' car; they take charge of the prisoners; they reach the station at the same time as the troops and repair at once to their assigned car. The officer of the guard receives orders from the commander concerning sentries to be posted at once and at the stations en route.

Distribution of the units. — The troops reach the station in column of squads and are formed in line; everybody, with the exception of officers, takes his place in the ranks. The platoon leaders see that proper room is left for men temporarily detailed, (loading fatigue party, orderlies, etc.), that the men do not leave the ranks, keep their intervals and remain in their assigned places. The officer sent ahead divides the command according to the accommodation of the cars, no distinction being made between the companies. The company commanders detail men in charge of each car and each compartment. These men take the names of the men who are to travel in their car and aquaint them with the number of that car.

After entraining, the number of the car must be plainly marked on the other side of the car and the letter of the occupying company also.

Entraining. — The troop is marched to the train in column of squads by a convenient way of access, so that each fraction of the column marching at a distance of 2 paces from the preceding one, may easily reach the car assigned to it and be halted facing it. Men must take care not to extend beyond the length of the car.

When the commander causes the « Forward march » to be sounded, the men place their packs on the ground. The man put in charge of the compartment enters the car with one man only. The rifles and packs are successively handed to them and placed at the opposite end of the compartment (on pegs and baggage straps) or under the seats and in the racks.

When the arms and equipments are thus placed, the man in charge of the compartment orders the other men to enter the car. He is responsible for their behavior during the journey and keeps them from leaving the car without permission.

Bugle signals. — **Halt :** Men are allowed to leave the car for a halt of 10 or 15 minutes.

Forward march : Men repair at once to their cars.

Issue call: Sounded at the halts reserved for the serving of meals. The mess sergeants and 2 men for each car go to the supply officer or his assistant. Rations are distributed **in the cars** under the supervision of the officers. The men cannot leave the compartment before the distribution is over.

For particulars concerning the allowances and composition of the meals see under head : « Subsistence ».

Regimental march: Detraining; same principles as for entraining; order reversed.

During short halts, wehre the bugle signal **Halt** is not sounded, the officer in command of the guard goes along the train and may allow a few men to leave the cars

CHAPTER XIII.
NOTES ON THE SERVICE OF THE REAR.

The purpose of the service of the rear is to assure the continuity of communication between the armies and the national territory.

The *army zone* is under the direct orders of the commander in chief.

The *zone of the interior* is under the authority of the minister of war.

The *lines of communication* (generally railroads, but also roads and navigable watercourses) are found in both zones. As to the railroads, they are divided into :

Railroads within the theater of operations (commander in chief) and *railroads of the interior* (minister of war) separated by the *line of demarkation.*

Line of communication by rail. — Going from the interior toward the front one finds the following establishments :

The *gare de rassemblement* or regional railroad station (one for each army corps region).

Station magasins (interior supply depôts), *arsenals, military bakeries;*

The *gare régulatrice* (regulating station on railroad) of each army, through which pass all supplies to receive their final destination.

Gares de ravitaillement (or refilling points) : terminals of rail or water transport, points of contact with the supply trains of the division and army corps. These are also the *gares d'évacuation* or evacuating stations.

« **Etapes** ». — If the railroad line does not extend sufficiently near to the troops, the supply is continued by a line of *étapes*. The refilling station is then called the *gare origine d'étapes* from which the supplies are sent by road or water to the «tête d'étape» or advanced refilling station.

Here the division and army corps supply trains are filled for transport to the distributing point, where the empty ration sections of field trains meet them.

CHAPTER XIV.
NOTES ON THE RULES OF WARFARE.

The laws of warfare were instituted under the chivalrous though mistaken idea that certain well organised nations had entirely risen from barbarism and that they would consider themselves bound b the fixture of their signatures to the international conventions to which they had freely consented.

An infinite number of facts, very carefully and officially checked, have proved that our troops and our countrymen are never able to rely on the observance of these laws, and that atrocities are due not only to individual violations dishonorable only to those who commit them, but are often premeditated violations, ordered in cold blood by persons in authority who have the moral protection of the highest powers of the nation with which we are at war.

Nevertheless we sum up those laws here :

1. In order that the idea of what war ought to be may develop in everyone the feeling of *hatred*, which ought to be his only sentiment when face to face with such an adversary; in order that a platoon commander should never under any circumstances, tolerate any relations except warfare between his men and the enemy. This duty is absolute, and has no exceptions save in the case of wounded men or prisoners who are not in a position to do harm by treachery.

2, In order that any transgressor of these laws, taken in the act, shall be the subject of an immediate report by the witnesses and then be sent to the division headquarters to be judged on the simple proof of the facts.

The laws of warfare are the result of the *Convention of Geneva*, the *Declaration of Saint-Petersbourg* and of the various acts of the Hague. All these diplomatic documents were signed by Germany, Austria-Hungary, Turkey and Bulgaria.

The following are the principal provisions :

The obligation to protect the wounded on the field of battle from pillage and ill-treatment; to respect military hospitals and hospital-trains; to respect all persons exclusively employed in the transport, treatment, administration and protection of the wounded, and in the case of such persons falling into the hands of their adversaries, not to treat them as prisoners of war; but to send them back with all their equipment as soon as their presence is not indispensable for the case of the wounded prisoners of their nation.

The prohibition against the use of any projectile weighing less than 400 grams, either explosive or charged with fulminating or inflammable material; of any projectile having for its single purpose the production of suffocating or deleterious gases, of any bullet which spreads or flattens on contact with the human body, such as the steel-jacketed bullet, the jacket of which does not completely cover the core (the inverted German bullet) or a bullet that is easily subject to incisions. (The French bullet being one solid piece of metal may be inverted.)

The prohibition against the use of poison or poisonous weapons (phosphorous shells); against killing or wounding an enemy after he has laid down his arms and surrendered unconditionally, against declaring that quarter shall not be given; against bombarding undefended towns or villages; agaisnt firing on churches. historical monuments, buildings devoted to the arts, sciences, charity, the care of wounded and sick and which are under the protection of a special sign which has been made known to the enemy.

As regards food, lodging and clothing, the prisoners must be treated on the same footing as the troops of the government that nas captured them. All that belongs to them (except weapons and military papers) must be left in their posession.

The following have the right of inviolability : the bearer of a flag of truce (i. e. the man authorized by one belligerent to parley with another, under the white flag), his bugler, his flag-bearer and his interpreter. He loses his inviolability if it can be proved that he has taken advantage of his privileges to provoke or commit acts of treachery.

A soldier who is not disguised may never be treated as a spy

PART V.

GENERAL DISCIPLINE.

CHAPTER I.

MEASURES TO BE TAKEN TO SECURE SECRECY AND TO COMMUNICATE INFORMATION TO THE HIGHER AUTHORITY.

A. **In order to secure secrecy,** all persons connected with the military service, either in cantonment or on the march are forbidden to throw away any paper or letter, etc., without previously destroying it. Papers that are crumpled and thrown away are not destroyed. Particularly useful information may be derived from envelopes and newspaper wrappers. The number of the regiment should never be inscribed on doors, etc., or on the movable signs that are sometimes used in cantonments. The letter of the company, the number of the platoon or group are the only things to be mentioned.

It is forbidden to answer questions asked by persons who do not belong to the army. Persons who show themselves too inquisitive, or offer drinks to men to get them to talk, should be taken at once to the company commander. It is impossible to judge what information may be and what may not be made public without danger. The best plan is to refrain from giving any information whatsoever. Soldiers must never complain in the presence of civilians. Such complaints if known to the enemy can but better the r morale. Even in the presence of persons who may seem uneducated or unintelligent, it should never be forgot en that it is dangerous to let the smallest bit of information drop: with such people it is even worse than with others, as they alter and exaggerate that which they have heard.

As a general rule a careful watch must be kept in the vicinity of cantonments, bivouacs or batteries over people wearing civilian clothes or unusual uniform whose person and manners appear suspicious. Any soldier who does not wear known insignia or brassards that show clearly who he is should be led to the guard and detained until his identity is established.

Men on furlough have to be cautious on the statements they make and the opinions they express on war subjects, keeping always in mind the evil use that may be made of any piece of military information.

It is to be remembered that it is almost impossible for the fighters to form a sound judgment of the action in which they have taken part.

Telephonic messages may be overheard by means of clandestine connections, or induced currents, if there is no return wire. Without special caution the telephone must not be used for the transmission of attack orders or secret messages.

No order, plan or map which might be of any use enemy is to be taken when going into an attack.

Lastly if taken prisoner, military honor most imperatively forbids giving the enemy any useful information. Neither physical nor moral suffering will be an excuse for the departure from a firm and silent attitude. Such an attitude if deliberately adopted will win the respect of the enemy after he has vainly attempted to overcome resistance.

Moreover, intelligence service notes mentioning, like ours, names and regiments of interrogated prisoners will one day fall into our hands. Woe be to those who return from their captivity with the proofs of their treachery to their country.

B. **Communication of information to higher authority.** — Any information or documents concerning the enemy must be reported **without delay,** whether or not considered as urgent and interesting. Abandoned clothing or equipment are examined. Reports of their numbers, marks on the outer facing as well as on the lining are sent to the military superior. Patterns and trimmings of uniforms, shoulder-straps, cockades, facings, pipings, hats or caps, anything that may be easily handled, are to be sent in with the reports.

Any one in command of a detachment first to enter a locality from which the enemy has withdrawn, seizes immediately all letters found at the post-offices or letter-boxes, papers of the town-hall, the station, post-office, etc. He tries to gather all documents abandoned by the enemy and to examine all signs that might help to identify the commands which have occupied the locality (inscriptions, etc.).

Any soldier, knowing of the existence of carrier-pigeons in a cantonment, reports the fact to his superiors. Whoever hears of the landing of a pilot-balloon must look for the letter which is probably tied to it.

C. **Interrogation of prisoners.** — Prisoners must be searched **as soon as possible** under the supervision of an officer so that they cannot destroy or throw away papers or valuable documents on their way to the rear.

Moreover it is absolutely necessary, as soon as practicable, to confine separately commissionned officers, N. C. O.'s and privates and forbid any intercourse whatever between them.

The complete interrogatory of the prisoners takes place at the division headquarters to which they must be sent, without delay.

The intermediary units, regiment, company, have however a particular and immediate interest in asking precise questions about the defensive organization formerly occupied by the prisoners in front of their own position : trenches, machine-guns, trench-mortars, gas emitters, dugouts, listening posts, observing-stations, place and nature of obstacles, telephone posts, hand grenade and bomb depôts ; the direction of telephonic lines, commanding officer's posts, positions occupied by supports, times and routes followed by relieving troops, fatigue-parties and meals; strength of the troops detailed in day and night service. Some of these statements may be verified on the spot through a periscope or from observing-stations.

To obtain information of this kind, prisoners should be taken apart from the others and one after the other.

On the other hand it is strictly forbidden that interrogatories taking place at company or even regiment headquarters should exceed those limits or deal with questions of general interest i. e. recruiting matters, number of officers or N. C. O.'s in the units, and places of actions, strength and composition of units and their former movements, moral state of the country. In fact the first interrogators have not sufficient information to detect at once false assertions on the prisoner's part and recall him to truer statements. A prisoner who has been able to tell lies without being seriously cross-examined will never confess later on that he has altered the truth, for fear of being severely punished. The officer in charge of the divisional intelligence service must therefore be the first one to deal with such subjects.

N. C. O.'s detailed to bring prisoners from the company to the battalion headquarters are given strict orders. No one is allowed to speak to the prisoners except the officer to whom they have been taken.

The same rule applies in the case of deserters.

. . . .

PART VI.

CANTONMENT REGULATIONS FOR INFANTRY.

CHAPTER I.

BILLETING.

A party of men detailed and prepared to find billets or arrange an encampment are called a billeting party.

A regimental billeting party is composed of :
The captain of the company detailed for the day.
The battalion medical officer of the day.
The battalion sergeant majors.

A company billeting party is composed of :
A quartermaster sergeant (fourrier sergeant).
A cyclist.
The mess corporal and two men for fatigue.
The guard goes generally with the billeting party.

When several bodies of troops are to occupy the same encampment, the senior officer among the parties takes charge. If a general headquarters are among the billeted troops, the control belongs, in case of equality of rank, to the officer commanding this staff billeting party.

This officer allots the billets to the different troops.

Duties of the billeting party commander. — The essential duty of the chief of the billeting party is to divide the premises at his disposal between the following elements :
Regimental headquarters,
Headquarters company.
Battalions.

Knowing the total strength of these elements (officers, soldiers, horses, wagons), he gives the command of the billeting party to the senior sergeant major and goes forward with the medical officer and several cyclists.

He goes to the town-hall and makes the allotment, following the information and the documents given to him by the mayor. (See Part V.). He does not enter into details. His only duty is to determine clearly the assignment of each battalion, or headquarters company, in order to avoid all discussion. He gives the central part to the battalion detailed for the day, and if expedient places the battalions in the order in which they will start the next day. He designates a house, in the center of the village, for the guard, generally the town-hall. He billets mounted units near the watering places, and the headquarters company near the places best fitted for the parking of wagons, and if he finds no stables, the picketing of horses.

Assisted by the medical officer, he gathers information upon the sanitary state of the village (men and horses), and upon the quality of the water. He forbids the use of all unsanitary houses, stables, wells and drinking fountains, and marks them with placards.

In case there is a river, he defines limits up stream and down for the drawing of water, watering of horses, and the washing of clothes.

He makes the necessary arrangements in case of a fire alarm (fire station).

When this first elementary arrangement is finished at the town-hall, if the billeting party has not yet arrived he makes a rapid inspection of the whole locality, after which he defines the allotment of the billets exactly.

He selects a place of assembly for the regiment in case of alarm, as a rule outside the village. He establishes a bulletin board to be given to the commander of the cantonment, and to be placarded at the guard house.

When the billeting party arrives, he orders sentries, to be placed immediately by the guard at the watering paces, the outlets of the village, etc. He indicates to the battalion sergeant-majors and to the «fourrier» sergeant of the headquarters company, the allotment of their billets, and gives them all the information and the orders which they should communicate to their units. He tells them how much time they will have at their disposal before the arrival of the column, and then sends them to their work.

He remains a short while at the Town-hall to decide any questions brought to him by the quarter-master sergeants.

If the enemy is distant and the rations have arrived, he begins the distribution to the mess corporals.

Finally he goes to meet the column at the prearranged time and reports to the regimental commander all the arrangements he has made.

Duties of the battalion sergeant major. — He secures the lodging of the battalion staff and horses (horses of the companies being excepted).

He points out to the fourrier sergeants the premises where he intends to establish himself with the battalion liaison party, and if there is a good location for it, selects a temporary jail.

He divides rapidly between the four companies the area given to the battalion, each company occupying both sides of the same street.

He reserves a house for the sick.

He selects an assembly ground for the battalion in case of alarm, from which access to the regimental assembly will be easy.

The sergeant major of the battalion detailed for the day must find a lodging for the colonel and the senior medical officer. The billeting of the regimental staff is done by the «fourrier» sergeant of the headquarters company.

Duties of the « fourrier » sergeant. — As soon as the «fourrier» sergeant knows the cantonment of his unit, he fixes an assembly point in the middle of the cantonment of the company, and he sends to his captain his cyclist or a man of the fatigue party to act as guide.

Such a system is particularly to be recommended, when the billeting party comes but little ahead of the troops. All means must be employed to hasten the entry into cantonment. Units are generally sent to the village as soon as the captain of the day has reported to the regimental commander, that his inspection is completed, but before the sergeant-major and the «fourrier» sergeant have been able to finish their duties and come back to their units. Led directly to its assembly place, the company stacks arms and waits at rest until all billeting operations are finished. The exact location of this point where all following assemblies must take place (distributions, inspections, alarms, etc.), is thus perfectly familiar to all the men.

This being done the «fourrier» sergeant visits the premises of his sector. He measures their capacity (2 meters long by o m. 75 wide for each man), he finds places for the officers and for their mess, and reserves rooms for the captain's liaison party and for the clerks.

He distributes the company as much as possible without breaking up the platoons, and posts all necessary indicating placards.

He selects places for the rolling kitchen, the supply and baggage wagons and the horses of the company (ammunition carriages are always in the park).

He notes the quantity of straw which is needed.

He takes to the guard a list containing the addresses of the officers and hands it to the sergeant major of the day, whose duty it is to report on the cantonment of the officers of the regiment.

Duty of the company commander. — The work of the «fourrier», sergeant being done, the company commander orders him to read to the company all orders and information relating to the cantonment.

He insists upon knowing the manner in which the liaisons with the battalion commander and between the captain and the platoons have been established.

He gives precise orders'to be executed in case of alarm.

He announces the duty for the day and for the next morning : platoon, officer, sergeant, and corporal, detailed for the day, men detailed to guard outlets of the town, management of prisoners, distributions, meals, inspections, calls, uniform, time after which soldiers will be allowed to circulate in the village, etc.

He orders the sergeant detailed for the day to make a list of the sick.

He orders the company to assemble at the pre-arranged place, ready to start at five o'clock the next morning, unless orders to the contrary be received in the afternoon or evening.

He orders the allotments of billets and commands each platoon leader to march off his platoon.

Duties of the platoon leader or leader of a group in cantonment. — He installs his platoon, or divides it up and sends the groups to their different lodgings; in this case, he makes the necessary arrangements so that each N. C. O. knows exactly where his men are located and each man exactly where he can find his corporal, his sergeant, his lieutenant. and the officers of his company. (When ranks are broken before this has been seen to, all liaison or unexpected communication becomes impossible).

He insists upon the establisment of liaison and on the instructions to be followed in case an alarm is given.

He orders the **immediate** digging of latrines.

Selection of places for kitchens.

Cleaning of the cantonment.

The arrangement of the straw, if possible before night, leaving a sufficient pathway for the men between the sleeping places.

He makes arrangements for lighting, either with lanterns belonging to the groups or with those lent by inhabitants.

He orders the preparation of buckets of water, for the immediate extinction of any accidental fire.

He takes any other precautions againts accidents, seeing to the solidity of floor-boards, ladders, banisters, etc., etc.

He orders the men into fatigue uniform, to wash themselves, and to clean their kits and arms.

No one is allowed to leave the cantonment until the time fixed by the captain.

The packs must be put in order for the evening assembly.

Before leaving the next morning, he should be sure:

That the N. C. O's have had the straw bundled up.

That there are no complaints against the troop.

That the latrines and fire-places are filled with earth.

That every soldier has his cold rations and his canteen filled.

Report on the accomodations. — As soon as the company has broken up, the captain makes a rapid inspection of the cantonment and sends a short report to the battalion commander :

1° What part of the cantonment he occupies,

2° State of the cantonment,

3° Straw,

4° Water,

5° Requests from the company-commander.

He then assures himself that the liaisons are in good order, and that the special orders for cases of alarm are well understood and have been communicated to the men.

Information and orders to be given to the troops before the occupation of the cantonment.

The places occupied (villages, etc.) by :
Regimental staff,
Headquarters company,
1st battalion,
2nd battalion,
3rd battallion,

Billeting..........
- Colonel :
- Field officer of the day :
- Captain of the day :
- Quartermaster officer :
- Supply officer :
- Doctor :

Duty..............
- Company detailed for the day :
- Color guard :
- Guard :
- Guard house :

Calls.............
- Morning :
- Day :
- Evening :

Distributions.....
- Bread :
- Meat :
- Forage :
- Wood :
- Straw (bedding for the men) :

Park..............
- Combat train :
- Field train :
- Horses :
- Inspection of horses :

Water.............

Sick..............
- Time of sick call :
- Place of sick call :
- Evacuations :

Post (letters).....

Place of assembly for the regiment in case of alarm.......

Prices of provisions..............

Police regulations..
- Hours when inns may be open to troops

Security orders...
- Outlets of village to be guarded :

Departure next morning

at..(place).., ..(date)..
Commander,

— 276 —

Particular cases.

Alarm cantonment. — Only ground floors and large well lighted rooms are to be used as emergency billets, the doors are left open, the men sleep dressed and equipped, the officers do not leave their men and everybody is ready to go without loss of time to the place of assembly.

Bivouac cantonment. — Each unit utilizes as far as possible, the premises which have been alloted to it, and those for whom there is not room bivouac in neighboring yards and gardens. Roads and lanes are not to be so used.

Bivouac. — Encampment commander orders the limits of the regimental bivouac to be marked out, and allots the areas to be occupied by the battalions and wagon trains.

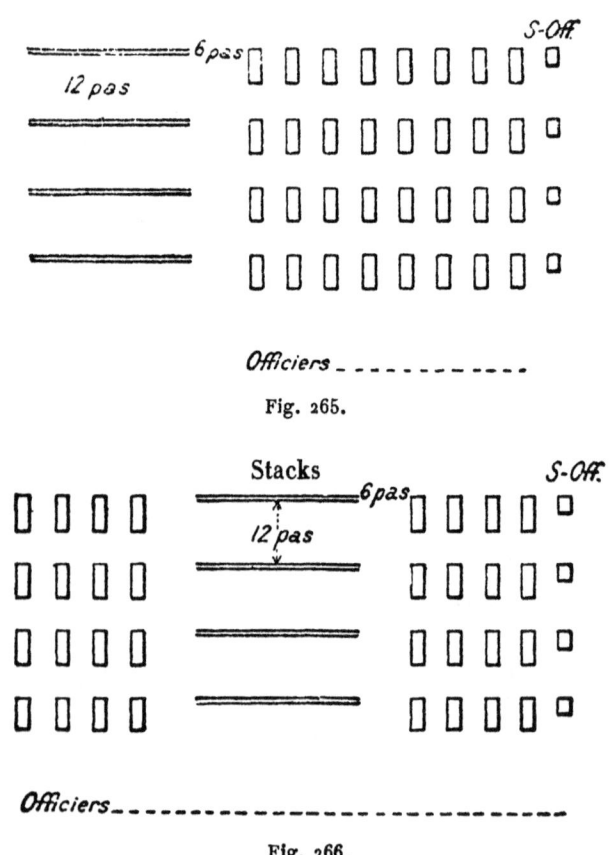

Fig. 265.

Fig. 266.

In the battalions, companies are placed in column, in line, or any other formation, according to tactical necessity, the distances and intervals varying whith nature and form of the ground.

For a **company** only, there are two regulation **bivouac formations,** either in column of platoons at twelve paces distance, or in line. A platoon bivouacing under shelter tents occupies a front double that of the stacks.

If a single company bivouacs in column, the half platoons camp to the right and to left of the stacks (fig. 266). If there is a double column or a line of columns, a whole platoon camps to the right or to the left of the stacks (fig. 265).

If the company bivouacs in line, the tents are pitched in two ranks, the odd numbered groups being in first rank. (fig. 267).

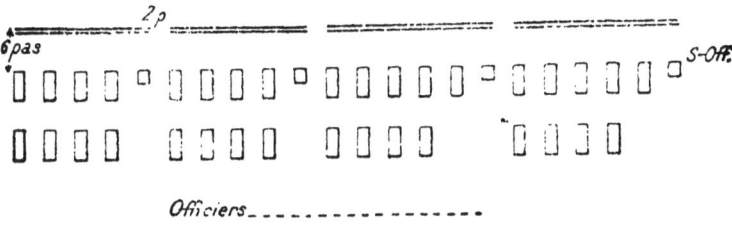

Fig. 267.

N.'C. O.'s. take their places to the right of their platoon; officers behind the troop, the combat train still further behind, and the kitchens either in front or behind, according to the direction of the wind.

CHAPTER II.

ADMINISTRATION IN THE FIELD.

Cantonment discipline. - Cohesion. — One of the aims of cantonment discipline is to develop cohesion in view of combat.

Without cohesion troops **cannot assault.**

Experience old as war itself teaches that cohesion is greatly developed in troops by the exact practice of a certain number of **rules,** whose principal and essential aim is to **form the habit of obedience in common** and to make this second nature.

On the contrary, if a soldier is allowed to have independent manners, to be unconstrained on the grounds that he is far from the enemy and that a certain negligence has no importance, cohesion is compromised.

A soldier at rest ought to enjoy a considerable freedom

permitted and directed by his superiors. But he ought never for an instant cease to be a soldier.

The material means to employ are : **To drill the troops frequently in close order,** require the fatigue parties to march in order, the soldiers **to salute regularly** and to be careful of their **appearance.**

A platoon trained to maneuver perfectly with rhythm and style takes pleasure in maneuvering and acquires self-confidence; keeps close together and never will disintegrate.

To be useful these exercises have to be frequent, varied and ended as soon as their aim is reached.

A soldier saluting boldly with a clear and loyal look respects his leader and will obey him. His salute says "Here I am."

He who avoids the salute or makes it carelessly, gives his leaders and comrades the impression of inefficiency and of one not to be counted on.

A soldier proud of his appearance shows that he is proud of his soldier's calling and of his regiment; he will be an honor to them. A man whose appearance is slovenly shows he has little self-respect and is just merely obeying orders, his comrades have no confidence in him and doubt that he will do his duty during the fight.

In the case of guard, more than in any other, the appearance should be exemplary and the manual perfect.

Such are the ideas which ought to guide the demands of platoon leaders while in cantonments, demands which are concise, never unreasonable or troublesome, but always the same and having as their avowed aim, **obedience.** In giving their care to **close order drill,** to the **exterior marks of respect** and to **appearance,** these officers are performing not only the service of interior administration but are creating cohesion and are doing a **tactical work.**

Appearance. — Appearance in cantonment must always be correct. A coat worn and patched may still be neatly kept, adjusted and buttoned with care. It is above all in accessories that care should be taken that they be in true military order; i. e., hat straight, hair neatly trimmed, cravat well set, clean puttees and shoes. N. C. O.'s should rectify the appearance of every untidily dressed man they meet, whether he belongs to their unit or to another. If his dress cannot be rectified (absence of cravat, buttons, insignia, rents) he should be sent back to his cantonment or post.

Above all, neglect and disorder must be repressed. A man working in his shirt sleeves is not slovenly, a man with clothes or shoes unbuttoned is slovenly.

A special dress is often ordered for wearing after evening meal (belt and bayonet, overcoat, etc.)

Among the requirements of good appearance must be considered the attitude on the street, a carriage upright and military without the hands in the pockets, etc.

Duty at cantonment. — Cantonment is under duty status from the reveille to the evening meal. The time free between exercises should be employed in maintaining neatness. Squad leaders must alway know where and how their men are occupied.

Besides morning and evening calls, a call is made during the day under arms and when not drilling.

Daily assembly for reading of orders and assignment of duty comes generally just before the morning meal.

An inspection is often made at time of assembly during the day.

Keeping up of cantonment. — For most of the prescriptions to be observed see Part IV, Chapter X, **Hygiene**.

To have a well kept cantonment, the entire area occupied by the company is to be divided among the four platoons, defining precisely the tasks of each, in order that no particular place in the street may be neglected. This being done, the platoon leaders divide the platoon fatigue work among the two sergeants who direct the necessary fatigue parties.

Establishment of the cantonment is profitably completed by the following measures:

By painting numbers upon every village house, these numbers making a singles series.

Placards upon each house or farm: cantonment for..... men, or stable for..... horses.

Placards at each watering point, aid station, etc.

Arrows showing direction of latrines, crematories, rubbish heaps.

It is sometimes advantageous to establish latrines far from houses: in this case a smaller **night latrine** will be established nearer, it will be lighted during the night and filled in every morning. During the day it can be easily required of the men to go 200 or 300 meters distant from their billet.

Memorandum for platoon leader. — Inspect platoon billets, approaches, kitchens, latrines.

Bodily cleanliness of soldiers, hair, care of feet.

Clothing, boots, leather accessories.

Inspection of arms and ammunitions.

— — reserve rations.
— — gas masks.
— — encampment material.

Inspection of material not issued uniformly to each soldier; i. e., tools, Filloux apparatus, rifle-grenade-tromblons, brownings, grenade baskets, etc.

Supervision of relations between soldiers and inhabitants.

Supplementary instructions of backward and poorly drilled soldiers of the platoon.

Care of sick and unfit.

1st Sergeant. Organizes and superintends tailors' and shoemakers' shops (dividing their time between the half-platoons).

Organizes barber shops.

Distributes soap, candles, etc. to the half-platoons.

Surveys cleaning of rolling kitchens.

Surveys evacuation of men to be sent back, having these take with them arms, kits, gas masks, one day's ration; and having them leave ammunition, tools and encampment material.

Half-platoon sergeant. — Makes up his call list and those of his corporals.

Inspects daily cleaning of arms and tools. Inspects cleaning of personal property. Minor repairs incumbent on the men themselves : buttons, seams, etc. Major repairs to be made in tailor's shop, to be verified on return. Cleaning of boots. Washing of linen, haversacks, ration bags, linings.

Superintends marking of all new clothes and bags.

Orders his men to be washed and shaved, to have hair cut.

To wear cholera belts.

To clean the cantonment : selecting himself fatigue parties, assigning to them their tasks, verifying their work.

Sees to it that all men are in the cantonment, working as ordered.

Whether the sick are following doctor's prescriptions.

He enforces the good behavior of his men in the village and obliges them to observe orders relating to inns and saloons.

He forbids smoking in barns and lofts, the lighting of fires near buildings and hayricks, the use of candles except in lanterns, canvas buckets to draw water from wells, noise after call to quarters, lights after taps.|

Chief of platoon detailed for the day. — Does not leave the cantonment.

Inspects distribution of food when the rolling kitchen is not working.

Assures the start of details and fatigue parties detailed for the day.

Inspects the new camp guard.

Inspects men leaving on furlough and sees that they do not carry away any explosives.

Reports evening roll call to the officer of the day at the camp guard house. On the march when halted for midday he selects places for fires and assures the speedy departure of the fatigue party in search of water (this fatigue party must have been selected during the previous halt).

Sergeant detailed for the day. — He sends prisoners to the guard house or previously appointed place and has them brought out at the proper time.

He receives and distributes letters, cashes money orders.

Lists sick men in sick book and goes with them to their inspection by the doctor.

Orders fatigue parties to the daily roll call and assures prompt departure. (Fatigue parties are ordered at first in the platoon detailed for the day, afterwards in the platoons detailed for the next day).

He oversees the distribution of rations to prisoners or to men on duty away from their units.

He calls the roll in the evening and reports to the leader of the platoon detailed for the day and to the lieutenant commanding the unit detailed for the day' if the battalion is alone.

On the march he goes with the fatigue party in search of water.

Corporal detailed for the day. — Is at the disposition of the N. C. O. in charge of quarters. (Sergeant detailed for the day).

CHAPTER III.

REGULATIONS AS TO THE GUARD AND SECURITY IN THE CANTONMENT.

General instructions. — Troops in the field do not render military honors either during the march or while at a halt. In cantonment or camp the guard renders the honors, but without music.

The commanding officer of the cantonment or camp has the same authority as the **commanding officer of a garrison.** If he is a colonel or a general he may detail a field officer as **camp adjutant** whose duty is analogous to the duties of the **adjutant of a garrison.**

Honors to be rendered by sentries, guards and pickets.

To render honors soldiers present arms.

Sentries present arms to the following :
1° To colors and standards;
2° To officers;
3° To armed troops;
4° To persons wearing the decoration of the Légion d'honneur;
5° To funeral escorts.

Sentries stand at attention for :
1° Warrant officers;
2° Persons wearing the military medal.

Guards and pickets turn out for :
1° Colors and standards;
2° General officers;
3° Commanding officer of the camp.

Interior guards render honors to the same and also :
To the regimental commander.

The strength of guards is :
In a regiment : 1 platoon..
In a battalion : 1/2 platoon. } commanded by its chief.
In a company : a group.... commanded by a sergeant.

Duties of particular sentries. — **The sentry over the arms** receives his orders from the local headquarters.

The sentry assigned to the colonel's quarters informs him of any unusual event happening in the camp. He looks after the color and permits its removal only by the color guard.

The **sentries around the regimental train** permit no one except the authorized personnel to approach the wagons.

Unit detailed for the day. — Consist of a :

Company in a regiment.......
Platoon or half company in a } commanded by the captain or the lieutenant
battalion.................. of the day.
It furnishes the guard.

The remaining portion of the unit of the day is called the **picket** ; it furnishes patrols, fatigue parties, and other detachments.

Pickets must be prepared at all times to fall in without delay.

Duties of the commander of the unit of the day. —
Makes distributions (helped if necessary by lieutenants).
Responsible for the police and general cleanliness of the cantonment (under adjutant or commander).
Has supervision of saloons and camp followers.
In charge of men in confinement (if they are formed by battalions or regiments).
Verifies exit guards.
Receives reports at evening call at post of the guard.
Fixes patrols and guard inspections (hours, routes, orders).

Exit guard. — Guard of an exit falls automatically to the nearest company, without special order to do so. Provisional sentries placed by the billeting officer on his arrival in the village, are relieved as soon as possible by this company.

Different companies establish liaison between each other to be sure no outlet is unobserved.

Exit posts. — Importance of these posts varies with the situation. Sometimes it is sufficient for a single sentry to be placed on the road; sometimes a barricade is built and strongly occupied (double barricade with a movable part for carriages and indirect passage for pedestrians. The strength of each post is calculated according to its needs.

The post is established in an alarm billet or in bivouac, **close to the sentry, who can easily call its commander.**

Each exit post is especially surveyed by the chief of the platoon which established it. This officer must give to the chief of the post very clearly **written** orders, which are taught to the men. He is responsible for drawing up these orders, for which he asks all necessary information of his captain, or officer of the day or the camp commander.

Orders for exit posts. — The orders for exit posts are very variable depending on the proximity of the enemy, traffic conditions, and agricultural work in progress.

Consequently the orders must be studied in every particular case and indicated clearly to the chief of the post so as to indicate to him clearly his line of conduct and the extent to which he will require passes from the following classes of persons :

1° During the day.

a) Officers.

b) Troops and regularly commanded fatigue parties.

c) Soldiers detached from the regiment.

d) Soldiers detached from other regiments.

e) Cyclists, motorcyclists, and couriers.

f) Motocars with generals' pennants or transporting generals.

g) Other military motorcars.

h) Civilians going to their work in the fields, on foot or with vehicles.

i) Other civilians travelling on foot or in vehicles.

2° During the night.

Same classes of persons.

It is to be determined between what hours «night» extends.

3° Traffic direction. To specify whether individual vehicles, convoys, horses at exercise, etc., may move in both directions or in only one direction.

The sentry uses his own judgement and discretion in such minor matters only as have been clearly indicated to him by his chief, and calls the latter in all other cases. Especially is it **mandatory to call the chief every time there is a paper to examine.** If the chief (N. C. O. of the guard) feels any doubt, he sends the individual or the vehicle to the officer of the day for the latter's decision.

In no case does the password replace the written pass or other authority required by the orders.

The **password** is used **during the night** to challenge soldiers alone or troops for whom the orders do not require a written pass (officers, regular fatigue parties, patrols, etc.). In all other cases the password is required, in addition to the written pass, which latter is the principal requirement to be demanded.

In the case of cyclists and messengers, the envelope they are carrying in the guarded direction serves as a written pass for them going and the signature of the addressee on the envelope serves to pass them upon their return.

During the night movement is generally forbidden to civilians and the exact password is required from men in uniform. The countersign must be kept secret and be given in a low tone. The name of any driver of a vehicle who gives the countersign carelessly, from his seat, is taken and reported.

Sentries must know to which villages the guarded road leads, in order to inform cyclists and driters.

The signal to stop carriages is made by standing in the middle of the road and moving the rifle up and down horizontally, with the arms extended. A flag may also be waved.

Sentinels at exits render honors during the day, the same as other sentinels.

Hunting. — Hunting is forbidden in campaign, as well to men in uniform as to civilians.

Aeroplane alarm. — When a signal service by bugle or other means has been organized vith a view to requiring everyone to hide upon the appearance of an avion, no one may disregard the precautions ordered. N. C. O's. who may be out, should, within their authority, require the men to place themselves in the shade of walls or under trees and not to resume their ways until the second signal agreed upon has been given.

PART VII.

INFANTRY IN THE TRENCHES

Infantry in the trenches is most often **in waiting.** This situation sometimes lasts for several months and allows it to be completely organized.

During shorter critical periods it is in its trenches **under attack** or **going out to attack.**

These three cases will be studied in their order.

CHAPTER I.

INFANTRY IN WAITING.

Plan of defense. — «The commander of all troops in waiting is obliged to consider beforehand the different missions he will eventually have to execute, to collect information relating to his situation and according to this information, reconnoiter the terrain or have it reconnoitered; so that he can, when it is time, come into action with the troops he commands without any loss of time and under the best conditions.»

These prescriptions show briefly the duties of the officers intrusted with the defense of a **strong point** as defined in part IV, chapter VI.

Each officer commanding a unit, large or small, must establish a **plan of defense,** aiming at overcoming superior forces on the terrain with which he is intrusted.

This plan must be made known to all immediate subordinates having to assist in its execution.

It is based on the knowledge of the enemy's line and of the terrain which he occupies, from which are derived :

The determination of the probable points to be attacked.

The choice of the main resistance points (active elements or segments) and the strength required to occupy it.

The preparation of counter-attacks.

The establishment of communications, supplies, evacuations and liaisons.

A paragraph of the plan of defense is entitled «**Plan of observation**». and has to do with organizing the land observation (See Part IV, Chapter VI).

The following principles should be considered in the **plan of defense :**

1° Defense in depth is accomplished by stopping the enemy on successive points skilfully chosen beforehand, where resistance has been prepared.

2° **Each portion of trench, each islet of resistance** (barricades, organized crossways, smaller works, etc.) **must have a leader responsible for its defense and maintenance.**

3° **Troops entrusted with the defense of an area of ground never under any circumstances abandon it.**

It is important not to have any doubt on this matter in the mind of the troops. The existence of stronger lines of defense to the rear, the moving of the company into **advanced posts** (groups or half platoons) or keeping **main bodies** more to the rear, **never** imply that advanced elements can take the initiative in falling back on the main body, even if they judge their positions exposed.

All resistance is to be made **on the spot, in the post that is given them,** and ended only when the troops are disabled or when they receive from the superior command express and authentic orders (preferably written) to occupy another post.

All such orders coming verbally by an uncertain way are not to be considered (orders to fall back are specially suspicious when coming anonymously along the line of skirmishers).

The conduct to be followed in case of attack is explained to the smaller detachments and the orders must always be very clear on this subject.

4° **All lost terrain is reconquered by counter attacks launched immediately, with troops specially reserved for this purpose.**

At a strong point (company) one or several re-inforcement platoons may have the missions of local **counter-attacking** in certain cases, set forth in the plan of defense of the strong point. The company in line with others does not have a **reserve.**

Counter-attacks are especially foreseen and launched by the battalion commander, who uses for this work the **reserves** from the center of resistance (companies, half companies or platoons).

The plan of defense of the center of resistance considers the probable places at which the enemy may penetrate the front of the battalion and provides for each case the suitable counter-attack. Each company or platoon receives a copy of the part of the plan relating to its task.

The mechanism of counter-attacks is explained below (Chapter II).

Reconnaissance of a strong point. — When a company is about to go into the trenches, the reconnaissance must be made during the day by the captain and the leader or N. C. O. of every platoon. An officer or a sergeant is sufficient to bring up the company during the night to the entrance to the boyaux.

The reconnaissance party includes moreover the liaison party of the captain and four guides (one for each platoon). The four guides will return to the rear to get the company at the place and time agreed upon, while the remaining part of the reconnaissance party will remain in the trench to study completely the plans of defense and the ground.

The four guides may also be furnished by the relieved company. In this case they are conducted without fail to meet the company coming to relieve.

This personnel can be reduced when the company is to become the reserve of the battalion at the center of resistance.

Plan of defense of the strong point. — The four platoon leaders, assembled at the command post of the captain, study the plan of defense of the strong point and receive the explanations of the captain commanding the relieved company. The captain allots his four platoons to the different **elements** of the strong point.

He orders the groups of grenadiers and automatic riflemen that it may be necessary to constitute outside of their accustomed platoons, according to the plan of defense.

Each platoon leader then goes with his man of liaison and his guide to the leader of the platoon he is to relieve.

The captain coming to relieve is in no wise obliged to base his arrangements and orders exactly on those of his predecessors, unless the latter were given by a superior authority. However, to make easier the relief during the night, always a delicate operation, it is recommended to relieve at first platoon by platoon and even group by group, and to delay until day the changes which the captain would make in the interior distribution of his strong point.

Plan of defense and orders to each platoon. — Each platoon leader reconnoiters rapidly the parts of trenches and the shelters his platoon will occupy as well as his command post. He sends back his man of liaison to the captain, and his guide to meet the company, after having shown to him the distribution of the groups. The guide returns through the boyau (with a written authorisation if circulation in one direction only is allowed) noticing along the way all necessary guide marks, placards, etc.

The platoon leader demands from the platoon leader who is being relieved an extract of the plan of defense relating to the trench or trenches occupied and makes with him a detailed examination of the terrain. This extract of the plan of defense comprises :

1° For platoons in first line : **the precise role of each trench element or islet of resistance whose defense is entrusted to the platoon** (for example : to sweep a part of the ground before it, or to flank one of the neighboring elements, etc.).

2° For the support platoons: **the fighting stations in case of alarm, the support to be given, or counter-attack to be launched, in the probable cases considered in the plan of defense of the strong point.**

Examples.— Figure 164 gives an exemple of the disposition of a company, taken from an actual case.

This disposition is more complicated than usual because of the salient and re-entrant angles that the ground and circumstances have given to the first line. Three platoons occupy respectively elements ABC, DEF, GHI. The fourth platoon is in support at K and L. The first line is held by five groups and two listening posts. Flanking with machine-guns or automatic rifles is prepared at M, M_1 and M_2. The central element DEF will receive, for example, the following orders :

To assure the guard and maintenance of the first line trench from R to S, the boyau EK as far as the crossway T and the boyau EI to U.

Half platoon at salient D : To watch and sweep the enemy line from N to G.

Group at the re-entrant E : To flank the portions ED and EA, defend the machine-gun M_1. In case the enemy has taken G, it fires in the interval GR.

Group at stockade F : According to orders, mans the portion DE, mans the portion EA, or, if the first line is taken, prevents the enemy from breaking from UES.

Figure 268 gives en example of a more simple disposition.

A quarter of the strength is on the line, the rest divided between the cover trench and the support trench. The platoon at the center and the support platoon alternate in occupying a redan and two little flanking works. Each of the two other platoons guards one of the trenches of the first line, and works its groups by roster.

General remarks. — The task given to a platoon enclosed by the others, in the trenches as in the fight, is always very simple.

But the difficulty is to communicate it to all concerned with such precision and clearness that at a given moment nobody will be turned aside from his duty by the foreseen or unforeseen circumstances, which will inevitably arise.

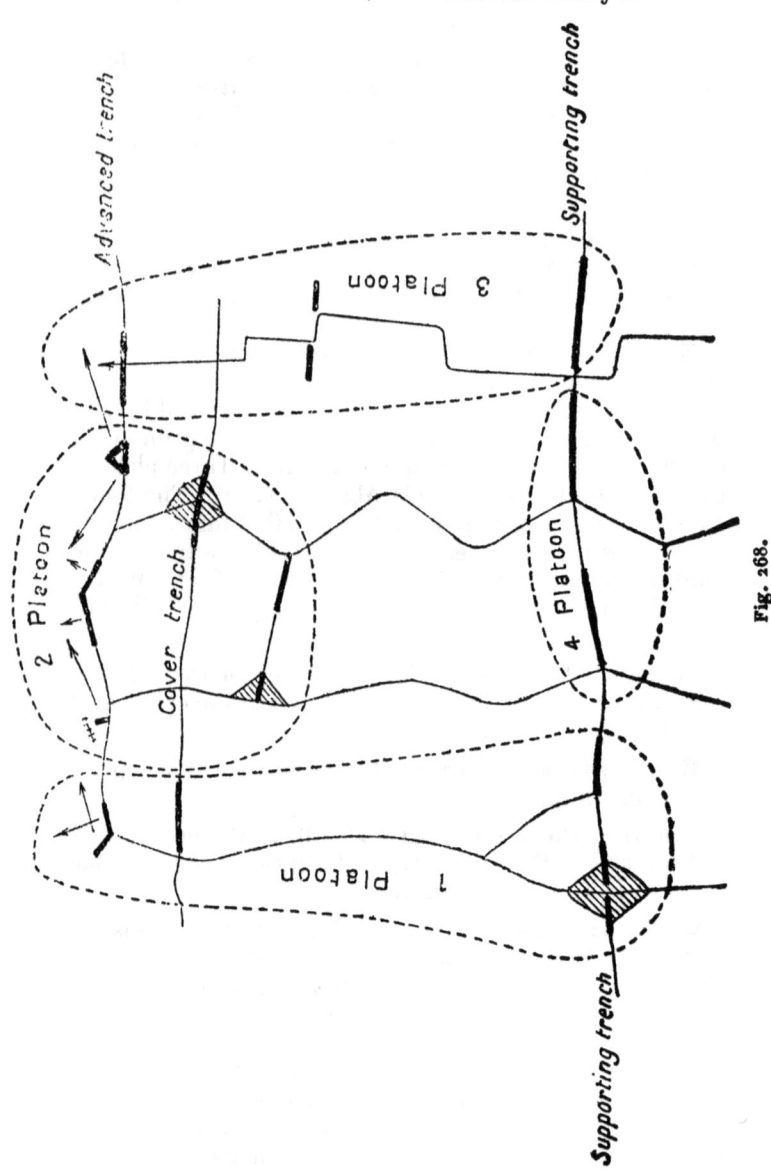

Fig. 268.

To do exactly what has been ordered, to realize to the letter what has been found necessary, is in the defense as in other operations of a platoon the whole secret of success.

Tactical memorandum of the platoon leader.

When the platoon leader has thoroughly grasped the particular part his platoon is to play in the whole defense, he easily deduces from it all tactical measures and details **which will be his constant preoccupation during his station in the trenches.**

He receives from his predecessor all information which may be summed up in the following memorandum, suitable for every leader of trench or lesser work.

1° **Extract of the plan of defense.** — Role of the trench in the whole position; detailed sketch of the organization; role of the neighboring platoons; liaison with them and with the captain.

2° **Defense.** — Establishment of the trench defense (stations of riflemen, field of fire, flanking works, machine-gun and automatic rifle stations, grenadier stations, trench mortar stations, and field to be swept; emplacements, value and capacity of dug-outs, defensive measures against gas attacks; nearest aid station).

Accessory defense works, chicane passages through the barbed wires.

Information concerning the enemy; sketch of the enemy trench; statement of observations; datum points.

Dangerous points, projectiles received, threatening mine works, unexploded shells.

3° **Watch.** — Stations of the watchmen, particular orders to certain watchmen, listening posts, patrols in front of the accessory defense works, rounds.

4° **Material.** — Recesses for cartridges and grenades, state of the grenades and the rockets, shields, periscopes, trench tools and destruction tools, different material the captain has permanently alloted, defense apparatus against gas, nearest water depôt.

5° **Works** under construction or ordered. Boyaux to be kept in repair at the rear.

6° **Places of latrines,** waste holes, cleanliness of the trench.

To facilitate the transmission of orders, every chief of a trench notes all the above points and gives them in writing to his successor.

Alloting the platoon between the first line trench and the support trench. — As the occupation of a strong point by the same company lasts several days, it is necessary to define clearly to each party (and in each party to each man) the periods of rest and the periods of duty, rather than to leave all men stationed in the trench in a situation of neither rest nor fighting. The principle is **to place in the parallel closest to the enemy only the men strictly necessary for the watch, for the wearing down fight, and for work** (strength being between one third and one sixth of the company). Other men are in the cover trench or in the support trench, resting or occupied in other work.

According to circumstances, the captain changes by roster the platoons of his company for first line duty, or better, gives to two or three of them placed in depth a position on the front, and keeps together in the cover trench one or two support platoons (see figs. 164 and 268). The platoon leader then organizes his service, alternating on the firing line groups or men (watchmen, grenadiers, automatic riflemen, etc.).

The only absolute rule is that **every first line trench must have at all times a responsible n. c. o. present in the trench,** and a severe discipline must be observed by the men in their fighting posts.

Relieve them as often as necessary, so that their attention may be continuous. Never leave in the fighting trench men whose turn has come to rest or sleep.

For the same reason, the captain details alternately an **officer of the watch** (platoon leader) whose duty it is to keep watch upon the whole front of the strong point (company officer of the day).

Establishment of the watch and wearing down firing. — The watch in the trenches aims not only at preventing the enemy from rushing out of his trenches, but at observing continually the details of his defensive organization and at taking advantage of his slightest movements to inflict losses.

Choice and training of watchmen. — Any man in a company can fill the role of sentinel at a bomb-proof shelter, but not everyone can be an observer.

Some are more qualified for it than others; ability is developed by exercise. **The drilling of good observers is one of the most important tasks.**

Watchmen must not only be able to see without being seen, but they must have tenacity and patience to observe.

Trench warfare permits the training of enthusiastic observers. The care of this training is given to the officers of the company, who control (every day) the service of their watchmen.

It is well to have them note down their observations.

Each platoon should have at its disposal at least 6 watchmen, of excellent sight and good shots. During the fight in the open field two of them go with the platoon leader and aid him, one observing continually the signals of the liaison man of the platoon who is with the captain. The four others may be scouts.

In the trenches they take their turn at the service of watchmen.

The company commander and the battalion commander use their men of liaison as observers. — These divide among themselves the terrain to be overlooked, observe the evolutions of the enemy, those of our troops, and the signals.

Whatever rank he belongs to, the leader indicates without delay to the superior authority (and to the artillery) the points giving a good view over the surrounding terrain.

The principal **dispositions for observation** are to be found in Part IV, chapter VI, «Principles of Field Fortification».

Necessity for a wearing-down fire. — A wearing-down fire should be the constant object of all platoon leaders and troops, and should not be slackened by fear of reprisals. **Trench warfare is not a suspension of hostilities or guard duty; it is a phase of the battle.**

Each enemy company should leave the trench with a loss of 20 men. The enemy should feel himself confronted by a vigilant hatred, and should know that we wish no rest until he is defeated.

The organization of a **wearing-down firing** with the tromblon VB has been thoroughly explained, with the tactical use of this arm (Part IV, chapter V).

Watchmen. — Watchmen always keep their rifles in their hands. Sitting is forbidden. They must remain continually at their posts, even under violent bombardments.

General orders are given them for the following emergencies :

Surprise attack, or attack preceded by bombardment.

Attack preceded by gas emissions.

Arrival of bombs.

Special orders are given to each post.

Watchmen for a sector. — Those called sector watchmen inspect a clearly defined part of the enemy defenses. Sectors constructed slightly slanting are recommended in order to protect the watchman when he has to shoot. The sectors should slightly overlap each other. Sector watchmen observe from a loop-hole placed slanting in the parapet, or with a periscope. A piece of mirror fixed to the end of a stick is also used to obtain a general view of the enemy trenches (See fig. 269).

The least change in the enemy lines (accessory defenses, ground dug up), or any indication of the preparation for an attack should be reported to the vatch officer.

Fig. 269.

The written order of every watchman-post is completed if possible with a panoramic sketch, in scale.

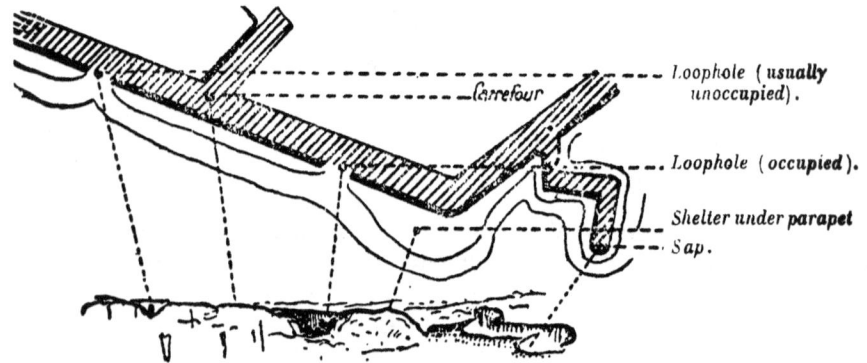

Fig. 270.

Watchers of registered aiming points. — Other watchmen inspect particularly the points to which their attention has been drawn by preceding observations and upon which one may hope to fire with success. They try to observe, without being observed, through a narrow and well hidden loop-hole.

Patient, attentive observation always gives valuable information upon the enemy's customs (**time for reliefs, supplies, etc.**).

Dust blown up by a shot, or smoke of a cigarette may

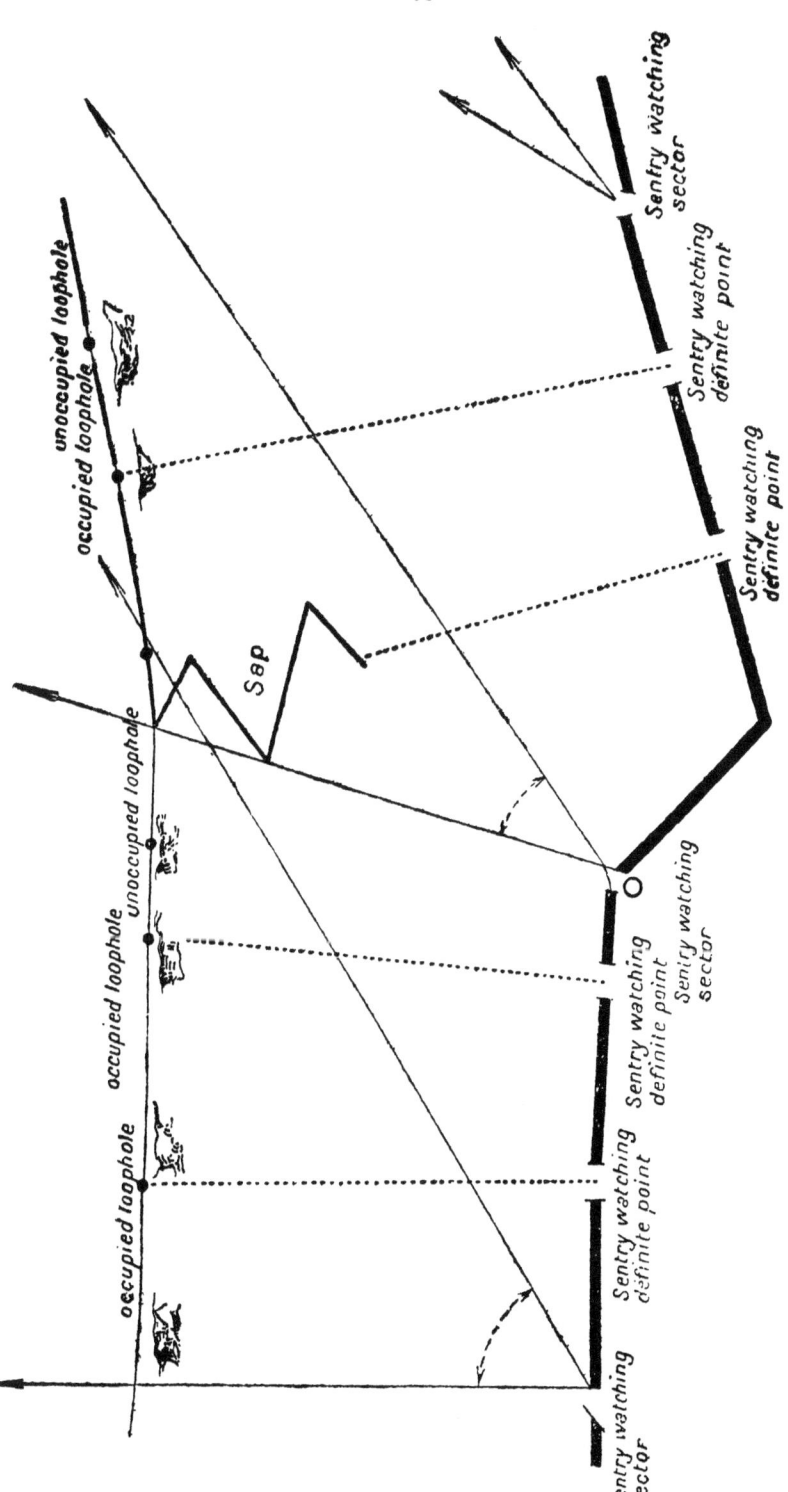

reveal a loop-hole habitually occupied, and it should be inspected with a field glass, and a rifle (upon a rack) or an automatic rifle trained upon it. Earth thrown up indicates a fatigue party, the establishment of a dug-out. A small earth heap and smoke reveal a dug-out. Study of the battle map and of the aerial photographs may allow one to locate on the terrain the crossways and the most important boyaux upon which it is always advisable to fire with trench mortars at hours when they are supposed to be occupied.

When the enemy is shelling our lines the curious will look through the loopholes to see the effect produced: it is the moment to catch them there. All means are good to attract them; shouting, dummies, simulated fire, placards, etc.

Watchmen try to find machine guns, flanking guns, trench mortars, observatories, etc., and to interpret ingeniously the least object or unusual sign appearing before them. This information is indispensible in case we attack, and also to insure the **daily wearing-down of the enemy.**

Listening posts or advanced posts. — These are used to watch over accessory defenses when they are very wide, or to flank the front of the trenches.

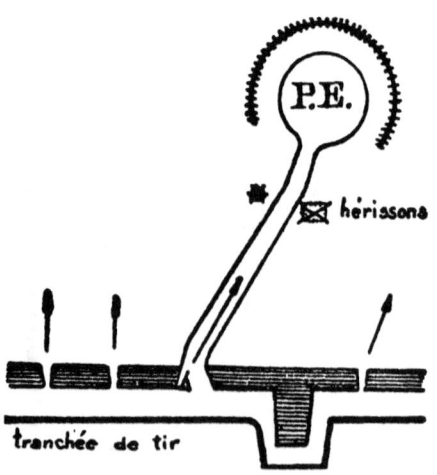

Fig. 272.

The boyau which connects them with the trench must be, in case of alarm, instantly blocked or barricaded by the sentinel who falls back after having given alarm (fig. 272).

Besides, it must be swept without any dead angle by the fire of a loop-hole specially established for this purpose.

The abuse of listening posts is to be avoided. They are easy aims for enemy raids and they take away from the firing line the station of several riflemen.

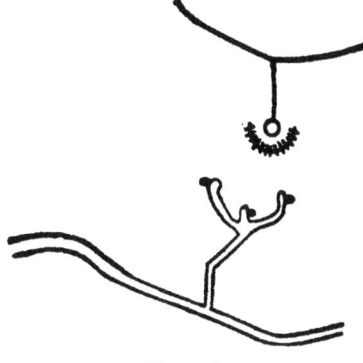

Fig. 273.

When they are opposite to enemy advanced posts they may be established with three platforms for grenadiers (fig. 273).

Watchmen in second and third lines. — Watchmen are posted near the post of command in the second and third lines for observing the whole ground and repeating the signals and the rockets from the first line.|

Patrols. — The watch is strengthened during the night by patrols whose field of action and strength depend on the proximity of the enemy.

They are armed with shot guns, brownings, and offensive grenades.

The captain or the major prescribes them. Their number should be sufficient to bring back any wounded or prisoners, and if necessary to establish a chain of men connecting them with their starting point.

They always have a definite mission : to go and reconnoiter such a point, to lay an ambush at such a place, to remain listening for a fixed time, etc. The success of a patrol depends on the choice of its leader; in him lies its will and audacity : patrols are his security and escort. It his he who must go and see.

They are to determine the time and the point at which they will get out from the lines (through the chicane passages prepared through the barbed wires, or from a listening post) the itinerary, the probable time and point at which they will return to te lines.

All this information is given, at the prescribed time, to the watch officers and to the neighboring companies, in order to avoid mistakes. Notice is given to the watchmen that the patrol may be obliged to fall back by an unforeseen itinerary.

The leader of the patrol must have a luminous compass. He places his men at varying distances according to the darkness of the night, so as not to lose them. He examines (before their departure) their equipment to see that it makes no noise. He communicates to them the mission and the conduct to be followed, and arranges with them a few very simple signals to be used. He may have a few rockets fired at stated intervals to light his way and guide his return.

All night patrols are preceded by an observation as complete as possible during the day.

Patrol duty is an excellent means of raising a soldier's courage. Volunteers are to be called for in exceptional cases only.

Establishment of a defense firing. — Habitually, only the active portions of the firing line are occupied, but the platoon leader should arrange for the possibility of manning the whole line and to **fire either through the loop-holes or above the parapet.**

A few traverses are loop-holed for the interior flanking of the trench. The means to block it are prepared. Those in which the boyaux end are specially defended.

In a loop-hole one should always see:

If it is not obstructed.

If it is well directed.

If it sweeps the ground.

If its height is fit for the man.

After several diggings out of a trench or a boyau, loop-holes often get too far from the bottom; they should be dug anew, or a step should be made. The loop-holes are previously allotted to the men, who are placed in order in the dug-out, the man lying nearest the outside of the dug-out having to run to the farthest loop-hole.

Establishment of the liaison. — The liaison between the platoon leader and the captain is made by runners (agents of liaison) or with signallers' flags. The company has two lanterns for signals, which are used to supplement the telephonic lines with the major and with a neighboring company.

Every telephonic line is supplemented by a visual liaison provided for in the plan of defense, which it is advisable to use once every day as a trial (for example: to report one of the daily statements).

Conventional indicative letters of the neighboring posts are asked of them.

Mechanical means having failed in certain circumstances does not excuse a commander's remaining in ignorance of important changes in the situation of his unit and his not haviug exerted his personal action over the direction of the events.

Organisation of the works. — The platoon is always charged with the keeping up of the trenches, parallels and boyaux it occupies, with the constant improvement of accessory defenses and with new works to be made upon the ground (mainly shelters).

The captain also allots among the platoons the maintenance of the boyaux at the rear and the general fatigue parties of the strong point, using preferably for this the support platoons.

The duty of the platoon leader is to divide the whole work among small parties each one with a leader. This leader is responsible for a well defined and practicable work. The platoon leader shows him during the day what he will have to do during the night; orders him to place all marks necessary to be able to find his way in the darkness. He sees if he has all wooden measures necessary to verify at any moment the dimensions.

The platoon leader suggests to the captain the new works he may find useful for improving the flanking and the boyaux. For example : in fig. 164, to join B and F.

Liaison with the neighboring platoons. — To develop **cohesion**, the platoon leader's duty is to have frequent and personal relations with the leaders of the neighboring groups, with the trench mortar party, the engineers working at the strong point, etc. He inspects observatories giving views over his ground and over the ground of units side by side with him.

To be able to give most of his time to these tactical occupations, he requires his N. C. O's. to assure themselves very exactly as to all details of trench duty and he gives hem the responsibility for it.

Internal service in the trenches.

Reliefs. — When the platoon arrives each group takes its place : the watchmen, the listening posts, N. C. Officer of the watch, execute the orders given for the night.

The platoon leaders and the commander of the relieved company retire only when they have given over the whole service and when their substitutes have given notice that they have no further need of them. The latter then become responsible and report to their immediate commander that the relief has been accomplished.

When the enemy attacks during the relief, the commander of the relieved units retains command.

Leaving the trench. The men are prepared before the relief. Be careful to take away all portable tools and encampment material. Grenades and cartridges exceeding the regular individual load remain in the trench. The trench is inspected to be sure nothing has been forgotten.

The trench, the shelters, and the latrines are to be left quite clean.

Defects noted during reliefs. — In a hurry to go, officers of the relieved units give incomplete statements of the orders. N. C. O's. relieving replace only the sentries and send the men into the dug-outs; they do only what is indispensable. The information given is very indefinite and often consists of indications on the degree of the enemy's activity. So, ill-informed and out of its bearings, the new garrison is for a time exposed to an attack, and sometimes fires on a portion of its own line.

Duty during the day and during the night. — The orders must be known by everyone beforehand. The numbers for day or night duty must be detailed by the company commander responsible for the defense of the strong-point.

During the day. — A certain number of watchmen are detailed; besides, a **detachment of pickets** may be detailed in each platoon or in the company. It is kept in readiness without taking any part in the fatigue parties or distant works.

During the night. — The necessary number of men is placed in the line between the watchmen to secure the protection of each trench.

Often the listening posts are kept only during the night.

Night and day a **N. C. O. is detailed for the watch** in each trench and an **officer is detailed** for the whole company.

Time table. — The platoon leader makes the timetable for the men not on duty. He orders them to rest in the dugouts or to be detailed for different works which he orders or which are prescribed to him. It is always known who is on watch, who is sleeping, and who is working.

Rounds and patrols. — Rounds aim at controlling the service in the whole of the company. They are done by the officers and N. C. O's (particularly by those of the support platoons). The company commander orders the number and the time for the rounds. A statement is made to him after each round.

The company commander also details the patrols. (See above).

Alarm. — An alarm is frequently given to be sure that everyone reaches his place rapidly and knows his duty. It is the best means to find out the weak places. Every day an alarm is given before daylight, followed by rollcall. Also, a gas alarm is given.

Dress. — The helmet must always be worn; the gas mask must be within easy reach of the hand; the men always under arms; the tools on the belt; the pack, the haversack, the waterbottle, the blanket, etc., set in order in the dug-outs.

Rifles. — In the first line trench, the rifle is never put aside. It is always retained even during the meals. In the other trenches, gun racks may be established near each dug-out door, or in the dug-out. It is forbidden for anyone to be in the boyaux without his rifle. During the night each man must keep his rifle beside him in the dug-out.

Rifles are never left in the loopholes, except rifles on racks. They are taken away when a bombardment is expected.

Rifles are hooded with a cloth cover tied to the bayonet hilt by a thread. **It is forbidden to put any kind of stop of paper, cloth, wood or grease in the bore.**

To avoid accidents and not to wear out the firing pin spring, the rifle never remains loaded. The magazine is always filled, usually with four cartridges only, to spare the spring.

Rifles are cleaned, greased and inspected every day. All the rifles in a group are never taken to pieces at the same time.

Cartridges. — Cartridge niches must be waterproof, and their place well known by everyone. Only a few packets are untied beforehand. It is strictly forbidden to stick cartridges in the earth.

The empty shells are taken up in every platoon and sent back to the matériel depot of the company commander.

Grenades and rockets. — They are placed in cases, if possible covered with zinc, well protected against the weather. Smaller niches large enough to hold a sack of ten to twenty grenades, are established at various places in the trenches, behind the barricades, in the dug-outs, etc.

It is well as a rule to put the cartridges and the grenades in **sandbags,** containing an invariable number. The following numbers are convenient :

    Cartridges 256 in each bag, weight   7 k. 500
    Grenades FI 10 in each bag,   —   7   500
    —   OF 20   —   —   6   »
    —   AB 1916, 6 in each bag, weight 4   »
    —   VB   10   —   5   »

This allotting allows these bags to be carried by a man, even loaded with his own equipment.

Men furnishing the ammunition supply tie two or four together to make a bag which is carried upon the shoulders or the arms.

This system is as practicable for the troops stationed in the rear as for the troops on the firing line during the battle.

During the night the watchman places the grenade bag open at his side, rolling down the mouth of the bag. In the morning he puts it back in the niche, all danger of surprise being past.

A few grenades are fired from time to time, to verify their state of preservation.

Materiel depots. — As a rule, one materiel depot only exists in every company (near the post of command of the company commander), but to avoid all waste, the leaders of the platoon or of the trench have collected into a little depot the tools put at their disposition and the trench material not in use for the time being.

A company depot should contain a minimum of 500 grenades, distributed in sandbags as explained above.

Combating waste. — It is necessary to repress severely all carelessness causing waste of material, and to make clear to everyone that the sum of carelessness and individual waste reaches a figure which no production at the rear can compensate for.

Ammunition left in the rain deteriorates or is lost in the mud or in unknown holes; one sometimes sees damaged bayonets and rifles used as supports, packs employed as sandbags, etc.

All material that cannot be used, all metallic pieces, leather, etc., must be collected in every platoon and daily sent to the company commander's depot.

Fatigue parties of rag pickers are sent into abandoned boyaux to bring back all things left lying around in them.

A man who finds, during a fatigue or a mission, a tool, any ammunition, any abandoned effect whatever, brings them back to his officer.

Reserve rations should never be eaten merely for pastime or without authorization.

All forms of waste must be severely repressed. It is a proof of idleness and lack of discipline.

Supplies. — At a fixed time, determined by the observation of the enemy artillery, a mess fatigue party of the company leaves the trench under the command of the 1" sergeant or « fourrier » sergeant and with the mess corporal. The N. C. O. has the party take back material that cannot be used, the empty cartridge shells, the arms of the killed and wounded, and gives them to the supply officer.

The distribution is made at a rendezvous arranged at the rolling kitchen, which is attended by another N. C. O. of the company who has remained with the combat train to receive the food and to see that it is properly cooked.

The distribution being made, the fatigue party comes back to the trenches in a group, mess corporal going ahead, while the N. C. O. must go behind. This N. C. O. reports to the company commander the return of the fatigue party and its division among the different platoons.

The platoon leader orders the operation of all means to heat the soup and the coffee (charcoal, brasiers, etc.). He orders all the mess tins to be shown to him, and he may be sure that if he succeeds, in spite of all difficulties, in making the food in the trenches agreeable, he will produce the best effect upon the morale of the troops.

Platoon leader's memorandum. — He is responsible for the defense of the trench, which he is to hold at any cost.

Role of his trench in the whole defense.

Bring up to date the orders and the plan.

Observation, inspection, watchmen.

Service for day and night. He details the N. C. O. on watch. Rounds, patrols.

Defense fire and wearing-down fire.

Flanking of frontal trenches and interior flankings.

He must keep the loop-holes in repair, the weapons and ammunition in good state. Grenades.

To look at accessory defenses; chicanes; mobile defenses prepared to block the boyaux.

Liaisons, rockets, signals.

Neighboring machine guns and trench mortars.

To keep the trench and the boyaux in repair.

To improve the trench and the dug-outs.

To propose new works and to execute them.

Material being used; material not to be used; waste.

Precaution against gas.

Alarm drill.

Half platoon leader's memorandum. — Detail by name for duties. Calls.

Assembly and start of fatigue parties to be furnished.

Allotting the men to the dug-outs. Placing the clothes and the straw.

Cleanliness of the trench and the dug-outs.

Taking the mud away regularly. Drains, sump-pits.

Burial of refuse. Struggle against rats.

Forbidding the least particle of food to be thrown on the ground or out of the trench.

Digging and cleanliness of latrines. Daily disinfection by the bearers.

Placards, telephone wires; care of all establishments.

Regular dress of men (watchmen, fatigue parties, resting men). Wearing the helmet, the rifle, the gas-mask, and the portable tools.

Daily inspection of arms and ammunition.

Equipment, camping material, tools, reserve rations.

Warming food. Making fair distributions.

Sickness. Soldiers excused from duty.

He makes known to the men the post of command of the platoon leader and the captain, the battalion aid station; the direction given to the circulation in the boyaux.

He has to be able to take unexpectedly the place of the platoon leader.

N.C.O. on the watch; memorandum. — Knows the exact role of his trench and the neighboring trenches. The directions to cover when firing. The aiming marks for the night.

He keeps the flare pistol and gives a light if a suspicious noise is heard.

Verifies the condition of the loop-holes.

He sees that the watchmen are alert, ears uncovered, rifles loaded, sound apparatus ready for gas alarms.

He verifies the orders, written or by word, which watchmen give to one another.

He knows the time of coming in and going out of patrols; their itinerary. He makes it known to the men.

Reports to the officer of the watch and his chief of platoon each incident and the arrival of a superior officer.

Gives to his successor the written orders and the panoramic sketch of the enemy line under surveillance. Gives it each time it is necessary to the chief of platoon, to be brought up to date.

Company «fourrier» sergeant or 1st sergeant; memorandum. — Receives from the «fourrier« sergeant of the relieved company the statement of the material to be taken in charge (inclusive of material that may be in the platoons).

— 305 —

Verifies it; gets receipt of the company commander, who becomes responsible for it.

Manages the matériel depot, notes the matériel received, the matériel given out, and the matériel used up.

He is always ready to fire the signal rockets when the company commander orders it.

He obtains information upon reports to be given and prepares them.

He identifies the dead, takes away their personal effects; makes a statement of these; gives it to the company commander to sign; and puts all the objects into the hands of the regimental officers of details. He leaves upon each corpse the identity disc. Orders them to be buried by the stretcher bearers, after having tied around their necks a bottle containing that which is necessary to identify them.

He takes away from the slightly wounded, camping material, tools, ammunition, material belonging to the company. They take away with them arms, gas-masks, kits, and supplies for one day.

He conducts the supply fatigue party (every evening).

He gives back to the supply officer all unserviceable material that he has gathered.

Battalion sergeant major's memorandum. — Takes in charge the material of the battalion commander's post of command.

Takes note of the established telephonic and visual iaisons.

Provides for rocket firing that may be ordered by the battalion commander.

Informs himself concerning the statements and periodical reports he has to prepare. He demands them of the companies in time.

He demands of the companies a duplicate list of the matériel they have in charge. He centralizes every morning their demands for materiel.

He regulates the service of the liaison men; makes them know every post of command and useful itinerary (colonel, neighboring battalions, companies, aid stations of battalion and regiment, observatories, telephonic stations of the artillery, etc.).

Company commander's memorandum. — The company commander is responsible for the defense of the strong point.

Plan of defense of the strong point. Sketch.

Extracts to be given to the platoon leaders.

Use of specialists ; grenadiers, automatic riflemen, signallers.

He limits to the minimum the secret documents being

kept in the trenches; provides for their destruction in case of an attack; never keeps the company fund in the trench.

Appearance and order of the trenches. Details the officer of the watch.

Prescribes the rounds. Proposes the patrols to the battalion commander.

He studies the possible improvements for the means of defense and counter-attacks, and for the establishment of the men in the trenches.

He studies the possible raids and the best use of the trench mortars.

He chooses and establishes the post of observation. He puts near it the post of command, the telephone station, the ammunition depot, the depot of water, supplies and materials.

He inspects the liaisons, telephonic, visual or others with the battalion commander and the neighboring companies, the liaison with the platoons, indication signals for each station.

He keeps personal relations with the trench mortar party, the machine gun company, the engineer, etc.

He knows how to command a barrage or a reprisal and all conventions relating to the rockets.

Daily statements. He notes the bombardments received, their origin, time, caliber, points of fall.

He requests all materiel.

CHAPTER II.

INFANTRY ATTACKED IN TRENCHES.

The men in the trenches may have to face two sorts of attacks: those executed by surprise and those that are preceded by violent shelling.

Both sorts may be prepared by a gas-cloud or by gas-shells,

Surprise attack. — Night or day surprise attacks can succeed only if lookout service is not properly done, when the men have not been sufficiently trained for the alarm, or if the accessory defences and flanking fortifications are insufficient. The enemy then takes advantage of the momentary confusion occurring, even among good troops, when they have relied too much on the idea that nothing will happen.

The preventive remedy for this is always to maintain the unit in the trenches in a fighting atmosphere by obliging it to keep up a wearing-down fight. The enemy thus harassed and deprived of rest has an acute sense of what must await him in front of intact trenches.

Attacks after shelling. — The attack comes most often after a shelling of extraordinary violence. It is executed on all the lines and communications of the first position and even on the lines and communications of the second position. Before each assault there is a heavy concentration of firing on the first objectives assigned to the infantry and a barrage fire kept up behind these objectives. The heaviest shells will be employed on the first line trenches. After a few hours or after a few days, the enemy will judge that the accessory defences are destroyed, that the trenches are levelled, and that the few shelters remaining unharmed contain defenders quite demoralized. Then he will lengthen his range, though still continuing the barrage, and his infantry will come rapidly out of the trenches and **running after his shells** reach our line.

To defend a trench thus wrecked and deprived of a part of its defenders is an extremely hard task and one which you must not fear to explain in advance in all its difficulties.

But numerous resistances, **victorious in spite of the most formidable attacks,** have proved that **brave defenders in small numbers can still occupy their ruined trench and stop the assaulting enemy.**

The most powerful artillery **diminishes** material means of defence and the morale of its defenders; but it cannot destroy **completely** either the one or the other.

The capacity for resistance of the real soldier remains always superior to material conditions.

Every man must endure shelling with stoicism and know that if he escapes he can **certainly,** with the aid of a few comrades and undamaged machine-guns, sweep the enemy's waves of assault **if at the proper time he is at his fighting post.** If the fighting post is destroyed, a shell hole will be chosen to protect him while accomplishing his mission.

Importance of good watchmen. — All depends on the watchmen's good work.

They must give warning immediately when the assaulting line shows itself; and the men must quit their shelters, with rifles loaded and grenades ready, before the enemy reaches our lines.

It is a question of seconds, not of minutes.

Observe the following rules:

1° **Every shelter must have a watcher in the immediate neighborhood, able to be seen and heard from the entrance of the shelter.**

2° **The watchman's post** built at the same time as the shelter, **must be protected** as strongly as possible.

3° **The watchman**, in turn watched by a man as relay placed at the entrance of the shelter, **must be replaced as often as necessary.** (This post being dangerous, every man in the shelter takes his turn.)

In addition to the watchman, a large periscope is installed, if possible, worked from the interior of shelter; but the periscope alone would be uncertain.

Do not rely on any signals, bells or wires of any sort, to give an alarm from a watchman placed at some distance from the shelter.

These rules must be applied for cavern-shelters and machine-gun emplacements, particularly as the trench's safety depends largely on the flanking works.

Liaison under shell fire from first line trenches to the captain and battalion commander. — Do not rely on the telephone, the wires will usually be cut.

Visual communication is unreliable on account of the wreck of the first line and of the huge dust clouds floating about it. You will be able, perhaps, to renew liaison after the **assault**, with the aid of lanterns kept till then in bombproof shelters. but you must not rely on this kind of communication to announce this assault.

The runner, especially the **doubled runner,** is the only means of communication reasonably certain ; but it is costly and not immediate. You must reserve it for a crisis.

It is only the runner who may bring a small sketch of the situation to the higher command, who awaits it with impatience.

Rockets are the best means of **immediate** communication, You must place some beforehand in available shelters, though it will be difficult to use them well in the first line, the rapidity of the assault often preventing their use. However, trust the watchman with two or three rockets asking for barrage, and a rocket-rack beside his sheltered post, with orders to fire the rocket as soon as the assaulters appear.

The best solution of communication is, for the command post of the captain on the supporting line and the battalion commander's command post on the redoubt line, to be provided with **armored observatories,** well placed so that the watchmen at these observatories may perceive the launching of the assault at the same time as the watchers of the first line.

Reinforcement of the first line. — Initiative of the supporting platoons. — The captain may immediately send his support platoons to the help of the first line, **a movement which must be studied and decided upon beforehand and every detail worked out;** but the execution of this movement would be very dangerous during shelling, before the range of fire is increased.

The leader of a support platoon must not wait for the captain's command to act. If he learns of the danger of the first line, otherwise than through the captain, he must execute upon his own responsibility the reinforcements previously arranged, and assume all communications, commands, etc., that are cut off at the critical moment.

In case nothing is perceptible from the captain's control post, and the battalion commander alone perceives the enemy's rush, all communications with his captain being cut off, he must then send one or two of his reserve platoons, fully prepared in advance for this emergency, to reinforce the platoons resisting the onset. These platoons should rapidly reach the first line, or replace the captain's reinforcements, if the latter have been able to reach the first line.

Use of barrage fire. — It is not sufficient that the first line defenders have taken a position to sweep the first assault waves; it is necessary to warn artillery that the time has come for a violent **barrage-fire** behind these first assaulters.

This barrage has its use in cutting them off from everything and preventing any support, supply or retreat.

Thus isolated, they are at our entire mercy, even though they have succeeded in our first line and in the trench supporting it.

Their successes will engage them with one or several **compartments** of our position (fig. 274 and 275) where they will be the prey of the front and flank fires, while awaiting our counter-attacks.

Officers must explain to their men, not by theory, but on the ground they occupy, these principles of barrage fire and the «compartimentage» of the position. The officers must show the men why they **should not be influenced by the first disagreeable impression, when they feel behind themselves an enemy who has broken through the lines to the right or left of those they themselves occupy;** for the enemy has on his flanks and behind him works that still hold out. His local success has in reality shut him in a «fire pocket» from which he will not be able to escape, unless our men get discouraged.

The tenacity of a few handfuls of men, even completely encircled in their defense works, will bring victory.

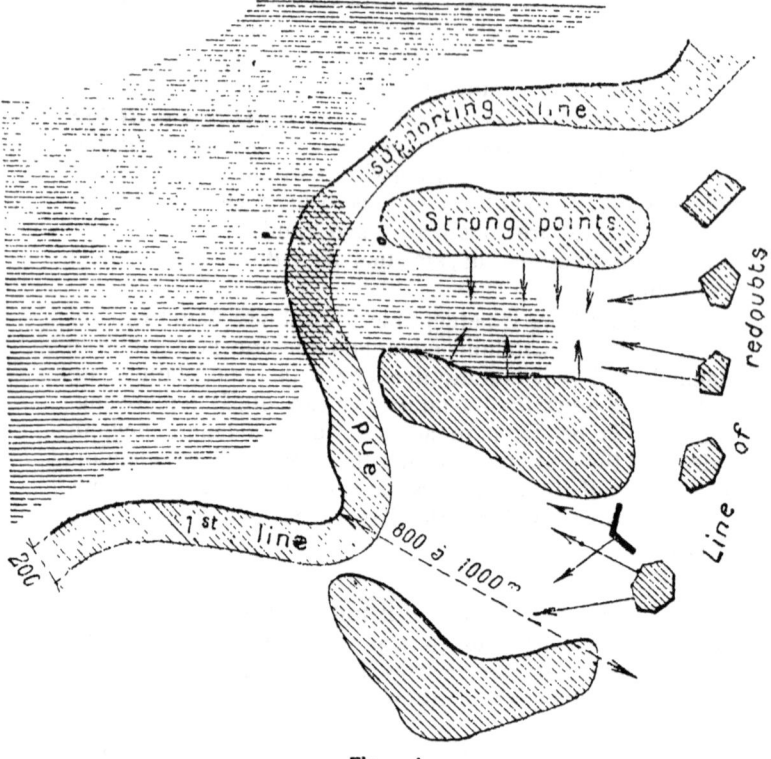

Fig. 274.

Launching the barrage fire. — Barrage fire is requested by every commanding post on perceiving the launching of the enemy's assault. It is requested by telephone or if the telephone is cut off, it is signalled for by rockets.

RULES. — **Each line must repeat, one after the other, the rocket signals seen in front until the barrage fire commences.**

In default of other information the captain and the battalion leader may demand barrage-fire and send up the supports as soon as they perceive that the enemy's fire range has increased and that his rifle fire is sweeping our first line.

If shelling is localized on the front of one or several of the resistance centers, the nearest centers must try also to watch the imminent assault and must warn the artillery concerned by their own telephones, which have probably remained intact. These lateral communications and observations, although indirect and longer, are precious if the direct means have not been able to work.

Carrier-pigeons are very little influenced by heavy shelling and may also be employed. The bird returns to a central dovecot and the message must mention exactly from which artillery group the barrage is asked, and in front of which part of the front it is required.

Signals between searchlights on earth and avions are employed when possible and will follow the regulations and methods mentioned in part IV, chapter IX, «Methods of liaison and signalling».

Counter-attacks. — The counter-attacks succeed the better and with smaller losses the more quickly they are launched, and must surprise the enemy before he can take breath or organise any defence.

They must start on the initiative of the men themselves, the transmission of commands and information being extremely uncertain.

Hesitation or delay is costly.

That is why it is necessary in the plan of defence of the center of resistance, to forecast the principal hypotheses of the enemy's invasion of our line of resistance. In every hypothesis try to foresee :

1° Which counter-attacks must be made;

2° Which units must execute counter-attacks (platoon or half-company);

3° The course to be pursued by each unit and its final objective.

The commander organizes this beforehand, **but it is practically the enemy himself who gives the signal for the counter-attack.**

The counter-attacks must be like the two jaws of a trap that shut up automatically, as soon as the animal has set foot on the spring.

Direction of the counter-attacks. — They may be frontal, as in the case of a support platoon which, sent to help a first line platoon, finds the enemy already in the trench.

The best results are those obtained simultaneously on both flanks and along the first line resistance trench. By a progressive attack with grenades in the fire trenches, cover trenches, support trenches, and in the boyaus, the enemy is attacked in the back, his retreat is threatened and the men who have managed to get through are surrounded.

Thus in case the enemy penetrates between C and D (fig. 275) we will forecast the following counter-attack :

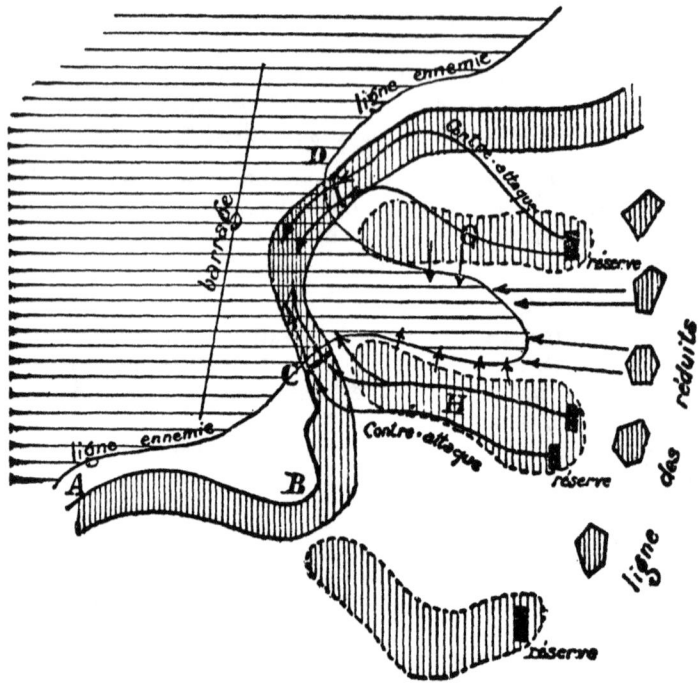

Fig. 275. — Lines of counter-attack.

barrage by group X in front of C and D; a column of 1 or 2 platoons starting from the work G, and attacking in the direction indicated by arrows N ⟶ S; another column starting from the point H, and attacking in the direction S ⟶ N. Details of execution must be arranged beforehand by the commander of the center of resistance.

Rebuilding of destroyed trenches. — After an unsuccessful enemy attack you must **always reckon that a second will follow rapidly;** and you must quickly repair the wrecked parapet. Sand-bags and trench-shields will allow rapid rebuilding.

Mine works. — If it is thought that a mine chamber is in a certain place (sounds heard during a very long time and suddenly ceasing), you must resolve to jump into the crater before the enemy. If the engineers say that the mine-chamber seems to be on the line directly beneath point M and that the average diameter of craters in this region is 30 or 40 meters, you must establish two trenches AB and BC, 10 or 15 meters outside the probable circle of the crater. One must evacuate the dangerous trench and prepare the men for jumping from AB and BC to the interior brim (fig. 276). From that position you hinder the enemy from occupying the crater. It is dangerous, however, to occupy it as the enemy often has a second mine chamber all ready, or else is able to build one rapidly by using his old branches not destroyed, although the branches under the crater itself are destroyed.

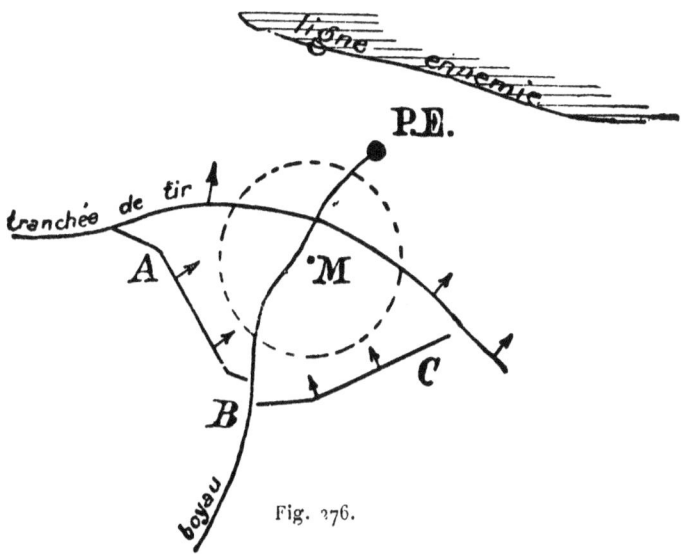

Fig. 276.

It would be wise to post beforehand two machine-guns firing towards direction PE tangent to the circle, and to have some VB grenades to sweep the interior of the crater by a curved fire.

Men on special duty and fatigue parties, surprised by an attack. — Isolated men or supply columns or workers surprised at some distance of their unit must put themselves immediately under the commander of neighboring unit, and remain at his disposal. The commander will incorporate them in his own troop, or will have them sent back to their unit by a N. C. O. bearing a written order.

Details surprised in their shelters. — Cavern shelters allow resistance under an intense shell fire, but their drawback is in hindering the soldiers' rapid issue. One must foresee that the enemy may be found at the outlet of the shelter, when you wish to regain the fighting positions. Each shelter must possess a small stock of grenades allowing one to clear the issue by force; every man must be well determined to act thus, and not to allow himself to be killed or asphyxiated by the intruders. Do not be alarmed by the enemy's having crossed over the trench, your companions will take care of them. Exterminate those in the trench, and take your place to fire on the second and third wave.

To assure exit from cavern-shelters, you may construct an armoured traverse-blockhouse of rails and concrete (fig. 277). A firing chamber communicating with the shelters controls by its fire the exits from the shelter.

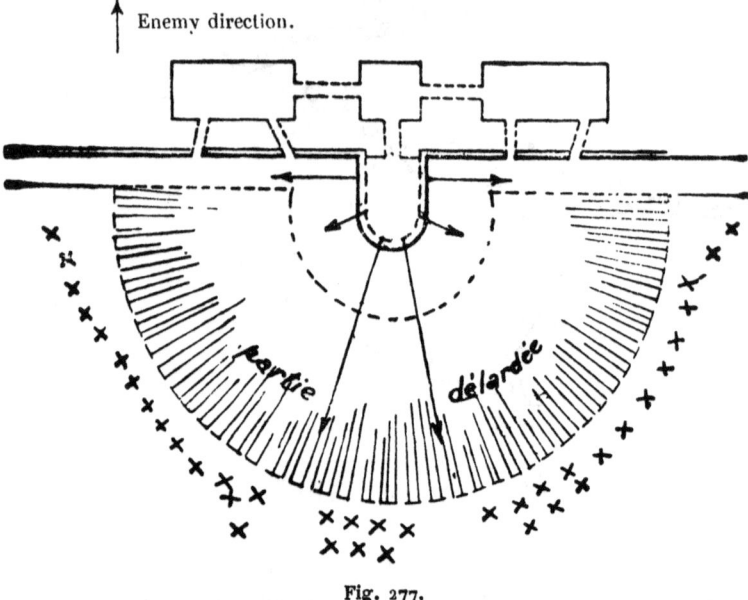

Fig. 277.

The surrounding ground is chamfered and accessory works of defence offer the enemy who has leaped into the trench, outlets in which he will infallibly be shot.

Defender's tenacity. — The defender must be resolved to fight till the end and **not to give up the fight, even though he believes those nearest him are overcome;** for beyond his neighbors they are other soldiers that still hold on and who will come to his help. Never judge a combat by what you see in the immediate neighborhood, but have entire confidence in your battalion and your regiment.

Not a parcel of ground should be voluntarily given up, no matter what the circumstances may be. A troop, even though surrounded, must resist to the last man, without falling back; each man's sacrifice is the first condition to victory.

PART VIII.

AN ATTACK UPON A POSITION BY THE INFANTRY.

CHAPTER I.
THE ASPECT OF AN INFANTRY COMBAT.

Infantry combat may take place :

In an offensive against lines long before organized by the enemy.

In every separate episode of the battle.

In an encounter during open field warfare.

In any case its action always consists in an attack on a position.

Artillery destroys; infantry overflows.

The principal action of infantry is the assault. All infantry tactics may be reduced to :

Preparation for the assault;
Execution of assault;
Following up the success.

The operations are successively repeated several times during the same combat : they may be expressed in a few simple acts, which must become instinctive with every infantryman.

1. — Preparations for assault.

The preparation consists of :

1° The approach to the enemy positions at assaulting distance,

2° The organization of the zone from which the assault can be launched.

The approach. — To approach is to bring a well ordered attacking force into contact with the enemy, and **exactly opposite its objectives.**

Under the present circumstances, the approaching movement has been carried on for months. It is sufficient (if such an operation has not yet been done) to carry the parallels of departure forward to within assaulting distance.

The most satisfactory **distance of assault** is to be determined according to the following facts.

It must not exceed 400 or 500 meters in order to shelter our assaulting and supporting forces from the artillery barrage fire. It must not be less than 150 meters lest our troops should suffer from our destructive fire on the enemy's first line,

The most satisfactory distance is about 200 meters.

This condition and the necessity of **facing the objectives** may demand a change in the front and the establishment of one or more parallel lines in front of the first line trench, if the front line trench is too far from the enemy's front line.

As a rule such works are to be avoided, especially those making necessary an advance of ground, which have the serious inconvenience of revealing to the enemy our offensive plans.

Generally it is more advantageous to start the assault from a greater distance, than to lose the benefit of surprise.

During the actions which follow the assault, the approach to the second line of the enemy or to any other position further behind, remains to be executed.

In this way the approach will be one of the constant problems of open field warfare.

The advance of the columns of attack will be executed in thin lines, or in lines of small columns, which by successive rushes advance with rapidity and in good order, under the protection of the artillery supporting the attack and the counter-battery artillery.

The result to be desired is that the infantry progressing in the very wake of the bursting shells of a well regulated artillery fire which forms a sort of shield, shall arrive in good order at the assaulting distance, assault without having to fire, and thus advance to the last objective assigned.

In trench warfare, things very easily go that way, when time and materiel have been at hand to completely crush all organization of the enemy before the attack.

In open warfare such a thorough preparation cannot be expected.

As a rule, in open warfare, the nearer you come to the enemy the slower and harder the movement becomes. Instead of moving together, the advance is made by rushes in small groups (platoons, and half platoons). Sometimes the skirmishers progressing one by one extend their line in a more advanced position.

When the infantry has been well trained the skirmishers

open fire only at short range, where they can see and take aim,

The officers and N. C. O's are the very soul of the advance; their spirit of determination and military education enable them to overcome the tendency to hold back and the anguish which besets the soldier who is to come out into the open. Together with the handful of men in close touch with them they take the lead in all attempts at advance.

Organization of the zone from which the attack is to be launched. — The zone from which the attack is to be launched consists of lines of trenches called **parallels of departure.** They must be dug close enough to each other that the most distant from the enemy's lines will fulfil the above mentioned conditions i. e. not to lie in his barrage; and they must be numerous enough to hold all the assaulting forces. Sometimes it proves advantageous to place there at the outset the second line battalions.

It is a well known fact that during the preparation of the attack the hostile artillery reacts very little. Consequently there is no necessity for the construction in the zone from which the attack is to be launched of shell proof shelters for the whole forces, nor of boyaus stretching too far in the rear.

On the contrary, it is necessary to resort to **camouflage**. as soon as the undertakings are begun.

The organization of the ground for an attack will chiefly consist :

Of the construction of observation posts, of command posts of platforms for trench mortars of light shelters for ammunition, food stores, and materiel in the first line.

The organization of communications (paths, boyaus of adduction and evacuation).

The organization of means of transmission (underground telephone, visual signals, messengers).

The organization of parallel lines capable of holding the assaulting forces on the day or on the eve of the attack.

In open field warfare the parallel of departure is constructed by the men in the first line. When it has proved impossible to come up during the day within assaulting distance of the enemy, the line from which the assault is to be launched is carried forward to its definite emplacement late in the evening. Such an operation must be performed in conformity with the principles ruling attacks.

The reserves are stationed in the **assembly trenches** organized as stated in Part IV, chapter VI, end of chapter.

II. — *The assault.*

The intensity of the efforts demanded of the storming troops and the successive attacks which they must deliver require an organization of depth. The various «échelons» thus constituted have been termed «waves», but this word does not at all imply a uniform formation. The foremost waves (generally the first and second ones) advance in extended order, the following waves may be in different formations for instance in lines of small columns.

On the other hand, to allow the command to be exercised easily in all échelons, the waves are made up of joined tactical units which are themselves formed in depth and not entirely deployed. Thus it is that a company or a battalion may be parts of several successive waves.

Consequently the formation for the assault is not constituted of echelons of stiff lines only capable of pushing straight forward, but on the contrary it consists of **tactical units placed side by side which can be directed and are even able to manœuvre.**

The waves are arranged quite close together in the first line and also the next parallels. They are there sometimes formed in double rank. They rush ahead at a short distance from one another so as to be able to cross the zone shelled by the barrage of the enemy in the shortest time possible. As a rule, the assaulting battalion leaves the parallel altogether and if need be, takes on the march, if there is room, the distances intended to exist between the waves.

These waves are not supposed to break automatically on the foremost wave; such an operation would have no other effect than giving the formation too exaggerated a density, this tending to increase the losses and mix up the units.

Therefore, when the first wave has gone over the first enemy lines, it continues its advance towards the objective assigned. The other ones follow up in good order without attempting to join the foregoing waves. **They are successively brought into action, if required, by the officers in command of the various units.**

III. — *Front breaking attack. — Following up the success.*

a) **The assault is followed by a fight inside the position.** — It is the breaking combat.

At certain points, the enemy gives in, at other places groups resist desperately.

The assaulting troops, gathered round the remaining officers, **rush through the gaps and surround the small centers of resistance.**

As soon as a trench has been captured the attack stops, but only long enough to re-form the groups, then the assaulting troops rush forward across stretches of ground lying open before them. Their strength is in their boldness.

These dispersed attacks bring the groups into contact with a new defensive line of the enemy. If the latter is manned they entrench themselves to establish a line from which others can launch an assault.

The attack of the new position is resumed with new troops, as previously stated.

Passing thru is an operation consisting in the assaulting battalions having their lines crossed thru by those of the reserve battalions, the latter thus becoming the first line.

This operation is performed either along a line of intermediate objectives (if the final objective is too distant for the same battalions to lead the attack throughout) or immediately after the attack, on the line of the most distant objectives assigned which the troops entrusted with the **tactical exploitation of the success** are ordered to cross.

It is regulated to the most minute detail by the **plan of attack** or by **the plan of tactical exploitation.** The difficulty lies in avoiding all confusion.

This operation is easily performed by well disciplined troops. It must be carried on very quickly, for on the line where it is executed it doubles, for a moment, the density and consequently the vulnerability of the troops.

The battalions thus overtaken become reserves or are left behind to garrison the conquered position.

If the attack has for its only aim the conquest of a wel determined position, the first line occupies the position and digs in, pushing forward only advanced elements. The supports come up to make certain the occupation of the conquered territory.

The attacks will generally be aimed at the enemy's artillery line, in order to disorganize his defence by silencing his guns.

The plan of attack indicates to every one in a firm and unconditional way which objective is to be reached.

That is a minimum line which must certainly be reached but beyond which the attacking troops can and must progress.

The **plan for the tactical exploitation** of the success established beforehand plans what is to be done immediately after the attack. It especially concerns those troops who follow up in the rear for that purpose.

Without waiting for them the troops having taken part in the **breaking combat,** as soon as they have reached the last objective assigned to them must **immediately push forward contact patrols** to reconnoiter the adversary's new position. If the results of the reconnaissance and their personal judgment of the situation show that the opportunity is favorable the commanders of the units of assault (**captains,** etc.) have the strict duty to **develop by their own means the success which has been obtained.** They will immediately report to their chiefs if they think the development of success can not be secured unless fresh troops are thrown in. Should the reconnaissances prove that the attack must limit itself to ensure the possession of the objectives carried, the assaulting units must immediately set themselves to the organization of the conquered ground. **The best way to reorganize conquered ground is to set regular parties to work on a judiciously rectified and marked out plan.** As much as possible avoid a new trench's being formed by joining a collection of individual elements dug in at random during the fight. Report without delay any artillery observation posts which will help in the preparation of the new position to be attacked.

Sometimes the attacking force disorganized by the combat and deprived of the majority of its officers, is engaged by converging counter-attacks. It has in such circumstances a tendency to fall back.

Conquered ground must be desperately defended, falling back is out of the question.

The troops must station and intrench themselves on those portions of ground from which they can withstand all attacks.

If surrounded, they must resist, until completely exhausted. Moreover, the first waves are immediately followed by a powerful line of machine guns, and supported by reserves.

REMARK I.

It is convenient to explain by means of an example what has just been said of the assault and of the combat inside a position.

Figure n° 278 represent assaulting troops having attacked in successive waves (V_1, V_2, V_3, V_4) and meeting beyond the first line TT with resistance of quite a different value (V_1 represents a line of assaulting platoons, each one of which may be disposed into two waves twenty paces apart).

In front of C the breach has opened. C runs as quickly as possible across the adversary's barrage zone and engages the intermediate line which he hopes to be able to rush in the same manner. If the resistance offered by the TT (trenches) and the barrage have caused V_1 and V_2 to slacken their pace and the waves to close up, they must be able to take more distance on the march in order to prevent any confusion while engaging the intermediate line and also to always keep room enough for manoeuvering. This «concertina movement» can as easily be performed by V_3 and V_4 in extended lines as well as in lines of small columns.

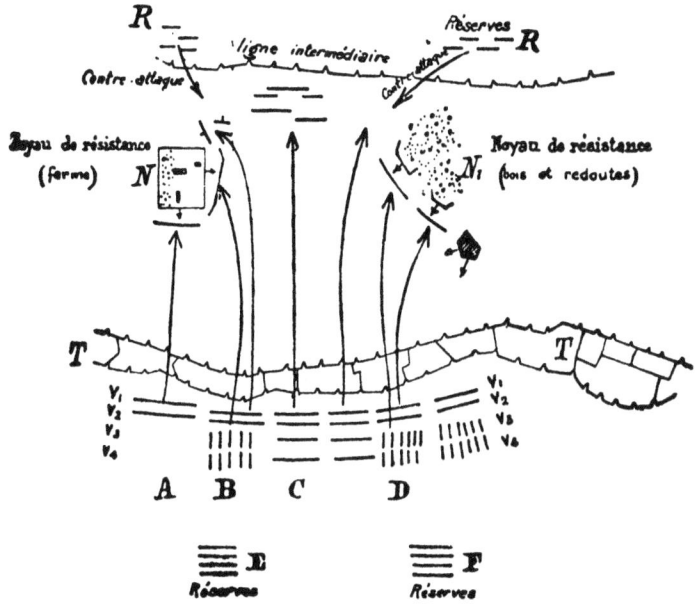

Fig. 278.

B troops have met a center of resistance N on their left flank which has not yielded. The support waves V_3 and V_4 have then manoeuvered to face the obstacle and have begun *to surround* it so as to permit the advance in the free space to go on. The new direction to be given V_3 and V_4 and their *manoeuvers* are here facilitated by the formation of small colums in line.

For D the same formation is necessary to allow the four waves to manoeuver by *wheeling* to the right and *attack* the center of resistance N_1, which has proved tenacious on that side and covers the interval with flanking fires which must be put out of action.

In front of A the first line has been brought to a standstill by N: in such a case reinforcing the line would often bring no other result than an increase in casualties. To reduce N, it is necessary to surround and attack it from the rear. This shows plainly how it happens that the density of the attacking infantry will generally be greater in front of the intervals than in front of strongly organized centers of resistance such as N and N_1.

Remark II.

For another reason it is necessary that strong reserves E and F should stand ready to push on in the intervals: it is the gap that may be produced by the quick advance of the units B and C. While the units placed on both sides (A and D) have had to engage the enemy on the outskirts of the centers N and N1 (fig. 279), if the enemy has sheltered any

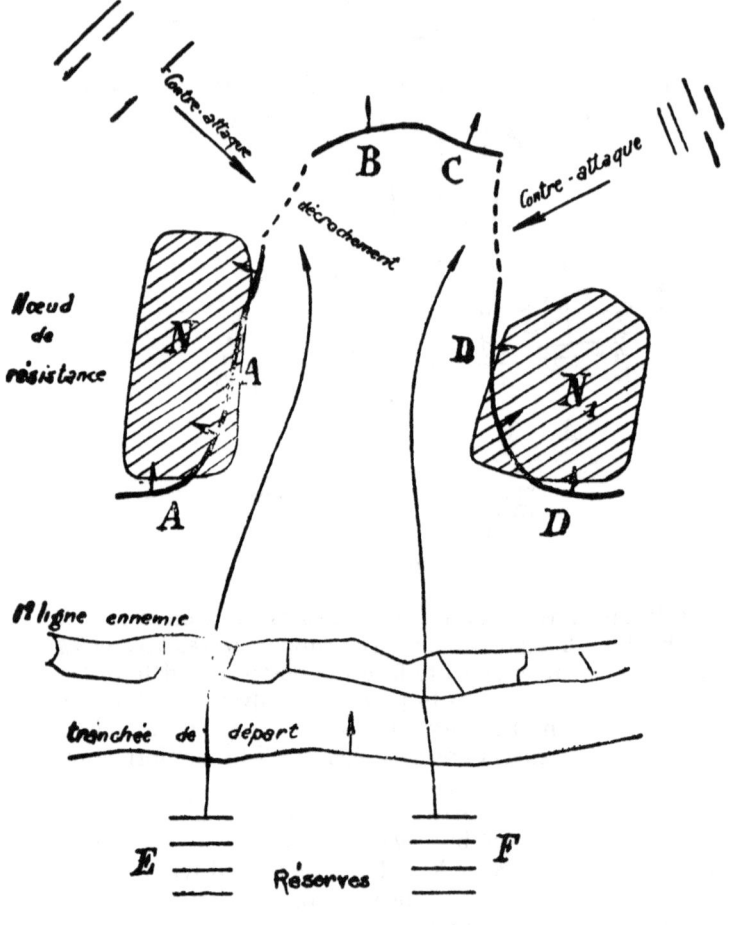

Fig. 279.

reserves behind these centers of resistance, which is probable, his counter-attacks on the gaps of the line will be dangerous. Such counter-attacks are to be prevented by pressing forward supports along the already conquered communication trench and by attacking without delay N and N1 at their most vulnerable spot which is their rear.

b) **Continuation of the fight at night.** — The night following the day of the attack generally causes a lull, which the enemy takes advantage of by entrenching and re-inforcing hastily.

Thus it is advantageous for the assailant to avail himself of the darkness to develop his advantages, to progress methodically wherever the enemy has given in, and to try and take the hostile organizations before they are strenghthened.

A night attack can take place only when in contact with partially destroyed or weak organizations or those still garrisoned by demoralized troops.

Every time troops rush undamaged trenches, well established and garrisoned by unshaken defenders it is necessary to prepare the attack by an efficient artillery fire. In this case they avail themselves of the night to accelerate the setting-up of all the means and even to begin the preparation with trench artillery.

Owing to the difficulties of advancing over unknown ground during the night, the attacks should never have a distant objective. They should generally be limited to the storming of a well determined point or of a well defined line of trenches.

It is impossible to have an attack executed by troops who have just arrived on the ground of action during the night as a thorough knowledge of the terrain is indispensable.

Night attacks are the direct province of the colonels and battalion commanders, for owing to the difficulty of the communications and the mixing up of the units, the action of brigade or division commanders is almost out of the question.

First of all the troops who have taken part in the attack must be again in good order. This is the duty of the officers who, going about the front, execute the necessary reconnaissance and inspire to all comfort by their mere presence.

The preparation for the attack, the collection of the necessary materiel, the placing of troops in position are performed after the usual procedure.

When the preparation is over, the line of infantry rushes forward with fixed bayonets without shooting.

Once the trench has been stormed it is immediately reversed. Star shells are shot up to reveal the territory ahead. The greatest care should be taken of the flanks.

It goes without saying that a solid garrison is always left in the trench of departure which is immediately connected with the conquered trench by boyaux.

Good order and silence are the chief conditions necessary to the success of any night operation whatever,

If the above mentioned conditions cannot be fulfilled, it is safer to give up the attack.

IV. — Notions on the part played by the artillery in the offensive.

3 roles.

Counter-battery artillery.
Artillery for the destruction of defensive organizations.
Artillery for the support of the infantry.

Counter-battery artillery aims at the **destruction** of the hostile batteries and in the meantime to be able to **neutralize** them effectively at any moment during the destruction. It diminishes the volume of counter-preparation and barrage fires of the enemy's artillery engaging either the batteries known beforehand or those which betray themselves during the combat.

Destructive artillery has the following aims :

1° To shatter the obstacles, to open wide gaps in the wire-entanglements, etc.

2° To ruin the principal organs of defence-strong points, post of command, observing posts, machine-guns, shelters and assembly trenches, etc., to shell the enemy's communications and establishments.

3° To demoralize the post's surviving defenders.

The work of the **destructive artillery** is determined before the attack.

The aim of the **supporting artillery** is:

1° To act as a **direct protection** for each assaulting troop; it is the shield behind which the infantry will advance. It prevents the defenders of the attacked zone from manning the parapets and placing their machine guns in position. A thorough agreement must be minutely established between the progression of the artillery fire and the progression of the infantry. The latter must follow **its shells and march in the very fire of its artillery.**

2° To act as a **complete screen to the attacking forces**, i. e. to cover them, both in front and on the flanks against any interference whatsoever which might come from the unattacked zones, to prevent all near or distant approach to the attacked zone, to catch under its rapid fire the gatherings and the counter attacks which might disclose themselves, and to prevent all supports, all reliefs, materiel and ammunition from coming up.

CHAPTER II.

COMBAT OF THE PLATOON AND THE GROUP.

The formation and **officering of the platoon**, its **progression in combat**, and the **assault** have been dwelt with in Part II, Chapter v.

Platoon firing is discussed in Part IV, Chapter iv, the beginning of which alone concerns the assault.

The **mission of the platoon in line with others is always quite simple and énergetic.**

A comparison of the line of skirmishers and the line of groups in column of files. — Skirmishers on one line are more closely in touch. They see one another and advance at the same pace towards the same dangers. If there is a space of a few yards on each side, the soldier can advance more easily and is better able to pick out a shelter for himself when the order to halt is given.

For crossing ground which is being shelled, it has been found better to advance in line at double time with a space as wide as possible between the men.

A distance of four or five spaces between men is the best formation for firing and attacking. This formation, however, creates parallel lines of men visible from a distance and, therefore, ought not to be used as a formation of advance under the fire of artillery alone.

As regards the **vulnerability** by infantry firing on this formation, it is impossible to state that **at short distances** one formation is more dangerous than the other. Everything depends on the position of the machine guns and the proportion of firing on the front and the flank.

The sheaf of the machine gun fire is very thick and very narrow. From the flank, it will play more havoc in a line than in a column; from the front the effect will be the reverse (fig. 280.)

From this it follows, that among the assaulting waves, which follow one another in close succession, the first ones may be in lines and the last ones in small columns (group columns by files.)

The small columns are more easily manœuvred than the line. The line, once it has been launched to attack, works well only straight ahead, while the small column can be easily directed and manœuvred in any direction even while attacking.

Small columns by files and by twos are used :

In approach formation, under artillery fire, obligatory on all terrains.

In fighting formation under infantry fire, only on thickly overgrown terrain of difficult crossing.

In assault formation, for the support waves which must be easily and readily manœuvred;

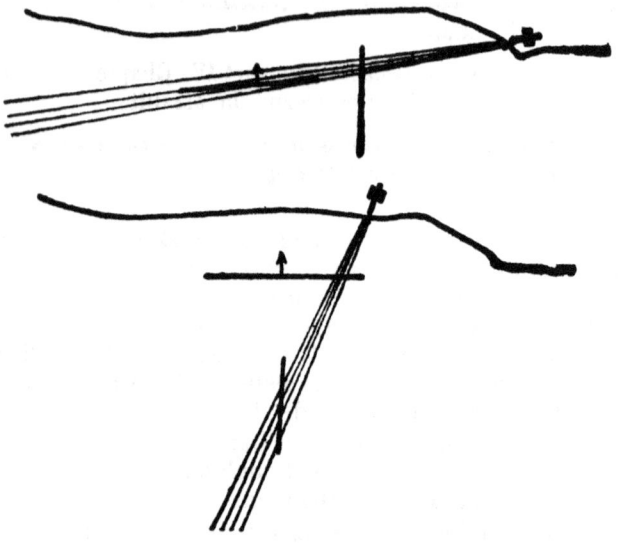

Fig. 280.

The great drawback of this formation is the dropping off of men, especially at the assault, and numerous and reliable file closers must be at hand. When it is necessary for the supporting party to march in lines of groups in file, it must start forward in line like those preceding it and then quickly be formed into a column. If this is not done all the men coming out behind one another from the same point in the trench choose inaccurate intervals between each other and lose all cohesion.

In short, under artillery fire, the formation of small columns is obligatory.

Under infantry fire, the choice between one or the other of the two formations will be more a question of good order than one of vulnerability.

Rôles and objectives which a platoon may be given. — The plans decided upon must tend to **paralyse instantly the defense at the same time from all sides.** Each German must suddenly find himself facing an American before having time to think of defending himself.

The platoon can fight as :

An **assault** unit,

A **supporting** unit.

Assaulting platoon. — In order to paralyze the defensh all important points must immediately be seized, whice points are :

The dugouts (dugouts under the parapet, and dugouts in the communication trenches in the rear).

The cross-roads.

The machine gun emplacements.

The command posts.

Photographs serve to give each platoon as successive objectives a series of these important points. Each N.C.O. receives a sketch on which these objectives are clearly indicated by colored pencil marks.

Each platoon marches straight toward its objective, never evades it, and never allows itself to be turned aside. **Boyaus are not to be entered** unless they have been given as a final objective. Attack them from the open ground.

When an intermediate trench has been taken, reform quickly a few meters beyond the parados and advance toward the next objective.

The principal lines on which the troops will have to effect these successive rallies are indicated beforehand by the captain, according to the plan of the enemy's boyaux.

The platoon must automatically reform after each stop.

Supporting platoon. — If the assaulting platoons have suffered severe casualties the supporting platoons reinforce them.

Otherwise, they try, during the combat and after the rallying, to station themselves on flanks of the company, in order to close up the gaps should there happen to be any.

If an assaulting platoon meets with resistance, the supporting platoon takes care to avoid encountering the same resistance. It tries to outflank the resistance and take it from the rear.

The struggle carried on by the first two waves must be rapid and confine itself to disabling the defenders who are in evidence in the trench and not leaving them behind their back. The rest of the work is done by the trench cleaners.

Formations to be taken.

1° When the platoon is an assaulting unit :

Its first line, commonly called a wave, is generally constituted by its first half-platoon (grenadiers and automatic riflemen.)

Grenadiers, in order to deal immediately with the enemy defenders, hidden either in the trenches or in shell holes.

Automatic riflemen, in order to handle with their fire the defenders coming in view, those running away, or those rushing up to counter-attack.

Its second line (second wave) consists of its second half-platoon :

The V. B. grenadiers, in order to create by their high angle fire a barrage ahead of the occupied front line or, behind the front line attacked, to reach the hiding enemies, too far distant to be reached by hand-grenades.

The riflemen (voltigeurs) in order to occupy the line reached by the first wave and settle with rifle and bayonet the individual fight started by their comrades of the first wave.

The chief of platoon advances with the second wave between his two squads of riflemen.

The distance between the two waves varies from ten to fifteen paces.

One may also, under certain conditions, be led to place the riflemen in the first wave, notably when the frontage of the platoon exceeds the normal front; it is then recommended to use them by squads so as to enclose the automatic riflemen's group on both sides.

2° When the platoon is a supporting unit :

It assumes a double line formation like the assault platoon, if it has sufficient numbers.

The chief of platoon marches ahead with the line constituted by the squads of the specialists, in order to be able to direct his platoon to the best advantage, according to the conditions revealed by the attack made by the preceding platoon (assaulting platoon). He deploys his groups or marches them in columns of files in order to be able to use them for a longer time.

When the supporting platoon has been diminished by one or two of the specialists'squads (as provided for below) its chief may find it advantageous to use it at as a single wave.

Combat of the platoon in the boyaus. — The struggle on terrain interspersed with trenches often leads groups of skirmishers to progress along the communication trenches instead of attacking from the open ground.

Hand to hand fighting in the communicating trenches is extremely slow because one man alone can be engaged at a time and the enemy falls back only step by step.

The weapon used in this fight is the grenade. The instructions of the grenadier (Part II, Chapter IV) and the tactical use of the grenade (Part IV, Chapter V) contain all necessary prescriptions.

Asaulting equipment. — The following dress for the assault is indicated here, for reference :

Clothes : Field service dress without the knapsack.

Equipment : Shelter-half carried over the shoulder flanket rolled inside the shelter-half.

Tool (hanging from the belt), sometimes two tools. (See picture).

Ordinary haversack (food supply).

Reinforced haversack (grenades and fireworks).

Canteen holding 2 quarts.

Supplementary canteen of one quart or a brandy flask.

Mask (hanging on the stomach, within reach, between the two cartridge pouches)

A second mask (if possible).

Sand bags (from two to five in number, and fastened on the shelter-half, in front).

Signal panels (for emergencies) or flares.

Drinking cup and spoon (in food supply haversack).

First-aid packet. } (In great coat pocket).
Soldiers hand book.

Identity discs (one around the neck, another around the wrist).

Day's rations. } (In food-supply haversack).
Reserve rations.

Ammunition : 120 rounds.

5 grenades (three hand and 2 V. B.)

Another combination consists in taking the haversack containing the food supply, shelter-half and the blanket.

If the weather is very wet it is useless to carry the blanket.

CHAPTER III.

THE COMPANY ENGAGED.

Results to be obtained from the new company armament.

The best results will be obtained, especially on the offensive, only when three primary conditions are fulfilled :

1° The weapons must act **in combination** with one another.

2° The **supply of stores and ammunition** must be assured.

3° The men must be **expert** in the use of these weapons.

The **combination** of machine guns, automatic rifles, 37 mm. gun and rifle grenades, force the enemy to lie close in his entrenchments while the grenadiers and the riflemen advance and engage in a hand-to-hand encounter.

The weapons of flat trajectory (i. e., machine guns, automatic rifle, 37 mm. gun) engage everything that shows above the ground, and the weapons of curved trajectory (hand and rifle grenades) engage everything that is below the surface. The riflemen complete the results and follow up the successes obtained by the specialists.

The perfect organisation of the **supply of ammunition** is necessary in order to secure sufficient ammunition for the various weapons at all times. The heavy and cumbrous material, now required to keep the new weapons supplied, makes its provision all the more delicate an operation.

Training is even more necessary with the new armament than with the old.

Arms of high efficiency are effective only when in the hands of **disciplined and courageous experts,** under officers with accurate knowledge of the weapons.

All must get the idea out of their heads that specialists are a race apart, whose role in daily life and in battle is different from that of their comrades; machine gun men, grenadiers, automatic riflemen, live and fight in the same ranks and in close union with the riflemen. Their training only is specialized.

The present day company, with all its weapons and a proportionate number of machine guns in support, can produce a far greater volume of fire than could the same unit at the beginning of the war. The difference is noticeable at medium distances and is striking at distances under 200 meters.

In the defensive the company can now hang on to its ground much more firmly whilst **awaiting the protection of artillery barrage**.

This last property is particularly valuable to infantry during the period when, after the capture of an objective, the artillery has not yet obtained sufficiently exact knowledge of the situation to enable it to afford support.

In the offensive, infantry has regained the power and manoeuvering ability which was so much reduced by the introduction of trench warfare. Once the artillery has breached the enemy's defenses the infantry can now dash forward into the latter and break up any local resistance and hostile counter-attacks **with their own weapons**.

Formations for approach, and approach.

1° **Formations for approach**. — The most usual formation is the **double column** at variable distances and intervals (two columns of 2 platoons each) the platoons in lines of groups (by file) or in lines of half-platoons (by twos or by file) [similar to U.S. squad and platoon columns].

The company may also be formed in line of half-platoon (by ones or twos).

2° **Approach** :

a) **In open warfare.**

As soon as the company leaves the marching column it takes the **formation for the approach.**

As soon as the artillery fire becomes efficient and in all cases when it comes into the infantry firing zone it takes **the formation for fighting.** However, over difficult or broken ground, it may keep the formation in small columns.

The lines of the ground peculiarly dangerous (roads, outskirts) are crossed by surprise (by the whole company) In this case the last units close upon the first which halts. The distances are resumed afterwards.

The captain tries to push the firing line as close as possible to the enemy.

He pays close attention so as to maintain order in the supporting platoons and profits by all occasions to retain control. He engages them as soon as he finds their support necessary to secure the continuation of the forward movement.

When on account of an efficacious fire he cannot change his place to give his orders, he tries to reach the group which is most favored by the terrain and push that one forward. He thus begins the movement of the company, which he continues to command, by signal if he has no other means.

b) **In trench warfare.**

The approach and the formation for combat take place under cover in the « boyaux » or underground and in the parallels of departure.

What follows deals with an attack prepared completely, starting from a system of trenches occupied for a long time and engaging an enemy also powerfully entrenched.

In the case of open warfare, the principles would be the same; the application would be changed by the fact that two enemies would occupy only improvised lines, almost without any communications to the rear.

Conduct of the fight and the assaults.

The front allotted to a company varies from 200 to 300 meters.

The company is generally able to place two assaulting platoons side by side in its battle front. It may also place three and occasionally four.

Platoons not forming part of the assaulting line become **reinforcing platoons.**

The **assaulting platoons** form the first two «assaulting waves» of the company, which act as described for the platoon.

Immediately behind the assaulting waves and at a distance of ten to twenty paces from the second wave come the parties for cleaning up the trenches; these form the cleaning up or third wave. (See below).

The remainder of the company (one or two platoons less any detailed as a cleaning up party) form one or two waves, according to their strength, for supporting or maneuvering waves.

The company commander moves at the head of the last mentioned.

Reinforcing waves follow the cleaning up wave at a distance of about 40 to 50 paces. (See fig. 277 *bis,* and fig. 277 *ter,* for conventional signs, fig. 17).

— 333 —

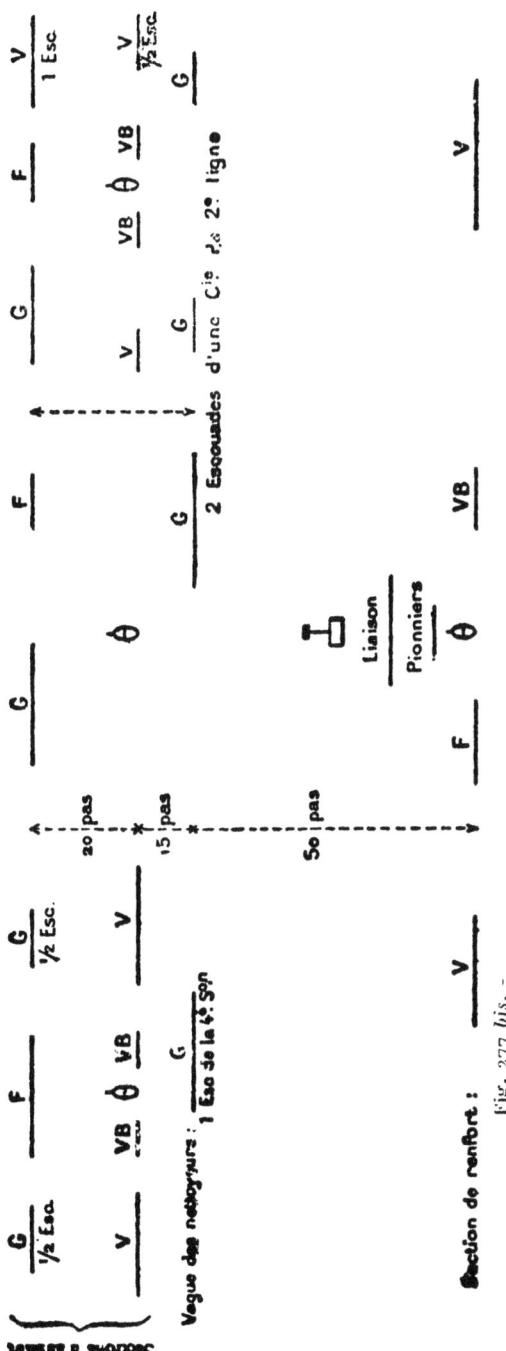

Fig. 277 bis.

— 334 —

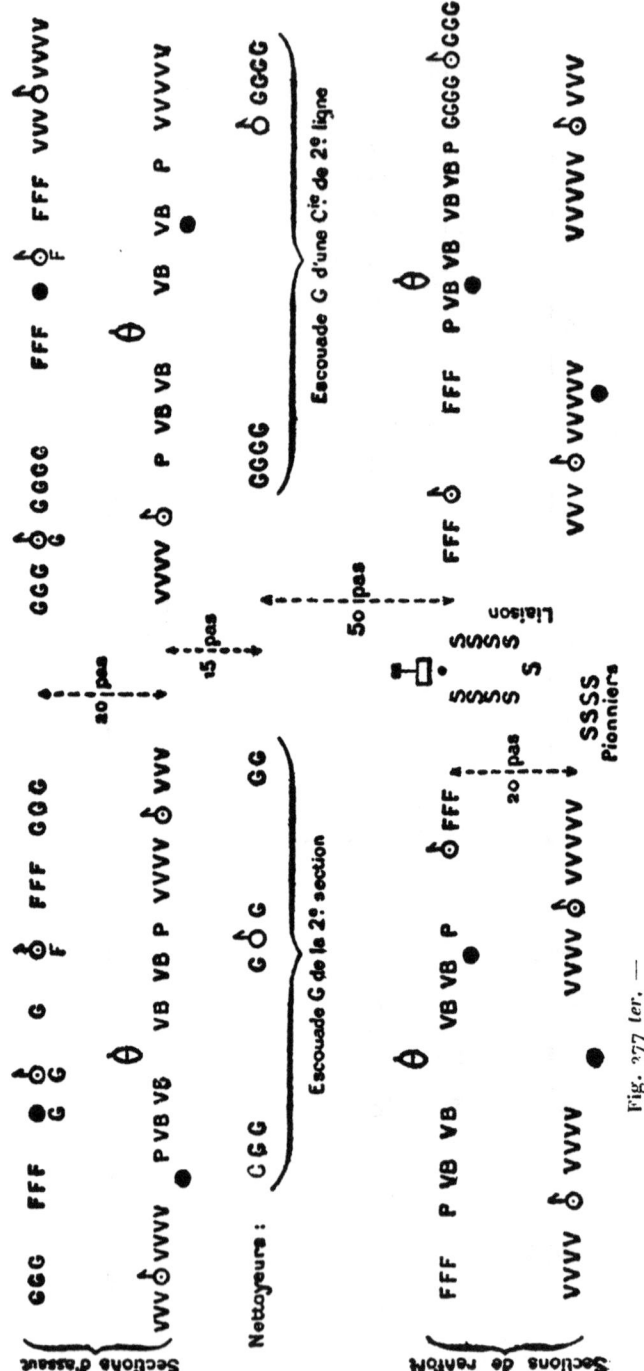

Fig. 277 ter. —

PLAN OF OPERATIONS.

The success of an attack depends on the accuracy with which it is carried out. A commander should draw up his plans in such a manner as to assure accuracy of execution.

The plan of operations is based on:

The mission assigned to the unit;

The obstacles to be overcome in order to assure success;

The means at the disposal of the unit.

The mission of the unit and any supplementary means which may be placed at its disposal are detailed in the battalion commander's operation orders.

The obstacles to be overcome are known nowadays in almost complete detail, thanks to excellent methods of observation and the information placed at the disposal of the troops by the staff (i. e. intelligence reports on the enemy's defences day by day, photographs, large scale battle maps, sketches, and information from various sources). All this information must be classified by the regimental commander and convenient extracts or reproductions freely distributed so as to reach all companies concerned. The company commander issues the necessary copies to his subordinates, sergeants included, and causes to be entered on each sketch the routes and succesive objectives of the unit in colored pencil.

The company commander issues the plan of operations for his company in the form of an operation order. This must be submitted for approval to the battalion commander without giving rise to papers and correspondence.

The details of the plan of operation determine:

1° The mission of the battalion, of the company concerned, and of the detached companies;

2° The number of assaulting platoons, the starting point of each and its role and objective;

3° The number and composition of cleaning up parties and their respective role in accordance with the orders of the battalion commander;

4° The distribution and respective roles of reinforcing platoons (from these the cleaning up parties will be taken) and the routes they are to follow;

5° Lines of attack of different units and their compass bearings;

6° Distance between different echelons;

7° Line along which company commander will move;

8° Time the assault is to start;

9° Method by which the artillery fire is to be timed to conform with progress of the infantry, especially the use of fireworks (rockets, cartridges);

10° How the platoons and company commanders are to keep each other informed of their respective positions;

11° Methods of communication with neighboring units;

12° The method to be adopted beforehand to mark out the front occupied either at some particular time or on some line agreed upon, or as required.

13° The occupation of the conquered positions and following up the success obtained.

14° Outfit to be taken.

15° Supply of ammunition, including V. B. rifle grenades and ammunition for automatic rifles and machine guns. Whether to be supplied under company or battalion arrangements; where these supplies will be drawn or delivered.

16° Situation of depots for wire, sand-bags, tools, etc., required for the organization of the new front; half-platoon of riflemen charged with its transport.

17° Evacuation of the wounded.

Remark. — In paragraph 9 of his plan of operation the company commander must explain to the men how the artillery fire will lift as the assault progresses and how in consequence the infantry must march, as it were, into the shell fire, following up the barrage as closely as possible.

Officers with the attack carry no swords; they will be dressed and equipped like their men with badge of rank as inconspicuous as possible.

START AND PROGRESSION INTO THE ENEMY POSITION.

At the precise time when the signal is given, the whole company must rise and start as a single man.

The two waves of each platoon, which before the start are generally in one parallel only, take their distances during the march, every one knowing exactly, beforehand, where he has to go.

The first wave follows the barrage. If the progression is normal, the company goes without any change in its original arrangement, all N. C. O's. trying to preserve this arrangement until the end. **Order must be preferred to rapidity.**

When the position is not yet ripe, when resistances are met, the captain tries to desintegrate it; he pushes parties into the free portions of the ground while he gives orders to others to attack the points of resistance in reverse.

These complete the work of the cleaning up parties and come back as soon as possible to their company.

Generally, the companies rally during the fight without stopping. In the combat the men try to join their remaining N. C. O's. These form again a line of skirmishers and the company is reorganized as soon as possible, every man joining his group.

As soon as contact with the enemy is lost, the captain sends out at once a scouting party or an organized unit, and supports them as closely as possible. He must act quickly; the scouting party has no other mission than to guard against surprises.

These patrols go along the boyaus without entering them, to find the flanking works which might be prepared there to sweep the intervals between the trenches.

The reconnaissance of the ulterior objectives is done by the progression of the fighting line.

How to keep the conquered ground. — When the company is checked by an obstacle stopping all progress, the captain must, before everything else, organize his company's positions very strongly, at a sufficient distance from the enemy's line for the artillery preparation. This establishment must assure the safety of the flanks and as far as possible contribute to the flanking of the whole front (with M. G. and A. R.)

During the day it is generally necessary to dig the ground at the place where the company has halted. During the night a better design is marked with stakes and pickets and when the supply of tools has arrived, laboring parties begin to prepare a normal trench, wire entanglements and flanking works. The captain thus puts his company in order, and forms a fraction ready for service, if he has none already. **He fully establishes his liaisons with the neighboring units.** In rear of the line built by the first line units, the supporting units create strong points with closed works formed from the system of enemy trenches already existing and surrounded with barbed wire and flanking each other.

One of the most important things is to find stations giving good views over the enemy position. The views from the flank are particulary interesting. **Observatories are immediately reported to the battalion commander who makes them known to the artillery.**

In order to facilitate the rapid drawing up of reports, the company commanders and the platoon leaders have a certain number of sketches of the battle ground and note pads giving printed information forms.

The use of detachments of pioneers and engineers. — When a detachment of pioneers or engineers is given to an assaulting unit, they are pushed forward like other troops, but they are considered as a reserve of technical workers to be employed at the proper time. They are not to be wasted.

These detachments may also be detailed for the digging of boyaus joining the parallel of departure to the conquered parallel, thus making a continuous covered way.

If there are electric connections or mine chambers in the conquered trenches, they are to be destroyed.

SPECIAL INSTRUCTIONS FOR THE SECOND LINE COMPANIES.

The chiefs of these companies must always **cover the flanks of the companies preceding them**, in order to allow the latter to give all their efforts to the pushing forward.

Besides, the chiefs of these companies rally all the supports of the assaulting companies.

They must engage themselves without orders, if necessary : to cover a flank, to follow up a success, to repulse a counter-attack, etc.

This coming into action without orders is done only in case of **urgent necessity :** as a rule the battalion commander orders the engagement of all his available units or of several of them to secure the following up of the forward movement. These units should not normally get out of his control to go against and engage in the first line, making its density greater and creating disorder.

This danger is to be specially avoided when the fighting line is stopped in front of a strong enemy point. In this case the reinforcement will often produce no result. The battalion commander will order the supporting company to maneuver by the flank, whenever possible. The supporting company must always be ready to execute immediately such a maneuver.

It may be useful for this purpose to place beforehand a part of the second line companies (supporting companies) behind the wings of the first line companies, with the idea of engaging the flank of the enemy, if the first line is stopped.

This has been explained above relating to supporting platoons.

SPECIAL INSTRUCTIONS FOR THE RESERVE COMPANIES.

The reserves (see fig. 278) are distinguished from the supporting companies and do not go with the assaulting waves. They generally replace the supports in the parallels of departure as soon as they are vacated. They must be able to prevent all giving way of the fighting line, particularly when a hostile counter-attack is launched.

The commander of a reserve unit stays generally at the post of command of the commander of the unit, directly in front of him, in order to be informed more rapidly and to send more quickly the orders the engagement requires.

All counter-attacks are repulsed by units, well in hand, posted and able instantly to give a powerful volume of fire.

The best means to stop counter-attacks is to keep detachments well in hand, well commanded, and with machine-guns in chosen places at the rear of the waves. They can work under better conditions here than in the first lines toward the establishment of their station. Great numbers are not necessary for this role as one or two platoons, and **above all machine guns,** are generally sufficient.

With a view to occupying the conquered ground, the reserves will immediately establish a series of strong points forming a second line. The battalion commander designates their station.

The battalion engaged.

The battalion commander places in the front line one, two or three companies, according to the front allotted.

Companies in second line assume a thin approach formation, moving to a great extent in lines of groups by file.

PLAN OF OPERATIONS.

The battalion scheme is based on the same rules, and alls under the same heads as that of the company.

18. In addition the battalion commander issues orders for the following:

19. Cleaning up the trenches and the evacuation of prisoners.

20. The employment of the M. G. company.

21. The employment of the 37 mm gun.

22. Occupation of the position won.

23. Reconnaisance of a further objective, and following up the advantage gained.

24. Replenishment of ammunition, etc.

25. Organization of liaison.

Cleaning up of trenches. — This is an extremely important operation and must be carried out methodically and speedily. Courageous men are required and energetic commanders.

The cleaning up scheme is drawn up by the battalion commander according to instructions issued by the regimental commander. It is founded on aeroplane photographs, which show the principal dug-outs of the enemy.

With this assistance, the battalion commander determines the strength necessary to clean up each group of dug-outs, detailing the unit to furnish the detachments and the duties of the latter when the cleaning up is completed.

As a rule cleaning up parties are made up of grenadier groups reinforced by a few riflemen; they are always under the command of N. C. O.'s.

In some cases the strength of a party may be half a platoon or a platoon and sometimes a complete company may be detailed to clean up some strong point of particular importance.

Cleaning up parties are never drawn from assaulting platoons, which must be kept intact. They are drawn from the reinforcing platoons or from companies or battalions in the second line.

In this case they are incorporated several days beforehand into the company they have to follow.

When the objective of the first line companies consists of two lines of trenches some distance apart, it is indispensable to detail separate cleaning up parties for each group. But whatever their objective, the **whole** of these cleaning up detachments march in the rear of the assaulting waves.

As they march in front of their regular unit and not behind it, they have its support when they meet any unforeseen resistance.

Once their particular task is completed the cleaning up parties may be employed on the preparation and occupation of the conquered trenches. In this case machine guns or automatic rifles are detailed to assist them.

Cleaning up parties move in lines or small columns, according to circumstances.

Frequent drills in cleaning up trenches must be carried out.

Among the dispositions relating to the evacuation of prisoners, their use as stretcher bearers may be foreseen. In this case they are given as support to the battalion surgeon.

The machine gun company is the powerful means at the battalion commander's disposal for completing by its fire effect the operations of his other units. He regulates its work:

At the opening of the attack, and during its progress.

In the occupation of the objective assigned.

1° **At the opening of the attack** the machine guns of the battalions of the first line accompany their battalion, according to the distribution previously ordered by the battalion commander, chiefly with a view to their installation on the captured front.

As a rule, they follow it, each section having a well defined role noted in the plan of operations. One may remain as reserve for an emergency or to replace a disabled platoon.

Automatic rifles will suffice henceforth to out-maneuver the enemy by their firing, as the machine guns are becoming more and more defensive weapons.

The machine guns of the battalions in the second line are placed, in advance, on the front from which the attack starts. Placed at selected points affording good fields of fire, they may be employed to advantage in covering the flanks of the first line battalions by directing a fire on any intervals which may occur between them, or more particularly on the outer flanks of the battalions situated on the wings of the whole attacking force.

When the form of the ground permits, it is also desirable to bring these machine guns into action against the enemy's second or third lines, his boyaux or his machine guns which show themselves. But all necessary precautions must be taken to avoid hitting or obstructing our own troops.

2° **When the attack has reached its objective** the battalion commander sends all or part of his machine guns to positions which have been pointed out beforehand, and which offer the best facilities by direct fire **and by flanking,** for holding the ground won either by his own battalion or those on either side.

To keep a secure hold on ground when it is conquered the fullest possible use should be made of the various weapons (machine guns, automatic rifles, and V. B. rifle grenades).

The arrangement of the companies along the front should tend to place the groups of automatic riflemen and rifle grenadiers in the first line and to keep the groups of grenadiers and riflemen in reserve to provide against counterattacks.

Furthermore, the battalion commander must distribute his M. G. company and groups of automatic riflemen and rifle grenadiers of the company or companies in reserve in such a manner as to increase the volume of fire available in the front line.

The 37 mm gun. Its use is explained in Part IV, Chapter v.

Plan of occupation of the conquered ground. — It is based on the instructions of the regimental commander drawn up in accordance with the scheme laid down by higher authority.

It will provide for the following:

Number of troops to occupy the position.

Their distribution in breadth and more particularly in depth. The distribution of M. G. and the 37 mm. guns.

Works to execute; constructions of trenches and especially boyaux; distribution of work to units.

To make known the sites for depots of all sorts of stores, tools, wire, pickets, logs, sandbags, etc.

Approximate position of different posts of command.

Reconnaissance of the ulterior objectives and following up a success. — The capture of the assigned objective is not the end of the battalion offensive. It is above all necessary:

To regain contact with the enemy.

To reconnoiter the enemy's new position.

To prepare and then carry out a forward movement with the idea of either securing a base of departure for a fresh advance, or of obtaining the fullest possible value out of the success already obtained.

Contact is regained and the new enemy position reconnoitered by **patrols** detached from the first line troops as soon as they reach the conquered position.

Their objectives are indicated by the battalion commander in the orders for the attack.

These patrols, composed of grenadiers and automatic riflemen and strengthened by riflemen, advance toward their objective. They occupy these objectives and form the skeleton of a fresh line, which is occupied and organized as quickly as possible.

Full advantage should immediately be taken of any gaps in the enemy's defences. Enterprising infantry will always find opportunities of completing an initial success by the seizure of strong points which would cost them dear the following day. It is particularly important **to seize immediately any point which the enemy has abandoned.**

The limiting of objectives does not imply the suppression of initiative.

The battalion commander must not lose sight of the fact that the exploitation of the success is not obtained by the infantry alone but by **combination with the artillery.**

Further progress, therefore, must be studied beforehand in concert with the artillery and worked out in fullest detail. Such is the object of the **plan of following up the success** as outlined above.

The necessity of sending back quick and frequent reports must be strongly impressed on all officers and N. C. O.'s.

Replenishment of supplies, ammunition and stores. — See Part IV, Chapter XI.

Remark I.

Referring to fig. 278 and to the remarks already made on the general physiognomy of combat, it will be seen that such a fight as described will be developed by the companies C, placed before an interval.

It must be observed that companies B and D being turned aside by the necessity of encircling the resistance point, N and N_1, other companies which continue to progress are obliged to extend themselves to cover the part of the front originally opposite B and D. In this way the first line is weakened just at a time when it is most exposed to hostile counter-attacks. Reinforcement is obtained by the reserves E and F, placed for the purpose behind the intervals.

Remark II.

Intervals easily broken in by the attack would become traps and fire-pockets if N and N_1 should continue their flanking roles. It is necessary therefore to annihilate them.

To completely conquer the fortified points would be too hard and hazardous a task and too difficult for the strength of companies like A, B and D. But it is sufficient if they neutralize the parts of N and N_1 which are really prejudicial, particularly the edges and the points from which reverse and flank fire can be delivered on the companies which have advanced.

Also the companies A employ different tactics, though they attack the front like the companies C; they will enter the enemy trenches and engage the enemy in the boyaux, which engages the enemy and does not need great effectives or heavy sacrifices. They must be very well supplied with grenades and sandbags. If they try, as do C, to conquer several successive lines of trench by attacking in the open, they would have numerous and useless casualties.

The companies B and D are obliged to execute a turning movement difficult but necessary. The objectives aimed at on the outskirt of the strong point are :

The parts which flank the interval;
The rear of the supporting point;

The turning movement is done, each platoon changing direction in its turn, so as to blind successively the flanking fires in front of which are advancing the units going towards the furthest objectives.

Afterwards the companies B and D operate like the companies A.

CHAPTER IV.

LIAISON DURING THE PROGRESSION.

Liaison with the artillery. — It is apparent from what precedes that an advance is destined to be stopped and is at the mercy of hostile counter-attacks, if abandoned by its artillery.

The artillery never abandons the infantry if it knows where the infantry is, and where it is necessary to fire to support or to defend it.

The composition and the role of the **observation and liaison detachment** sent by the **artillery group** to the **infantry regiment** it supports has been given in Part IV, Chapter ix.

Liaison with the higher command. — **To inform the commanding authority of the places reached by the most advanced elements** is one of the most difficult problems.

The company and battalion commanders in the first line must employ all possible means to solve this problem. Upon it depend their salvation and their victory.

The successive changes of the posts of command must be foreseen, with their improvement by the pioneers, the installation of the telephone lines which are to lead to them, and the exterior indications which will enable messengers to find the post of command, etc.

A well trained personnel for the transmission (signallers, agents of liaison, runners) is specially instructed for the attack which is being prepared.

All means of communications are minutely established beforehand and the replacing of the bearers of special material if they should be disabled, etc.

These means of communications which have been studied in Part III, Chapter ix, and Part IV, Chapter ix, are:

Telephone;
Signal rockets and cartridges;
Sound signals;

Searchlights, shutter panels;

Pigeons;

Runners.

Also, Bengal fires, panels or searchlights to send signals to avions and balloons which transmit them to the commanding authority.

It must be remembered, as far as this last means is concerned, that the avion rockets are only for signalling to the infantry; the balloon and the avion of one's division must be perfectly well known.

Always remember that the commander is waiting impatiently for the least information and that he can intervene only when he knows the situation.

No chance to communicate is to be neglected and several different means are to be employed simultaneously.

Before asking for artillery fire or making signals to show the contour of the first line, **the company must be sure that there are no friendly detachments in advance of it.** In the confusion of battle, supporting or counter-attacking troops who are poorly informed and sustaining losses are inclined prematurely to believe that they have arrived on the first line; if they then blunderingly open fire or call for a barrage, terrible results follow.

Liaison with the neighboring units. — The rules for this liaison are given in the last paragraph of the plan of operations of the battalion commander (see above).

This liaison is particulary important when the neighboring unit belongs to another regiment. In each unit an instinctive tendency leads troops to draw closer to the center, even when the objectives have been chosen with the greatest care so as to avoid that tendency. Consequently it is useful to post a half-platoon, a platoon or even more, abreast of the second line, on the flank of the battalion, for the purpose of maintaining contact with the neighboring battalion or regiment.

The chief of this platoon forms it in small columns, observes with care what happens and widens its front or deploys it abreast of the first line when a noticeable gap is produced between the two battalions he is entrusted to keep in contact.

Personnel with the battalion commander and with the company commander. — The division of the company into fighting platoons and soldiers not included in those platoons and the large increase in the number of specialists (signallers, pioneers, etc.) has resulted in surrounding the captain or the battalion commander with a number of men who become an encumbrance around the post of command and in combat, unless a place has been designated in which they shall wait until needed.

This personnel, which may be called **company commander's group, battalion commander's group**, must always rest, march and maneuver as a little platoon. under command of a N.C.O. in the company, or of the sergeant major in the battalion.

These men should habitually march in the same relative positions in order that their presence may be readily verified, their replacement assured, and that they may be found when needed. During combat they avoid surrounding their chief, they take formation which resembles the other detachments of the company. They are required to march to their allotted place and to leave it only when they are called.

The following tables are given by way of explanation and memorandum :

Company Commander's Group.

	NOT INCLUDED in FIGHTING PLATOONS.	
	Corporals.	Soldiers.
Corporal, chief of the Co. commander's group...	1	"
First group agents of liaison. — Drummer and buglers..........	"	2
First group agents of liaison. — Cyclist..................	"	1
2d group for signals and observation. — Signalman..................	"	2
2d group for signals and observation. — Observers	"	3
3d group... Pioneers	"	4
4th group runners. — For the company...............	"	4
4th group runners. — For the battalion (d)...........	1	4
(d)		

The detachment of battalion runners is sent to the battalion commander only when he asks fort it.

— 347 —

Battalion Commander's Group.

		BELONGING to the BATTALION STAFF.				BELONGING TO.	
		O.	N.C.O.	Corp.	Sold.	Hq. Co.	The Cos.
A. At the battalion commander's post of command :							
1st group. command.	Adjutant	1	"	"	"	"	"
	Sergeant major	"	"	"	"	1	"
	Mounted orderlies	"	"	"	"	2	"
2nd group. Agents of liaison.	Supply sergeant.......	"	"	"	"	1	—
	N.C.O. agent of liaison of the M.G. company.	"	"	"	"	"	"
	Cyclists (motor)	"	"	"	"	(a) 3	"
3d group. Telephonists.	Sergeant	"	"	"	"	1	"
	Corporal	"	"	"	"	2	"
	Telephonists.........	"	"	"	"	10	—
4th group. Signalmen.	Signal men..........	"	"	"	"	4	*
5th group. Runners.	1-Co. : 1-L. corporal, 4 runners..........	"	"	"	"	"	(b) 5
	2-Co : 1-L. corporal, 4 runners..........	"	"	"	"	"	(b) 5
	3-Co : 1 corporal, 4 runners.............	"	"	"	"	"	(b) 5
6th group. Pioneers.	1 pioneer corporal	"	"	"	"	1	"
	8 pioneers...........	"	"	"	"	8	"
7th group. Liaison with the artillery.	For records..........	"	"	"	"	"	"
	Variable strength......	"	"	"	"	"	"
B. At the aid station of the battalion :							
Medical officer......................		1	"	"	"	"	"
Hospital sergeant....................		"	1	"	"	"	"
Hospital attendant...................		"	"	"	"	"	(c) 4
Cyclists..		"	"	"	1	"	"

(a) One sent to the regimental commander.
(b) This number allows the battalion commander :
  1. To give to the regimental commander 1 lance corporal, 4 runners ;
  2. To keep with him 2 such teams.
(c) They rejoin their company if it is detached.

PART IX.

PURSUIT AND WAR OF MOVEMENT.

The present form of warfare should not be considered as definitive. Troops should be prepared in the event of operations developing on a wider and more considerable scale than those at positions only a few kilometers distant. The rout of a vanquished army will afford an opportunity for pursuit, in the course of which it will once more be necessary to march, halt, and guard.

The data necessary for the operation of a small infantry unit are to be found:

For marching, in Part II, Chapter vi.

For halting, in Part VI.

It now remains to sum up the methods for **insuring security on the march and security at a halt.**

Security.

The object of security is:

1° To give to the chief the time and space requisite for making his dispositions.

2° To protect troops on the march, or in camp against any surprises.

In case of immediate contact with the enemy, the judicious distribution of forces, with view to a battle, is the best guarantee of security, and such is particularly the case in trench warfare where security, properly speaking, is reduced to listening posts and watchmen.

At a distance from the enemy. security is guaranteed by **detachments of security,** (advance-guard, flank-guard, etc.) whose mission it is to gain, by their resistance, the time required by the chief to make his dispositions.

These detachments protect themselves while on the march and when halted by smaller detachments (supports of advance-guard, outposts) while fractions of cavalry placed at their disposal attend to scout duty (divisional cavalry).

These methods of protection cannot be made the object of precise rules; the effectives, the distances, the disposition, and the missions of detachments of security depend on the distance of the enemy and his moral situation.

— 349 —

Point. 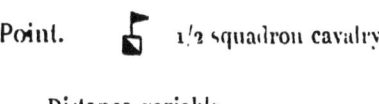 1/2 squadron cavalry.

Distance variable.

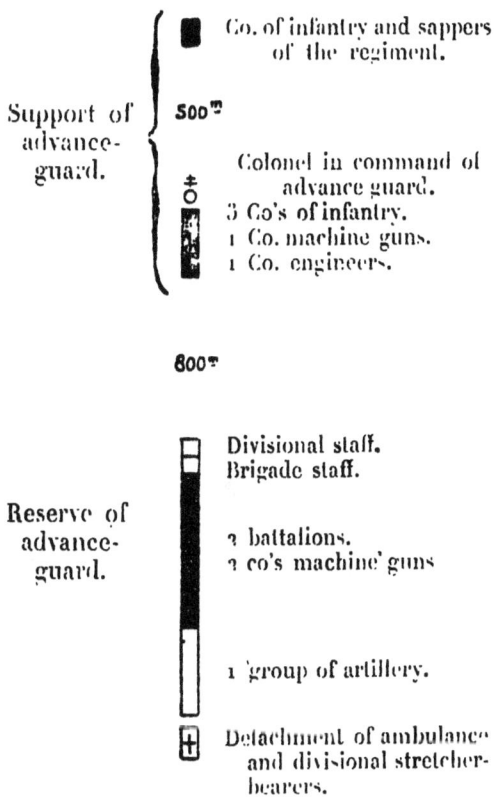

Support of advance-guard.
{ Co. of infantry and sappers of the regiment.
500ᵐ
Colonel in command of advance guard.
3 Co's of infantry.
1 Co. machine guns.
1 Co. engineers. }

800ᵐ

Reserve of advance-guard.
Divisional staff.
Brigade staff.

2 battalions.
2 co's machine guns

1 group of artillery.

Detachment of ambulance and divisional stretcher-bearers.

1500ᵐ

Main body of the column

Fig. 281.

— 350 —

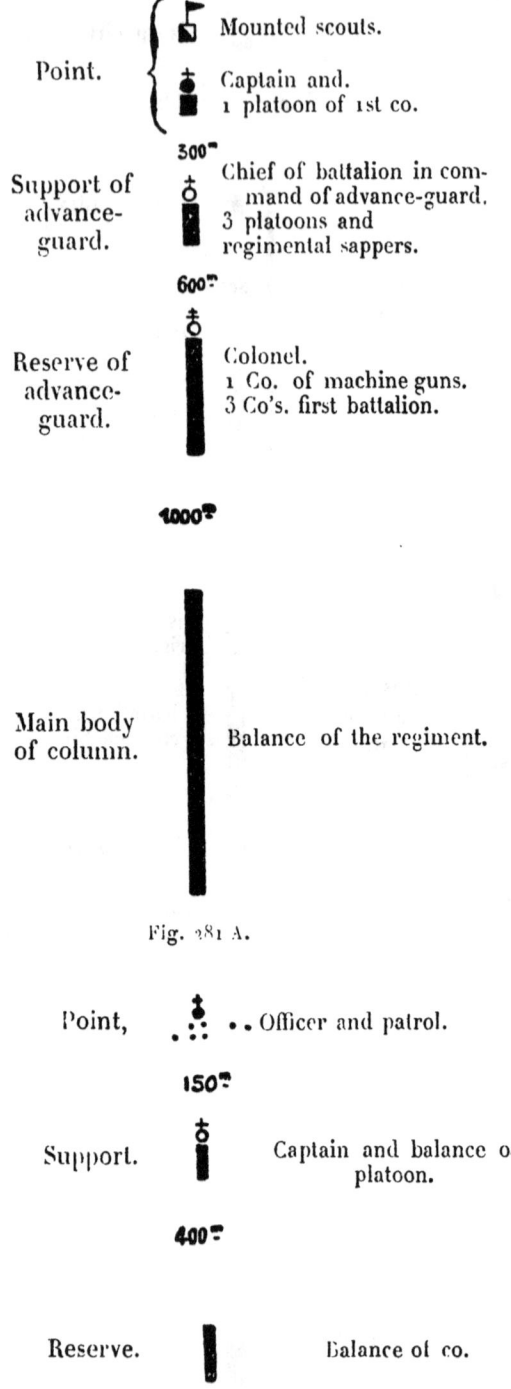

Point.		Mounted scouts. Captain and. 1 platoon of 1st co.
	300ᵐ	
Support of advance-guard.		Chief of battalion in command of advance-guard. 3 platoons and regimental sappers.
	600ᵐ	
Reserve of advance-guard.		Colonel. 1 Co. of machine guns. 3 Co's. first battalion.
	1000ᵐ	
Main body of column.		Balance of the regiment.

Fig. 281 A.

Point,		Officer and patrol.
	150ᵐ	
Support.		Captain and balance of platoon.
	400ᵐ	
Reserve.		Balance of co.

Fig. 281 B.

CHAPTER I.

PROTECTION ON THE MARCH.

The protection of a column is assured by detachments named as follows : advance-guard, rear-guard, flank-guard, according to the position they occupy in front, behind or on the flanks of the column.

Advance-guard. — When distant from the enemy the task of the advance-guard consists only in clearing the roads and in giving an easy passage to the advancing column.

When near the enemy, it must be able to fulfil any duty that is required **in the order of battle,** for instance : to attack the enemy and force him to deploy, to seize the strong points necessary for the formation of the whole, dislodge the enemy; sweep away the first resistance of an enemy posted, etc.

It must act quickly and if necessary engage all its units.

The advance-guard comprises as a rule :

The cavalry detailed to the column.

A part of the infantry varying from a sixth to a third of the column; some engineers and artillery.

It is apportioned into the **point.** support and reserve of the advance-guard; each of these echelons being about a third or a quarter of the one following.

The distances between them and between the advance-guard and the main body of the column are very variable and are determined after the following considerations : each division should be sufficiently distant from the following one to protect it in the greatest possible degree from a surprise, sufficiently close to be supported in good time, so as not to be destroyed singly.

The advance guard in its entirety is placed **on the march** under the order of one officer who is the **commander of the advance-guard.**

The officers commanding the different units march with the fraction which precedes the one which they actually command. They keep in liaison with all the units.

The figure 281 gives examples of divisional, regimental and company advance-guards.

Another disposition of the advance-guard. — The advance-guards set forth above correspond in a general way with displacements operating at a certain distance from the enemy.

When the advance-guard enters into cannon range of the enemy, or when an engagement seems imminent, it marches **on guard** in a semi-deployed formation which allows scope to deploy instantly in any direction where the enemy should present himself. It thus avoids flank movements, particularly dangerous in the presence of the enemy, which (otherwise) would be necessary at the moment of deploying, in order to pass from march formation to battle formation.

Note. — The formations as indicated here vary of course, according to circumstances, and according to the information which has been gathered concerning the enemy.

Rear-guard. — In a forward movement, the rear-guard fulfils the function of noting what happens in the rear of the column and covering it against a rear attack by cavalry.

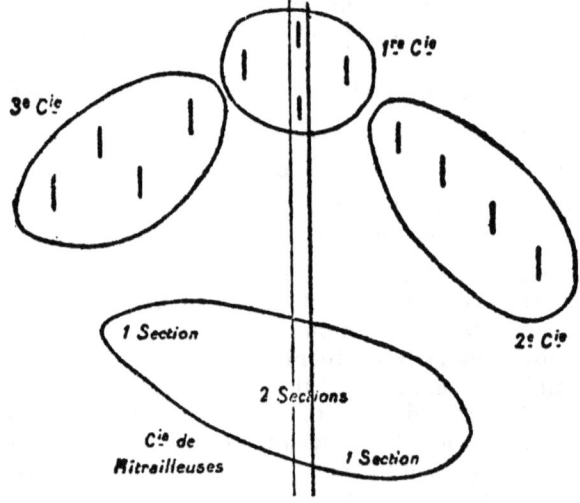

Fig. 282.

The ordinary composition is : two companies and some mounted troops for a division; one platoon for a regiment.

If the column retires, the rear-guard is made up like the advance-guard in a forward movement. Its object is to permit the column to escape punishment from the enemy and to avoid an engagement. It must hold out to the last man if necessary, without counting upon support from the main body. It must not retire until the column is out of reach.

Flank-guards. — The flank-guards are required to protect the uncovered flank or flanks of a column.

When only mild attacks by light detachments are expected, the cavalry may be sufficient for this task.

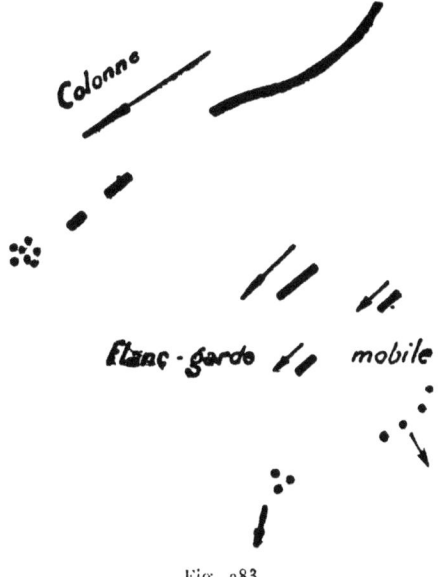

Fig. 283.

When a possible attack is to be feared the flank-guards comprise troops drawn from the vanguard or main body of the colomn.

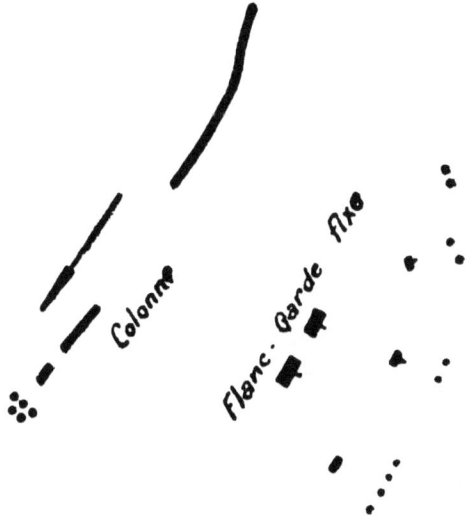

Fig. 284.

According to their instructions flank-guards are **fixed** or **mobile.**

The mobile flank-guards march parallel to the column; either abreast at the main body or abreast of the advance guard, and at a distance analogous to that separating the vanguard from the main body (fig. 283.)

The fixed flank-guards occupy on the exposed flanks the points from whence the enemy might molest and hinder operations; they draw up in an échelon formation, protected (fig. 284.)

Support and point of advance-guard. — When the column does not comprise cavalry, the infantry will depend upon its own resources for safety.

Particularly in the case of an isolated regiment, the company forming the support of the advance-guard detaches an advanced point of infantry to which may be added a part of the mounted scouts of the regiment.

Mounted scouts. — The regiment possesses 12 mounted scouts, they are distributed by the colonel, according to the needs of the units under his command.

Their principal duty is to insure security on the halt, on the march and in battle. They are patrol, flanking and liaison troops, mounted so as to travel faster and further and with less fatigue than the foot soldiers whom they replace.

During the halts they push forward to a nearby crest to reconnoiter.

Their role is not to fight, but to give information.

They should be employed as carriers of orders or special messengers exceptionally, and only when there are no cyclists available.

Platoon point of advance-guard. — The point of infantry is composed of a platoon or half-platoon commanded by an officer.

The officer marches at a distance of 100 to 150 mètres in advance of this fraction with a group of scouts to whom are attached some mounted scouts or cyclists. This group of scouts is arranged like a reconnoitering patrol and performs equivalent duties.

The officer receives communication of the itinerary and all information concerning the terrain and the enemy. He is furnished with a map. He is responsible for the route. He is given a guide if necessary.

Rules for scouts. — March with your rifle in your hand, magazine loaded; be active.

Visit rapidly all shelters and covers in the line of march, do not waste time in searching minutely small obstacles that are able only to conceal small bodies of troops incapable of endangering the troops.

Arrest all suspects. Send all isolated individuals to the chief of the point, who after a summary interrogatory, will have them conducted to the officer commanding the main guard.

Clear the route of all small obstacles. Notify the fractions in the rear and the pioneers if their help is required, take a position in advance of the obstacle and keep watch while the passage is re-established. The commandant of the advance-guard will determine the probable duration of the delay.

On the top of a slope, halt under cover, look ahead before advancing.

Rapidly cross all small defiles. March on the upper edge of ravines or sunken roads; the point takes up its position beyond the same and searches the surrounding by means of patrols.

On reaching a bridge the chief of the point makes an investigation to ascertain whether the bridge has been in any way recently damaged (inspect piles, and beneath arches).

The woods are searched as far as possible without straying too far from the route and without thus being overtaken by the column.

On arriving in a village, creep silently into the first house, capture any resident and conduct him to the chief of the point.

To search a house in detail, take a turn around the house, then send two men in to search it while the others guard the exit, visit every room, cellar and garret, always taking care to be preceded by the resident.

In case of an encounter with a small enemy patrol, drive it back or lie in ambush to capture it.

If the enemy is stronger in number, take position and notify the fractions that follow; opening fire if necessary.

If the enemy retires, follow him and do **not lose contact with him.**

Remark. — The complete execution of all missions that have been mentioned above is possible only to the scouts of an isolated platoon or company reconnoitering and regulating accordingly its speed of march.

In the general case of a column advancing at a speed of 4 kilometers an hour, the scouts should advance much more quickly as they risk being overtaken by the oncoming column.

The following method permits them to execute their duty without retarding the march of the vanguard : when some of the scouts have to quit the road to examine a cover, a quarry, a clump of trees, pursue a retreating enemy patrol, etc., at a signal from the chief of the point, the sergeant replaces the missing scouts of the patrol by men sent up from the point. The first patrol fall in with the left of the the company when it passes or at the next hour's halt. This way of proceeding assures also the frequent relief of patrol, and even that of the platoon that constitutes the point, relief is necessary on account of the very active service required of them.

Point and support. — These fractions have received instructions in the event of an encounter with the enemy : they hold themselves accordingly in readiness to deploy and engage rapidly.

The commander of advance guard marches as a rule with the support.

Connecting files. — Each fraction of the vanguard will detail the necessary men (one or two men together) to keep in touch with the preceding fraction. The men leave more or less space between them; they wait at the corners of the roads, crossings, etc. Their duty is a delicate one to perform properly.

If the scouts on the point stop, these men signal : « Halt». This does not mean that the support and the rest of the column successively should stop. This is not an order that they give, but a warning. If the point stops, the support must, on the contrary proceed further on, to give assistance; the prescribed intervals are resumed little by little.

All the intervals must be shortened during the night.

CHAPTER II.

SERVICE OF SECURITY. — OUTPOSTS.

The principles of outposts and advance guards are identical. Outposts are drawn from the troops to be covered and consist generally of units amounting to from one sixth to one third of the total effective. Outposts are placed towards the enemy in echelons of decreasing strength from front to rear ; under their protection the remainder of the troops march or rest in security.

To the three echelons of the advance guard, **reserve, support** and **point,** correspond the three echelons of the outpost **reserve, supports and outguards.**

Advance guards, flank-guards and rear guards, habitually become outposts when a halt is made. During a halt the advance guard is sometimes re-inforced by units from the main body. The commander of the advance guard becomes the commander of the outpost.

If the march is resumed the next day, the outposts remaining at their stations are overtaken by the new advance guard, then assemble and take their place in the column as it marches by. If the troops do not move, outpost duty generally lasts 24 hours. Relief always takes place by day and at different hours.

Duty of outposts. — Outposts have a double mission to **watch** and to **resist**. They must not seek battle, but they must sacrifice themselves to give the troops they are covering time enough to make dispositions, and they must not cease to resist unless they are ordered to do so.

Outposts far from the enemy. — Far from the enemy when the army corps cavalry reconnoiters at one day's march ahead, the mission of security only remains : security results from the disposition of the cantonments echeloned in depth. Each cantonment is protected by **entrance guards.** (See Part VI). A few posts are pushed forward in the principal directions to be watched.

Outposts at a short distance from the enemy. — When an attack is expected, resistance by the outposts is

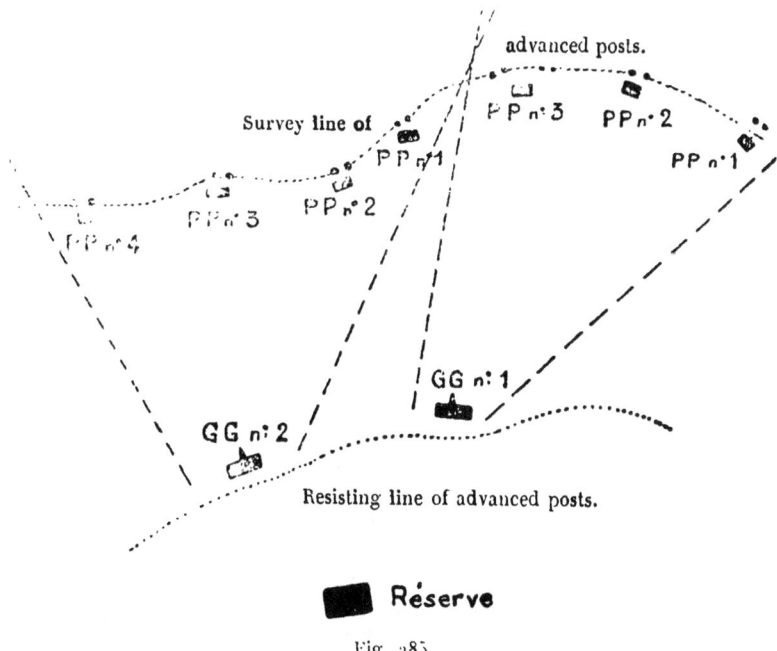

Fig. 285.

of the greatest importance, and in the exposed directions a more complete disposition for the combat is taken. (See fig. 285).

Combat outposts. — At the end of a day of battle, when contact is maintained with the enemy, security and observation are gained by combat outposts, which are posted **without waiting for further orders.**

Units in the first line remaining in the immediate proximity of the battelfield, or on the battlefield itself, protect themselves, each on its own account, by platoons which in their turn push forward the necessary sentries and listening posts.

Co-operation of the cavalry. — The cavalry which has formed part of the point of the advance-guard, assumes charge of all or part of the distant **reconnaissance,** to relieve the infantry of the task; but only during the day. During night it takes its position in the rear.

Establishment of outposts. — At the end of a march, the outpost service is established as soon as the advance guard has reached the places assigned to it in the **halting order.** Establishment takes place under the protection of the cavalry or of advanced elements of the advance-guard.

The officer in charge of the outpost issues his orders **according to the map,** that is:

Mission of the outposts and what to do in case of attack.

Mission of the cavalry.

Approximative disposition and sector of observation **for each support.**

Disposition of the outpost reserves.

Information of the enemy and the neighboring units.

Liaison to be established; points to be especially watched, etc.

Countersign and parole, signals for recognition.

Upon receipt of orders the officer in charge of each support or reserve, sends his unit as soon as possible towards the emplacement assigned, every outguard covering itself by a small advance-guard.

The company commander points out to his lieutenant on the map the temporary emplacements to be occupied in guarded halt, then rides out in advance of his troop to **reconnoiter the terrain.** During this reconnaissance he fixes the definite emplacements, then returns to his troops to take up and settle in detail the apportionment of duties.

The chief of each outguard, and each commander of support or reserve, **sends as soon as possible** his report and the sketch of his installation. Supports and reserves remain under arms till the outguards are stationed and the liaison established. The outpost commander inspects the arrangements made, then takes position with the reserve.

The password at the outposts. — The password, is composed of the countersign and of the parole, as a rule issued by the army corps H. Q. If it arrives too late the outpost commander gives a temporary password and reports to the general of division and to the neighboring outposts. He does so when he suspects that the password has been overheard by the enemy.

Outpost reserve. — The outpost reserve is, as nearly as possible, constituted of **one half of the effective** forming the outposts.

According to the orders received, it reinforces the supports being attacked, holds when the supports fall back or attacks.

It installs itself in alarm cantonments or in bivouacs.

It has a **camp guard**, and there all distribution of supplies and stores is made to outpost troops.

Support. — The general line of supports determined by the commander of outposts is called the **outpost line of resistance.**

The usual effective strength of a support is one company. Each outguard has a well determined **sector.** A road or an important point is never given as a limit for a sector.

The support has a defensive mission which most often consists of resisting on the spot to the end; therefore it organizes itself strongly, digs trenches, and sends forward only N. C. O's and men strictly necessary for the establishment of small posts and patrols.

Resistance is prepared in all details and **against any eventuality.**

A support ought not, as a rule, to abandon either its mission or its sector, to go to the help of a neighboring support which is being attacked. It assists if possible by flanking fire, but redoubles its vigilance on its own front.

The support is located ouf of the enemy's sight close to the prepared fighting station, and either in alarm billets or in bivouac. The men remain fully equipped day and night.

The **picket** is about one-fourth of the total strength of the support and is a fraction held ready to march at the first signal. The picket supplies a sentry over the arms and, if expedient, the men necessary for observing the signals from the outguards.

The liaison with the outguards, the neighboring support and the reserve is to be most carefully established.

Outguards and sentries. — Every outguard must have at its head an experienced N. C. O. A very important outguard may be commanded by an officer.

Outguards do not form a first line of resistance

in front of the support. They are only intended to make certain the surveillance over the sector assigned to them, and to give warning of the approach of the enemy. In case of a surprise attack they fire and avoid falling back directly on the support in order not to restrict the latter's field of fire.

The effective of each outguard is limited to the number of men absolutely indispensable for the sentries and the patrols necessary for watching over its own sector.

The outguard generally supplies one **double sentry**, rarely two or more. In the latter case a single additionnal sentry is detailed at the post if it is not located near one of the double sentries. The emplacements chosen for the sentries must insure the maintainance of a very strict watch (if need be on the top of a tree, a hay-stack, etc.).

The general line of the sentries is generally designated as the **outpost observation line.**

Sentries attempt to conceal themselves provided that this does not interfere with their powers of observation. They keep constantly alert and their attention is not to be distracted from their watch even by the appearance of an officer; they do not pay honors. They may be allowed to leave their haversacks behind them at the outguard. The magazines of their rifles are always loaded, but they shoot only when they distinctly perceive the enemy or when attacked. They fire also on anyone who disregards the orders given thems.

By night they must neither sit nor lie down.

The location of the outguard is determined by the location of the sentries; it must be such as to allow easy communication both with the sentries and with the support. Generally it is advantageous to establish the outguards on the roads or quite close to them. Their emplacements must be concealed from the enemy's sight in so far as is possible.

At the outguard the men remain constantly equipped and keep their arms within reach. At night a part of the effective, at least half of them, remain constantly awake and on the watch; the remainder may be allowed to sleep for a few hours. N. C. O's. rest in turns. Lighting fires and smoking are generally forbidden.

The food is prepared at the emplacement of the support and is carried to the outguard.

How to challenge and recognize when on outpost duty. In addition to their protective mission, outposts must enforce the strictest observation of the following orders:

No one is allowed to cross the line of sentries without being challenged by the chief of the outguard or the support under conditions fixed below.

Consequently **sentries stop every isolated person or every group passing in their neighborhood.**

Chiefs of outguards accompany to the line of sentries detachments, isolated soldiers sent out on missions, or persons provided with passes. After having challenged them, they allow isolated soldiers, patrols and rounds to come into the lines day and night. During the day they permit the entrance of detachments which form parts of the outpost troops and also those for which they have received special orders.

The commander of the support himself recognises the detachment coming in during the night. He allows them to penetrate only if they belong to troops covered by the outposts, if their chief is the bearer of written orders, or if there is not the slightest doubt as to their identity.

To challenge, sentries cry out by day as well as by night: **Halt!** If one does not stop, they cry out as a second warning: **Halt or I fire!** Should this second injunction not be heeded, they fire.

If the oncomer stops, they inform the chief of the outguard but deny all approach.

The outguard leader challenges by the cry « **Who's there!** ». When the answer has come such as: «Friend», soldier or detachment from such and such a regiment, or patrol or rounds, or when the proper signals have been exchanged, he shouts: « **Advance one with the countersign** ».

If the persons thus held up form parts of small groups of isolated soldiers, the chief of outguard allows them to approach only one by one.

If a detachment, round, or patrol is challenged its leader must come forward alone; his troops are kept back at a certain distance until they are permitted to advance, after the chief has been recognised.

By night when a detachment comes up, the chief of out guard causes the support leader to be informed.

Even when the countersign has been given him in answer to his challenge, the chief of outguard must take all possible precautions to make sure of the identity of the persons he is qualified to recognise. Should the least doubt arise, or should the persons held up be unable to give the countersign, the outguard chief then has them taken to the support commander who examines them, causes them to be searched if need be, and sends them under escort to the officer in charge of the outpost.

The support commanders act in like manner whenever they have to challenge.

Whatever his rank may be, the chief of a troop held up by the outposts must answer all questions that are put to him to verify his identity.

Recognising of rounds and patrols.

The chief of outguard, after having required the countersign, answers with the parole.

This is to be done **by day as well as by night**, when rounds, patrols, or troops in arms happen to meet.

They challenge in the following manner : the chief who first catches sight of the round, patrol, or troop cries out : **Halt!**, then, **Who's there?** If the answers comes: «France, round, patrol or detachment from such and such a regiment», he cries out : **Advance one with the countersign**, receives the countersign from the chief of the round, patrol, or troop whatever the rank of the latter may be and answers by the parole. Both words are to be exchanged in a low voice. They are often superseded by signals or sounds agreed upon.

Patrols. — Patrols are detachments of variable strength, which outguards, supports, and if need be the reserve, send forth ahead of the line of sentries to keep watch over the parts of the ground lying out of the latter's sight, or to observe the enemy's movements while in contact with him.

Patrols, on principle, constitute the **mobile element of the watch.** They may, however, according to the orders, keep motionless for a time of variable duration, either to observe better, resting on points of vantage, or to **lie in ambush.**

The orders issued to each chief of patrol before he starts explain :

The precise object of his mission.

The approximate itinerary to be followed or the sector to go over.

The points which he must not go beyond or the approximate duration of his mission.

The countersign and parole and the signals.

Patrols are always composed of at least three men led by a corporal, a N. C. O., or an officer if need be. Intelligent, clever men, able to find their bearings, are chosen in preference to others.

The commanders of the supports or of the reserve determine the number, time, and itinerary of patrols according to the strength of their troops, the nature of the terrain, and the possibilities of attack.

Whenever he deems it necessary, a chief of outguard may also send out patrols.

Patrols have to march cautiously and noiselessly, stop-

'ping often either to listen or to find their bearing. They observe with great care the terrain they go over.

At night or in broken ground small infantry patrols generally never go more than a kilometer ahead of the line of sentries. Should circumstances require them to be pushed further ahead, their strength must be increased.

About day-break, patrols must be more frequent and their reconnaissances are to be pushed further; they return only by broad daylight.

Patrols avoid engaging the enemy and still more being cut off. Therefore, they come back by another road. If they meet with an enemy inferior in numbers they try to make prisoners after having drawn the enemy into an ambush. If the enemy is in strength the patrols warn the outguards in the rear and fall back continuing their observations as they do so.

Every chief of patrol imparts to his men the password and the signals so that each one may come back by himself should the patrol be dispersed.

Upon returning he reports what he has observed to the officer who assigned him to patrol duty. All important intelligence is communicated to the officer in command of the outposts.

When the outposts are to remain several days on the same terrain the time of departure and the itinerary o. the patrols are changed each day.

Examining post. — Occasionally on the outguard line a special post called **examining post** is established, charged with questioning all isolated men, deserters, etc., and generally speaking all persons not connected with the army but desiring to enter the lines.

Its emplacement is as a rule on the main approach. It is made known to the chiefs of outguards who send there all suspected soldiers and all civilians.

General prescriptions relative to outposts.

1° **Once in touch with the enemy, patrols led by officers, if need be, must keep in contact with the enemy.** — If the enemy seems to have slipped away, a report should be sent without delay and patrols sent at once in order to remove all doubts.

2° Outpost troops do not render honors.

3° During the night, on being alarmed by the sentries over the arms, the outguards, the reserve **camp guard.** and the support **picket,** fall in under arms for all patrols rounds and troops of all descriptions coming toward them.

4° One hour before the dawn, all outpost elements fall in under arms. Call the roll.

5° All intelligence about the enemy is immediately reported, quite independent of the prescribed periodical report.

6° The supports, the outguards of the same supports, and the sentries of the same outguard are numbered from right to left.

Night duty. — Sentries being unable to see clearly at night are to be supplemented by frequent patrols.

Night emplacements may differ from day emplacements; more advanced so as to give more time to take up defensive positions. These emplacements are to be reconnoitered during the day and occupied at nightfall. Place sentries by day on vantage points to see great distances, at night place them on the counterslope that they may see what comes over the crest.

Highways and roads are practically the only possible ways of access for-troops of any importance during the night and in a country little known. They must be strongly held by the reserves and supports : ambuscades are to be prepared ahead, the towns and villages crossed by these roads must be occupied and garrisoned.

The installation of outposts by night. — Can be done only by the map, and consists in the occupation, in important directions, of points of the terrain well registered and easy to find, such as buildings, bridges, crossways, etc. Liaisons must be made especially secure. Unlike the procedure by day when each element marches directly to the place assigned to it, supports pass through the reserve emplacement, and outguards through the support emplacement that they may become familiar with them.

At day-break, reconnoitering of the ground and rectifications.

Memorandum for the double sentry. — As a fixed sentry : hide and observe.

As a mobile sentry : if necessary the mobile sentry **may** leave his place to see concealed parts of the ground, to communicate with the neighboring sentries and the chief of outguard.

1° **General instructions**

Eyes and ears on the watch : see but do not be seen.
Never wrap up the head.

Rifle with loaded magazine ; bayonet fixed during the night.

When to shoot. (Tactical instruction to the isolated soldier.)

Sitting or lying down is absolutely forbidden during the night.

No honors to be rendered; whenever a superior comes near, continue observation of the enemy.

How to challenge; summoning the chief of post to recognise parties arriving.

2° **Special instructions :**

Mnemonic method of the « cross ».

In front, sector to be watched over (a sketch if possible), a fixed datum point in the direction of the enemy, names of villages, rivers, woods, to be seen in front, names agreed upon to designate certain objects which will be used as datum points, (i. e. ball shaped trees, black-road).

Right and left, sentries and neighboring outguards.

In the rear, emplacement of the out guard and of the support, their numbers, and indirect ways of access to them.

Call and correspondence signals with the outguard.

Hours of arrival and departure of announced patrols.

Who is to be allowed to pass during the day (officers belonging to the outpost battalion), who is to be challenged. « Challenge everyone at night. »

Memorandum for the sentry over the arms. — Observe the sentries' signals. — Repeat them to let the sentries know that they have been understood.

Inform the chief of everything that comes near, and of all incidents perceived anywhere about.

Honors are not to be rendered.

By night, cry out : « **Turn out the guard** », whenever a patrol, round, or troop is approaching.

Memorandum for the chief of the outgard. — In front : Mission of the outguard, sentries to be detailed, special orders given them. Sketch of the outguard sector.

Right and left : emplacements of the neighboring outguards : Examination post.

In the rear : emplacement of the support; the indirect way along which it is possible to fall back while leaving the field of fire of the support entirely free.

How to behave in case of attack : orders given in consequence.

Assignment of duties : sentries, patrols, assistant chief of post, men allowed to sleep.

Length of sentry duty, and time appointed for the relief of sentries, never relieve at one time both men of a double sentry.

Report of installation forwarded at once to the captain.

Prescribed daily reports.

Parole and countersign. How to recognise.
Food supply.
Material organization of the outguard. Camp latrines.
Outfit. Men equipped day and night : state of arms and ammunition.
Questions to be put on the general instructions of the sentries.
Rounds and patrols. Anticipate mistakes liable to be made by sentries.

PART X.
METHODS OF INSTRUCTION.

CHAPTER I.
TRAINING IN THE BILLETS IN REAR OF THE LINES.

Aims in resuming the training. — Life in the trenches, although it seasons the soldiers, is a poor preparation physically and morally for the assault.

Physically the men become dull and have no opportunity to keep up their suppleness and their agility.

From the moral point of view, to avoid useless casualties the soldiers are required to accustom themselves to be prudent and this may react upon them when the moment arrives for them to fight in the open field. Besides that, each group or platoon lives in its own trench, somewhat separated from the others, at the expense of the cohesion of the company, which it is impossible to assemble every day.

As a matter of fact, troops can only be trusted for an assault when their hearts and legs have been trained for it.

Consequently, the troops coming to the rear, after a few days rest and after the necessary cleaning up, must employ their time conteracting the effects of inaction in the trenches. The training is resumed in order to thoroughly reshape the troops for the forward movement, the **offensive fight and the assault being necessarily the chief aim of all effort.**

Qualities to be developed in assaulting troops are agility, agressive spirit, boldness and cohesion.

Memorandum of the exercises to be performed in view of offensive combat and assaults. — Preparatory exercises developing the soldier's agility and personal value: these are performed individually or in rather small detachments in order to point out easily the individual faults.

Review of the mechanism of progression. Rushes. Fire.

Hand to hand fight drills for small groups of riflemen.

Fighting drill for the platoon and the company, in order to train not only the troops, but above all the officers and N. C. O's.

Training in field fortification.

Exercices developing cohesion : close order.

Moral instruction.

Drilling in specialities.

16..

Sports. — Assault is generally made on broken up ground; the infantryman will have to cross wire entanglements, shell craters, fallen trees, ruined houses, barricades, obstacles of all kinds; this requires great agility.

The instructor must develop the agility by means of all sport available, races, obstacle races, steeple chases, games, climbing upon pendicular slopes, jumping ditches and scaling walls, races through woods, thickets and bushes, wrestling.

Lungs and legs must again be rendered fit.

Exercises should be performed without or with full equipment.

These exercices must be executed daily and are independent of the regular every day drill.

Bayonet fighting. — Very lively fencing, against dummies, while running, over difficult ground, etc.

If possible a wood 100 or 200 meters long is organized and filled with different obstacles, (tree trunks, stretched wires, branches bent down and interlaced, etc.); dummies are hung concealed or not. A note is made of the time required to rush through and strike every dummy.

Practice in finding breaches, use of the Filloux apparatus against the barbed wire entanglements.

Exercises in fixing the bayonet, in any position : running, lying down, etc.

Firing. — Great importance must be attached to rifle firing when training. It must not be neglected under the pretext that other apparatus has taken its place as a weapon of war. The rifle is still the surest means of killing a man within 400 meters. Hence, rifle firing must be practised and the men must become excellent marksmen, however much the specialities might rightly appeal to them. In many cases when the supply of grenades is exhausted and the automatic rifles are fouled, the faithful and solid old rifle will be always ready.

a) Accurate firing in view of improving the skill of the snipers and the wearing down fire in the trenches. Rapid aiming or very careful aiming with rifles on rest, on sandbags, without taking their eyes from the target. A shot accurately fired at a movable target (the rifleman having his weapon supported, the target is pointed out to him, the command « fire » is given and the rifleman is allowed one to five seconds to aim and fire). Moving or disappearing targets. Rifle firing competitions.

The rifle practice is carried out in quarries or in front of high embankments; a distance of from 30 to 50 meters is sufficient.

b) **Firing during a hand to hand fight.** — (Practice without cartridges, special precautions should be observed). Attack while firing at very close range, extra rapid aiming to anticipate that of the enemy, and firing before he can, at the same ime aiming sufficiently correctly to be certain of hitting him The rifleman must always be able to tell where his line of sight was directed when he fired.

The assaillant who is exposed unsheltered to the fire of an ambushed enemy very often looses his head and turns from left to right not knowing what danger he has to face. He must be accustomed to keep cool, to locate the enemy and to take rapid decisions. He should pratice with several riflemen who lie at a short distance away in a trench or behind some obstacle, who make a pretence of attacking or disappear or barely show themselves.

The same exercise may also be carried out, the assailants being supplied whith cloth balls to replace grenades.

c) Filling the magazine in every position, while walking or running.
Jamming.

d) Firing with the automatic rifle. Every man must have fired several cartridges with an automatic rifle.

e) Practice in firing the German rifle, if possible.

Grenades. — All men should be trained to throw the grenades ordinarily in use.
Never miss an opportunity of teaching the men how to throw the German grenades.
Training for hand fight, as above.
Supplying with grenades a team of grenadiers.

Review of technique of approach. — Rapid formation into lines of groups by files, or in lines of half-platoons by files or twos. Long marches over ground strewn with obstacles.
Assembly behind a narrow shelter, deployment when leaving it.

Review of technique of fighting and assault. — Individual rush : reach a shelter and leave it without being seen.

Rapid deployments of the group in all directions starting from any formation whatever, at different intervals.

Marching without a stop, at wide intervals, the skirmishers being well lined up (zone of infantry fire, under the protection of our artillery). Changes of direction at small angles, avoiding closing up towards the pivot (group training).

Different kinds of rushes :

a) Long rushes (80 to 100 meters) alignment and intervals strictly observed, groups always at double time (same case as non-stop marching). Utilization of the terrain during the stops without taking into consideration alignment or intervals.

b) Rapid rush up to 50 meters at full speed to a cover pointed out, under effective infantry fire.

c) Rush by small detachments 4 or 5 men strong, starting only when the former group has reached the cover (used to pass through an artillery fire on registered points; dangerous on open ground under effective infantry fire).

d) Infiltration man by man by the same way (under an efficacious infantry fire, on well covered terrain only).

e) Progression man by man, every one chosing his own way and reaching the pointed out cover (under an efficacious infantry fire, through a terrain strewn with many small covers such as dung heaps, shell craters, etc.)

f) Rush by two or three thin lines in succession (to go through a swept open space, when the line of skirmishers is too dense to make one single rush), the successive lines should be designated, such a one... such a one..., or such and such a group ; or the men of such and a such a company, when the companies are mixed.

Faults to be avoided in rushing : men starting at random ; showing the enemy a rush is intended ; closing in ; allotted front only partly utilized ; incorrect alignment ; stragglers.

Exercices of hand to hand fight for little groups of skirmishers. —

These are to be combined with the practice of point blank firing. It is a mistake to think that, the assault being launched, it is sufficient to rush on head down and bayonet fixed and to get along some way or other. In fact, the close proximity of man to man, the unforeseen appearance of one or two enemies, or the least surprise, disconcerts the soldiers unless they have been accustomed to be astonished at nothing, to keep cool and determined and to face every unforeseen circumstance.

The training for the hand to hand fighting is performed over a ground specially prepared for it or over a very uneven terrain As many obstacles as possible are placed upon it. The enemy is represented by a group of seasoned soldiers having already fought in assaults and knowing how the enemy appears to the assaillants eyes. An N. C. O. leads each group in order to note every fault, to keep order and prevent any accident; bayonets should not be fixed.

The groups of grenadiers, automatic riflemen, and riflemen are separately trained, afterwards they are assembled in one or two waves, taking the formation which may be employed during attacks.

The drill is composed of :
Starting from the line of departure for the assault.
Running towards the enemy.
Charge, breaking through the wire entanglements.
Contest on the opposite trench.
Leaping over the trench and rallying on the further side.
Incidents to be provoked during the exercise :
Enemies appearing when the wire entanglements are being overrun.
Enemies coming out from their dugouts to take their fighting stations.
Hidden machine gun, suddenly coming into action.
Throwing of grenades, etc.

The following points should be strictly observed.
The soldier should rigidly fix his attention upon the trench against which he is marching, he should fire first as soon as , rifle appears, run to the adversary whose head has disappeared cover him with his rifle and if the enemy tries to rise again he should use his bayonet. If no enemy is directly opposed to him, he should go and help his neighbors by attacking the enemy from the flank. He should jump over the trenches and not go down into them. He should not leave behind him any enemy who can shoot the assailants from behind.

This exercice must only last a few minutes. It is performed with all the spirit necessary for an assault. The N. C. O. notes the individual mistakes and makes his observations at the end of the drill.

Patrol training. — Patrols for exploring far away, preceding an imaginary assaulting wave, carried out on open ground. They consist of men of the different specialities; they should follow the communicating trenches leading up to the enemy, try to foresee his offensive actions, surprises on the flanks, the machine-guns, etc.

Night patrols going between our accessory defensive works and those of the enemy. Ambushes to catch similar enemy patrols.

Firing by platoon, by group, or by assaulting wave.
(See Part IV, Chapter III.)

Firing at remote objectives, with single aiming point. Change of objectives. This practice is but seldom used.

Firing during fighting at close quarters, without any permanent objectives; in executing this the soldiers fire at anything that appears in the line of their objective. This is a general case.

It must be explained that the assaulting platoon need not fire before the first line is taken as the artillery takes care of that. In order to continue the attack afterwards and to follow up the success, the platoon must frequently open fire; then the artillery fires much farther on.

Neighbouring detachments should go forward, alternately opening fire to help one another.

Flanking fires performed by a posted troop, should be directed at all targets appearing in the zone which is being covered.

The orders relative to the fire transmitted all along the firing line.

Organization of combat drill for platoons and companies.

Duty of instructors. — Organized drills should conform to the following principles:

All drills must be performed with a particular objective; for example, the teaching of a certain phase of combat.

Given a situation in which the position of the enemy and of the company is simply and clearly defined. Suppose as a rule that the company is in line with others.

The officers and the men must clearly understand the situation as defined, the objective of the attack, the method to be employed in executing the attack, and the duty of each individual.

There should not be action on both sides. The enemy is purely figurative and plays only a passive part; he is placed by the instructor, who decides upon his action, chooses proper signals to make to him and uses them to bring on a series of incidents, so as to compel the troops to execute movements that he wishes to teach them.

To practice an engagement at close quaters, the enemy is represented by dummies and a party of soldiers who retire just before the time of the onset. Actually represent machine guns.

The instructor gives his subordinates all liberty in their action, without interrupting the continuity of the combat, confining himself to figuring the casualties, which will be represented as fairly heavy, especially if the attack hesitates and goes slowly.

When the exercise is over, the instructor draws from it principles of operations, and points out the faults; the exercise it repeated if neceessary, or any part of it in detail, wich is not sufficiently understood.

Automatism in fighting. — One can not insist too much on the neccessity of studying throughly and unceasingly the most frequent and ordinary situations in combat, but do not labor under the delusion that a manœuver will be successful on the fighting ground because it has been successful on the drill ground. Under fire, casualties sustained are very heavy; the mind is confused; the attention wanders; so that the company must master beforehand a series of instinctive actions, which they will perform automatically, in the absence of any leader and without stopping to think.

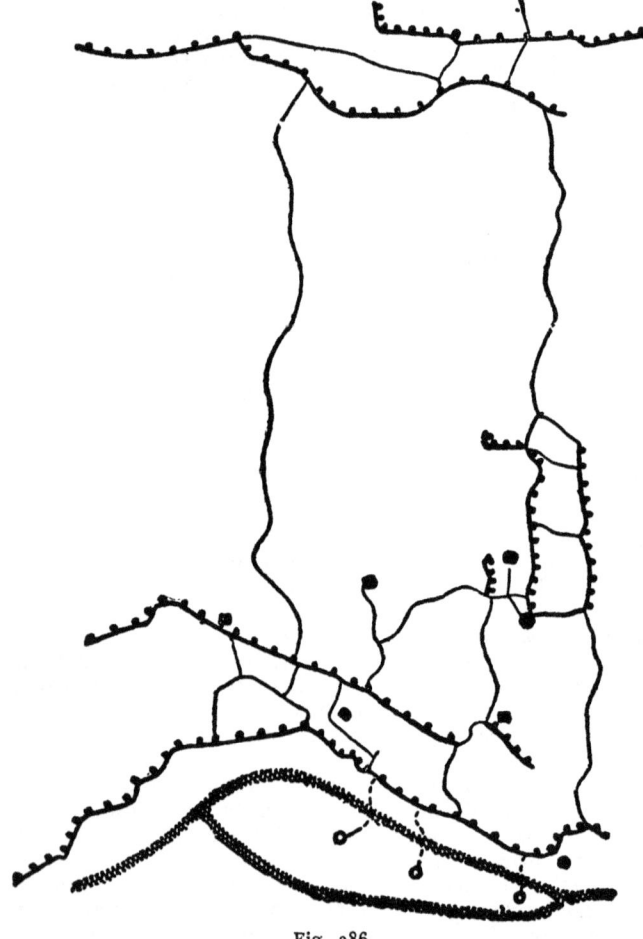

Fig. 286.

This necessary instinct is acquired by unceasing practice.

To prevent monotony in the execution of the drills, vary the initial situations and incidents; using, however, the same principles in the same energetic way as though the attack were real.

In the execution, keep as near as possible to reality. Do not teach by saying what should be done : «I should send a patrol», «I should dig a boyau.» Send the patrol, dig the boyau. End the exercise with a parade.

Organization of the terrain. — It is impossible to execute any combat drill without actually representing on the terrain some German defensive organization.

Each battalion will prepare the terrain to such a width and depth that it can execute a complete battalion action in its different situations (first line, reserve). Lay out lines of defense, 800 to 1000 meters apart (fig. 286).

The plan of the hostile trenches will be constructed according to the battle map, especially if one is apt to be obliged to attack them.

According to the time you have at your disposal the trenches and the boyaux will be laid out or simply traced with the plow, excepting at certain points where you wish the combat to assume the aspect of a real battle and to represent real situations.

Lay out or represent accessory defenses. Locate the first line on a ridge and the other defensive organizations on the counter-slope. The storming party will thus frequently have to solve the difficulties of rallying and reorganizing, and of resuming the offensive against the second line on terrain unknown to it, except by the maps and sketches arranged from photographs.

Principal platoon and company exercises.

A. *Advancing toward assaulting line*.

1° Approaching under artillery fire. — Exercise to be developed over two or three kilometers, taking for objective the prepared terrain or some line of woods. It will be agreed in advance to represent artillery fire by bugle calls, signifying intense fire (rafale), fire on first line, fire on second line, diminishing fire, cessation of firing, etc.

Object: to cross in order and without marked losses the zone of artillery fire.

Normal formation of approach (line of small columns), 150 to 200 meters between echelons.

The occasional use of the line of skirmishers in strict alignment at long intervals, for the first line.

Crossing spaces swept by shell fire : in prolonged rushes, halting only during rafales, and avoiding fire by forward movement.

Crossing lines whose range has probably been found (crests, roads, outskirts, etc.) : 1° By surprise : a rapid and prolonged rush; 2° If there is sufficient time : by crossing in small groups without drawing the attention of the enemy and by making use of natural shelters and safe passage ways.

Lateral movements ordered by captains and battalion leaders so as to avoid a zone particularly swept; by platoon leaders, to make use of a road in a defile. Return to line of march.

Faults to be avoided : instinctive rushing upon the head echelon to escape forward ; lateral movements not ordered.

2° Advance through the zone of infantry fire under the protection of intense and efficient artillery fire. — Exercices to be studied most carefully as being the normal method of advancing 1200 or 1500 meters and also the means of advancing towards the second line after carrying the first, when the artillery can continue its support.

Object : reforming rapidly within storming distance and without firing.

Normal formation for combat : riflemen at a distance of five paces, the platoon forming one or two waves according to the front given. Platoons of first line, platoons of reinforcement at 100, 150 or 200 meters in the rear.

Prolonged rushes by entire company in strict alignment.

Halts are to be made only during very violent rafales. The only real protection from artillery is found at assaulting distance.

Faults to be avoided : premature doubling up, confused crowding of waves on the first line ; wave having doubled up with the one preceding to profit by cover, and not retaking its distance, when the former advances again ; prolonged stops by a platoon that has found cover and delays there.

3° Advancing through the zone of infantry fire with insufficient protection by artillery. — A case exceptional in the attack of the first enemy line, but frequent in the advance after the carrying of the first position, liaison with the artillery being difficult. It is then necessary to make up for the lack of artillery by rifle and machine gun work. Advance with the combined fire : « marching fire ». Fire of automatic riflemen on the march, the majority of automatic riflemen of the company in the front wave.

Object of exercise : to carry the firing line within storming distance and reforming it successively on firing positions more and more advanced.

Locate in advance, from a distance, fovorable firing positions (banks, hedges, furrows of the ground, or freshly plowed earth, which is easy to dig into).

Rapid organization of a firing position.

Extremely rapid and imperceptible movements between two successive firing positions. Stop long enough on a firing position to execute an effective fire, so as to protect the movements of other units.

Practice platoons protecting each other in pairs, one firing, the other rushing forward.

Or one wave doubling up under shelter before advancing in two thin lines, the first one reaching the firing position, the second joining it later.

General movement if the enemy's fire slackens or becomes ineffective.

Faults to be avoided : stopping in open terrain without completing the rush Firing position to be reached improperly indicated to the men.

4° Advance by night. — Object : To profit by the darkness to get troups within storming distance.

Advance in silence, by small flexible columns. Some patrols will creep noiselessly into contact. Deployment at assault intervals only, or instantaneously, when the advance is discovered.

Transmission of orders verbally by single file.

Faults to be avoided : noises of all kinds. Insufficient liaison between small columns. Errors in direction.

5° Construction of a line of trenches, rifle pits, etc., at storming distance.

— This exercise should not be separated from exercises 2, 3 and 4, but should terminate the same systematically (reread the first part of the Sapper's school, Part II, Chapter VIII).

Make an improvised parallel of departure. Fatigue parties and riflemen. Tracing and laying out the work.

At night : details workers and watchmen,

B. Assault on and combat in the enemy positions.

The following exercises are performed upon a prepared terrain, where a parallel of departure is established with steps leading out.

6° Assaulting platoon.

— Extract from the plan of operations, the part which relates to the platoon under consideration. Clear information is given upon the portion of the trench to be attacked ; if the hostile terrain is sufficiently known, allot the tasks (dug-outs, cross-roads, minenwerfer, etc.). Duties and places for the groups according to their specialties.

The platoon being on its position in one line in the same parallel, advances as a unit at a given instant and in a single mass, the second wave letting the first get about twenty meters ahead ; every man taking exactly the place to wich he has been assigned.

This separation of the two waves at the start is difficult to perform and must be seriously studied and often rehearsed.

The charge. The duties of grenadiers, automatic riflemen, riflemen. They put the accessory defenses out of action. They assault the enemy trench and put it out of action without entering it ; rally the men lying down 10 meters further on. Resume the forward march.

It is a special case when the parallel of departure is oblique to the enemy trench.

7° Supporting platoon.

— The supporting platoon advances behind the platoon which assaults, simultaneously with it. It takes up a similar formation and takes the same distances.

It re-inforces the assaulting line beyond the conquered trench.

According to the strength of the assaulting platoon, the supporting platoon goes forward with it or resumes its distance in the rear.

Mistakes to be avoided : closing up, and doubling up too soon the first wave of the platoon with the second.

The case must be studied in which the assaulting platoon and the supporting platoon waiting in a single trench have to take up, on advancing, a formation in four waves.

8° Assault performed by a company furnishing assaulting platoons and supporting platoons. — The waves work simultaneously (four waves) and are followed by a cleaning up platoon.

They put out of action successive trenches ; clean up important points ; carry the fight to the last part of the position.

There must be automatic rallying, outside of the trenches, of the parties scattered by the local fighting.

At the start for the second line, the waves are reformed during the march.

Various incidents to be developed (see below).

9° Following up success. marching against successive positions. — The companies are boldly pushed forward through the breaches on the heels of the enemy, although they must always be on guard against surprises.

Various incidents to be developed (see below).

Marching : reestablishment of the order, liaisons with the neighboring companies, allotment of new duties.

Patrols following the boyaus towards the enemy and guarding against surprises.

Taking of the second line in the same rush, or advance on the second line, following the principles laid down in exercise No. 3. and establishment of an improvised parallel at a distance suitable for assault.

Mistakes to be avoided : timidity before a terrain or obstacles which are not as well known as the first line. Lack of decision when unexpected incidents arise. Deviating from the original direction of the attack.

10° Second line company. — Advance across conquered terrain. Groups of grenadiers or automatic riflemen pushed singly up to the line of the first waves.

Reinforcement of these waves, if they have stopped in front of the second line.

They emerge from their line as from a new parallel of departure to storm the second enemy line.

Machine guns following the second line company and entering into action on its flanks.

Study as shown above the debouch from the trenches at the same minute as the first line company and the taking of prescribed positions, starting from a congested and confused situation in the parallels of departure.

Fault to be avoided : a premature engagement without the order of the battalion commander, the only commander of the supporting companies (except in exceptionally urgent cases.)

11° Other duties of a reinforcing company. — *a)* Protection of the first line companies' flanks. Changing direction to right or left upon a center of resistance which has not surrendered. Study in detail this movement, which is difficult to execute, by successive platoons (fig. 287).

If possible, complete the encircling movement by attacking also the rear of the center of resistance. Silence his flanking fires by jumping into his first trench and there opening the combat in the boyaux. Insist upon the difference between this tactical movement and that of the waves of assault.

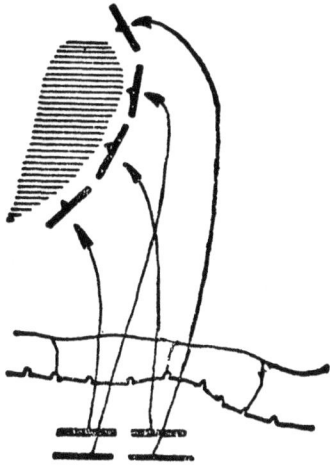

Fig. 287.

b) Return the fire of a counter-attack directed on the flank or behind the first waves.

12° Particular cases.
a) An isolated company executing an assault on a limited objective (raid).
Arrangement in three lines: reconnoitering wave, automatic riflemen and grenadiers at six or eight paces; waves of assault, denser, composed especially of grenadiers; waves of materiel porters, men told off to bring back prisoners, etc.

b) Platoon or even company in a single wave: after casualties; or else to approach the second line if it has not been possible to rally by platoon after the attack of the first line. Division of the command.

Incidents to bring about in the course of exercises-6 to 12. — Machine guns appearing in front and on the flank.
Firing of flanking pieces under casemate.
Artillery barrage.
Gas shells.
Small grenade counter-attack.
Firing at back of assailant by enemy neglected in rear.
Center of resistance encountered, flanking fire by a boyau.
Barricade.
The fire slows down.
Offensive return the enemy.
Intervention of our attillery.

13° Exercices for passing through. — Very important exercises whose object is explained in Part VIII, Chapter I, paragraph 3.
To be executed for practice by two companies forming three

or four waves each, the reinforcing company becoming the first line company.

Be sure to follow with entire battalions, as in the case in actual combat.

Exercices in field fortification.

The preparation of terrain necessary for practising assaults necessitates, at the beginning of a period of instruction, the review of the regular methods of detailing fatigue parties and digging trenches. In particular, sapping ought to be reviewed and correctly practised without changing anything in the required method set forth in the « School for sappers, »

All these exercises include, in short, the progressive setting to work that would have to be done in an actual case.

Also suppose the case in which individual rifle pits have to be transformed into a continuous trench.

Execute, in addition, the following night exercice :

Establish yourself firmly, by night, at assaulting distance during the course of a combat.

The immediate proximity of the enemy precludes the use for ordinary working parties.

Send patrols to establish contact.

Under their protection, the officers stake out the line with orderlies lying down.

Distribution of tools to the rear. Placing of the workmen brought up by files ; they put their rifles behind them, bayonets fixed.

Patrols replaced by watchmen or listening posts.

Use of the luminous compass to trace the boyaux to be provided leading to the rear.

Exercises in close order.

Exercices in close order are intended to develop the spirit of subordination and immediate obedience, as well as the sense of solidarity and complete cohesion among the men of the same unit.

Each time the men go out for drill or return from it, have them execute some movements taken from Part II, Chapters V and VI.

Review especially the various platoon and company formations, and the correct and rapid passage from one formation to another. Do not come to a full halt in close ranks unless certain movements frequently needed have been forgotten.

Require of the men an energetic and proud carriage, a neat handling of arms and complete immobility.

This result being obtained, it is unnecessary to review all the movements provided by the regulations for platoon and company.

These movements have been included in Part II, Chapters V and VI, only for reference to the text of the drill regulations in case of need, and especially for the use of battalions of recruits and in regimental depots.

Moral instruction.

The officers should get their men together and talk over with them the situation of our armies and the efforts of our allies. Try to give a clear idea of facts and men, show the reasons we have for being sure of final success and how the daily efforts of each one must bring it closer.

Gather subjects for talks from the «Bulletin des Armées,» the bulletins of information furnished by the battalion leaders, and from other publications.

History of the regiment from the beginning of the war. Decorations and citations that it has won; examples of bravery and devotion to the flag.

Hatred of the Barbarian, of the treacherous adversary, of the men who murder children and wounded.

Develop the spirit of subordination and unquestioning obedience, overcome weariness; extol good temper, and deserve it of men who constantly laugh at fatigue and privations, which is harder than to risk one's life from time to time.

Instruction of the company specialists.

N. C. O.'s. — Reading of maps and plans. Showing the ground form with contours and hachures, practical instructions to be given on the terrain, map in hand.

Drawing up of very simple sketches without contours, and reports.

Grenadiers. — Review of special training, under the direction of the battalion grenadier officer.

Drill on prepared terrain:

1° *Defense of a trench with grenades.* — Placing of the grenadiers, grenade recesses, establishing a barrage with grenades.

2° *Combat in the boyaux.* — March in the boyaux, conquest and defense foot by foot.

3° *Grenade assault on a prepared trench.*

4° *Cleaning up a trench by taking it on the flank.*

5° *Execution of a raid.*

Formation for marching on open ground by day and night.

Rapid approach after preparation by artillery and trench mortars.

Surprise attack by night.

Rapid cleaning up of trench, guard during the cleaning.

The organization of supplies will constitute one of the principal objects of each drill.

V. B. Grenadiers. — Firing exercises:

Learn to judge without plumb-line or graduated tripod the inclinations of the rifle that correspond to the principal distances.

Firing of the 4 V. B. battery:

Concentration of fire upon a particular objective; dispersion of the fire of four rifles to form a barrage at 150 meters, at

100 meters, the four grenades falling at 25 meters, one after the other, in the direction of the front.
Rapid execution of an emplacement for V. B.

Automatic riflemen. — Arrange a trench at the foot of the butt, allowing silhouettes to appear and disappear.

1° *Individual firing exercices :*
Shooting with rest shot by shot or by small rafales of two or three shots.
Marching fire on fixed silhouettes : shot by shot;
        by small rafales of 3 or 4 cartridges,
        by long rafales of 5 or 6 cartridges.
Same fire marching over broken terrain.
Fire while advancing, jumping from one shell crater to another, spaced at 10 meters.
Sweeping fire, on 3 or 4 silhouettes appearing along the trench.
Assaulting fire. Fire several clips and replace them while on the march. Train the automatic rifleman on distances ranging from 50 to 200 meters.

2° *Exercises by crews.* — By crews, by double crews, advancing in their platoon, by groups of four crews and more.
Repeat advancing fire and assaulting fire.

3° *Taking down, maintenance and jamming.* — To be thoroughly understood.

Crews of signalers. — Knowledge of the Morse code.
Choose an emplacement (utilization of terrain), find the correspondant, transmit messages in all positions and by all methods (flags, lanterns, etc.), change post (first one crew, then the other).
Role of the crews during the advance of the whole regiment : crews changing places simultaneously.
Repeat these exercises by night.
Signaling between infantry and avions (see Part IV, Chapter IX).

Runners. — Add runners posts to signalers posts, and have them work together.

Observers, watchmen, liaison agents. — Mentioned for the sake of completeness.

CHAPTER II.

INSTRUCTION CAMPS AND DEPOTS.

The subjects wich the new soldiers are to be taught have been assembled in Part II.
As soon as the mechanism of a movement is summarily known the instructor should devote his attention to the application of il in combat and assault drills with the possibility of executing alt or part of one of these exercises mentioned hereabove in Chap-

ter I. In a word, never teach a movement for its own sake ; but show very plainly at the earliest opportunity its application to a situation of war.

All new soldiers receive the same general instruction.

Each recruit should be proficient in throwing grenades and at the same time should be instructed in one of the specialities praticed by the company ; so that he could at any moment replace a grenadier, a V. B. grenadier or an automatic rifleman.

Moreover, special instruction is given to a certain number, chosen according to their aptitude, which enable them to supply the specialists for the regiment as below :

Telephonists, signallers, liaison men.	1/10 of the effective.
Machine gunners.	3/10 // // //
Sapper-pionneers and bombardiers.	3/10 // // //

The instructions for old soldiers in the depots should not differ from that which is taken up in the cantonments behind the front.

www.ingramcontent.com/pod-product-compliance
Lightning Source LLC
Chambersburg PA
CBHW070958160426
43193CB00012B/1828